The Russian Origins of the First World War

The Russian Origins of
the First World War

Sean McMeekin

The Belknap Press of Harvard University Press
Cambridge, Massachusetts · London, England

First Harvard University Press paperback edition, 2013

Library of Congress Cataloging-in-Publication Data

McMeekin, Sean, 1974–
The Russian origins of the First World War / Sean McMeekin.
p.   cm.
Includes bibliographical references and index.
ISBN 978-0-674-06210-8 (cloth : alk. paper)
ISBN 978-0-674-07233-6 (pbk.)
1. World War, 1914–1918—Causes.   2. World War, 1914–1918—Russia.
3. Russia—Foreign relations—1894–1917.   4. Imperialism—History—
20th century.   5. World War, 1914–1918—Campaigns—Eastern Front.
6. World War, 1914–1918—Campaigns—Middle East.   I. Title.
D514.M35   2011
940.3'11—dc23   2011031427

For Ayla

Contents

Maps

Abbreviations

ATASE — Askeri Tarih ve Stratejik Etüt Başkanlığı Arşivi (Archive of the Turkish General Staff). Ankara, Turkey.

AVPRI — Arkhiv vneshnei politiki Rossiiskoi Imperii (Archive of the Foreign Policy of the Russian Empire). Moscow, Russia.

BD — *British Documents on the Origins of the War, 1898–1914.* 13 vols.

BOA — Başbakanlık Osmanlı Arşivleri (Ottoman Government Archives). Sultanahmet, Istanbul, Turkey.

DDF — *Documents diplomatiques français* (French Diplomatic Documents). Third Series (1911–14). 41 vols.

GARF — Gosudarstvenny Arkhiv Rossiiskoi Federatsii (Government Archive of the Russian Federation). Moscow, Russia.

HHSA — Haus-, Hof, und Staatsarchiv (Diplomatic Archives of the Habsburg Empire, [Austria-Hungary]). Vienna, Austria.

HS — "Hoover Stavka." Collection "Russia Shtab Verkhovnogo Glavno Komanduiushchego" (Stavka, or Russian Military Headquarters), Hoover Institution Archives, Stanford, California, United States.

IBZI — *Internationale Beziehungen im Zeitalter des Imperialismus. Dokumente Aus den Archiven der Zarischen und der Provorischen Regierung* (International Relations in the Age of Imperialism. Documents from the Archives of the Tsarist and Provisional [Russian] regimes). 8 vols+.

KA — *Krasnyi Arkhiv* (The Red Archive). Secret Documents from the Tsarist Archives, especially the running "diary" of the Imperial Russian Ministry of Foreign Affairs. 106 vols.

KP   *Konstantinopol' i Prolivyi. Po sekretnyim dokumentam b. Ministerstva inos-trannyikh del* (Constantinople and the Straits, According to Secret Documents from the Former Ministry of Foreign Affairs). 2 vols.

KW   Kriegsarchiv Wien (Austrian Military Archives). Vienna, Austria.

OAU   *Österreich-Ungarns Aussenpolitik von der bosnischen Krise 1908 bis zum Kriegsausbruch 1914* (Austria-Hungary's Foreign Policy from the Bosnian Crisis of 1908 to the Outbreak of the War of 1914). 9 vols.

PAAA   Politisches Archiv des Auswärtigen Amtes (Political Archive of the Imperial German Foreign Ministry). Berlin, Germany.

PBM   Peter Bark Memoirs. Columbia University Rare Book & Manuscript Library. Columbia University, New York, United States.

PRO   National Archives of the United Kingdom. Kew Gardens, London, United Kingdom. Although it has been several years now since the Public Record Office was renamed the National Archives, for the sake of tradition, and to preserve common currency, I refer to it in this book as the PRO.

QO   Archives of the Quai d'Orsay (the French Ministry of Foreign Affairs). Paris, France.

RAT   *Razdel Aziatskoi Turtsii. Po sekretnyim dokumentam b. Ministerstva inos-trannyikh del* (The Partition of Asiatic Turkey, According to Secret Documents from the Former Ministry of Foreign Affairs).

RGVIA   Rossiskii Gosudarstevennyi Voenno-Istoricheskii Arkhiv (Russian Government Military-Historical Archive). Moscow, Russia.

TRMV   *Tsarskaia Rossiia v mirovoi voine* (Tsarist Russia in the World War). Secret Documents from the Former Ministry of Foreign Affairs.

VSHD   Vincennes. Service Historique de la Défense (French military archives). Vincennes, Paris, France.

Author's Note

Because the story is told mostly from Russia's point of view, I have referred consistently in the book to Constantinople, as Istanbul was still called in the pre–World War I and wartime era, even by Ottoman government officials. Still, I can assure my Turkish friends that when I speak of the city as "Tsargrad" it is very much in Russian-ventriloqual scare quotes. As for the capital of tsarist Russia, it will be referred to as "St. Petersburg" or simply "Petersburg" up to the outbreak of war in August 1914, after which I follow its Russification (and de-Germanicization) to "Petrograd." (Fortunately, in the current narrative, we do not also have to reckon with Soviet-era "Leningrad.") With most other cities I have used the contemporary form, with the modern equivalent initially mentioned in parentheses, thus "Adrianople (Edirne)" or "Kharput (Elâzığ)."

For Russian-language words, I have used a simplified Library of Congress transliteration system throughout, with the exception of commonly used spellings of certain famous or frequently repeated names (e.g., Izvolsky not Izvolskii; Trotsky not Trotskii; Yanushkevitch not Ianushkevich; Yudenich not Iudenich; Yuri not Iurii). I have also left out "soft" and "hard" signs from the main text, so as not to burden the reader.

With regard to Turkish spellings, I have generally rendered the "c" phonetically as "dj" (as in *Djavid* and *Djemal*) and used the dotless ı where appropriate (it sounds a bit like "uh") to differentiate from the Turkish "ı," which sounds like "ee." Likewise, I have tried to properly render ş (sh) and ç (ch) to help readers puzzle out pronunciations, even if these letters are really post-1928 concoctions of Atatürk's language reforms. It is impossible to be consistent in all these things; may common sense prevail.

Until the Bolsheviks switched over to the Gregorian calendar in 1918, Russia followed the Julian calendar, which was thirteen days behind the Gregorian by the early twentieth century. The Ottoman Empire traditionally used a modified version of the Islamic lunar calendar, with years dated from the time of Mohammad's exodus from Mecca *(hejira)* in 622 AD—although it switched over to the Julian version of solar calendar dates in the nineteenth century. Sensibly, Ottoman archives provide translations of the old dates to modern Gregorian ones (e.g., 1332 = 1914, for most months, with solar month-dates also indicated), although Russian archives generally do not so translate. To keep things simple, I have used Gregorian dates consistently throughout the text, with the exception of certain major pre-1918 dates in Russian history, which Russian specialists may know by the "old" dates, in which case I have given both dates with a slash, as in 3/16 August 1914, where 3 is the Julian and 16 the Gregorian date.

Finally, a note on 1914-era diplomatic terminology. "Chorister's Bridge" is shorthand for the Imperial Russian Foreign Ministry, just as "Whitehall" stands for the British Foreign Office (and government). The "Wilhelmstrasse" represents the German Foreign Office (and the Chancellery), the "Ballhausplatz" (or, shortened, "Ballplatz") means the Austro-Hungarian government, "Quai d'Orsay" the French, and "the Sublime Porte" or "the Porte" the Ottoman. I have tried not to overuse these terms, which have something of a cliquish sound about them. Still, to avoid incessant repetition in the text, they do have their place.

All translations from the French, German, Russian, and Turkish, unless otherwise noted, are my own.

Essentially the great question remains:
who will hold Constantinople?
—Napoleon Bonaparte

History from the Deep Freeze

CONSIDERING THE IMPORTANCE of Russia's war of 1914–1917 for the subsequent history of the world—from the collapse of the Ottoman Empire and all that followed in the Middle East to the rise of Communism—it is curious how little is widely known today about the thinking of policymakers in Petrograd during the conflict. It has been fifty years since the publication of Fritz Fischer's *Griff nach der Weltmacht* in 1961 (literally "Grab" or "Bid" for World Power, published in English as *Germany's Aims in the First World War*) and, judging by the Fischer-esque tone of a recent boomlet in popular books on the First World War, historians are still in Fischer's shadow, massaging the same basic argument about German responsibility for the conflict. Although few scholars accept any longer Fischer's extreme thesis that World War I was a premeditated "German bid for world power," histories of the war's outbreak still invariably focus on decision making in Berlin and, secondarily, Vienna. For scholars and general readers alike, the war of 1914 remains essentially Germany's war, in which Russia plays, at most, a passive role: fear of Russia's demographically unstoppable "Slavic hordes," who were due shortly to be mobilized far more rapidly after the enactment of Russia's Great Army Programme of 1913, swings the Germans into preemptive action. As for what Russia's leaders hoped to accomplish by going to war in

1914, most histories of the conflict have little to say, beyond vague mutterings about Serbia and Slavic honor, treaty obligations to France, and concern for Russia's status as a great power.[1]

The gap in public knowledge of Russia's war aims owes much to the deep freeze into which her revolution and civil war thrust historical scholarship on the war generally. Not until 2015 or so (we are told) will the first volume of Russia's official wartime history finally appear, and even this schedule is believed by few Russians. Several Soviet scholars produced specialized monographs on wartime operations, but the subject always took a backseat to social and economic history in accordance with the ideological imperatives of Marxist-Leninism. Military history is just now coming back into fashion in Russia: there is a lot of catching up to do.[2] So sparse is the literature in the West, meanwhile, that searching for books on Russia in World War I turns up mostly books on the *Second* World War. Only one or two general narratives on the eastern front have been completed in the last thirty years, and almost none before.[3]

The poor scholarly output on tsarist Russia's war effort is not surprising, in view of the difficulty of archival access in Russia until very recently and the fact that so few Russian-language monographs exist to guide researchers on their way. The same cannot really be said, however, of Russia's wartime diplomacy. Since Trotsky's revelation of the "secret treaties" of the Entente powers in 1917, and the publication of vast troves of secret Russian diplomatic correspondence by the Bolsheviks in the 1920s, the world has known the basic gist of Russia's war aims, if not all the particulars. Russian specialists have known about these documents for decades. They have been mined with particular enthusiasm in Germany, where scholars for understandable reasons have often sought to problematize the Versailles "war guilt" thesis used to levy a colossal reparations bill (the last installment of which was paid in 2010). Since the fall of the Soviet Union in 1991, western and Russian scholars alike have discovered even more relevant material in the tsarist archives, such that there is now more formerly secret material available on Russia's war aims in 1914 than on those of any other power. Strangely, however, most general histories published in recent decades ignore Russia's war aims almost entirely, in a way those published before 1961 did not. In a real sense, historical understanding of the First World War may be said to have regressed after the

Fischer debate taught several generations of historians to pay serious attention only to Germany's war aims.[4]

In similar fashion, in most of the myriad books, novels, and films dealing with the notorious Sykes-Picot Agreement of 1916 and its impact on the greater Islamic world, one hears scarcely a word about the Russian side. That Britain and France conspired together to destroy the Ottoman Empire is taken as a given in most books on the modern Middle East, especially those inspired by Edward Said's famous critique of western attitudes in *Orientalism* (1979). Although not untrue, so far as it goes, the now-ubiquitous narrative of western perfidy in carving up Asiatic Turkey is nonetheless deeply misleading, for it leaves out the main character in the drama. To tell the story of the collapse of the Ottoman Empire without mentioning the role of Turkey's age-old Russian enemy, as some authors do, is like writing a history of the fall of the Soviet Union in 1991 without reference to American foreign policy and strategy in the Cold War.[5]

Just as the military history of the eastern front has been smothered by historians' understandable focus on the titanic drama of the Russian Revolution, Russia's own war aims have been buried in popular modern histories underneath the explosive postwar history of the Middle East under British and French imperial tutelage. As a matter of historical malpractice, however, the latter case of negligence is the more serious. It is possible (if hardly ideal) to explain the Russian Revolution in mostly domestic terms, with only passing reference to military developments on the eastern front between 1914 and 1917. Few historians really do this anymore: the cardinal theme in recent scholarship is the continuity between "Russia's Great War and Revolution," as one major scholarly initiative terms it, a "continuum of crisis" between 1914 and 1922.[6] By contrast, the last hundred years of history in the lands of the former Ottoman Empire—stretching from European Thrace and the Aegean and Black Sea littorals to Anatolia, "Turkish Armenia," the Caucasus and Persia, Mesopotamia and Palestine—is arguably impossible to record without reference to Russia's aims in the First World War. And yet few contemporary historians of the modern Middle East seem familiar with any but the most general outlines of tsarist Russian foreign policy.[7]

Even the basic chronology of the First World War cannot be properly understood without grappling with the war aims of Imperial Russia. From the Sarajevo incident that sparked the July crisis, to the mobilization drama surrounding the war's outbreak, the unrealistic timetable of the Germans' Schlieffen Plan and the bogging down of the western front in trench warfare, the sanguinary tragedy of Gallipoli, the Armenian massacres of 1915, the Sykes-Picot Agreement of 1916 and the subsequent carve-up of Asiatic Turkey, until the Revolution of 1917, all of the most notorious—and enduringly explosive—events of the war were intimately related to Russian foreign policy. Trenches, Verdun, and the poppies of Flanders field may be the lasting images of the Great War in western imagination, but it would be difficult to argue today that anything of lasting strategic importance was at stake in the Franco-German clash in Flanders. That action's lack of identifiable foreign policy goals helps explain why the carnage there seemed so senseless and so badly scarred the men who fought and bled there. But can one really say the same of the struggle for Gallipoli, "Turkish Armenia" and the Transcaucasus, Baku, Teheran, Baghdad, Damascus, Palestine, and Suez?

From the perspective of present-day residents of these places, the First World War appears not as a kind of senseless civil war between European nations which have now long since learned to live in peace—what we might call the standard European Union narrative—but more like a deliberate plot to disrupt and dismantle the last great Islamic power on Earth, Ottoman Turkey. One does not have to credit the wilder conspiracy theories to realize that there is a certain grain of truth here. What were the Italian and Balkan wars fought by the Turks in 1911–1913, after all, but a kind of opening act for the world war of 1914, in which great powers threw in with the smaller ones already fighting to dismember the Ottoman Empire? If one takes the long view, bracketing the global conflict between the Italian invasion of Ottoman Libya in 1911 and the Treaty of Lausanne in 1923 that finally granted Turkish independence (with the renunciation of Turkish claims over many former Ottoman territories), the First World War could very easily be labeled "The War of the Ottoman Succession."

This is the story told in the records of the Imperial Russian Ministry of Foreign Affairs, a story that has been hiding in plain sight ever since Trotsky first burgled the archives in 1917. It has been available to any scholar who reads Russian (or German, as many of the Soviet-produced volumes of tsarist documents have been translated into that language).[8] Drawing on these materials, along with still-unpublished documents now open to the public in Russian and European archives, I contend in this book that the current consensus about the First World War cannot survive serious scrutiny. The war of 1914 was Russia's war even more than it was Germany's.

CHAPTER ONE

The Strategic Imperative in 1914

Everywhere you feel the fear of something threatening; something dangerous and repulsive is imminent, a consciousness of an approaching catastrophe. All feel it, including those who are preparing it.

—F. A. Rodichev, May 1914[1]

The road to Constantinople runs through Warsaw.
—E. N. Trubetskoi[2]

The shortest and safest operational route to Constantinople runs through Vienna . . . and Berlin.
—Quartermaster-General Yuri Danilov[3]

I F THERE IS A dominant cliché in current thinking about the outbreak of World War I, it is German fear of the "Russian steamroller." Chancellor Theobald von Bethmann Hollweg's anxiety about the growth of Russian power is amply confirmed in both his correspondence and in the Riezler diaries, in which he is overheard muttering, "Russia grows and grows. She lies on us like a nightmare." From the raw data, it is easy to see why policymakers in Berlin felt time was not on their side: Russia's population had grown by forty million since just 1900, and was approaching 200 million to Germany's sixty-five. By the time the Great Program was complete in 1917–1918, Russia's *peacetime* army (already Europe's largest in 1914, at 1.42 million) would number 2.2 million soldiers, or roughly triple the size of Germany's.[4] Russia's economy, although still only fifth-largest in the world (behind Britain, France, Germany, and the United States) was growing at a "developing economy" rate of nearly 10 percent annually, rather like China's is today. Measured in output of coal, iron, and steel, Russia was already fourth (having passed France) and inching up inexorably to first rank. Just looking at a map was enough to induce terror in Russia's neighbors: according to a famous calculation the Romanov Empire had grown by fifty-five square miles a day—20,000 a year —since 1683, primarily west, south, and southeast. It was not hard to extrapolate forward a geopolitical map on which Russian territory included half of China, Afghanistan, northern Persia, Anatolia, Constantinople and the Straits, Austrian Galicia, and Eastern Prussia.

Like all clichés, this one rests on a kernel of truth. Russia's population, economy, and her military strength *were* increasing in size each year. Bethmann Hollweg, an intelligent and well-traveled man, was not paranoid: he had visited Russia himself in July 1912 and witnessed her growing industrial might firsthand. In an era when military budgets were—even in autocratic Russia—subject to parliamentary and public scrutiny, it was easy to compare the strengths of European armies. The size of the Imperial Russian Army in 1914 and its basic mobilization timetable was no secret, although whether or not Russia really could mobilize as fast as her generals claimed was an open question.[5] Nor were the implications of the Great Program enacted in 1913 secret: by 1917, Russia would theoretically be able to mobilize roughly one hundred divisions for battle within eighteen days of mobilization, only "three days behind Germany in overall readiness."[6] In strictly military terms, one can see why German military planners concluded Russia would be easier to beat in 1914 than three or four years later.

International relations, however, are not conducted in a vacuum. As Russian policymakers knew perhaps better than their western European counterparts, what matters in geopolitics is not the absolute growth in one country's demographic, economic, or military power, but its relative growth compared to other powers.[7] And here the Russian steamroller cliché begins losing plausibility. There was just one European power that had prodigiously increased in strength vis-à-vis all its rivals in the previous half-century, and it was certainly not Imperial Russia, which had lost two major conflicts (the Crimean War of 1853–1856, and the Russo-

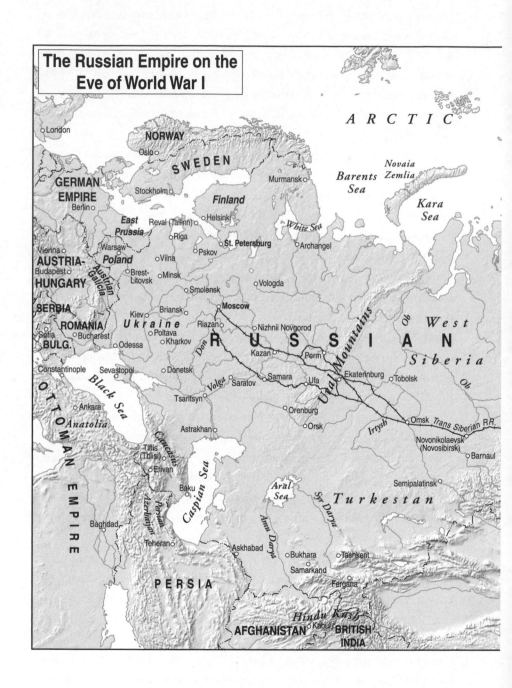

The Russian Empire on the Eve of World War I

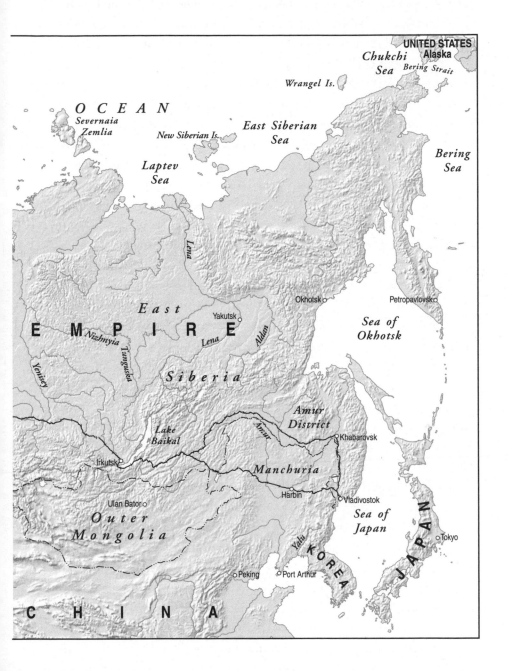

UNITED STATES
Alaska

*Chukchi
Sea*

Bering Strait

Wrangel Is.

O C E A N

*Severnaia
Zemlia*

New Siberian Is.

*East Siberian
Sea*

*Bering
Sea*

*Laptev
Sea*

Lena

Okhotsk ○

Petropavlovsk ○

East

Yakutsk ○

E M P I R E

Nizhnyia

Lena

Aldan

*Sea of
Okhotsk*

Tunguska

Yenisey

S i b e r i a

*Amur
District*

Khabarovsk ○

*Lake
Baikal*

Amur

Irkutsk ○

Manchuria

Vladivostok ○

Ulan Bator ○

Harbin ○

*Sea of
Japan*

*O u t e r
M o n g o l i a*

Yalu

K O R E A

J A P A N

○ Tokyo

○ Peking

○ Port Arthur

C H I N A

Japanese War of 1904–1905) and won a conspicuously hollow victory in a third (the Russo-Turkish War of 1877–1878, in which Petersburg's gains were largely nullified by Bismarck and Disraeli at the Congress of Berlin). Had not the Franco-Prussian War of 1870–1871 heralded a new geopolitical era, with Germany decisively passing France as the greatest military power in Europe—a development that led the Russian General Staff to convene an unprecedented "strategic conference" in 1873 designed to produce a plan for preserving the Romanov Empire against the German threat?[8] Were not the German use of railways and the near-universal literacy in the ranks of the Prussian army both revolutionary developments in military effectiveness—developments that had not only embarrassed France but made Imperial Russia (with her paltry rail network and a literacy rate of 30 percent as late as 1913) look positively outdated? Had not the German economy exploded in size since the 1880s, surpassing even Britain's, to trail only continent-sized America? Did not German heavy industry dwarf that of her eastern rival, with—despite the latter's three-to-one edge in population—her production of coal still nearly ten times that of Russia, and her annual output of coal and pig iron four times as great?[9] Were not the Germans now world leaders in everything from pharmaceuticals to automotive technology to—perhaps more significantly—ever-more destructive explosives and ever-more accurate (and longer range, and larger caliber) artillery? The words Krupp and Skoda alone were enough to terrify infantrymen who might have to face Germans. Fear of the growth of Russian power? Judging by the outcome of the war on the eastern front between 1914 and 1917, the growth of *German* power would seem to have been the more plausible nightmare.

The "growth of German power" was no less visible on the diplomatic playing field, at least as perceived in Petersburg. Bethmann Hollweg and his diplomats may have felt that they had been dealt a series of defeats at the hands of France and England (most recently following the Agadir incident of 1911, when, as the chancellor lamented, in return for acquiescing in French domination of Morocco, the Germans had received "an immense number of square miles of tropical marshes" in the middle of Africa).[10] But these should have been balanced out by clear German victories over Petersburg, such as the Russian climb-down over Austria's 1908 annexation of Bosnia (enforced by an unsubtle German threat in March

1909), and more recently the Liman von Sanders affair of winter 1913–1914. Liman von Sanders, a German officer appointed to command the Turkish army corps defending the Straits, had ultimately been allowed to stay on (at an elevated rank which rendered Liman "overqualified" to command a single Turkish army corps) despite a passionate protest from the Russians. The Russians, for their part, felt they had suffered through a series of diplomatic debacles since the humiliating military defeat in the Russo-Japanese War—the Bosnian annexation, the Balkan wars (from which Russia herself had gained nothing tangible, despite the gains of nominal proxies like Serbia), and the Liman affair—but with no compensating victories to cushion the defeats.

Of course, diplomatic gains and losses could be a matter of interpretation. In a seeming paradox, many politicians in both Berlin and Petersburg felt that they had lost in the Liman affair, for example, while Russia and Austria-Hungary were almost equally frustrated over the muddled outcome of the Balkan wars. To some extent, the perception that one was losing ground was chronic in the classical era of great power diplomacy, when crises were usually evaluated in zero-sum terms. Diplomats everywhere were supremely sensitive to the slightest slip in their country's status, which might imply a victory for rival diplomats (even if these rivals believed themselves to have lost).

The sense of losing ground, however, was felt more by some powers than by others. France and Britain both ruled over fairly stable, far-flung colonial empires acquired gradually over several centuries, to which the only real neighboring rivals (aside from each other) tended to be decaying imperial has-beens like Spain and Portugal, or lesser powers such as Belgium. Neither Paris nor London had a real strategic interest in the Balkans, scene of the most serious diplomatic crises of the past half-decade. The Eastern Question—the struggle to manage the collapse of the Ottoman Empire, which all powers expected to be imminent—was for neither France nor England terribly urgent. London had long since wrested control of Ottoman Egypt and the Suez Canal, which together formed the linchpin of British global communications. In June 1914, Britain signed an agreement with the Porte that divided the Arabian Peninsula into Ottoman and British spheres of influence, with the latter including the entire southern coastal area between Aden and Qatar. London had little further interest in Asiatic Turkey besides the quiet economic penetration of Mesopotamia and southern Arabia. Some French imperialists, it is true, did look on Syria and Lebanon with greedy eyes, but Parisian capital was already so dominant in the Ottoman Empire that the absorption of the Levant into the French sphere of influence seemed to be only a matter of time. In terms of imperial prestige and the basic state of the game, Britain and France were essentially "status quo" powers in 1914, with their imperial appetites largely sated.

Berlin and Petersburg, by contrast, were both heavily invested in the Eastern Question and knee deep in the Balkans (even if, in the case of Germany and the Balkans, mostly at second remove via Austria-Hungary). Neither the Germans nor the Russians were anywhere near satisfied in terms of imperial appetite, nor feeling particularly secure in their current positions. The ambitions of pan-Germanists—largely shared by Bethmann Hollweg, the General Staff, and the Wilhelmstrasse—to dominate "Mitteleuropa" and "Mittelafrika," along with Asiatic Turkey, are well known.[11] Much less well known are the goals of Russian imperialists of the time, but they were, in their way, just as ambitious. Since the Russo-Japanese War, Petersburg had made surprising gains in the Far East, with Japanese recognition of Russian supremacy in northern Manchuria in 1912, China reluctantly granting autonomy to Mongolia under strong Russian pressure the same year, and the British consenting to Russian administrative oversight in Harbin in 1914. London also agreed to cede to Petersburg a "zone of influence" north of the Hindu Kush in Afghanistan.[12] Meanwhile, Russia's imperial penetration of northern Persia was rapidly creating a fait accompli on the ground: Russian settlers and syndicates had already acquired title to three-quarters of the arable land in "Persian Azerbaijan," thanks to judges installed by Russian diplomats already behaving as imperial pro-consuls.[13] The Armenian reform campaign of 1913–1914, which alarmed both the Porte and Berlin, was a scarcely disguised Trojan horse for the expansion of Russian influence in Turkish Anatolia. Finally, Russian plans for seizing Constantinople and the Straits were well advanced and universally supported by policymakers by 1914, even if the Black Sea fleet was not yet strong enough to carry them out.

Just as German and Russian ambitions were roughly matched in terms of scale, so, too, were the fears of policymakers on each side that these ambitions would be sundered by a coalition of hostile powers. Kaiser Wilhelm II, Bethmann Hollweg, and the German generals famously, and by no means unjustifiably, complained of "encirclement," the sense of feeling ringed in by hostile powers (England, France, and Russia). Less well known, although just as significant, was the fear of encirclement felt in Petersburg. If anything, the Russians had a better case than the Germans to complain of *Einkreisung:* the Romanov Empire's long and ragged borders butted up against no less than five powers, either actively hostile (Germany, Austria-Hungary, Ottoman Turkey), recently hostile (Japan), or certain to be hostile if she ever got her act together (China). This was not even to count the Raj—British India had, of course, been Russia's principal strategic antagonist ever since the Napoleonic Wars, and, if Delhi instead of London were driving British policy, would have remained hostile still. Even while negotiations were underway in spring 1914 to forge a closer strategic relationship between London and Petersburg, flare-ups of the old antagonism continued, especially in Persia, where the cynical Accord of 1907 had never really been taken to heart among British and Russian officials on the ground. As the July crisis deepened, French diplomats were terrified that Russia's ongoing land grab in northern Persia would ruin the fragile accord between London and Petersburg just when Paris needed it the most.[14]

It is only when we sense the *fragility* of Russia's strategic position in 1914 that we can begin to make sense of her behavior during the July crisis. As Lord Durham, an unusually level-headed British ambassador to Petersburg, had once observed at the height of Great Game tensions, "the power of Russia has been greatly exaggerated. There is not one element of strength which is not directly counterbalanced by a corresponding ... weakness."[15] Durham's was and remained a minority opinion among British policymakers, who tended to overestimate Russia's strengths both when they were anxious for India's defense and when they were hoping to unleash her "Slavic hordes" against Germany.* The very size and ex-

---

* Compare Lord Durham to Sir George Buchanan, British ambassador to Russia before and during World War I, who advised London in April 1914 that "Russia is rapidly becoming so powerful that we must retain her friendship at almost any cost."

tent of the Romanov Empire meant that her borders were well-nigh impossible to defend. Russia's seemingly inexorable imperial expansion into Central Asia in the 1860s and 1870s, which led Russophobes in London to believe that some grand design was afoot targeting India, had in fact been propelled largely by the self-perpetuating strategic problem of border insecurity. "Every time a tribe was pacified," as one military analyst observed, "Russia was exposed to attack from the peoples who lived on the other side of the frontier cordon."[16]

Russia's more recent imperial expansion into eastern Turkey and northern Persia had reproduced the same strategic conundrum, as new enemies appeared on the frontier to replace those already incorporated inside the borders of the empire. The years before 1914 saw one crisis after another erupt on Russia's southern borderlands, with an ever-changing array of antagonists: now Kurdish depredations against Armenians and other Russia-friendly Christians, now Ottoman raids across the frontier of "Russian Persia" in pursuit of pro-Russian Kurdish tribesmen, now unrest among Russia's own Caucasian Muslims, particularly Tatars and Azeris believed to be receiving covert support from the Turks. When Russia's foreign minister Sazonov was asked in November 1910 by the British chargé d'affaires in Petersburg whether he believed the German chancellor's assurances "as to Germany never having encouraged Turkey in her aggressive action in Persian territory, and in the direction of the Russian frontier," Sazonov replied incredulously, "you do not suppose that I am sufficiently naïf to believe in them?" If, as Sazonov suspected, Turkey's anti-Russian maneuvering in Persia and the Caucasus was indeed being encouraged and financed by the German government—which was now insisting ominously on extending the German-dominated Baghdad Railway to the Persian frontier—one can hardly blame the Russians for paranoia about Berlin.[17]

The problem with railways, from the point of view of Chorister's Bridge, was that they upset Russia's traditional strategic advantage: geographical isolation. One of the key objectives of Russian diplomacy in the decades before 1914 was to *block* strategic railway building, particularly in Turkish Anatolia and Persia, so as to circumvent mobilization of hostile forces near Russia's borders. The Anglo-Russian Accord of 1907 had neutralized possible threats from Persia and Afghanistan in theory, but

Asiatic Turkey, believed to be under German influence, was another matter entirely. To the chagrin of both kaiser and sultan, the Baghdad Railway had been diverted southwest at great cost by way of Konya—failing entirely to exploit a pre-existing line running from the Asian shore of Constantinople to Ankara—precisely because of Russian objections to a line running anywhere within a country mile of the Caucasus. In 1906, Sazonov's predecessor, Alexander Izvolsky, had proposed a straight-up bargain with Berlin: Russia would "allow" completion of the Baghdad line so long as the Germans promised never, ever to build railways in Persia. It is true that this proposal was modified by Sazonov in November 1910 to appease the Germans, with Russia agreeing that the Baghdad Railway might be connected to the planned Russian Tiflis-Teheran line (which then ran as far as Djoulfa, on the border, toward Tabriz), crossing into Persia near Hanekin. In exchange the Germans promised not to countenance further "aggressive dispositions" by Austria in the Balkans. But Sazonov's bargain was just as cynical as Izvolsky's: in reality the Baghdad line had, by 1910, not yet bridged the Taurus and Amanus mountains through Cilicia and Syria, let alone been extended into Mesopotamia, where construction had not even begun. There would be plenty of time for the Russians to renege on this deal if the German line ever did get too close to Persia.[18]

Still more dangerous to Petersburg was the German rail network in Eastern Prussia and even, potentially, her own expanding network in Russian Poland. From the destructive wars with Sweden in the seventeenth and eighteenth centuries to Napoleon's invasion of 1812, Russians had learned at great human and material cost how vulnerable her western borders were. The great northern European plain was the last place Russia liked to fight her wars, not simply because there were few natural obstacles there to slow down invading armies, but because on her western border she faced European armies usually more advanced than her own. Building new lines in Russian Poland—or double-tracking the existing lines there—was certainly in the best interest of France, whose military planners were desperate to speed up Russia's mobilization on the German border. But accelerating the movement of men and war matériel across Poland was not necessarily in Russia's own interest, if (as was assumed in many realistic war-gaming scenarios dating back to the 1870s) the German army happened to capture it. Russia's updated Plan 19 for mobilization in a European war, approved by Tsar Nicholas II in 1910, actually *assumed* the Germans would capture almost ten provinces of Russian Poland.[19] Russian anxieties about German invasion are aptly illustrated in the gauge break at Brest-Litovsk: to this day trains crossing into Russia must wait in the station for an hour or more as their carriage is widened to fit the wider tracks.

Fear of what we might call the "German steamroller" colored Russian war planning and diplomacy to such an extent that the pacifist inclinations of the last two foreign ministers before 1914, Izvolsky and Sazonov, were (quite mistakenly in both cases) taken on faith in Paris and London, where both men were regarded as "liberals." As Sazonov later recalled with characteristic duplicity, "at the time when I joined the Russian Government [in 1910] there was no trace in St. Petersburg of the existence of any party which desired war."[20] As regards war with Berlin, this was doubtless true, as borne out in the Bosnian crisis of 1908–1909, when Austria's foreign minister, Baron Alois Lexa von Aehrenthal, had embarrassed Izvolsky by claiming that Vienna's unilateral annexation of Bosnia had the latter's imprimatur (the Russian thought he had negotiated a secret quid pro quo, with Vienna offering to support Russia's goal of revising the Berlin Treaty of 1878 to allow Russian warships free passage through the Straits).[21] Deposed from his ministerial post in Petersburg, the humiliated Izvolsky would play a major—and by no means pacific—role in the July crisis of 1914 as Russia's ambassador to France. (Upon learning that Russian mobilization had been declared, Izvolsky reportedly exclaimed, "This is my war!") Russian planning for a war of aggression against the Ottoman Empire was in full swing even as Izvolsky complained of Germanic bullying—in part to restore Russian prestige after the defeat in the Russo-Japanese War. In February 1908, addressing a special conference of the heads of the government, Foreign Ministry, army, and navy, Izvolsky himself mooted the idea of invading Turkey if a crisis were to break out on the Balkan peninsula. To his disappointment, Petr Stolypin, the chairman of the Council of Ministers, declared "categorically" that, due to the continuing social fallout from the 1905 revolution, "Russian mobilization was impossible at the present time, under any circumstances." Nevertheless, Russian concentration proceeded apace, so as to overcome then-Turkish superiority in the Caucasian theater. Later that year, Russia's chief of the General Staff, F. F. Palitsyn, quietly "ordered an automatic mobilization of Russian forces in the Caucasus if Turkish army formations on the other side of the frontier reached a certain density."[22]

Although Stolypin continued urging the generals to be patient, Russian plans to conquer Turkey received a major fillip with the Young Turk "Revolution" of July 1908, which was assumed at Chorister's Bridge—correctly, as it turned out—to have fatally weakened the regime of Abdul Hamid II (the sultan was deposed the following April, in conditions approximating civil war in Constantinople, and replaced by a figurehead, Mehmed Reshad V). The fall of the last true Ottoman sultan produced a kind of manic glee in the Russian General Staff, where war gaming for the occupation of Constantinople—which had largely ceased following the sinking of the Russian Baltic and Pacific fleets in the Russo-Japanese War—now resumed with a vengeance. The mood of the time was well captured in a General Staff memorandum of October 1910 that outlined plans for seizing Constantinople: first the rail and telegraph lines to Adrianople and Ankara would be cut by "agents from the Christian population" (Macedonians and Bulgarians in Europe, Greeks and Armenians in Anatolia), whereupon Russia-friendly Christians in the city would "burn down all the wooden bridges spanning the Golden Horn and set fire to Stambul"—which predominantly Muslim district was, conveniently for Russian purposes, blanketed "almost without interruption with wooden houses" *(pochti splosh" iz" derevyannyikh domov)*. The Christians of Pera would then rise, in coordination with a Russian amphibious landing. Once Russia's Black Sea fleet had secured the Straits, it would herald the "annihilation of Turkish dominion on the Balkan peninsula."*[23]

Russia's rulers, then, were hardly pacifists by inclination. Their preferred opponents were Persians, Turks, and Central Asian Khans and tribes of Turkmen—not simply because these enemies were easier to fight

---

* Showing that the "annihilation of Turkish dominion" was something more than a rhetorical flourish, this exact phrase occurs three separate times in this document. Variations of this phrase occur in nearly all Russian naval and army policy papers on amphibious operations targeting Constantinople.

The Polish Salient

SWEDEN

Gotland

Öland

BALTIC SEA

Bornholm

Estonia

Gulf of Riga

Riga

Courland (Latvia)

Düna (Dvina)

Dvinsk

Memel

Lithuania

Kovno

Vilna (Vilnius)

Wilja

Danzig

Königsberg

East Prussia

Allenstein

White Russia

RUSSIAN

Grodno

Niemen

To Moscow 540 m.

Tannenberg

Vistula

Lomza

Bialystok

Baranovichi

Oder

Notec

Torun

Narew

GERMAN

Posen

Vistula

Novo Georgievsk

EMPIRE

Frankfurt am Oder

To Berlin 150 m.

Posen

Warsaw

Bug

Brest Litovsk

Pinsk

Pripet Marshes

Pripet

EMPIRE

Kalish

Russian Poland

Warta

Lodz

Ukraine

Silesia

Breslau

Oder

Pilitsa

Ivangorod

Wieprz

Lublin

Kovel

To Kiev 190 m.

Lutsk

Rovno

Dubno

Krasnik

Bohemia

Austrian Silesia

Vistula

San

West Galicia

Cracow

Jaroslaw

Lemberg (Lvov)

Przemysl

Moravia

Carpathian

East Galicia

Dniestr

AUSTRIA-

Mountains

Vienna

HUNGARY

Danube

Czernowitz

Bukovina

Budapest

Tisza

Transylvania

0   50   100   150 miles

than Europeans, but because there were real, if ever problematic, gains to be had from beating them. Stolypin's famous 1909 remark that Russia needed "twenty years of peace" to complete her economic modernization in reality referred conditionally, like Sazonov's professions of pacifist intentions, to the prospects of a *European* war on Russia's vulnerable western borders. Meanwhile, Russia's perennial skirmishing on her eastern and southern borders would continue, as land syndicates and proconsuls continued the quiet imperial penetration of Anatolia, Persia, Afghanistan, Chinese Turkestan, Mongolia, and Manchuria. The recent war with Japan had been an imperial setback, of course; but it had only concentrated Russian expansion more neatly on her southern and southwestern borders.

Expansion to the west, by contrast, had only created problems for Russia. Poland was the suppurating wound of Russian military planning, subject of hundreds of anxious analyses and endless war gaming. A glance at the map is enough to grasp why: the "Polish salient," a bulge of territory 230 miles long by 200 miles wide, thrusts directly between German Eastern Prussia and Austrian Galicia, its flanks undefended by natural frontiers. In strictly military terms it made little sense for Petersburg to hold onto "Congress Poland" at all, as Russia's smarter generals realized. V. A. Sukhomlinov, Palitsyn's successor as chief of the General Staff (who had then pruned its power and taken over planning as war minister), and his assistant General Yuri Danilov reoriented Russia's deployments eastward into the Russian heartland with the updated Plan 19 of 1910, going so far as to demolish Polish fortresses, tempting the Germans into a war of attrition *à la Napoléon* if they were foolish enough to invade. (An important side benefit was that the Caucasian army, facing Turkey, was effectively doubled in strength, from two to three army corps.)[24]

Not surprisingly, the Sukhomlinov strategy sent Paris into a flat panic, raising the hackles of Russian Francophiles like V. N. Kokovtsev, then chairman of the Council of Ministers, and Grand Duke Nicholas, then inspector of cavalry, who teamed up to save the Franco-Russian alliance by vociferously repudiating Sukhomlinov's plans and rescuing at least some fortresses such as Novogeorievsk and Ivangorod, which guarded the railway bridges over the Vistula, from his wrecking crews.[25] Plan 19, however, endured into 1914. The famous stimulus for strategic railways

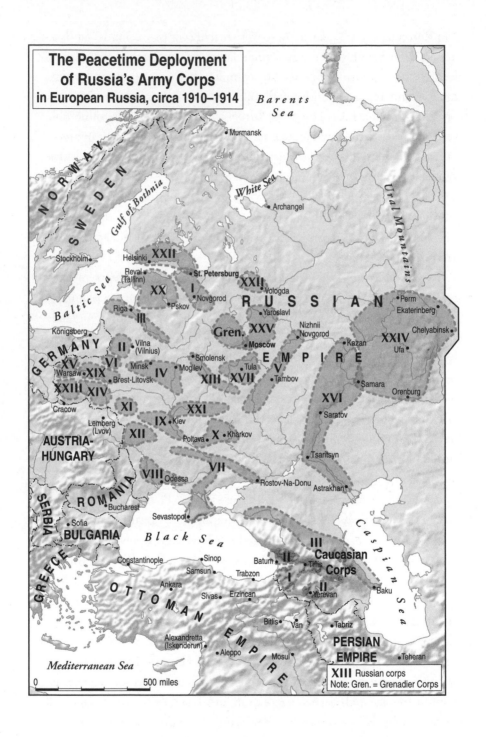

The Peacetime Deployment
of Russia's Army Corps
in European Russia, circa 1910–1914

Barents Sea

NORWAY

SWEDEN

Gulf of Bothnia

White Sea

• Murmansk

• Archangel

Ural Mountains

• Stockholm

• Helsinki

XXII

Baltic Sea

• Reval (Tallinn)

XX

I

• St. Petersburg

XXII

• Vologda

R U S S I A N

• Perm

• Ekaterinberg

• Riga

III

• Pskov

• Novgorod

• Yaroslavl

Gren. XXV

Nizhnii Novgorod

• Kazan

XXIV

• Chelyabinsk

• Ufa

• Königsberg

GERMANY

II

• Vilna (Vilnius)

• Moscow

E M P I R E

• Smolensk

XV

VI

• Minsk

IV

• Mogilev

• Tula

V

• Samara

• Orenburg

XIX

• Warsaw

• Brest-Litovsk

XIII XVII

• Tambov

XXIII

XIV

XI

XXI

IX

• Kiev

XVI

• Saratov

• Cracow

Lemberg (Lvov)

XII

• Poltava

X

• Kharkov

AUSTRIA-HUNGARY

VII

• Tsaritsyn

ROMANIA

VIII

• Odessa

• Rostov-Na-Donu

• Astrakhan

SERBIA

• Bucharest

• Sevastopol

Caspian Sea

• Sofia

BULGARIA

Black Sea

III

Caucasian Corps

GREECE

• Constantinople

• Sinop

• Batum

II

• Tiflis

• Samsun

• Trabzon

I

• Baku

OTTOMAN

• Ankara

• Sivas

• Erzincan

II

• Yerevan

EMPIRE

• Bitlis

• Van

• Tabriz

• Alexandretta (Iskenderun)

PERSIAN EMPIRE

• Teheran

Mediterranean Sea

• Aleppo

• Mosul

| 0 | 500 miles |

XIII Russian corps
Note: Gren. = Grenadier Corps

in Poland in the army's Great Program of October 1913 was provided at French insistence—after all, it was French capital paying for it. Building up the Polish railway net, however, was never a *Russian* priority. (In fact, the Russians refused to build any railways at all west of the Niemen, fearing they would fall into German hands.)[26] Had Sukhomlinov had his way, every last one of Poland's fortresses would have been razed to the ground, with money wasted on their 5,000 heavy fortress guns spent instead on mobile artillery in the field.[27]

Poland's strategic importance for Russia was, in reality, more symbolism than substance. Since the 1870s, Pan-Slavist propaganda had created monstrous new pseudo-obligations for Russian foreign policy. Even moderate "national liberals" like Sazonov worried that increasing German or Austrian influence over Russian Poles would call into question the loyalties of Slavic protégés like the Serbs and Bulgarians, not to mention subject-Slavs such as Ukrainians. Taking the precepts of national liberalism still further, "neo-Slavists," like Grigorii Trubetskoi, head of the Foreign Ministry's Near Eastern department, wanted Russia to offer autonomy to Poland out of Slavic solidarity. If Congress Poland ever fell under Germanic influence, the thinking went, then Russia could kiss her influence in the Balkans goodbye. Any setback to the Bulgarians or Serbs might loosen the bonds holding Poland in Petersburg's orbit. Conversely, Russian gains in the Balkans (or Turkey) would excite expectations among Slavic minorities in Austria-Hungary—Czechs, Croats, Poles, Serbs, and "Ruthenes," that is, "Little Russian" Habsburg subjects, as the Russians called them (or "Ukrainians," as most would later call themselves).[28] Ideally, in neo-Slavist thinking, Russian foreign policy should aim for the "deliverance of the Slavic peoples from their shackles: Turkish, Hungarian, and German" and the "union of these peoples in a powerful Slavic federation."[29] Or as Grigorii's like-minded brother E. N. Trubetskoi memorably put it, "The Road to Constantinople runs through Warsaw."[30]

It may have sounded like a fantasy, but Russian imperialists were dead serious about dismembering Turkey—and, in the wake of the apparent ineptitude of the Ballplatz during the Balkan wars of 1912–1913, Austria-Hungary too. As the French chargé d'affaires in Petersburg observed in March 1914, "little by little the scales fell from the eyes of Russian policymakers [during the Balkan wars] .. the lamentable performance of Austria laid bare that Vienna was powerless and that the only real power in the Triple Alliance lay in Berlin."[31] Tsar Nicholas II himself told the British ambassador in April 1913 that "the disintegration of the Austrian Empire was merely a question of time."[32] As Sazonov recalled of the atmosphere in the capital after the Balkan wars, "in society circles . . . in close touch with . . . Court and military centres, there was a rooted conviction that a favourable moment was approaching for settling with Austria-Hungary."[33] By April 1914, *Novoe Vremya,* Petersburg's most influential newspaper,* was openly advocating the dismemberment of the Habsburg Empire, which had come to seem just as inevitable as the collapse of Ottoman Turkey.[34] Making a war of conquest against Austria still more enticing was the fact that a high-ranking traitor, Colonel Alfred Redl, had sold the Russians a genuine copy of the Austrian mobilization plan against Russia in 1913.[35] Austrian Galicia was as tempting to Russian generals as the Polish salient was to the Germans: by seizing it, the Russian army would no longer have to worry about its exposed Polish flank, and then maybe all those fortresses could do some good after all.

That Russian lust for Austrian Galicia, circa 1914, was not mere journalistic gossip is confirmed by Maurice Paléologue, the recently appointed French ambassador to Russia. In early May 1914, Paléologue felt compelled to report to Paris a conversation with "an influential member of the Council of Ministers" (probably A. V. Krivoshein, the minister of agriculture) in which Paléologue had asked the Russian minister what might transpire if Franz Josef I, the long-serving Habsburg emperor, were ever to step down due to old age. Before he could even finish asking his question, Paléologue recalled, "[Krivoshein] interrupted me: 'First of all, we would be obliged to annex Galicia. Our minister of war, General Sukhomlinov, explained to me just the other day that the possession of Galicia is indispensable to the security of our frontier. And besides, it is basically Russian territory" *(et puis, c'est un pays foncièrement russe).*[36]

There were two "Eastern Questions," then, which competed for the attention of Russia's strategists in 1914. It would be wrong, however, to

---

* On its board sat not only Peter Bark, the finance minister, but also Alexander Guchkov, who headed the Octobrist Party in the Duma.

mistake the greed with which Sazonov and the generals viewed the impending collapse of the Ottoman and Habsburg empires for anything like confidence that Russia would be the real beneficiary. Russian statesmen had been haunted for decades by the disastrous outcome of the Crimean War, when Tsar Nicholas I's nominal Austrian ally had betrayed him by ordering his troops to evacuate Romania while his armies were in battle against Britain, France, Sardinia, and the Ottoman Empire—just six years after Russian troops had helped Vienna suppress a Hungarian nationalist uprising. This "fear of the Crimean coalition" was replaced, after 1878, with dread of the even more bewildering "Congress of Berlin syndrome," wherein, despite Russia having for once fought a war against Turkey in which no enemy coalition had coalesced, diplomatic defeat had nevertheless been snatched from the jaws of victory on the battlefield. In the 1910 General Staff memorandum cited above, the author vows not to "repeat the cardinal mistake of 1877–1878": by invading Turkey overland through the Balkans (rather than by sending a rapid amphibious landing force directly to Constantinople), Russia had given the powers too much time to assemble the vaguely hostile coalition that led to the Congress of Berlin. In any future war, the Russians would have to strike much more quickly.[37]

The First Balkan War provided a critical dry run for Russia's military planners. It is worth examining the crisis in some detail, for in nearly every important particular it prefigured Russia's options in the July crisis of 1914. Capitalizing on the dispersal of Ottoman forces resulting from the ongoing war with Italy, Montenegro declared war on Turkey on 8 October 1912, followed nine days later by Serbia, Bulgaria, and Greece. Pressed to the limit, the Porte was forced to sign an armistice with Italy on 15 October 1912, which might have enabled reinforcements to be routed to Ottoman Europe but for the stunning rapidity of the coalition advance. On 22/23 October, the Bulgarians broke through at Kırk Kilise, opening up a path across Thrace to the final Ottoman defensive lines at Çatalca, just thirty-seven miles from Constantinople. On 24 October, the Serbs routed the Turks in Macedonia. On 8 November, the Greeks entered Salonica, reducing Ottoman-controlled Europe in effect to the Gallipoli peninsula, the capital itself, and several fortress strongholds, such as Adrianople (Edirne), which were now surrounded by the enemy.

As the Balkan crisis deepened in November 1912, the threat of a general European war began to loom. Austro-Hungarian troops in Bosnia-Herzegovina and Dalmatia were placed "on a war footing," while Austria was also reinforcing its Galician garrisons facing Russia at Cracow, Przemysl, and Lemberg (Lviv or Lvov). Many expected the Germans to react more strongly than this, with their ostensible client state, Turkey, threatened with oblivion. (It had not escaped anyone's notice that the French-manufactured Creusot rifles and guns deployed by the Serbs and Bulgarians had apparently outperformed the Turks' weapons, made by Krupp and Skoda.) And yet Kaiser Wilhelm II, for all his famous Turcophilia, had soured somewhat on the Ottomans since his friend, Sultan Abdul Hamid II, had been deposed in 1909; he declared the Germans' policy as a relaxed one of "free fight and no favor," that is, that they would simply let the battles run their course. Without the requisite backing from Berlin, Vienna famously sat out the Balkan wars, even after the armies of her archenemy, Serbia, reached the Adriatic coastline on 15 November 1912, threatening what was by any reckoning a serious national interest, Austrian control of the Adriatic Sea. It was her passivity at this crucial stage of the First Balkan War, more than anything else, that convinced so many policymakers in Petersburg of Austria's strategic impotence.

The contrast with Russian behavior during the First Balkan War could not be more striking. The coalition advance in Ottoman Europe was ostensibly a triumph for Chorister's Bridge. Russia's notorious minister to Belgrade, Nikolai Hartwig, was widely believed to be the mastermind of the predatory Balkan coalition. And yet, so far from following the kaiser's policy of "free fight and no favor" even as his Ottoman clients were being routed, Russia's leaders had improbably reacted with near hysteria as Hartwig's Russophile coalition was routing the Turks. Having already sanctioned a dangerous "trial mobilization" in Poland as the war first broke in October, on 22 November 1912 Russia's war minister, Sukhomlinov, prepared orders for a full-on yet "partial" mobilization of the military districts of Warsaw (that is, Russian Poland, targeting Austrian Galicia), Kiev (Russian Ukraine, targeting same), and, intriguingly, Odessa (from which an amphibious operation in Constantinople might be launched). The idea, almost identical to the one that would be mooted in July 1914, was for Russia to appear to mobilize "against Austria alone," so as not to alarm the Germans. On 23 November 1912, after "asking Sukhomlinov to wait another day," Tsar Nicholas II convened an emergency meeting of his senior ministers, including Army Chief of Staff General Yakov Zhilinskii, Sazonov, Krivoshein, and Kokovtsev, the chairman of the Council of Ministers, to discuss the war minister's "partial mobilization" plan. After Kokovtsev, the conservative chairman, explained that such a mobilization would inexorably lead to general Austrian mobilization, to be followed by German mobilization and thus a European war, the Crown Council vetoed Sukhomlinov's plan, thus averting what might have been the Great War—of 1912.[38]

Why was it Russia, and not Austria or (as Fischer suggested) Germany,[39] that nearly plunged Europe into war in November-December 1912, at a time when her Balkan clients were sweeping all before them? Despite appearances, the advance of the Balkan armies into the Thracian plain was, in fact, more dangerous to Russian interests than to those of any other power. For an ambitious king-conqueror, like the self-styled "Tsar" Ferdinand of Bulgaria, to inherit the mantle of Byzantium was the *last* thing Russian statesmen wanted. (Ferdinand in fact kept a full Byzantine emperor's regalia in his closet, made to order by a theatrical costumer, for just such an occasion.) Russia had sent troops—at Turkish invitation—to protect Constantinople from the forces of Khedive Muhammad Ali as Egypt swept across Anatolia in 1833, and, with Bulgarian troops nearing the city from the European side now, she threatened to do so again. Even as Sukhomlinov was getting the army ready for action, on 26 October 1912 Russia's naval minister, Ivan K. Grigorevich—with the apposite patronymic of Konstantinovich—wired Tsar Nicholas II with a request to place the Black Sea fleet under the command of M. N. Girs, Russia's ambassador to the Porte, so that he might summon it at a moment's notice to Constantinople. The tsar agreed.[40] The danger was not simply that the Bulgarians threatened to conquer "Tsargrad" without Russian help, but that the approach of any enemy army to the gates of the capital posed a risk to the Christian population of the capital. Sazonov had already received requests for Russian protection from the Greek Orthodox patriarch, along with various western governments, including the United States, Belgium, and Sweden, who feared for the safety of their ambassadorial staff. In this sense, the Bulgarian advance, dangerous though it was, also provided Russia with an opportunity—a pretext by which Russia might seize the Straits by force. As Sazonov explained in a long memorandum to Kokovtsev, Sukhomlinov, and Grigorevich on 12 November 1912, conquering Constantinople would give Russia a "global position which is the natural crown of her efforts and sacrifices over two centuries of our history." Such a crowning strategic triumph, Russia's foreign minister continued in the most grandiose vein of national liberalism, might also "bring healing to our internal life, [and] would give the government and society those achievements and that enthusiasm which could unite them in the service of a matter of indisputable pan-national importance."[41]

Sazonov's vision of a dramatic storming of Constantinople, seductive though it was to pan-Slavists and national liberals, was still premature in 1912. Sufficient naval carrying capacity was lacking. Then, too, even if enough ships could be found, the army chiefs, Sukhomlinov and Danilov, had made clear their opposition to any major diversion of troops from the European front, such as would be necessary to mount a proper amphibious strike. It was not that either man was against conquering Constantinople. Rather, they had a different idea as to how to go about it. As Danilov put it in what we might call the military version of national liberal neo-Slavism, "The shortest and safest operational route to Constantinople runs through Vienna . . . and Berlin."[42]

Nevertheless, Sazonov had laid down an important marker in Russian Straits policy. Having first seriously though unsuccessfully broached the idea of an amphibious landing in November 1912, and then once more (again unsuccessfully) after the Ottoman garrison at Adrianople fell on 27 March 1913, Sazonov would admonish the service chiefs repeatedly over the coming months that Russia's Black Sea fleet must be made ready to intervene decisively at the Straits at a moment's notice—if need be, denying them to Bulgaria.[43]

For all the hype about pan-Slavic solidarity created by nationalistic Russian newspapers, the Straits/Bulgaria issue shows it to be largely hollow. Sazonov was arguably the leading exponent of national liberalism and its pan-Slavic themes in the Russian government, and yet when push came to shove, he was willing to throw fellow Balkan "Slavs" overboard if Russia's national interests were threatened. Bulgaria was a Slavic client state literally created by the force of Russian arms in 1878. Bulgarian staff officers had, as recently as the summer of 1912, conducted joint planning exercises with the Russian General Staff for invading Turkey.[44] During the Second Balkan War, launched in June 1913, Bulgaria was rapidly overwhelmed by Greece, Romania, Serbia, and Turkey—in what appeared to all Europe as a rebuke to Russian prestige and pan-Slavism. And yet Bulgaria's comeuppance in the Second Balkan War was regarded with seeming indifference at Chorister's Bridge, whereas the Bulgarian threat to the Straits in the First Balkan War had produced a veritable war scare in Petersburg. With hardly a touch of regret, after the imposition of the draconian Treaty of Bucharest in August 1913, Sazonov assumed Bulgaria matter-of-factly to be a hostile power, due both to Sofia's revanchist designs on territory lost in this treaty to Greece, Romania, and Serbia; and, more significant, her evident desire to conquer Constantinople without Russian help.[45]

Even Serbia itself, Russia's ostensible casus belli in July 1914, was of purely symbolic interest to Russian foreign policy properly understood. Of course, Russia had no wish to see "heroic little Serbia" carved up by hostile neighbors such as Austria-Hungary or Bulgaria, but neither did she wish to see Serbia herself aggrandized. During the first Bosnian crisis, in 1908, Serbia had demanded territorial compensation in exchange for recognizing Austria's annexation of Bosnia-Herzegovina: Izvolsky refused to back Belgrade.[46] Had Russia truly wished to "fight for Serbia," the time would have been in October 1913, in the aftermath of the Second Balkan War, when the Austrians at last showed enough spine to demand that the Serbian army withdraw from Albania, in effect to deny Serbia access to the Adriatic. Instead, Sazonov quietly went along with this Austrian démarche because Russia had no interest in seeing Serbia so aggrandized. Denying Belgrade its coveted port access to the Adriatic in fact became one of Sazonov's principal foreign policy goals following the Second Balkan War, to the extent that he quietly intrigued to restore Albania to *Ottoman* control so as to weaken Serbia.[47] Not the least (apparent) irony of the July crisis of 1914 is that Petersburg plunged into war on behalf of the very country her diplomats had been lobbying against for months.

To assume that Russia really went to war on behalf of Serbia in 1914 is naïve. Great powers do not usually mobilize armies of millions to protect the territorial integrity of minor client states. To take an obvious example from recent history, it beggars the strategic imagination to believe that the United States–led coalition truly fought the First Gulf War to reconstitute the internationally recognized boundaries of Kuwait. The "New World Order" of universally sanctified borders was a useful rhetorical fig leaf to cover up the sordid-but-necessary business of restoring order and predictability to Persian Gulf oil supplies and deterring further aggression that might disrupt them.

Likewise, Russia's real interests in July 1914 could not possibly have been as ethereal as her public posturing about "Slavic honor and the Serbs." An extensive survey of Russia's diplomatic correspondence in the months before the Sarajevo incident does not reveal undue concern with any sort of Serbian problem, nor, indeed, is concern voiced in the months after July. (Revealingly, one of Sazonov's first diplomatic moves following the outbreak of the world war was to pressure Serbia to cede Macedonian territory to Bulgaria.)[48] What it *does* reveal is a widespread obsession, bordering on panic, with the Straits question. Following the Italian and the two Balkan wars, it was now universally assumed that Turkey would not last for long in the face of the belligerent hostility of its neighbors. The question was, which power would swallow which pieces of the carcass as the Ottoman Sick Man was carved up? And for Petersburg, the question was starker still: who would now control Constantinople and the Straits?

Because of the centuries-old Russian interest in "Tsargrad" as the "Second Rome" of Orthodox Christian dreams, the Straits obsession of Russian policymakers like Sazonov in the early twentieth century has sometimes been mistakenly assumed to be romantic. In fact, Russia's designs on the Straits, unlike her shadowy pan-Slavic pretensions in the Balkans, were a matter of cold, hard national interest. Not for nothing had Izvolsky nearly plunged Petersburg into war in the first Bosnian crisis after Vienna reneged on Aehrenthal's promise to support Russia's desired right of passage into the Mediterranean for its warships (while failing to offer even nominal backing for Serbia's demand for territorial compensation).[49] In economic terms, the importance of the Straits for Russia was stark and true. Although calculations differed on the exact figure, something approaching half of Russia's burgeoning export trade was, by 1914, routed via the Black Sea, Bosphorus, and Dardanelles to world markets.[50]

When, in summer 1912, the Porte had briefly closed the Straits to shipping during the Italian-Turkish War, Russia's vulnerability had been painfully exposed: the volume of Black Sea exports dropped by one-third for the calendar year 1912, and revenue likewise dipped 30 percent, from 77 million pounds sterling (or nearly 800 million rubles) to 57 million (less than 600 million rubles). Heavy industry in the Ukraine, dependent on supplies imported directly through the Straits via the Black Sea, had nearly ground to a halt. Although the Straits remained open for commerce during the two Balkan wars, the general disruption to trade was already so damaging that Russia's export revenue in 1913 was still 20 percent lower than in 1911.[51] Because this revenue paid for the imports of manufactured components on which Russian industry increasingly depended, not least in the Ukraine and south Russia, the evaporation of the Black Sea export trade had devastated Russia's recently favorable trade balance, with a surplus of some 430 million rubles in 1910 plummeting to 200 million in 1913. At this pace, Russia's balance-of-payments surplus threatened to erode within a year or two, which would undermine her industrialization drive and, with it, her goal of remaining a great power.[52]

To understand the overriding importance of the Straits question for Petersburg, however, we must go beyond numbers. Russia's principal Black Sea export was grain. Over 20 million tons was shipped in both 1911 and 1912, of which nearly 90 percent was exported through the Bosphorus to world markets: the health of her entire agricultural economy now depended on unfettered Straits access. Stimulating grain production was, moreover, the key to Stolypin's social reforms, which envisioned the creation of a stable class of successful peasant producers who would serve as a bulwark against anarchic social revolution. Ever since 1907 (and particularly following Stolypin's death in 1911) these reforms had been overseen by Stolypin's star protégé, Agriculture Minister Krivoshein. Krivoshein was universally believed to be the most powerful policymaker in Petersburg in 1914. In February he maneuvered his own creature, the elderly figurehead I. L. Goremykin, into power as chairman of the council, over the more pacifistic Kokovtsev, who had become a punching-bag for Russian nationalists because of his passivity during the Balkan wars. Krivoshein was a notorious Germanophobe: the French loved him. His

overriding priority was protecting Stolypin's land reforms, both by protecting the domestic grain market against German competition and by
ensuring unrestricted access to the Straits for exports.[53]

In view of Russia's increasing export-economy vulnerability and burgeoning Germanophobia in the Council of Ministers, it is not hard to see
why rumors about the imminent appointment of Liman von Sanders (and
forty-odd other German officers) to command the Ottoman Straits defenses in November 1913 struck Petersburg like a thunderclap. Already on
high alert lest the ungrateful Bulgarians usurp Turkish authority in Constantinople, Russia was now faced with the frightening prospect that her
most powerful enemy would soon possess a chokehold at the Straits over
her export economy, on which depended everything else. In discussions
of the Liman affair, Sazonov's famously belligerent reaction to the news
is sometimes dismissed as exaggerated because of his personal anger at
having been duped (he had recently passed through Berlin, and Bethmann Hollweg had not told him of Liman's upcoming appointment).[54] In
fact Sazonov was legitimately terrified in November 1913, and not simply because a German officer was being sent to strengthen—and possibly
take over—Ottoman Straits defenses. In a series of dispatches from the
Porte that month, Ambassador Girs informed Sazonov ominously that
the Turks were arming themselves to the teeth to avenge recent battlefield
losses. The new government, dominated by members of the Committee
of Union and Progress (CUP), had just signed a new deal with Krupp for
guns which, presumably, would be mounted onshore at the Bosphorus
and Dardanelles. The Italians, despite the recent hostilities, were now
selling guns and even three small warships to Turkey.[55] Most worrying of
all were the two state-of-the-art dreadnought-class battleships being built
for Turkey in British shipyards, the launching of even one of which, the
Naval Staff had pointedly warned Sazonov as early as 1912, would immediately make obsolete Russia's entire Black Sea fleet.[56] These dreadnoughts were expected to arrive in Constantinople, Girs informed Sazonov in an urgent 27 November 1913 dispatch, by March or April 1914.
All this, coupled with the prospect of an experienced German officer directing the shore defenses of the Bosphorus, meant that Russia's window
for seizing the Straits might soon close forever. "In the event of a crisis,
which must sooner or later transpire in Turkey," Girs warned Sazonov,

"the [improved] Turkish fleet will be able to strike a decisive blow against us. This blow will not only be devastating to our Black Sea fleet, but to our entire position in the Near East, the unassailable right to which we have acquired through centuries of immeasurable sacrifices and the shedding of Russian blood" *(bezspornyiya prava na kotoroe priobreli vekovymi niezmerimyimi zhortvami i prolitoi za nikh' russkoi krov'yu).*[57]

The timing of the Liman appointment alone was enough to produce panic in Petersburg. Just in the preceding eighteen months, Russia had seen Turkey close the Straits to her shipping during the Italian war; two Bulgarian offensives which, over Russian objections, had reached the shore of the Sea of Marmara, within sight of Constantinople; a major Turkish naval import drive, funded by (the Russians assumed) Berlin; and now a German mission to modernize the Ottoman army, including the Bosphorus shore defenses. It is little wonder that Sazonov took fright, warning the tsar on 6 December 1913, in a memorandum clearly influenced by the dire tone of Girs's recent dispatches, that "the state which possesses the Straits will hold in its hands not only the key of the Black Sea and Mediterranean, but also that of penetration into Asia Minor and the sure means of hegemony in the Balkans."[58] It was with these colossal stakes in mind that Sazonov, in a historic 6 January 1914 memorandum to Tsar Nicholas II, for the first time mooted the idea of provoking a European war over the Straits question, which would lead to the sharing out of Turkey among the powers of the Triple Entente: "If our War Minister and our Navy Minister believe it possible to risk complications, in the case, of course, in which France should decide to support us with all her forces and England lent us adequate assistance, we can now today engage on a confidential exchange of views on this question [the occupation and possible partition of the Ottoman Empire] with these two Powers." The idea was for Britain to land troops at Smyrna (Izmir), France at Beirut, and the Russians at Trabzon, ostensibly to pressure the Porte into expelling the Liman mission, but in reality as a prelude to partition. As the official Russian draft aide-mémoire phrased it ominously, "we would remain there until the fulfillment of our demands."[59]

At a historic meeting of the Russian Council of Ministers held one week later, Sazonov, War Minister Sukhomlinov, Naval Minister Grigorevich, Army Chief of Staff Zhilinskii, and Chairman Kokovtsev openly discussed the possibility of provoking a European conflagration over the Liman affair. Of the principals only the by now notoriously pacifistic Kokovtsev—who, significantly, would be ousted in February—spoke energetically against the prospect of a European war, which he thought would be "the greatest misfortune that could befall Russia." When Kokovtsev asked the generals, "Is the war with Germany desirable and can Russia wage it?" Sukhomlinov and Zhilinskii replied "categorically" that "Russia was perfectly prepared for a duel with Germany, not to speak of one with Austria." The crucial point to Sukhomlinov was that although "perfectly prepared" to wage war, Russia in reality would not have to fight alone: "it would more probably be a matter of settling accounts with the Triple Entente." Backing up the war minister, Sazonov informed everyone that France's departing ambassador, Théophile Delcassé, had assured him that "France will go as far as Russia wishes." Unlike in the Crimean War, when Russia had faced a hostile coalition encompassing nearly all of the other great powers, France and England, her principal opponents then, would this time be on her side—unless, that is, London finked out in the crunch, which would ruin everything. Sazonov himself considered British intervention a certainty "in the case of any setbacks in the military operations of Russia and France," but Kokovtsev was not willing to risk sparking a European conflagration in the absence of guarantees. In the end, the Council of Ministers resolved to continue negotiating with Berlin about Liman's appointment, resorting to war only if "the active participation of both France and England in joint measures were ... assured."[60]

Sazonov and the Russians, to be sure, ultimately backed down in the Liman affair, consenting to an awkward compromise on 16 January 1914 that saw the German promoted to inspector-general of the Ottoman First Army (rendering him overqualified to command a single corps, such as the one responsible for Straits defenses). But to conclude from this that Russia had buckled again in the face of German pressure, as some in Berlin and Vienna unfortunately surmised, was to misread the situation entirely. The weeks following the Liman compromise saw not only the fall of Kokovtsev, whom many nationalists blamed for backing down in the Liman affair, but also the famous "press war" between Russia and Germany, with nationalist newspapers in Berlin and Petersburg all but urging their leaders to take the plunge into war.[61] Not least, there was a historic joint army-navy planning meeting that February in Petersburg, chaired by Foreign Minister Sazonov and attended by Girs, the ambassador to Constantinople, that aimed to make Russia's Black Sea naval and amphibious forces strong enough to seize Constantinople on their own—ungrateful Bulgarians, German-Ottoman inspector-generals, British dreadnoughts, and all.

The basic upshot of the 8/21 February 1914 "special conference" in Petersburg—the appropriation of 102 million rubles by the Duma in March to accelerate the development of Russia's Black Sea fleet, pursuant to seizing the Straits in the coming years—was never really secret.[62] Sazonov even discusses the meeting in his memoirs, admitting openly that the principals agreed that "they considered an offensive against Constantinople inevitable, should European war break out." The problem which (Sazonov claims) emerged in the course of the discussion among the military and naval staffs was that "we did not possess the means to take swift and decisive action, and that years would elapse before we were in a position to execute the plans we had in view." This revelation left Sazonov feeling "greatly depressed." And so, far from constituting (as in the postwar German critique) any sort of "plot against the integrity of the Ottoman Empire and a threat to European peace," the Russian plans hatched in February 1914, Sazonov concludes, were "wholly defensive" and of a "peaceful character."[63]

In the admittedly competitive field of disingenuous and misleading First World War memoirs, this crucial passage in Sazonov's *Fateful Years* must rank near the top of the list. By claiming that the February 1914 conference was a one-off, Sazonov cleverly implies that Russian plans to seize the Straits were hatched only in response to German provocation, in the form of the Liman mission. "The formidable symptoms of Turkey's approaching disintegration," he writes, "which Germany had foreseen, and was ready to take advantage of—obliged Russia to consider the measures to which she might at any time have to resort to in defence of her own safety."[64] In fact, as Sazonov himself had informed Tsar Nicholas II in a secret telegram only two months previously, serious Russian operational planning to seize Constantinople by force dated back to 1895–1896, when they had been kicked off in hopeful response to the first major wave of Armenian uprisings and subsequent massacres.[65] Alas, Sazonov informed the tsar, Russia's amphibious carrying capacity, in the form of warships and merchant marine vessels, was not then sufficient.[66] Eighteen years later, it was *still* not quite sufficient, but not for lack of trying. The February 1914 conference may have been the first one Sazonov attended in person, but for Naval and General Staff officers, joint Straits-seizure planning conferences were a dime a dozen. Just six months previously, the Naval Staff had promised the army that the Black Sea fleet could provide enough transport ships to ferry 127,500 soldiers (including 3,500 officers), 44,000 horses, 288 guns, and 11,200 horse-drawn wagons from Odessa to Constantinople. To accomplish this feat, they would add to the existing fleet by quickly commandeering 115 civilian ships from Russia's Merchant Marine. All Black Sea port officials were already under naval command. True, it would take sixty days for all the men and war matériel to reach the Ottoman capital, but the first "echelon," comprising a bit more than a single army corps (30,000 to 50,000 men), including a full division's artillery component, could put ashore by Day 15, weather conditions permitting.[67] By February 1914, "zero hour"—the day on which the first Russian amphibious landing forces would put ashore at the Bosphorus—had been accelerated to M + 10.[68] The plan to seize Constantinople and the Straits, perhaps the single greatest operational priority of the Russian Naval Staff (although not also the Army Staff) in the last decade before the First World War, was self-evidently not a "defensive" operation, contrary to Sazonov's protestation in his memoirs.[69]

As for Sazonov's contention that Russian intentions in February 1914 were "peaceful" because she was not yet ready to wage war, this is an even greater howler. Russia's naval minister, Grigorevich, had personally assured Sazonov on 2 January 1914, at the height of the war scare over Liman, just four days before the foreign minister first mooted the idea of going to war in his own memorandum to the tsar, that "the fleet is ready for wartime operations."[70] The conference held the following month, moreover, was a war planning session. The issue addressed by Russia's top diplomats, generals, and naval admirals on 8/21 February 1914[71]—a meeting convened by order of His Majesty Nicholas II, under the chairmanship of Sazonov himself—was, according to the original transcript, "the possibility of the Straits question being opened, even quite possibly in the near future" *(byit' mozhet' dazhe v blizkom budushchem)*. Ideally, the

Straits "question" could be answered without a general European war, but no one in the room was in any doubt that the question *would* soon be answered, and by war. The one given in all scenarios was this: among Russia's "enemies" would be found, "first and foremost, the Turks" *(Takovyim prezhde vsego yavit'sya turki).* For this reason the cardinal priority of the Naval and Army Staffs was the acceleration of the mobilization timetable against Turkey: the expansion of amphibious forces available on the Black Sea littoral, up to at least three full army corps; intensified artillery training in the Odessa district; the acceleration of the landing of the first amphibious "echelon" from M + 10 to M + 5; the building or sudden importation of dreadnoughts into the Black Sea fleet; and the extension of Caucasian rail lines up to Oltu on the Turkish border, via Kars and Sarıkamış. Far from betting that "years would elapse" before a crisis would "force" Russia to seize Constantinople, Sazonov and the service chiefs were preparing for a war with Turkey *right now.*[72]

There are several important observations to be made here. The first is that, at the last planning conference of Imperial Russia's leading civilian and military officials before the July crisis, there was no mention of Serbia and only passing reference to the mobilization timetable against Germany and Austria-Hungary. The strategic issue of the day was clear and unambiguous: Constantinople and the Straits. The second point is that, despite all the hue and cry about Russia's Army Great Program of October 1913, and the (soon to be announced) Naval Program of March 1914—neither of which would be completed before 1917 at the earliest—Russia's leaders were under no illusion that they would be able to wait that long before going to war. True, none of Russia's three Black Sea dreadnoughts-under-construction, the *Empress Catherine II, Emperor Alexander III,* and *Empress Maria,* would be ready for several years. But apart from re-stating the obvious need to finish building these modern warships in the Black Sea (and the commissioning of a fourth, the *Emperor Nicholas I,* along with two light cruisers), five of the six points resolved at the February conference concerned immediate, short-term mobilization measures. And all six points related to the Ottoman Empire.[73]

Why the sense of urgency? Contrary to Sazonov's clever insinuation about German provocation, the real impetus behind the February 1914 conference came from Turkey. For years Russia's staff officers had observed Ottoman naval developments with foreboding. The British Naval Mission to Turkey, inaugurated in 1908 and headed by the formidable Admiral Arthur Limpus, was just as offensive to Russian sensibilities as Liman's German Army Mission, and arguably a good deal more dangerous. As early as 1911, Russia's naval attaché was reporting that "skeleton crews" were being trained by English instructors to man British dreadnoughts as soon as they arrived in the Sea of Marmara. One Ottoman navy training manual, translated into Russian and sent to the Foreign Ministry, displayed a worrying level of sophistication, encouraging Turkish petty officers to hone their physical sang-froid by playing competitive team sports (the Turks had apparently taken to heart Wellington's line about Waterloo being won "on the playing fields of Eton") and requiring that they all learn English and spend at least two to three years in England.*[74] This sort of thing might not have mattered a great deal, except for two key facts. First, by January 1914 Turkey had no less than *five* imported dreadnoughts on order. Three of these five were being built in England: the *Reshad V* and the *Rio de Janeiro,* originally contracted to Brazil, the latter soon to be renamed the *Sultan Osman I;* and the *Almirant-Latorre,* originally contracted to Chile. Two more were under construction in the United States (the *Rivadia* and the *Moreno,* first contracted to Argentina), and Turkey was rumored to have another one in the hopper on top of these. Second, by the terms of the Berlin Treaty of 1878, as Izvolsky had reminded Aehrenthal during their ill-fated diplomatic dalliance in 1908, Russia was not allowed to send warships through the Straits, even in peacetime, which meant she could not import dreadnoughts into the Black Sea. And the earliest possible launch of the first Russian-built Black Sea dreadnought, the *Empress Maria,* was the end of 1915 (a wildly optimistic scenario). By this time, Grigorevich warned Sazonov in a top-secret memorandum on 17 January 1914, Turkey would have launched "at least three, if not four ships of the line of the dreadnought class." Moreover, because the Turks' three state-of-the-art British ships all mounted thirteen-and-a-half inch guns—the *Sultan Osman I* would mount more guns than any ship ever afloat—they would greatly outclass the Russian

---

* Turkish naval officers would also now all learn to swim. That this needed to be stipulated says a great deal about the historic limitations of the Ottoman navy.

ships' twelve-inch guns, which also lacked a "superfiring imposition," meaning the Turkish dreadnoughts could fire larger shells not only farther but faster. Here, Grigorevich wrote Sazonov on 19 January 1914, was the real "crisis of the 'Eastern Question'": as soon as the *Reshad V* or the *Sultan Osman I* passed through the Dardanelles, the "Turks would have undisputed mastery of the Black Sea."[75]

If Germany had a narrow window of opportunity in 1914 to preempt the Russian army's Great Program, then Russia's own window was still narrower. Delivery of the first British-Ottoman dreadnought was expected within weeks. The *Sultan Osman I* had in fact already been launched to sea; its dispatch in Turkey awaited only the imminent completion of proper docking facilities in Constantinople, being built by British firms, Vickers and Armstrong Whitworth.[76] Making Turkey's naval expansion drive still more frightening to Petersburg, it was not only British and American shipyards who were supplying Constantinople, and not only British firms who were modernizing its port. Three cruisers had been ordered from an Italian yard in 1914; two submarines were on order from Germany; and even a French firm, Norman, was building six mine-sweepers for the Turks.[77] As if to rub salt in Russia's gaping strategic wound, *Le Matin* cheerfully announced on 29 April 1914 that Armstrong had just contracted a new, fourth Turkish dreadnought order. This latest, greatest British battleship to grace the growing Ottoman navy would be styled, as if to strike terror in the hearts of Russian Christians, *Muhammad the Conqueror*.[78] With friends like these, why did Russia need enemies?

The saga of the British dreadnoughts contracted to Turkey—even while a British Naval Mission was modernizing the Ottoman navy and British firms were upgrading the naval port facilities of Constantinople—illustrates, as nothing else could, just how precarious were the strands of the strategic "alliance" between London and Petersburg. It was almost as if, during the Cold War, a close American ally (say, Britain) had decided to sell nuclear weapons to the Soviet Union, and to send a team of advisers to show Soviet engineers how best to deploy and target them. So over the top were these latest insults from perfidious Albion that Russia's diplomats were not sure quite how to protest them. Shortly before Nicholas II ratified the Russian naval expansion program targeting Turkey on 5

April 1914, the tsar and Sazonov had discussed naval issues with Britain's ambassador, Sir George Buchanan, but only in the most general terms. As if trying to camouflage their concerns about the growth of Turkish naval strength, both the tsar and his foreign minister had emphasized the *German* threat to Russian Straits access, each man citing "secret military information" without specifying the source.[79] The only clue the Russians were willing to offer about their fears of Turkey's dreadnoughts was a request lodged with Buchanan by Grigorevich, the naval minister, that Russia be allowed to buy two of the Armstrong dreadnoughts originally contracted to Chile. Revealingly, Buchanan reported this request to Sir Arthur Nicolson on 16 April 1914 in apparent ignorance that the warships in question were in fact under contract to Turkey. While the British ambassador knew *something* was afoot—he informed London that "it is quite a new departure for Russia to order battleships abroad"—he had no inkling of the real grounds for Grigorevich's unprecedented démarche. Whether deliberately misinformed by the Russians or unable to connect the dots, Buchanan concluded merely that Russia's dreadnought request "shows the serious view she takes of the international situation."[80]

It was not until May 1914, following the stunning headline in *Le Matin* about *Muhammad the Conqueror,* that Sazonov finally worked up the nerve to instruct Count Alexander Benckendorff, his ambassador in London, to ask the British government why they seemed intent on destroying Russia's entire strategic position. Remarkably, Sazonov did not even mention the dreadnoughts in this first formal protest, dated 8 May 1914. He confined his complaint to the Admiral Limpus mission, which he hoped Benckendorff might (ever so politely) convince Sir Edward Grey, His Majesty's Foreign Secretary, to recall, as part of some prospective Anglo-Russian naval agreement. And yet at no point, Sazonov insisted with an eye on public suspicions in Britain of the Liberals' embrace of autocratic Russia, was Benckendorff even authorized to use the sensitive word "agreement" *(soglashenie).* Not until two weeks after this did Benckendorff finally broach the issue of the Armstrong dreadnoughts with Grey, explaining Russia's impossible strategic position, being unable herself to import dreadnoughts through the Straits. By this time the Russians had learned that another English firm, P. S. White, had contracted to build two 1,500 ton minesweepers, also for Turkey. Compounding Benckendorff's difficulty was the fact that Winston Churchill, the First Lord of the Admiralty, was out of town for much of May, which gave Grey a convenient excuse to continue putting him off. Finally, on 12 June 1914, Grey passed on Churchill's reply. Predictably, Grey and Churchill washed their hands of the problem, claiming—they were laissez-faire Liberals, after all—that the British government could not legally interfere with private business contracts.[81]

The Russians received the worst of all worlds from the British blow-off in June 1914. Not only would construction on the Ottoman dreadnoughts proceed, but Admiral Limpus himself would travel to Britain in late July to escort the *Sultan Osman I* back to Turkey.[82] Meanwhile, the (in fact entirely fruitless) negotiations between Benckendorff, Grey, and Churchill had put the Germans on high alert about a mostly imaginary Anglo-Russian Naval Convention, as Benckendorff warned Sazonov in an ominous dispatch on 26 June 1914—just two days before Archduke Franz Ferdinand was murdered in Sarajevo. Although Benckendorff and Grey had patiently explained to Prince Lichnowsky, Germany's ambassador to London, that the recent negotiations in fact had had little to do with any Anglo-Russian naval agreement—much less joint maneuvers—Germany's press barons had concluded just this and were on the warpath again.[83]

There is an interesting passage in one of Fritz Fischer's books in which the author downplays the importance of "'strained Anglo-German relations' resulting from Anglo-Russian negotiations toward a new naval agreement." Fischer is right to point out that "negotiations on the [Anglo-Russian] naval agreement were by no means as far advanced in June 1914" as some pro-German authors have claimed. It is curious, nonetheless, that Fischer's emphasis here is on the *English* naval threat to Germany. Russia figures, as usual in accounts of the July crisis, as a passive, disembodied actor, important only insofar as her admirals succeed (or do not succeed) in coordinating naval operations with Britain in the Baltic.[84] Fischer is just as ignorant as the Germans were in 1914 about Russia's actual foreign policy concerns. Her diplomats' main priority in naval negotiations with London was not coordinating actions in the Baltic, but rather staving off the threat to Russia's position in the Near East posed by Britain's modernization of the Ottoman navy.

Had Germany's leaders known how worried the Russians were about

the Turkish dreadnoughts that were about to make Russia's Black Sea
fleet obsolete and close off the "Straits window" forever, they might have
laughed off the most recent press hysteria. Bethmann Hollweg may not
then have been so paranoid about the "growth of Russian power" in July
1914. But how could he have known this? Not even the British knew what
the Russians were really afraid of. On 12 June 1914 Grey had pointedly, if
bizarrely, reassured Benckendorff that London had no wish to see the
Turkish navy become stronger than that of *Greece*.[85] If it did not occur to
Grey that the Russians were legitimately afraid of the growth of the Ottoman fleet, despite Benckendorff having stressed this (albeit hesitantly and
with great delicacy) for weeks, how could Lichnowsky or Bethmann Hollweg have intuited the Russians' concerns on their own? Diplomats, attachés, and spies can assemble great masses of data about a hostile power's
armaments, railways, ships, and mobilization schedules, but they cannot
peer into the hearts of men. Russian fears of the growth of Turkish naval
power (thought to be in the service of German interests) were no less ra-
tional or irrational than German fears of the growth of Russian power, but
the Russians' fears may have been more threatening to Europe's fragile
peace because they were invisible to everyone but themselves.[86]*

A state whose policymakers nurse grudges against both its enemies
and its friends is a dangerous animal, ready to pounce at the first fright or
whiff of opportunity. Russia in 1914 was a country with much to lose, but
for which the risks of inaction seemed, by June or July of that year, to be at
least as great, and possibly greater, than those of action. It was a country,
in other words, whose rulers would not shrink from going to war to improve her precarious position in a hostile international environment.

---

* By contrast, the Russians knew perfectly well how concerned the Germans were. As Russia's ambassador to Berlin, Sergei N. Sverbeyev, reported in March 1914, "the growing power
of Russia is arousing the gravest fears in Berlin."

CHAPTER TWO

It Takes Two to Tango

The July Crisis

It is militarism run stark mad . . . Whenever England consents,
France and Russia will close in on Germany and Austria.
—Colonel House, 29 May 1914[1]

Sazonov explained, that reversing the [Russian] mobilization order
was no longer possible, and that the Austrian mobilization was to
blame.
—Friedrich Pourtalès, 29–30 July 1914[2]

Your Majesty, it cannot be done. The deployment of millions cannot
be improvised . . . Those arrangements took a whole year of intricate
labor to complete, and once settled, [they] cannot be altered.
—Helmuth von Moltke, 1 August 1914.[3]

O N SUNDAY, 28 JUNE 1914, the 525th anniversary of medieval Serbia's terrible defeat by the Turks on the fields of Kosovo Polje, a
young Serbian peasant named Gavrilo Princip fired two shots into the
bodies of Archduke Franz Ferdinand of Austria and his wife as they
toured the Bosnian capital of Sarajevo, wounding both fatally. Because
Ferdinand was heir to the Habsburg throne of Austria-Hungary and a
man of controversial views in his own right, echoes from the "Sarajevo
outrage," as it soon came to be known, reverberated quickly across European capitals. Accusations and counter-accusations flew between Bel-

grade and Vienna, spreading from there at second and third remove to Berlin, Petersburg, Paris, and London, as a growing mountain of rumors, half-truths, and obfuscations rapidly obscured the true nature of the crime. Lies about Sarajevo continued circulating for years afterward before the truth slowly emerged.

By now, the basic outlines of the Sarajevo conspiracy are well known and little disputed. It is clear, to begin with, that Princip did not act alone. The assassin and his six accomplices (one of whom also tossed bombs at the archduke's motorcade) belonged to Young Bosnia, an offshoot of the Black Hand ("Union or Death"), a secret organization headed by Colonel Dragutin Dimitrijević ("Apis"), Serbia's head of military intelligence. The Black Hand had trained Princip and his fellow conspirators; provided them with guns, ammunition, and explosives; and helped smuggle them and their equipment across the border into Bosnia. That Apis knew of and supported the plot was established in a legal sense by Serbia's own government-in-exile, which put Dimitrijević on trial at Salonica in 1917 and executed him after he openly confessed to the crime. While this does not necessarily prove he was guilty, it is noteworthy that nearly everyone in Serbian politics circled the wagons around Apis's guilt following the war. In part, the scapegoating of the intelligence chief may have been designed to deflect unwelcome attention away from other Serbian leaders' complicity in planning (or at least not doing anything to prevent) the Sarajevo outrage. Since details tracing threads of the conspiracy to Belgrade began emerging in the 1920s, few informed observers have doubted Apis's—and thus semiofficial Serbian—culpability in the crime. No serious historians do today.[4]

To say that there is a basic consensus now about Serbian complicity in Sarajevo, however, is not to say that there was anything like agreement on the subject in 1914. Just as generals must often make rapid-fire battlefield decisions in the "fog of war," so must statesmen navigate crises with imperfect intelligence, not only in the sense that not all relevant facts can usually be known but that many things presumed to be facts are not true at all. To evaluate the decisions made in European capitals in July 1914, one must therefore disentangle not only what actually happened when, but what the relevant policymakers knew (or thought they knew), and when they knew it.

To a considerable extent, this work has already been done with regard to both Austria-Hungary and Germany, who usually figure as the guilty parties in the drama. Decades of research and analysis have established a fairly reliable timeline of both intentions and decision making in Berlin and Vienna. The key events have entered the historical lexicon. First came the "Count Hoyos mission" to Berlin, which resulted in the notorious "blank cheque," wherein Kaiser Wilhelm II promised on 5 July 1914 that Germany would stand by Austria if she attacked Serbia (a position seconded by Chancellor Bethmann Hollweg the next day). This assurance was followed by a parade of "injured innocence" as German leaders took their vacations (the kaiser departing on his Norwegian cruise, Helmuth von Moltke continuing his annual cure at Carlsbad, Bethmann Hollweg summering on the family estate at Hohenfinow in Brandenburg, where Kurt Riezler overheard his remarks about the "growth of Russian power").[5] Next, a kind of "gap in the record" opened in mid-July, during which the papers of the principal German and Austrian conspirators fall silent, followed by a premeditated forty-eight-hour ultimatum from Vienna dispatched to Serbia on 23 July 1914, cooked up in quiet (and presumably undocumented) collusion with Berlin, so as to ensure rejection. Finally, the Austrians declared war on Belgrade on 28 July, which prompted Russia's mobilization and German counter-measures, thus plunging Europe into general war.

Although the issue of German war guilt proclaimed in the Versailles Treaty of 1919 was reopened by a flood of confessions regarding Serbian complicity in the Sarajevo outrage in the 1920s, and by revelations from the Imperial Russian archives opened by the Soviet government after the war, Fritz Fischer's bestselling indictment of Germany's bid for world power (*Griff nach der Weltmacht*) largely closed the door again. Although Fischer, predictably, found plenty of critics in Germany, for the most part western historians have endorsed at least a modified version of his thesis. David Fromkin, for example, answers his own question in *Europe's Last Summer: Who Started the Great War in 1914?* (2004): "Briefly and roughly stated, the answer is that the government of Austria-Hungary started its local war with Serbia, while Germany's military leaders started the worldwide war against France and Russia that became known as the First World War or the Great War."[6]

Convincing as it is on the surface, however, there have always been se-rious problems with the full-on thesis about Germany's deliberate launch-ing of a world war. As even its supporters realize, the botched execution of the Austro-German plot to isolate and punish Serbia hardly suggests brilliant, "cold-blooded" design. The original plan conceived by Beth-mann Hollweg during the Count Hoyos visit in early July was to forge a fait accompli, a chastisement of Serbia by Austrian arms to be completed before the great powers could react. Bethmann Hollweg was clear from the start about the objective of localizing the conflict. While Moltke, a no-torious pessimist, was less sanguine about the prospects for limiting the war's scope, he too chimed in from Carlsbad with the hope that "Austria must beat the Serbs and then make peace quickly."[7]

It was Austria's own prevarication in July that undermined the Ger-man strategy. Count Stefan Tisza, the Hungarian minister-president, was notably cool to the idea of a punitive invasion, unless Vienna could first prepare the ground diplomatically. It was largely to win over Tisza that Count Leopold von Berchtold, the foreign minister, was forced to work up the carefully worded ultimatum to Serbia, the composition of which to Tisza's satisfaction cost Berlin and Vienna precious time. Berchtold and Bethmann Hollweg originally wanted to send Serbia Austria's terms be-fore the French presidential summit in Petersburg, scheduled for 20 to 23 July, so that (in the words of Riezler, channeling Bethmann Hollweg) "France, recoiling from the real possibility of war, will counsel peace in Petersburg."[8] Tisza, however, did not approve the text until 19 July, the day before the summit began, which ruined the plan: to issue the ultima-tum while President Raymond Poincaré was actually meeting with Sa-zonov and the tsar would be dangerous, allowing France and Russia to coordinate war measures in the passion of the moment. Its release instead on 23 July, immediately following Poincaré's departure, was the worst scenario of all, making the ultimatum appear premeditated (which it was). Moreover, it allowed Russia to act in full confidence of France's support, but without the slightest restraining counsel from France's president or, perhaps more important, from René Viviani, a Radical of distinct pacifist inclinations, who after the triumph of the Left in recent elections held the offices of both prime minister and foreign minister. By the time the ulti-matum ran its course on 25 July 1914, nearly a month had passed since the

Sarajevo murders, which made Austria's declaration of war on Serbia appear (especially to London) cynically calculated rather than a lashing-out in the first flush of anger over the assassination of the archduke. We know, of course, the way the story turns out, with Russia standing by Serbia, France by Russia, and finally Britain by France and Russia. But this—a world war—was hardly the way the Germans *wanted* the story to turn out. Bethmann Hollweg had called the bluff of the Entente powers. To his profound disappointment, they did not blink.[9]

An even bigger hole in the middle of our current understanding of the origins of the war relates to the Russian role in the July crisis. Although the modified Fischer thesis nicely elucidates how and why both Austria-Hungary and Germany exploited the July crisis for their own ends (even if botching the plan's execution), it explains nothing about either French or Russian behavior. The biggest documentary gap in the July crisis is not, contrary to popular belief, Bethmann Hollweg's missing papers (the thrust of his thinking is clearly elucidated in both the Riezler diaries and in many other documents dating to July 1914) or evidence relating to Austro-German collusion over the Serbian ultimatum (which is in fact copiously documented in the diplomatic archives of both Berlin and Vienna), but records relating to the crucial four-day French presidential summit with the tsar and his foreign minister in Petersburg from 20 to 23 July 1914. Not a single scrap from this summit has ever surfaced, despite extensive research by both Soviet scholars and the editors of the official French documentary collection on the outbreak of the war.[10] In similar vein, there are conspicuous gaps in the dispatches of Maurice Paléologue, France's ambassador to Petersburg, lasting an entire week following the archduke's assassination. Paléologue did not report on Sazonov's reaction to the news from Sarajevo until 6 July 1914, and he omitted the entire period of the presidential summit from the 20th to the 23rd. The second gap is particularly suspicious, considering that planning for the July presidential summit had been underway for six months. Somehow Paléologue saw fit to dispatch to Paris no less than eight "urgent" telegrams in mid-July relating to the precise wording of Poincaré's presidential toast to be delivered at the gala dinner for the tsar at Peterhof Palace (the last of which, on 19 July, stipulated that the word *cordial* would be substituted for *empressé*), but he had not a single thing to say afterward about what the president and tsar actually talked about.[11] (Alexandre Millerand, then defense minister, later recalled asking Poincaré, "But what did you say to the Russians?" after the latter returned to Paris. "I never succeeded in making him tell.")[12] Rounding out the picture of selective recordkeeping inside the Franco-Russian alliance, there are substantial gaps in Russia's own diplomatic correspondence with its envoys in Paris and Belgrade in July 1914, in the latter case for ten whole days following the assassination of the archduke on 28 June.[13]

Did the Russians have something to hide? The gaps in the record strongly suggest a good deal of purging took place after 1914. Missing files from Imperial Russia's Ministry of Foreign Affairs are particularly noteworthy, in that following the October Revolution, Soviet researchers had no compunction in publishing the most incriminating documents they could find in order to indict the benighted "imperialism" of the old regime.[14] Sazonov's memoirs are little help. In typical fashion, the Russian foreign minister plays dumb as he narrates key July events, pretending, for example, that he had no inkling whatsoever of Austria-Hungary's ultimatum to Serbia before he was officially informed of it by her ambassador, Count Friedrich Szápáry, on 24 July 1914.[15]

This is almost certainly untrue. Just as the German government falsely claimed that it had not known of the ultimatum before Vienna dispatched it to Belgrade, it served Russian and French interests to feign ignorance when Austria's terms were finally announced. The wonder is that anyone has ever believed this, particularly after it was revealed that Russian cryptographers had broken the Austrian diplomatic codes.[16] Sazonov's denial of prior knowledge reads today a bit like Captain Renault's famous aside in Casablanca: He was shocked! Shocked! to learn that Austria planned to punish Serbia for the Sarajevo outrage. Likewise, Entente protestations against the ultimatum invariably stressed the fact that Vienna and Berlin must have colluded over its exceptionally harsh terms, judging from the Germans' public endorsement of the ultimatum after the fact. *Of course* the Austrians and Germans colluded over its terms: they were close military allies. That is what allies do.

So, too, did France and Russia collude, both before and after the Serbian ultimatum. Because many of the relevant records have gone missing, it is not easy to document exactly how they did so. But this is no reason not to make the attempt with those materials we do have, which, especially now that the Russian archives are open, are just as abundant as the German and Austrian files, and more reliable than the (quite possibly doctored) Riezler diaries used to make the case for German "premeditation." While any conclusions must necessarily remain cautious, there is more than enough evidence to reconstruct a basic narrative of Russian intentions during the July crisis.

A good place to begin is with reactions to the events in Sarajevo. There has always been something suspicious about Russian denials of foreknowledge of the assassination plot. Russia's military attaché in Belgrade, General Viktor Artamonov, was out of town on 28 June 1914, giving him a convenient alibi but a strange one, considering that the whole point of Archduke Ferdinand's ill-fated visit to Bosnia was to kick off Austrian military maneuvers in Herzegovina, which would have been of great interest to Russia's official military observer in Serbia. A Serbian army colonel close to Apis later claimed that Artamonov had given Apis a green light for the Sarajevo operation, telling him "Just go ahead! If you are attacked, you will not stand alone." Artamonov expressly denied saying this when later questioned by Luigi Albertini, although he did admit to having been "in practically daily contact with Dimitrijević" whenever he was in town, and noted further that "in the little Belgrade of the time, where public life was confined to a very few cafés, the plot could not have been kept secret" (these last are Albertini's words, rendering Artamonov's remarks). Albertini, after extensive interviews of all the principals, concluded that "Artamonov was told of the plot, if not directly by Dimitrijević then by some other informant." Unlike Artamonov, Nikolai Hartwig, Russia's notorious minister to Serbia, *was* in town on 28 June, and at least one historian, L. C. F. Turner, thinks it "impossible" that Hartwig, "the constant guide and mentor of the Serbian Government" throughout the Balkan Wars, "was not consulted . . . and did not have detailed knowledge of what was afoot."[17]

Whatever the truth about prior Russian knowledge of the Sarajevo plot, the reaction of Russian officials at the time does not suggest that the news took them greatly by surprise, nor that they were sympathetic in the least to the Austrians following the assassination of the Habsburg heir apparent. In the days following the crime, Austrian diplomats throughout the Balkans reported a distinct lack of condolences being expressed by their Russian counterparts.[18] In Rome, the Russian Embassy was the only one of all the great powers not to fly the flag at half-mast in honor of the slain archduke.[19] Likewise, the tsarist legation in Belgrade refused to lower its flag, even during the official funeral requiem for Franz Ferdinand.[20] So far from condoling with his Austrian counterparts, the Russian legation secretary there told the Bulgarian military attaché that Franz Ferdinand's death "should be regarded as a boon for the monarchy," in view of the archduke's (in fact entirely fictional) warmongering reputation. Wilhelm Ritter von Storck, the Austrian chargé d'affaires in Belgrade, felt compelled to report this Russian diplomat's apparent endorsement of the Sarajevo murders "in case this man may one day be accredited Ambassador to Vienna."[21]

Hartwig, Russia's minister to Serbia, who is usually credited (if that is the right word) with having single-handedly assembled the predatory coalition that launched the First Balkan War, was no kinder. Whether he knew of the plot or not, Hartwig was unperturbed by the news of the Sarajevo murders on 28 June 1914: he hosted a bridge party that evening. According to the Italian consul in Belgrade, Hartwig then told pretty much everyone in town that Austria was well rid of the archduke.[22] In light of Hartwig's views on the Bosnian question expressed the previous winter, it is not surprising that he refused to condole with Ritter. "After the question of Turkey," Hartwig had opined then in the flush of Vienna's humiliation in the Balkan wars, "it is now the turn of Austria. Serbia will be our best instrument. The day draws near when . . . Serbia will take back *her* Bosnia and *her* Herzegovina."[23] Not until 9PM on 10 July 1914, a full twelve days after the Sarajevo murders, did Hartwig finally visit the Austrian legation to condole with the Habsburg minister, Baron Giesl von Gieslingen, who had returned from Vienna earlier that day. The Russian denied holding the bridge party on 28 June, and told Giesl it was untrue that the Russian legation had refused to lower the flag during the memorial service for the archduke (although Giesl's Italian and English counterparts later confirmed that the original story about the flag was true). There followed a brief reconciliation between the two men, which lasted ten or fifteen minutes. As if in penance for his sins against the peace of Europe, at about 9:20PM that night the notoriously bellicose Russian minister collapsed and died of a massive heart attack (unless, that is, he had been murdered by the Austrians inside their legation, as much of the Serbian press immediately concluded).[24]*

Sazonov was more subtle than Hartwig in his response to Sarajevo. The line he pursued was that, while the murders were horrible, one must remember that Russians were the first and greatest victims of political assassination. As Sazonov told the Austrian chargé d'affaires in early July, "No country has had to suffer more than Russia from outrages prepared on foreign territory. Have we ever claimed to employ against any country the procedure with which your newspapers threaten Serbia?"[25] Showing impressive coordination between Petersburg and Paris, President Poincaré argued along identical lines to Austria's ambassador to France, Count Szecsen von Témerin, on 4 July 1914, recalling the anti-Italian mania that had swept through France following the assassination of President Carnot by an Italian anarchist in 1894.[26] Disregarding the ongoing flood of revelations from Vienna about Serbian government complicity in the Sarajevo crimes (many of which were, admittedly, premature or inaccurate),[27] Sazonov stuck to this line all through July, at one point telling Friedrich Pourtalès, the German ambassador, that for Austria to demand justice from Serbia was akin to Russia invading Sweden or Switzerland because so many Russian revolutionaries had sought refuge there.[28] It took a certain chutzpah to claim, after the Sarajevo outrage, that Russia was the real victim of terrorism. Sazonov was clearly up to the challenge.

The attitude in Russian "official circles" regarding Austria-Hungary in the weeks following the Sarajevo murders, Pourtalès reported to Berlin from Petersburg on 13 July 1914, was one of "boundless contempt for the conditions prevailing there." "Not only in the press, but also in society," the German ambassador observed, "one meets almost only with un-

---

* Giesl himself overheard the following story from another customer while visiting (one hopes, incognito) a Belgrade barbershop several days after Hartwig's death: "Giesl has brought an electric chair from Vienna which causes the immediate death of anyone who sits down on it and leaves not the slightest trace." Others accused the Austrians of poisoning Hartwig: although as it turned out, he had not survived long enough to be served dinner or drinks. The Russian consumed only two cigarettes during his brief interview with Giesl, the butts of both of which were immediately turned over to his grieving wife to allay her suspicions about foul play.

friendly judgments on the murdered Archduke."[29] The lax security of the Sarajevo motorcade hardly spoke well of Habsburg military efficiency. The Balkan wars had taught Russia's generals that the Austro-Hungarian army was a paper tiger. At the height of the German-Russian press war in March 1914, Pourtalès had reassured Berlin that the anti-German hysteria was French-inspired. "The desire to settle accounts once and for all with Austria-Hungary," by contrast, was in his view "doubtless much more widespread."[30] Moreover, Russian anti-Austrian sentiment had teeth behind it: for all the media saber-rattling against Berlin that March, Russia had then conducted menacing military exercises on the Austrian, not the German, border.[31] By April 1914, Kaiser Wilhelm himself was concerned, passing on to Bethmann Hollweg a rumor he had picked up "from an authentic source" that Russian cavalry officers had just bought up 30,000 horses in Hungary. The kaiser's fear was that Russia would use Serbia or Montenegro as anti-Austrian proxies to ensnare Germany in a European war.[32] The kaiser's fears of a Russian first strike were not without foundation, if we recall: *Novoe Vremya*'s advocacy that month of the dismemberment of the Austro-Hungarian empire; the tsar's prediction the previous year that "the disintegration of the Austrian Empire was merely a question of time"; Hartwig's recent remark that "it is now the turn of Austria"; and Krivoshein's vow to Paléologue in early May 1914 that Russia would seize Galicia as soon as opportunity struck. Although recent historical works, colored by both the Fischer debate and by our knowledge of how the Second World War began in 1939, invariably paint Germany as the natural aggressor in 1914, that is not how the strategic situation looked to most neutral observers at the time. Colonel House, the American presidential envoy who famously spoke of European "militarism run stark mad" on 29 May 1914, expected that, in the event of any serious crisis, "France and Russia will close in on Germany and Austria," not the other way round.

The contemptuous attitude of Russian leaders toward Austria must be kept in mind when examining the way they handled the ultimatum crisis. Despite the "shocked, shocked!" tone of the official response, no one in Petersburg was surprised in the least by the terms given Serbia. There is compelling evidence that Sazonov—or at least his *chef de Cabinet,* Baron Moritz Schilling—knew the basic gist of Austria's demands as much as a

week in advance. (Sazonov, like seemingly everyone in Berlin, was on va-
cation from 14 to 18 July 1914.) Nikolai Shebeko, the Russian ambassador
in Vienna, reported to Petersburg by telegram on 16 July that "the Austro-
Hungarian Government at the conclusion of the inquiry intends to make
certain demands on Belgrade," and asked for urgent instructions as to
how he might forestall any such demands.[33] That same day, Schilling also
received a similar warning in person from the Italian ambassador to Russia, Marquis Carlotti di Riparbella.[34] Schilling was sufficiently perturbed
by these warnings that he rushed to the train station to apprise Sazonov
of the situation upon the latter's return to Petersburg the morning of 18
July.[35] Later that day, Sazonov told Sir George Buchanan that "anything
in the nature of an Austrian ultimatum to Belgrade could not leave Russia
indifferent," which suggests he knew exactly such an ultimatum was coming.[36] Even the basic timing of the Austrian ultimatum was, in all likelihood, known to the Russians, whose cryptographers had decoded three
Austrian telegrams between 14 and 17 July enquiring as to the date Poincaré would be leaving Russia following the presidential summit.[37] To sum
up the state of the diplomatic game on the eve of Poincaré's arrival in Petersburg: the Austrians and Germans had colluded together on the terms
offered Serbia, and (following the delays caused by the need to placate
Count Tisza) Vienna planned to issue the ultimatum as soon as the
French delegation left Petersburg on the night of 23 July 1914. The Austrians knew when Poincaré would take his leave from Russia, and what
they would then do. The Russians knew (roughly, at least) what the Austrians would do, and exactly when they would do it.

So what did Poincaré, the tsar, and their foreign ministers talk about?
Bland official communiqués notwithstanding, they must obviously have
discussed the upcoming ultimatum in detail and prepared a joint response of some kind. From letters and telegrams dispatched to and from
Petersburg during the period in question, and even from Paléologue's
published "diary" entries (if not, alas, from Sazonov's memoirs), we have
a fairly accurate picture of the mood of the meetings and the subjects
under discussion, if not exactly what was said. There is, first of all, the
German ambassador's notorious 21 July letter to Bethmann Hollweg on
which Kaiser Wilhelm scribbled some of his famous marginalia, in which
Pourtalès warned Berlin of Sazonov's stiffening attitude. "If Austria-

Hungary was determined to break the peace," Sazonov told Pourtalès, "she should realize that this time she would have to reckon with Europe." (Opposite this passage, Kaiser Wilhelm II scribbled, "No! but with Russia, yes!") Showing that he knew just what the Austrians were in fact about to do, Sazonov responded to Pourtalès's protestations that Serbian rights would be respected with a threat of his own to Vienna: "whatever happens *there must be no talk of an ultimatum.*"[38]

If this was the state of Sazonov's mind at the beginning of the presidential summit, it is not surprising that his position had stiffened even further following several days of talks and toasts with the French delegation. President Poincaré was a man of courage and firm convictions, who—not unlike many Russian nationalists—had pointedly criticized Sazonov's submissive attitude during the Balkan Wars.[39] Ambassador Paléologue, a close friend of Poincaré's, had been expressly appointed to Petersburg in order to press Sazonov into a harder anti-German line. As then–Prime Minister Gaston Doumergue had instructed Paléologue in January 1914 prior to his departure for Russia, "War can break out from one day to the next . . . Our [Russian] allies must rush to our aid. The safety of France will depend on the *energy and promptness* with which *we shall know how to push them into the fight.*"[40] True to form, it was Poincaré and Paléologue, not Sazonov, who had the first belligerent run-in with the Austrian ambassador, the normally mild-mannered Hungarian Count Friedrich Szápáry, who had returned to Petersburg just one day before Sazonov. Where Sazonov had found Szápáry "docile as a lamb" when they spoke on 18 July,[41] Poincaré judged the Hungarian count much more harshly when he met with him three days later. "I'm not satisfied with this conversation," Poincaré told Paléologue after speaking with Szápáry, "the Ambassador has obviously been instructed to say nothing . . . Austria has a *coup de théâtre* in store for us. Sazonov must be firm and we must back him up."[42] Szápáry himself was no less dismayed by Poincaré's tone, reporting to Vienna that "the President's threatening attitude . . . in contrast with the circumspect bearing of Sazonov, confirms the anticipation that M. Poincaré will exercise anything but a calming influence here."[43]

Although Szápáry may have been deceived by Sazonov's "circumspect bearing" before the arrival of the French delegation, he was right to fear the impact of Poincaré's uncompromising attitude on the Russian foreign minister. On the night of 22–23 July, Sazonov reported the following to Shebeko in Vienna: "From my discussions with [Poincaré] it clearly emerges that also France . . . will not tolerate a humiliation of Serbia." Noting that he already had credible information that "Austria was planning to undertake measures against Serbia," Sazonov instructed Shebeko to warn Vienna "cordially but firmly" of the "dangerous consequences which must follow any such measures of a character unacceptable to Serbia." The French and English ambassadors to Austria, Sazonov added, would shortly make statements in the same sense.[44]

Alas, Sazonov's warning—what we might call his antiultimatum ultimatum—did not reach Berchtold in time to forestall the dispatch of the actual ultimatum the next day.[45] It does, however, give us a very good idea as to what was secretly resolved at the French-Russian summit. The anti-ultimatum ultimatum was clearly not a unilateral Russian idea. Sazonov's warning was repeated almost verbatim in Viviani's own instructions to Alfred Dumaine, France's ambassador to Vienna, in his first dispatch after embarking at sea on the *France,* time-dated 24 July 1914. What is interesting about this document is that, due to the Austrian trick of waiting until the French delegation left Petersburg, Viviani did not yet know of the text of the 23 July Serbian ultimatum when he wrote it. "No avenue must be neglected," Viviani instructed Dumaine, "to prevent an [Austrian] demand for retribution or any set of conditions foisted [on Serbia] which might . . . be considered a violation of her sovereignty or her independence."[46] Considering that Viviani, a quasi-pacifist, was of far milder temperament than Poincaré and Paléologue, we can safely conclude that Sazonov's antiultimatum ultimatum also had the unequivocal backing of the latter two men (if they were not indeed its real authors).

Of course, to say that French and Russian leaders conspired together in Petersburg (unsuccessfully) to preempt the Austrian ultimatum to Serbia is not the same thing as saying they had resolved to go to war. Clearly, however, both Poincaré and Sazonov were willing to *risk* war by refusing to countenance Austria's demands on Serbia—and they came to this decision before, not after, reading the actual text of the ultimatum. Paléologue's diary gives a sense of the atmosphere in Petersburg during the French visit, and "pacific" would not be the word to describe it. Here is his entry for 23 July:

Review at Krasnoïe-Selo this morning. Sixty thousand men took part. A magnificent pageant of might and majesty. The infantry march past to the strains of the *Marche de Sambre et Meuse* and the *Marche Lorraine.*

What a wealth of suggestion in this military machine set in motion by the Tsar of all the Russias before the President of the allied republic, himself a son of Lorraine! . . . Poincaré was seated on the Tsaritsa's right in front of the tent. The few glances he exchanged with me showed me that our thoughts were the same.[47]

Paléologue and Poincaré were not the only ones swept up in the martial fervor. At a banquet given the previous night by Grand Duke Nicholas, Paléologue recalled being told by the grand duke's wife, Grand Duchess Anastasia Nicolaievna Romanova: "There's going to be war. There'll be nothing left of Austria. You're going to get back Alsace and Lorraine. Our armies will meet in Berlin. Germany will be destroyed!"[48] True, this was the word of a Montenegrin princess, who could hardly be said to speak for the Russian government. Then again, she was the wife of the man who would soon take over as commander-in-chief of Russia's armies. He must himself have said something similar.[49] The views she expressed certainly accord well with the common view of Russian nationalists in 1914 that Austria's (if not necessarily also Germany's) days were numbered—a view prominently shared, as we have seen, by the tsar, *Novoe Vremya,* Nikolai Hartwig, and A. V. Krivoshein, the senior member of the Council of Ministers.

Sazonov himself was no less bellicose. Sazonov's reaction upon first learning of the Austrian ultimatum at about 10AM on 24 July 1914 is justly famous: *C'est la guerre européene!*[50] Considering the importance of Sazonov's own actions in the hours after he made this remark, this has the air of a self-fulfilled prophecy. On 18 July, when Sazonov had told Buchanan that Russia could not remain "indifferent" if Austria issued "anything in the nature of an ultimatum" to Serbia, he had added ominously that if she did so, Russia "might be forced to take some precautionary military measure."[51] True to his word, by 11AM on 24 July Sazonov had already instructed Nikolai Yanushkevitch, the chief of Russia's General Staff, to make "all arrangements for putting the army on a war footing," in order to have a partial mobilization plan written up and ready in time for the meeting of the Council of Ministers planned for 3PM that afternoon.[52]

Sazonov, clearly taking the idea from War Minister Sukhomlinov's partial mobilization plan against Austria alone discussed by the tsar's senior ministers (and nearly implemented) during the First Balkan War in November 1912, would insist that day in the Council of Ministers and for a week afterward that Russia could and did premobilize (and then mobilize) her army against Austria alone: a key corollary was that the Warsaw district *not* be mobilized so as not to alarm the commanders of the German Eighth Army in East Prussia. In fact, such an order was "folly," as the chief of the Russian army's mobilization section, General Sergei Dobrorolskii, told his boss Yanushkevitch between 11AM and noon, just minutes after the latter had promised that it *was* feasible to Sazonov—impossible both in the general sense, in that Plan 19 required mobilization against Germany and Austria simultaneously with no variant separating the two, and in the more specific sense that it was physically impossible to mobilize against the Austrian border without extensively using the Warsaw railway hub, which would inevitably alarm the Germans.[53]

It has been suggested that Yanushkevitch's error, if that is what it was, set in motion a disastrous chain of events that led to world war. Because he had been promoted to this position only five months previously (Yanushkevitch had not been present at the fateful war-planning conference of 8/21 February), Dobrorolskii's boss may have been less than fully versed in the details of Mobilization Plan 19. "Had Yanushkevitch from the beginning warned Sazonov of the mistake he would be making in proclaiming partial mobilization," Albertini has argued, Sazonov would never have got the Council of Ministers and the tsar to approve just this, "with incalculable consequences."[54] L. C. F. Turner has added several important wrinkles to Albertini's argument, suggesting that both Sazonov (a civilian) and Yanushkevitch (an incompetent) were ignorant of the real strategic implications of Sukhomlinov's partial mobilization plan, the activation of which must invariably force Austria to order general mobilization and thereby invoke German mobilization, pursuant to bilateral treaty obligations. Turner notes further that it was to Russia's advantage *not* yet to mobilize, so as to allow the Austrians to become fully entangled in the Serbian campaign (according to their own Mobilization variant B, for "Balkans," as opposed to R, for "Russia"), which would leave Austrian Galicia nearly defenseless and thus put the Central powers "at the mercy of the Entente." Interestingly, the French General Staff had explained the favorable strategic implications of an Austrian activation of Plan B to Poincaré back in 1912, but neither Paléologue, nor General Laguiche, France's military attaché in Petersburg, had done anything "to enlighten the Russian General Staff"—doubtless because, as Turner explains, France's own military planners were pushing for an immediate Russian offensive toward Berlin, and did not want to give the Russians any excuse to prevaricate.[55]

Intriguing as the Albertini-Turner story of Russian ignorance and incompetence is, there is good reason to believe that Sazonov himself knew perfectly well what he was doing when he proposed Sukhomlinov's "partial mobilization" plan to the government—that is, that he was knowingly plunging Russia into war. Sazonov, after all, had been present at the emergency ministerial council held at Tsarskoe Selo on 23 November 1912, when Chairman Kokovtsev had warned everyone that the "partial mobilization" plan, by forcing Austria to order general mobilization, could not but lead to a European war. As Kokovtsev had concluded his winning argument then, "no matter what we chose to call the projected measures, *a mobilization remained a mobilization,* to be countered by our adversaries with actual war." Sazonov, impressed by Kokovtsev's reasoning, had then chimed in that Russia should not, therefore, have ordered such a fateful mobilization without consulting first with France.[56]

This time, unlike in November 1912, Russia *had* consulted with France —not just with her ambassador, but also with her president and prime minister (the latter also foreign minister). The belligerent Poincaré, his willing tool Paléologue, and (perhaps because he was outnumbered by them) even the leftist Viviani had all just given their imprimatur to whatever counter-measures Sazonov might order to Vienna's ultimatum. This time, too, there was no Kokovtsev in the Council of Ministers to overrule him. Sazonov had his "blank cheque," and he would now cash it. There is an interesting passage in the memoirs of Peter Bark, Russia's finance minister, in which Bark describes what happened when he called at the foreign ministry the morning of 24 July 1914. Sazonov himself was unavailable (it is likely he was then meeting with Yanushkevitch to discuss the partial mobilization plan), and so Bark spoke with Sazonov's chief of staff, Baron Schilling, instead. Bark asked straight away, "Was there any likelihood of war?" Schilling answered immediately, Bark recalled, that *"Sazonov considered war unavoidable."* This remark could be apocryphal, of course. Its veracity, however, is backed up by hard evidence—in fact the very same kind of evidence which has recently been offered as proof that Bethmann Hollweg premeditated a European war, namely last-minute maneuvers to get Russia's financial affairs in order:

> I asked [Schilling] whether he thought matters would move quickly since, in that case, I should have to take immediate steps to ensure the transfer of the Russian Treasury funds deposited in Berlin. Baron Schilling advised me to make immediate arrangements to that effect ... I [signed] the papers necessary for the immediate departure for Berlin of foreign ministry officials who were to arrange for the return to Russia of Russian state funds deposited [there]. In addition, I told Nikiforoff to wire at once to Berlin to transfer to Petrograd and Paris the balances held by us on Current Account with our Berlin correspondents. I gave similar instructions to the Governor of the State Bank, Shipov. These steps enabled us, before the outbreak of hostilities, to recuperate Russian State funds and the balances of the Russian Treasury amounting to 100 million rubles.[57]

The fact that this decision was taken *before* the Council of Ministers met on the afternoon of 24 July is of cardinal importance. So, too, is the fact that Sazonov instructed Yanushkevitch to begin preparing for partial mobilization before the cabinet meeting. These actions—clearing the financial decks for war, and mobilizing the army by stages—constituted together three of the five resolutions passed by the council that afternoon. The first two, both uncontroversial, dealt with negotiating a "temporary postponement" of Serbia's ultimatum deadline, and the need for Serbia to show restraint. Far more significant, Resolution 3 inaugurated the "Period Preparatory to War" in four military districts (on this much more below), which Sazonov had already instructed Yanushkevitch to begin preparing. Resolution 4 "charged the War Minister [Sukhomlinov] without delay to speed up the stockpiling of war materials for the army." Resolution 5 instructed Bark to do precisely what he had already done on Sazonov's orders, namely repatriate funds held in what would soon be enemy countries. These critical three resolutions had already been decided on by Sazonov, who was himself, by longstanding (if increasingly inaccurate) reputation, one of the least bellicose members of the council. There was no doubt whatsoever that Krivoshein, the notoriously belligerent Germanophobe, would support Sazonov's strong stand (significantly, Krivoshein had supported Sukhomlinov's partial mobilization directive on 23 November 1912, before being overruled by Sazonov and Kokovstev).[58] To use a parliamentary analogy, Russia's foreign minister brought his bill to the floor only after he knew he had the votes to secure its passage.

Bark's memoirs are the principal source we have for what was said that afternoon. While the decision to begin preparing for war was almost certainly taken by Sazonov before the ministers met, Bark's recollection of the meeting is still an invaluable source for understanding why that decision was taken. Far from blaming the July crisis on recent, possibly contingent events like the Sarajevo murders and the Austrian ultimatum, Sazonov argued that "there were deep-seated causes of conflict between the Central European powers and those of the Entente." Russian weakness in each crisis since the war with Japan had provoked Germany's aggressive behavior: the Serbian ultimatum was only a "pretext that would enable her to prove her superiority by the use of force." Russia, Sazonov reminded the other members of the Council of Ministers,

> could not remain a passive spectator whilst a Slavonic people was being deliberately trampled down. In 1876 and 1877 Russia had fought Turkey for the liberation of the Slavonic peoples in the Balkans. We had made immense sacrifices with that end in view . . . If Russia failed to fulfill her historic mission, she would be considered a decadent State and would henceforth have to take second place among the Powers . . . If, at this critical juncture, the Serbs were abandoned to their fate, Russian prestige in the Balkans would collapse utterly.[59]

Krivoshein spoke next in much the same vein, making a "profound impression" on the cabinet with his argument that Russia's government must take a stand or be crucified by the public for its pusillanimity. "Public and parliamentary opinion," Krivoshein intoned, "would fail to understand why, at this critical moment involving Russia's vital interests, the Imperial Government was reluctant to act boldly." Reassured by Sukhomlinov and Grigorevich, respectively, that Russia's army and navy were ready, the Council resolved to issue a stern warning to Austria that Serbia's fate "could not leave Russia indifferent." The resolutions taken by the Council of Ministers, including the financial and military measures mentioned above, were signed into law by Tsar Nicholas II at the Crown Council held at 11AM the following morning at Tsarskoe Selo.[60]

Was Serbia really the "vital Russian interest" of which Krivoshein spoke? Certainly, for the sake of Russia's strategic credibility, it made sense to back up the tsar's verbal warning that any violation of Serbian independence "could not leave Russia indifferent" with at least a *threat* to mobilize against Austria. As Turner has argued, this would have been the best move not only politically, as it would put the onus for starting a European conflict entirely on Vienna if and when she declared war on Serbia, but also in purely military terms: delaying Russia's mobilization would have led the Austrian armies to commit fully to the Balkans, thus leaving Galicia free for the taking. But a *public* threat to mobilize is not what was decided in the Council of Ministers on 24 July 1914, but rather a *secret*, large-scale mobilization of Russia's army—and its navy. Why, after all, if Sazonov and Krivoshein wished merely to safeguard Serbia's independence, did they mobilize not only thirteen entire army corps—a force of some 1.1 million men—but also the fleets of the Baltic and Black Sea, neither of which bodies of water were contiguous at any point to Austria-Hungary (or Serbia, for that matter)? Why did they include Odessa alongside Kazan, Kiev, and Moscow among the four military districts in which the ominous-sounding "Period Preparatory to War" was inaugurated—a district where recent operational planning focused on amphibious operations against Constantinople?[61]

All this, meanwhile, is only what the Council of Ministers and the tsar had resolved on officially (but not yet publicly; even the impending partial mobilization would not be announced until 28 July). In confidence, Sazonov must have told Yanushkevitch to do much more than this. From the journal of the Russian General Staff meeting held the night of 25 July

1914, we know that "full mobilization" of the four districts was to proceed automatically when Austrian troops crossed the Serbian border. Meanwhile, not only Moscow but also St. Petersburg, a city nearly a thousand miles from the Austro-Hungarian border (and still farther from Serbia) was placed under martial law. Everywhere in Russia, training maneuvers were broken off and troops recalled to quarters. Cadets enrolled in Russia's military academies were immediately promoted officers, thus not only filling gaps in the army's command structure with new subalterns but also "freeing for active service in the field many mature officers who had hitherto been detailed on educational work."[62] Yanushkevitch emphasized that all of these tasks should be carried out "energetically" and stipulated crucially that, if necessary, mobilization officers "would be permitted . . . to overstep the boundaries laid down in the 'Period Preparatory to War' regulations."[63] Taking the hint, General Dobrorolskii had already wired Zhilinskii in Warsaw, instructing him to recall all troops in his district to quarters. At 1AM the night of 25–26 July, the Warsaw district (that is, Russian Poland) was placed under martial law. Later that night—at 3:26AM—Yanushkevitch wired Warsaw that the morrow (26 July 1914) would mark "the beginning of the 'Period Preparatory to War' in the entire region of European Russia," covering all *six* of the main military districts—Warsaw, Vilna (Vilnius, i.e., the Baltic area), Kazan, Kiev, Moscow, and Odessa.[64] What this meant in practice was that "All fortresses in the Warsaw, Vilna, and St Petersburg districts were placed 'in a state of war,' frontier guards were brought up to strength and the frontier posts were fully manned, censorship and security measures were tightened, harbors were mined, horses and wagons were assembled for army baggage trains, depots were prepared for the reception of reservists, and all steps were taken to facilitate the impending mobilization."[65] The Period Preparatory to War inaugurated on 26 July further allowed for the "call-up of the three youngest classes of reserves in areas threatened by enemy action," including, significantly, Russian Poland west of the Vistula.[66] Expanding the net of Russia's "intended partial mobilization" still further, on 27 July 1914 Yanushkevitch wired Tiflis command that the Period Preparatory to War was now also in force for the military districts of Omsk, Irkutsk, Turkestan, and the Caucasus.[67] Russia may have begun mobilizing in Omsk and Tiflis even earlier than this, as Norman Stone, drawing on Austrian sources, concluded: "There is also certain evidence to suggest that the Russians began to mobilize considerably earlier than they made out: at a comparably early stage in the Lemberg campaign, Austro-Hungarian units took prisoners from Siberian and Caucasian units, which could scarcely, in view of Russia's great transport problems, have reached the West if mobilized only at the end of July."[68] Manfried Rauchensteiner, a leading Austrian historian of the eastern front, went still further than this, arguing that the unexpected speed of Russia's mobilization against Austrian Galicia in August 1914 suggests that "the Russians began mobilizing towards the beginning of July and systematically prepared for war."[69]

An early, secret mobilization of this kind was entirely consistent with the understanding of the Period Preparatory to War by the members of Russia's General Staff—and by Tsar Nicholas II. "It will be advantageous," a secret military commission had reported to Sukhomlinov on 21 November 1912, shortly before the war minister first drew up orders for a partial mobilization against Austria alone, "to complete concentration without beginning hostilities, in order not to deprive the enemy irrevocably of the hope that war can still be avoided. Our measures for this *must be masked by clever diplomatic negotiations,* in order to *lull to sleep as much as possible the enemy's fears.*"[70] The language of the official "Regulation Concerning the Period Preparatory to War," signed into law by Tsar Nicholas II on 2 March 1913, was almost identical. The Period Preparatory to War, as stipulated by Russia's generals and approved by her sovereign, "means *the period of diplomatic complications preceding the opening of hostilities,* in the course of which all Boards must take the necessary measures of preparation for security and success at the mobilization of the Army, the Fleet, and the Fortresses, as well as for the march of the Army to the threatened frontier." These measures included, crucially, the calling up of reserves to frontier divisions (as in fact occurred on 26 July 1914). The reserves were mobilized not on the orders of the tsar but simply on the say-so of the war minister, Sukhomlinov. Frontier troops were then

> to be instructed as to the uniforms and probable dispositions of the enemy. Horses are to be reshod. No more furloughs are to be granted, and officers and men on furlough or detailed elsewhere are to return

at once to their troop divisions. Espionage suspects are to be arrested. Measures to prevent the export of horses, cattle, and grain are to be worked out. Money and valuable securities are to be removed from banks near the frontier to the interior. Naval vessels are to return to their harbors and receive provisions and full war equipment.[71]

The closer we look at Russia's so-called Period Preparatory to War that began on 25 July 1914, the more it looks like, well, mobilization. This is certainly what it looked like to Paléologue, as he recorded in his diary that very night (although without, apparently, reporting these observations to Paris): "At seven o'clock this evening [25 July] I went to the Warsaw station to say goodbye to Isvolsky who is returning to his post [Paris] in hot haste. There was a great bustle on the platforms. The trains were packed with officers and men. *This looked like mobilization.* We rapidly exchanged impressions and came to the same conclusion: 'It's war this time.' . . . the cities and Governments of St. Petersburg and Moscow have been declared in a state of siege."[72]

This is how Russia's Period Preparatory to War looked to the Austrians and Germans, too. As early as 3:25PM on 26 July 1914, Germany's military attaché, Major D. Eggeling, informed Berlin that mobilization had been ordered in Kiev and Odessa.[73] Habsburg consuls in Kiev, Moscow, and Odessa sent in reports of Russian mobilization measures on 27 July 1914.[74] All through that day, Pourtalès received alarming reports from his own consuls. Although he was unsure whether reserves had been called up yet (as in fact they had been, at least in the frontier divisions), a full Russian artillery division had been seen marching westward from Kiev, and another cavalry division leaving for Dubno. From Riga, Pourtalès learned that the Düna (Dvina) river had been mined, and that all rolling stock had been commandeered for the army. A letter from the German consul in Moscow dispatched that day (but received much later) reported that the telegraph office was no longer allowing the Germans to send encrypted messages to Berlin.[75] Giving particular cause for concern, the German consul in Warsaw telegraphed at 3:45PM on 27 July that "All troops have been recalled from maneuvers STOP Much infantry including also cavalry units were sent via the Brest station towards Lublin and Kovel STOP The entire night hundreds of military vehicles went up and down the avenue of Brest-Litovsk . . . Yesterday the artillery stores in the Citadel blew sky high."[76] Rounding out the impression of menace, Germany's aide-de-camp to the tsar, General von Chelius, had reported the previous evening (26 July) from Tsarskoe Selo that

> During the afternoon review it was announced . . . that maneuvers would be called off for tonight, and that troops must return [to base]. General Adlerberg, the Governor of St. Petersburg, broke off and said *he had to go to attend to the "mobilization."* Baron Grünwald, the Court Equestrian Officer *(Oberstallmeister),* a man very sympathetic to Germany, sat next to me at dinner and said, "the situation is very serious; *I am not allowed to tell you what was decided* earlier today, but *you will soon learn of it by your own accord;* you may assume, though, that the outlook is grave."

Grünwald concluded his ominous remarks by taking leave of Chelius with the parting sentiment, "hopefully we will meet again in happier times."[77]

Of course, even if we can now prove, based on the foregoing evidence, that Russia began secretly mobilizing its armed forces on 25 July 1914, this does not necessarily prove that the tsarist government had resolved on war. Because it was so slow, even a Russian general mobilization did not entail immediate hostile action on foreign soil in the way German mobilization did, due to the stringent time requirements of the Schlieffen Plan (as modified by Moltke).[78] But it was precisely because of this comparative slowness that ordering an early, secret mobilization was so crucial to the Russians. As Bruce Menning discovered, the last war gaming exercise of the Russian General Staff before the war, held in Kiev on 20–24 April 1914, concluded that Russia would have "assembled only half its forces" on the European frontlines by M + 16, by which day the Austrian mobilization would be complete (German mobilization was expected by M + 13). The "complete assembly" of the Russian armies would only occur by M + 26. It is true that Russia, by Danilov's calculations, would enjoy superiority of 20 percent in men, and still more in guns, over the Austrians and Germans: but this would matter little if her mobilization "lagged at least thirteen days behind that of Germany and ten days behind that of Austria-Hungary."[79] By launching her mobilization on 25 July 1914 (or even earlier, as Stone and Rauchensteiner have suggested), Russia's generals had gained precious time—time they desperately needed to offset the enemy's speed advantage.

The Germans, in turn, were just as desperate to preserve this advantage. As Holger Herwig sums up the imperatives of the Schlieffen Plan, "All was predicated on speed . . . a delay of just seventy-two hours in railway mobilization and deployment could spell disaster."[80] For this reason any evidence that Russia was secretly mobilizing early was bound to terrify Moltke and the German generals. And the German Foreign Office, one historian estimated, received twenty-eight separate reports of Russia's mobilization measures between 26 and 30 July, "no less than sixteen of which related to the Russian frontier against Germany." The Admiralty and General Staff received still more than this.[81] Thus when both Ambassador Pourtalès and Germany's military attaché, Major Eggeling, confronted Sazonov on the night of 26 July with reports that "several Russian army corps have been sent towards the western border in accordance with a mobilization directive," and Sazonov "guaranteed" the one, and gave his "word of honor" to the other, that "no such mobilization order had been issued," the Germans had reason to believe that he was lying through his teeth.[82] True, Sazonov was a civilian, and so he conceivably could have been ignorant of mobilization details. But Russia's war minister, Sukhomlinov, also summoned Eggeling on 26 July to reassure him, apparently with a straight face, that "not a horse was being requisitioned, not a reservist called up."[83] True, the Russian order for general mobilization may not yet have been publicly decreed; but *some* kind of mobilization was clearly underway. Did these deceitful denials constitute a deliberate ploy for time—time Russia needed to overcome Germany's speed advantage—or were Russian leaders sincerely interested in dampening German suspicions to avert a European war?

Probably only Sazonov himself knew the real answer to this question. Like Bethmann Hollweg and the kaiser on the German side, like Tsar Nicholas II himself, Russia's foreign minister was prey to cold feet in the tense last days of peace. Szápáry and Pourtalès reported contradictory signals emanating from Sazonov between 25 and 28 July, a period that, in retrospect, appears similar to the "phony war" of 1939–1940. Both ambassadors recorded doubts that Russian morale would hold if war erupted, citing widespread reports of labor unrest that swept through St. Petersburg in July—a wave that had peaked during the French presidential summit. Pourtalès's reports on this score have entered the lexicon of "German war guilt," the idea being that Berlin urged on the Austrians against Serbia because the Germans thought the Russians would not fight.[84] Offering a slightly different and surprising opinion, Fritz Fischer has argued that German plans to launch a world war were nearly upset at the last minute by Russia's "unexpected backing down."[85]

These arguments, like others relating to German responsibility for the war, are riddled with contradictions. If the Germans thought and hoped that Russia would stay out of the Balkan conflict, how was Berlin guilty of premeditating a world war? If Bethmann Hollweg and Moltke did not think that Russia would really fight over Serbia, why were they so alarmed about reports of Russia's secret mobilization, which began pouring into Berlin on 26 July? Why did the Germans protest these mobilization measures to Sazonov, with mounting indignation? And why would Russia's foreign minister deny these reports with such vehemence, if he was anxious to bluff Berlin into believing Russian morale was stronger than it in fact was (rather than anxious to conceal the truth about Russia's secret ongoing mobilization)?

Pourtalès himself was far from sure as to what the Russians were really up to. His reports about Russian intentions oscillated between alarm and reassurance, not because he was trying to mislead Berlin but because he was trying to make sense of contradictory information. The night of 27 July, for example, an audience with a visibly calmer and conciliatory Sazonov suggested to Pourtalès that the Russians were having second thoughts. There was no sign, he reported, of public enthusiasm for war in the streets of St. Petersburg. The next day he reported to Berlin that mobilization was underway and picking up speed, that reserves were being called up, and that cavalry units were seen mustering horses in Courland (Latvia), near the borders of East Prussia. It is noteworthy that the second, alarming message was dispatched immediately by telegram; the first, with the reassuring tone, was a letter dispatched more slowly by courier.[86]

Far from being egged on by falsely optimistic reports from Pourtalès, Berlin was hearing, on balance, far more bad news than good from their ambassador in Petersburg.

The most likely explanation of the growing divide between Berlin and Petersburg in the last days of July 1914 is also the simplest one. Russia inaugurated the Period Preparatory to War on 25 July in order to prepare for war. The Germans, picking up reports that Russia was indeed preparing for war (while not announcing any such thing to the world), protested strongly over the following days because they thought that Russia was secretly preparing for war. As Dobrorolskii, chief of the Russian army's mobilization section, himself recalled of the period following the decision for "partial mobilization" on 24–25 July, "the war was already a settled matter, and the whole flood of telegrams between the Governments of Germany and Russia represented merely the stage setting of a historical drama."[87] It would seem churlish not to give Dobrorolskii the benefit of the doubt as to Russian intentions. He was, after all, the man responsible for mobilizing Russia's army in 1914. But even if we are not willing to do so, it remains true that as early as 26 July the Germans had reason to believe, based on evidence received from multiple sources, that Russia was preparing for war.

This matters greatly. An important argument advanced by supporters of the modified Fischer thesis is that the timing of Russia's decision for general mobilization on 30 July and its public announcement the next day was ultimately immaterial: Moltke and the generals had already decided on German mobilization before the Russians did. Fischer himself claimed that the Russian proclamation on 31 July was a tremendous stroke of luck, allowing Bethmann Hollweg to bamboozle Germany's Social Democrats into believing that Russia had drawn first blood—whereas in fact Bethmann Hollweg had already been won over by Moltke to mobilization by 9PM the night of 30 July. "Sazonov," Fischer concludes, "had put this trump into his hand."[88] Imanuel Geiss added another layer to Fischer's argument, claiming that the key decisions were made in Berlin as early as 29 July, following Sazonov's announcement of partial mobilization against Austria on 28 July, in response to Vienna's declaration of war on Serbia. While Fischer was right that Bethmann Hollweg did not give Moltke the green light for mobilization until 30 July, Geiss points out that the chancellor himself threatened to mobilize in a dispatch to Pourtalès on the 29th, and also agreed that day to inaugurate the "situation of the threatening danger of war" *(Kriegsgefahrzustand)* on 31 July—akin to Russia's Period Preparatory to War. Herwig has recently backed up Geiss's key claims.[89] The famous exchange of "Willy-Nicky" telegrams between kaiser and tsar between 29 July and 1 August "was thus," as Geiss argues, "from the German viewpoint, hardly more than part of the diplomatic manoeuvre to brand Russia as the aggressor and of the propagandist manoeuvre to smooth the way for German general mobilization."[90]

All this is true, so far as it goes. But it does not go very far if the goal is to prove that the Germans beat Russia to the punch. If decades of research have by now proven only that the decision to mobilize was made in Berlin by Moltke and Bethmann Hollweg (if not yet the kaiser) as early as 29 July, this is still *five full days* after Sazonov, Yanushkevitch, and the Council of Ministers made Russia's decision to begin secretly mobilizing in the districts adjoining Austria-Hungary (including, still more secretly, also the Warsaw and Baltic districts, targeting Germany), along with the mobilization of Russia's Baltic and Black Sea fleets. It was not, *pace* Fischer, Geiss, and Herwig, in reaction to Sazonov's public declaration of partial mobilization against Austria on 28 July that the Germans first took counter-measures, but rather after receiving four days of reports that a much broader secret mobilization was already underway, despite Sazonov's increasingly implausible denials.[91] The key to the puzzle was Poland, where Russian military preparations were so blatant that even Entente sympathizers noticed them. As the Serbian military attaché to Berlin recalled,

> On July 28, in company with several Serbian officers, I arrived at Warsaw [from Berlin]. As far as the German frontier, not the slightest indication was seen of military measures. But immediately after crossing the frontier [into Russian Poland], *we noticed mobilization steps being undertaken on a grand scale* (assembly of freight cars in several stations, military occupation of the railway stations, massing of troops in several cities, transport of troops, mobilization signaling). When we arrived at Brest-Litovsk, July 28, the state of siege had already been proclaimed.[92]

On 29 July, Germany's consul in Warsaw reported to Bethmann Hollweg that "Russia is already fully in a state of preparation for war ... the troops ranged against Germany are assembling between Lomza and Kovno along the Niemen, while those ranged against Austria are assembling at Lublin and Kovel [in present-day Ukraine] ... The Warsaw-Kalish line [to the Prussian border] and the Warsaw-Vienna tracks have been blanketed with infantry and sappers, who are laying mines under the roadbeds."[93]

Many French leaders, too, knew what was going on with Russia's secret mobilization, but they played along with Sazonov's game to dupe the British. Contrary to some historians' claims to the contrary,[94] Paléologue had reported to Paris by the evening of 25 July 1914 not only that the ministerial council at Tsarskoe Selo had decided that morning "in principle" to mobilize thirteen army corps against Austria, but also the cynical corollary that this mobilization would not be made public until Austria-Hungary declared war on Serbia. In a stunning admission that has escaped the notice of nearly all historians of the war's outbreak, France's ambassador added in his 25 July report that "meanwhile secret [Russian military] preparations will begin today" *(Les préparatifs clandestines commènceront néanmoins dès aujourd'hui)*. France's military attaché, General Laguiche, was posted liaison that same day to Krasnoe Selo to Russia's war minister, Sukhomlinov, and her future commander-in-chief, Grand Duke Nicholas, which put France fully in the loop as Russia's secret mobilization proceeded.[95] Considering that Jules Cambon, France's ambassador in Berlin, had reported to Paris the night of 25–26 July that "any mobilization orders issued in Russia will certainly be followed by mobilization orders in Germany"—without himself knowing, like Paléologue, that Russia had already given these orders—we may conclude that anyone in Paris able to connect the dots knew Russia had already resolved on war.[96]

Laguiche had figured this out for himself by 2PM on 26 July, which means that everyone at the French ministry of war to which he reported the following had cottoned on by that night, too (Laguiche's encrypted telegram was received in Paris at 4PM). "Secret military dispositions," Laguiche had been told, were already underway in Warsaw, Vilna, and St. Petersburg, that is, along the entire northern front against East Prussia. The decree placing Moscow and Petersburg in a "state of siege" (martial law) had, revealingly, been accompanied by a "list of subjects which news-papers are forbidden to mention," every one of which was to do with on-going mobilization measures against Germany. Summing up the Russian plan for arranging the opening of hostilities, Laguiche explained, "The Minister of War [Sukhomlinov] has repeatedly assured us of his desire to leave to Germany the initiative in launching an attack on Russia. Our in-telligence from Berlin suggests that they are indeed planning to take this initiative."[97]

The French, then, were willing collaborators in Russian plans to launch a war with Germany in which the latter would appear the aggres-sor. With the British, Sazonov's task was tougher. Just as Bethmann Holl-weg was keen that Russia was seen to mobilize first so that that the Social Democrats would not oppose war credits in the Reichstag, to ensure London's participation in the war Sazonov had to hide from the British any possible hint that Russia had mobilized first and without prior Ger-man or Austrian provocation. Amazingly, he seems to have succeeded in doing so simply by not telling them. The closest Sir George Buchanan came to sniffing out the truth was in a dispatch on 26 July, when he in-formed London that the "Governments of St. Petersburg and Moscow have been placed in a 'state of extraordinary protective activity.'" This vague-sounding measure had been taken, Buchanan explained to Grey, "ostensibly in view of strikes" (this is the lie Sazonov must have told him). Mildly suspicious, the British ambassador speculated that, since "strikes here are practically over," the measure may have been "concerned with intending mobilization."[98] Earlier that afternoon, Grey had been told by Germany's Ambassador Lichnowsky that Berlin had "received informa-tion that Russia was calling in 'classes of reserves,' which meant mobiliza-tion." Grey dismissed Lichnowsky's complaint out of hand, telling him that "we had no information as to a general mobilization or indeed of any mobilization immediately." With curious conviction, Grey further as-sured Lichnowsky that the Russian "*Ukase* to mobilize 1,100,000 men has not been issued." This was not only expressly untrue, but the spe-cificity of Grey's comment suggests the British may have heard some-thing after all. At any rate, Grey was clearly uninterested in investigating further.[99]

Even had Grey been interested in learning the truth, his ambassador to

Russia was not up to the task. With revealing vagueness, Buchanan reported on 28 July that he had picked up a report of "Forces of infantry leaving Warsaw for frontier," without explaining which forces, or which frontier.[100] Completing the circle of British ignorance, Sazonov chose to send his utterly disingenuous 28 July 1914 announcement of "partial mobilization" of the districts of Odessa, Kiev, Moscow, and Kazan (which measure was supposedly issued in retaliation for Austria's declaration of war on Serbia) to London not through Buchanan or even Benckendorff, his ambassador to Britain, but by way of the Russian chargé d'affaires in Berlin, who forwarded the message on to London with something less than great haste. (Buchanan himself later recalled pointedly urging Sazonov that day "to refrain from any military measures which might be construed as a challenge by Germany," still utterly oblivious that such measures had been underway for three full days already.)[101] Benckendorff did not finally pass on Sazonov's "partial mobilization" announcement until late afternoon on 29 July, and even then he gave it to Sir Arthur Nicolson, not His Majesty's Foreign Secretary Sir Edward Grey, to whom one might think such a critically important message would have been delivered.[102] Only by nightfall on 29 July 1914, four and a half days after the actual decision was taken by the ministerial council at Tsarskoe Selo, and more than *five* full days after it had originally been resolved in the Council of Ministers, were the British informed that Russia had begun mobilizing four military districts against Austria alone—a mobilization that in fact had long since expanded well beyond the boundaries specified, encompassing by 28 July all of European Russia plus Siberia and the Caucasus, the Baltic and Black Seas, and particularly Poland.

It was a masterful performance. With the incuriosity of Buchanan and Grey assuring that the British cabinet and Parliament (and perhaps more important, the British public) had no idea Russia was already mobilizing, Sazonov's public urging of restraint on Serbia—he convinced the Serbian government to accept all but one of the conditions of the ultimatum (the last one, which would have allowed "Austro-Hungarian agents or authorities" to participate in Serbia's own investigation into the Sarajevo crime) —was all that was needed to convince London that Russia's intentions were peaceful. In a classic sleight of hand, the ultimatum drama in the Balkans so obsessed British diplomats between 24 and 28 July that none of them paid the slightest attention to what was happening in Russia at the time. In a revealing non sequitur, Grey concluded his 26 July audience with the German ambassador in which Lichnowsky had complained of Russia's aggressive mobilization against the German frontier by proposing a conference between the leaders of England, France, Germany, and Italy, which would somehow prevent Serbia, Austria, and Russia from fighting one another.[103]

It is easy to understand Grey's position. The First Balkan War had indeed been wound down by an international conference in London. And yet Grey had failed to note the significant differences between the circumstances then and now (and that the vaunted Treaty of London, signed on 30 May 1913, had not prevented the outbreak of the Second Balkan War scarcely two weeks later). Whereas, in 1913, the problem had been one of getting the Balkan states and Turkey to come to terms so as not to prolong the Balkan war and draw in the great powers, in July 1914 the great powers themselves were driving events. While Austria was preparing to invade Serbia, while the enormous wheels of Russia's military mobilization against both Germany and Austria were being set in motion across the Eurasian continental expanse from Siberia to the Caucasus, from the Black Sea to the Baltic, British diplomats pursued the chimera of an international conference to mediate the Serbian dispute peacefully—to which Austria and Russia, the two powers most directly interested, would not even be invited.[104]

It is important to emphasize Sazonov's success in deceiving Grey about Russia's peaceful intentions. The Serbian ultimatum had been conceived in Berlin and Vienna as the centerpiece of the Austro-German plan to win a quick coup against the Entente. Because Sazonov had sniffed out the ultimatum early, he instead used it as a smokescreen to distract London from Russia's military preparations, ruining Bethmann Hollweg's efforts to keep Britain out of the war. While London's entry into the war was finally decided in August by the Germans' foolish decision to violate Belgian neutrality due to the dead weight of the Schlieffen Plan, even this may not have been possible politically had Sazonov not done his diplomatic homework. As Buchanan himself had told Paléologue on 28 July, "I have just been begging Sazonov not to consent to any military measure which Germany could call provocative. The German Government must be saddled with all the responsibility and all the initiative. *English opinion will accept the idea of intervening in the war only if Germany is indubitably the aggressor.* Please talk to Sazonov to that effect." Paléologue responded, suggestively, "That's what I'm always telling [Sazonov]."[105] It does not seem to have occurred to Buchanan that he was being deliberately misinformed about "provocative military measures" already under way for three days before 28 July 1914 by Sazonov and Paléologue.[106]

It is possible, of course, that even had Buchanan been clever enough to see through the French-Russian deception, England would have entered the war regardless. Only Moltke and the German generals were responsible for the suicidal strategic stupidity of invading France by way of Belgium. Still, we must consider the possibility that they may never have put the hair-trigger Schlieffen Plan into action had their strict timetable not been threatened by Russia's secret early mobilization against Germany—and by London's failure to so much as notice it, even while British diplomats minced no words in their criticism of Austro-German bullying in the Balkans. Had Grey or Buchanan protested to Sazonov about Russia's threatening moves in Poland, Bethmann Hollweg might have convinced the generals to postpone enactment of the Schlieffen Plan in order to win time in his efforts to drive a wedge between London and Petersburg—a postponement in which the nervous and ever-hesitating Kaiser Wilhelm II would happily have acquiesced. The Russians might then have been forced to pull back advance units in sensitive areas like Poland, much as the French did on the German frontier, in part to appease British skeptics (who evidently paid much closer attention to French behavior than to Russian). Instead, the obvious pro-Russian partiality displayed by English leaders completed the ring of Germany's perceived encirclement by the Triple Entente—an encirclement previously exaggerated but now an undeniable fact. With Russia off to a head start, the French fully on board, and Britain blindly going along, there was no conceivable reason for the Germans to wait.

Sazonov's game of deception gives us a good idea of what the Russians were really up to in July 1914. Whereas Berlin and Vienna had initially hoped to forge a localized fait accompli in Serbia before the powers could react, Sazonov's own strategy was more ambitious: it envisioned a European war, in which he must line up the most favorable coalition possible. As Winston Churchill wrote in *World Crisis,* "the manoeuvre which brings an ally into the field is as serviceable as that which wins a great battle."[107] By manipulating London into the war, Russia's foreign minister had added to the Franco-Russian coalition not only Britain's expeditionary force of six divisions but, more significantly, the world's most powerful surface navy, making possible a blockade that could throttle the economies of the Central powers. Then, too, London was the world's leading financial center, which meant the Entente would have no difficulty raising loans to pay for the war, even as the Germans would have to resort largely to the printing press. On the overriding diplomatic question of July 1914 —British belligerence or neutrality—Sazonov had outwitted Berlin and Vienna both, and it was not even close.

The upshot of Sazonov's masterful diplomacy was one of Russia's ideal war-gaming scenarios. On the night of 28 July, just hours after Sazonov had sent off his phony announcement of "partial mobilization," Yanushkevitch wired the commanding officers of all of Russia's military districts that "30 July will be proclaimed the first day of our general mobilization. The proclamation will follow by the regulation telegram."[108] The *general* mobilization the Russian high command had thus decided on by 28 July—more than three days before Germany even began its *pre*mobilization—was for "a war with a coalition" ("variant 4"), in which the participation of both Britain and France was assured, and in which— as Yanushkevitch revealingly wired to Tiflis on 29 July 1914—"Turkey does not *at first* take part" *(sluchai voinyi . . . v' kotoroi Turtsii snachala uchastiya ne prinimaet).*[109] With the German economy cut off from the world by the inevitable British blockade, *Novoe Vremya* predicted shortly following Britain's entry into the war in August, "the German empire will not be able to wage war for more than several months."[110] By then, the thinking went, Russia would have secured her Polish flank by seizing Austrian Galicia, while France had tied down German strength long enough for the Russians to pick off enough of lightly defended East Prussia to barter for German acceptance of Russian gains in Galicia and, if possible, at the Straits and in eastern Turkey, where Russia's Caucasian army now stood poised, and fully mobilized, to strike.

It was a brilliant plan, which just barely came off. Russian plans to outmobilize Germany were nearly scotched by the tsar's last minute reservations as he and the kaiser were exchanging their famous telegrams. There is no reason to doubt the good faith of Nicholas II, a man of honor if not exceptional intelligence, in attempting to call off the dogs of war. And yet the poor autocrat was in over his head. When "Nicky" wrote to "Willy" at 1:20AM the night of 29–30 July that "the military measures which have now come into force were decided five days ago," he gave the game away.[111] "So that is almost a week ahead of us," Kaiser Wilhelm II concluded: "the Tsar . . . has been secretly mobilizing behind my back . . . That means I have got to mobilize as well!"[112]

Far from a misinterpretation of the facts, as historians have long claimed, the kaiser's deduction was essentially correct, if not on all points.[113] In fact Russia's final, irreversible decision for general mobilization had been taken earlier that evening (29 July), at a conference attended by Yanushkevitch, Sukhomlinov, and Sazonov between 7PM and 9PM at the Russian foreign ministry. The tsar was apprised of the decision shortly after 9PM by telephone, and immediately granted his approval. It is true that the tsar changed his mind an hour later (again), and insisted on switching back to "partial" mobilization, which produced a series of confusing orders and counter-orders on through the day of 30 July. But the key decision for general mobilization had already been taken on 29 July (if not even earlier, in Yanushkevitch's 28 July telegram which envisioned general mobilization on the 30th) by Sazonov, Sukhomlinov, and Yanushkevitch, who were the real drivers of Russian policy.[114]

Between midnight and 2AM on the night of 29–30 July 1914, just as poor hesitating Nicholas was inadvertently confessing the truth in his own telegram to the kaiser, Pourtalès called on Sazonov to issue one final protest at Russia's secret mobilization. Taking a markedly cynical tack, the Russian foreign minister proposed a new round of time-consuming diplomacy—suddenly becoming interested in Grey's appeal for four-power talks to mediate the Austro-Serbian dispute—shortly before telling Pourtalès point-blank that "reversing the [Russian] mobilization order was no longer possible."[115] Eerily reminiscent of Moltke's reply to the hesitating kaiser one day later that the German mobilization timetable "cannot be altered," Sazonov's own claim is yet more significant because, unlike Moltke, he was a civilian theoretically ignorant of mobilization timetables. By blurting out the truth about Russia's early mobilization to Pourtalès just hours after the tsar did the same to the kaiser, Russia's foreign minister had removed any last doubt in Berlin that Russia meant war—and that she hoped to beat the Germans off the mark. Sazonov had done his job in arranging the most favorable belligerent coalition possible and giving Russia a head start. Now it was up the army.

CHAPTER THREE

Russia's War

The Opening Round

[It appears] that the Austrian forces ranged against us are weaker than those we war-gamed against.
—General Nikolai Yanushkevitch, August 1914[1]

CARL VON CLAUSEWITZ was right when he said that no battle plan ever survives first contact with the enemy. It is equally true, however, that initial plans have much to tell us about a country's war *aims,* however greatly these are altered by onrushing events—by what Clausewitz called "friction," that accumulation of unforeseen obstacles, happy and unhappy accidents, and unexpected enemy maneuvers that will overwhelm even the best-laid battle plan. Before the clash of arms begins, we may evaluate a nation's priorities by asking where it concentrates the bulk of its forces, and what areas it leaves comparatively barren. Other clues may be found in the strategic objectives of the first major offensives, whether or not they succeed, and in the size of the force and the number of resources allocated to them. We may also decipher the hidden goals governments have in mind by examining their secret correspondence with allies and neutrals, especially in the early stages of a war, when all things still seem possible. Paradoxically, it is in the often delusional states of mind characteristic of early stages of a conflict that we must look for belligerents' real objectives. Only in its ideal war-gaming scenarios can we form a picture of what Clausewitz might have called a country's *true* war aims, before battlefield friction confuses them.

Going back to the beginning is particularly important in the case of Russia's war aims in 1914 because they were so thoroughly smothered by the famous German victory at Tannenberg. The basic template of our diplomatic understanding of the First World War—German expansionist aims on both the eastern and western fronts, as laid out in the notorious "September program"—grew directly out of Germany's battlefield victories in the first month. Had these battles gone the other way—had the Russians reached the lower Vistula in East Prussia (as General Maximilian von Prittwitz, the commander of the German Eighth Army, famously predicted they were about to do before he was cashiered for losing his nerve), and the French plunged deep into Alsace-Lorraine even as the German right wing had gotten bogged down in Belgium, or if the German center had been overwhelmed in the Battle of the Frontiers—then historians would have argued then and even now over the goals of French and Russian expansionism in 1914, rather than about Bethmann Hollweg and the September program. To assume that the crushing German victories of the war's first month were inevitable is the worst kind of hindsight. It is an assumption belied not only by the well-known *réveil national* optimism at the outset in the French high command (shared by some though not all generals at Russian Stavka) and Moltke's correspondingly famous pessimism, but by the material facts: the Germans were greatly outnumbered and outgunned, with their entire army, however formidable in reputation, boasting fewer battalions than the French, let alone the colossal Russian army, and deploying fewer artillery guns than the supposedly inferior Russians (6,004 to 6,700).[2]

Russia's generals could be forgiven, therefore, for assuring the tsar in July 1914 that Russia could win. Sazonov had brilliantly arranged the enemy coalitions in what was arguably Russia's best war-fighting scenario since the eighteenth century, if we compare the belligerent blocs of 1914 to the coalitions in Russia's last great power wars, whether in 1812 (Russia against Napoleonic France at the height of its strength, plus her Prussian and Austrian proxies; Britain only peripherally engaged) or in 1853 (Russia against Ottoman Turkey, Britain, and France, with Austria hostile). If we compare the strategic potential of the coalitions of 1914, it was not even close: the economic output of the Entente dwarfed that of the Central powers, and by a considerable margin—and this was not even to count superior Entente access to war credit in the bond markets of London and (later) New York.[3] To be sure, Russia's leaders, like everyone else, expected a short war in 1914, but this gave them all the more reason for optimism. Under the strain of the inevitable British blockade Germany was not expected to hold out for more than several months.[4] During those months, meanwhile, it was France, not Russia, that would bear the brunt of Germany's military might, giving the Russians a virtually free hand to settle accounts with Austria or Germany, in whatever order they chose.

Of all the myths that cloud understanding of the First World War, the hoariest of all must be the notion that Russia "fell on its sword for France." Born, like so much of the war's mythology, in the murky legend of Tannenberg and the Russian tragedy of 1917 to which it seemed to point the way, this cliché must be put to rest at last if we are to understand Russia's war aims in 1914.[5] Although it is true that Moltke pulled back two corps from the western front in the initial panic produced by the Russian invasion of East Prussia, in strategic terms this brought the balance of concentration between Germany's main war fronts down from nearly ten to one in favor of the western front to more like seven or eight to one. The whole point of the Schlieffen Plan, after all, was to knock out France before the Russians could mobilize, leaving only a token force in East Prussia. Even as the crucial right wing of Count Alfred von Schlieffen's original design was subtly weakened by Moltke both before and during the August 1914 offensive, the Schlieffen Plan was the greatest possible gift to the Russian army. The basic facts, though well known, bear emphasis. Even as the Germans threw over seventy divisions into the August 1914 offensive against France and Belgium—seven entire armies, totaling more than a million and a half men—the Russians, wielding by the thirtieth day of mobilization some ninety-eight infantry and thirty-seven cavalry divisions on the eastern front, a force larger than 2 million, faced (in addition to Austria-Hungary's anything but fearsome forces) only one German cavalry and eleven German infantry divisions, or about "a tenth of [Germany's] total strength." As Moltke had warned Count Franz Conrad von Hötzendorf, his Austrian counterpart, in February 1913, "the centre of gravity of the whole European war, and consequently the fate of Austria, will be decided not on the Bug [river] but definitely on the Seine."[6] Of course, it was the Germans who had arranged things this way. Even so, the metaphor which best describes the strategic landscape of August 1914 is clearly that of France falling on its sword for Russia, and not the other way round.

This was no accident. From the earliest days of the Franco-Russian alliance, the expectation in both Paris and Petersburg was that France would have to do the bulk of the heavy lifting against Germany. The original military convention signed in 1892 had envisioned the French army mobilizing 1.3 million men against the Germans, with Russia—despite her much larger population base—contributing only 700,000 or 800,000. General N. N. Obruchev, the Russian signator of the agreement, insisted to Tsar Alexander III that Russia retained "absolute freedom of action" to deploy the bulk of her strength against either Austria or Germany, as it was not clear how a European war would begin (the convention covered the case of a German attack on France, but also that of an Austrian move against Russia, if Vienna were supported by Berlin). The "final text of the Franco-Russian military convention," concludes George Kennan in his classic study of the subject, "had some strange and disturbing features, placing largely in Russian hands . . . the power to unleash a major European war whenever this might suit Russian purposes."[7]

Try though the French did in the intervening years with generous inducements financial, political, and diplomatic, they never did convince the Russians to concentrate the bulk of their forces against Germany. Although Plan 19 did provide a sort of pivot option where the Fourth Russian Army could be deployed by way of the Warsaw railway hub either north against East Prussia (variant "G" or *Germania*) or southward against Austrian Galicia (variant "A" or *Austria*), Russia's generals had rigged this game heavily in favor of the southern option, which was the default or "automatic" deployment (that is, a "G" mobilization, unlike an "A" one, would have to be "specially ordered"). Only in the extremely unlikely event that Germany chose to attack Russia first—a scenario seriously entertained by almost no one in either Paris or Petersburg—would the northern variant of Mobilization Plan 19 come into effect.[8] The reason Stavka privileged the southwestern front over the northwestern was as obvious as it was damaging to French interests: Russia simply had no territorial ambitions in East Prussia, nor a reasonable expectation that she could best the Germans there in a fair fight. By contrast, the Russian seizure of Austrian Galicia was the first operational priority of Russian military planning against the Central powers, and (especially now that Stavka possessed the Austrian mobilization plan sold by Colonel Redl) was expected to be achieved without much difficulty. It should have been no surprise to anyone that Russia concentrated two-thirds of its available forces on the southwestern front in August 1914 (four army groups, altogether about 1.2 million men). In contrast, Russia invaded East Prussia with a force barely half this size, comprising only the First and Second Armies. Twenty-two years after the Franco-Russian military convention had first been proposed, Russia had contributed almost exactly what she originally promised against Germany (though, significantly, 25 percent less than her generals had promised the French in 1912–13): about 600,000 troops. This made up less than a third of her available forces in the European theater and constituted barely a third the size of the army that France, from a population base one-fourth the size of Russia's, was putting in the field against the common enemy.[9]

That the Russians were able to get away with this, even while overmatched France and little Belgium (reinforced only by Britain's tiny expeditionary force of six divisions) faced the brunt of the German assault, speaks volumes as to the relative leverage of each side in the Franco-Russian alliance. Russia could do basically whatever it wanted on the eastern front while France was obliged to accept whatever small assistance against Germany she might offer. Untroubled by even the possibility of a German invasion at the outset of the war, Russia could use the Warsaw "pivot" to send more or fewer divisions northward into Eastern Prussia; she could do so with more or less haste; she could deploy them westward from Warsaw instead (as the French would have preferred), targeting Berlin directly; her troops could fight their way tooth and claw across East Prussia, or retreat to the Russian border as soon as they encountered the first serious resistance. Once the dust had settled over the early battles, Russia could then offer to fight on, or threaten to sign a separate peace with the Central powers. With any of these decisions—particularly the last, that of whether or not to continue the war—Russia enjoyed colossal negotiating leverage with Paris and London, as wartime diplomacy would soon bear out. By contrast, the only way France could have put pressure on her Russian ally was by succumbing to the massive German invasion, which of course was no option at all. The Schlieffen Plan, even in its less extreme version modified by Moltke, had put every trump in Russia's hand. How she would use them was entirely up to Danilov, Yanushkevitch, Sukhomlinov, and Grand Duke Nicholas.

From the view of Stavka, the Russian headquarters established at Baranovichi, the unfolding situation in August 1914 was—at least until Tannenberg—almost too good to be true. The token force the Germans had left behind to defend East Prussia, Prittwitz's Eighth Army, appeared to be just as small—and inviting to attack—as expected. As Yanushkevitch informed Zhilinskii, commander of the northwestern front, on 10 August 1914, initial reconnaissance revealed that the Germans had only four infantry corps in Eastern Prussia, plus a few reserve divisions.[10] Against this, even the half-hearted Russian force facing the Germans deployed nine full army corps, including ample cavalry divisions—those fearsome mounted "Huns" which so obsessed the kaiser and other paranoid Germans before the war. In infantry-divisional terms, the Russian advantage was twenty-nine and a half to eleven, and ten to one in cavalry. Because each Russian division contained sixteen battalions, to twelve for their German counterparts, the Russian battalion advantage was still greater, about 480 to 130. In artillery, the breakdown was more lopsided still: 5,800 Russian guns against 774 German.[11] As Sukhomlinov wrote in his diary on 9 August 1914, as these facts were becoming clear, "it seems that the German wolf will quickly be brought to bay: all are against him."[12]

Meanwhile, Conrad had botched the Austro-Hungarian mobilization so badly that IV corps of Böhm-Ermolli's Second Army, supposed to be the hinge of the Galician campaign in the case of a war against Russia, was bogged down in Serbia until the end of August, to the Russians' delight. Little wonder that Yanushkevitch gleefully reported on 23 August to General Nikolai Ivanov, commander of the southwestern front, that extensive reconnaissance showed "that the Austrian forces ranged against us are weaker than those we war-gamed against."[13]

In part the Austrian mobilization debacle was owing to logistical ineptitude. The curious principle adopted by the army's railway command that trains were all to move at "maximum parallel graphic"—the highest speed of the slowest train on the worst line (about ten miles an hour)— ensured that even in the best-case scenario troops would reach the front "at a speed less than that of a decent bicycle." But more fundamentally, the famous botching of the Austrian mobilization was the result of Conrad's painful dilemma: Austria's real strategic objective was to knock out Serbia, but her German ally wanted her to concentrate her forces against Russia. In a revealing demonstration of where the negotiating leverage lay between the Central powers, Conrad's demand to keep the Second Army engaged in Serbia, where hard fighting was underway between 16 and 20 August 1914, was overruled by Emperor Franz Josef under heavy German pressure. To the horror of Austria-Hungary's beleaguered railway technicians, after detraining on the southern front most (though not all) of the Second Army was, on 18 August, at a crucial stage of the Serbian campaign, re-routed northward by stages to Galicia.[14]

France's generals, by contrast, pleaded in vain for the Russians to mount their principal offensive against Berlin. Instead, the Russians conducted a tactical withdrawal from the area of Poland west of the Vistula in order not to risk too exposed a salient between the Austrian and German fronts—a maneuver that certainly did not please anyone in Paris. To be sure, the Russian mobilization on the northwestern front, due largely to its head start, was rapid and even ahead of schedule: Zhilinskii reported by 10 August that both the First and Second Armies would be ready for action by the following day, only the twelfth day of Russia's (officially proclaimed) mobilization, nearly four days before Russia was required by her treaty obligations with France to invade East Prussia (although this announcement shortly proved to be premature).[15] But Russian superiority was still much less than it could have been because the northwestern front was given much lower priority than Austrian Galicia. With Pavel Rennenkampf's First Army and A. V. Samsonov's Second Army advancing separately into East Prussia, the former heading due west from the Niemen River near Kovno, the latter northwest from central Poland, the Russians threatened to envelop the German Eighth Army in a pincer movement. Unless they could stay in contact, however—a prospect made supremely difficult by the fifty-mile barrier of the Masurian Lakes that would open up between them for several days—the First and Second Armies would individually enjoy at most marginal superiority over the German Eighth Army. As it turned out, many second-line and reserve divisions were distrusted by the generals at Stavka, and so were left behind the front "kick-

The Initial Mobilization Pattern
on the Eastern Front, August 1914

SWEDEN

Öland

BALTIC SEA

Gulf of Riga

Estonia

Riga

Courland
(Latvia)

Düna (Dvina)

SIXTH Petrograd Garrison
and Reserve formations

Dvinsk

Memel

Lithuania

Kovno

Vilna
(Vilnius)

Wilja

Königsberg

EIGHTH
(Prittwitz) East

Danzig

Prussia

White Russia

FIRST
(Rennenkampf)

RUSSIAN

GERMAN

Allenstein

Masurian
Lakes

Grodno

Niemen

To Moscow
540 m.

site of Russian
HQ (Stavka)
Yanushkevitch

EMPIRE

Vistula

Tannenberg

Torun

Notec

Lomza

Narew

Bialystok

SECOND
(Samsonov)

Baranovichi

(Zhilinskii)

EMPIRE

Posen

To Berlin
150 m.

Posen

Vistula

Novo Georgievsk

forming

Bug

Brest
Litovsk

Pinsk

Pripet Marshes

(Woyrsch)

Kalish

Warsaw

NINTH

Russian

Lodz

Warta

FOURTH
(Salza)

Pripet

Ukraine

Poland

Ivangorod

Wieprz

FIFTH
(Plehve)

(Ivanov)

Kovel

SEVENTH
Kiev-Odessa
Garrison and
Reserve

Silesia

Breslau

Oder

Pilitsa

Lublin

Krasnik

Lutsk

To Kiev
190 m.

Rovno

Dubno

Kummer Group

Vistula

FIRST
(Dankl)

San

Jaroslaw

THIRD
(Ruzski)

Austrian
Silesia

Cracow

West

Jaroslaw

Lemberg (Lvov)

THIRD
(Brudermann)

EIGHTH
(Brusilov)

Moravia

Galicia

Przemysl

FOURTH
(Auffenberg)

Carpathian

Mountains

East

Kövess Army
Corps Group

Dniestr

AUSTRIA-

Galicia

Czernowitz

Prut

Siret

Vienna

Danube

HUNGARY

SECOND
(Böhm-Ermolli)

from Serbia

part of Böhm-Ermolli's
Second Army

Bukovina

Moldova

Budapest

Tisza

Transylvania

0   50   100   150 miles

ing their heels": garrisoning fortresses, guarding supply lines, and so on. By the time they actually came in contact, each Russian army was inferior to the Germans' Eighth Army: Rennenkampf's First Army reduced to six and a half effective divisions, Samsonov's Second Army to nine and a half. Had several corps from the Russian Fourth Army been seconded to East Prussia, the Russians could have enjoyed superiority vis-à-vis Prittwitz's Eighth with either their First or Second Army. Zhilinskii might even have been able to bridge the "Masurian Lakes" gap, avoiding the danger of a lasting separation between Samsonov and Rennenkampf that would allow the Germans to attack them in sequence. Even the new Russian Ninth Army, being assembled in Warsaw from troops arriving from the Russian interior in accordance with Yanushkevitch's 7 August directive, ostensibly in preparation for an invasion "in depth" of Germany—its task, Grand Duke Nicholas promised Paléologue, was that of "bearing down on Berlin as soon as the southern armies have succeeded in 'holding up' and 'fixing' the enemy"—was routed instead to the southwestern front in late August. So far from "falling on the sword for France," Russia's generals failed to field even one single army larger than the Germans' token force in East Prussia, so keen were they to strike instead in Austrian Galicia.[16]

The Russian armies on the southwestern front, by contrast, enjoyed every superiority imaginable against their Austrian opponents. Conrad, like Moltke but unlike Yanushkevitch, faced a two-front war. Even had Conrad not deployed his Fifth and Sixth Armies (and, until 18 August, his Second) against Serbia, the forty effective divisions of the entire Austro-Hungarian army were inferior to the fifty-plus the Russians were able to throw into the invasion of Galicia. After being reinforced by the Second Army's partial redeployment from Serbia at the end of August, Conrad still had only thirty-seven infantry and ten cavalry divisions on the Galician front, many exhausted from their recent redeployment, facing fifty-three and a half comparatively fresh Russian infantry and eighteen cavalry divisions.[17]

If the odds in East Prussia were—slightly—in the Russians' favor, in Galicia the Austrians were fairly up against it. The front, to be sure, was nearly 200 miles long, and neither side had particularly good intelligence on the other's deployments. This allowed Conrad's First Army, under the command of General Viktor Dankl, to meet the Russian Fourth Army in roughly equal strength south of Lublin at the Battle of Krasnik on 23–25 August, leading to an initial Austrian victory that impressed Conrad and Yanushkevitch alike. After a confusing series of maneuvers on the flanks of the colliding armies, however, the crushing Russian superiority in the theater (particularly farther east, where Austria's Third Army faced the Russian Third and Eighth Armies nearly alone) began to tell. Lemberg, capital of Habsburg Galicia, fell on 2 September, and a general Austro-Hungarian retreat began on 11 September 1914—almost exactly concurrent with the German withdrawal from the Marne on the western front. So overwhelming was the reversal on the southwestern front that the Russian Fourth Army, thought to be in disarray after its defeat at Krasnik, joined the general pursuit. To Dankl, it seemed "as if the [Russian] casualties had risen from the dead."[18]

While the military situation in East Prussia remained fluid, the meticulously planned Russian occupation of Austrian Galicia was now well underway, slowed down only by the crushing size of the occupying army. Russia now had "more troops in Galicia than it could feed or move."[19] Considering that securing Austrian Galicia was Russia's principal war aim in eastern Europe, it is remarkable that it was largely achieved in less than the six weeks the supposedly hyper-efficient Germans allotted to the Schlieffen Plan, which had failed just as spectacularly as the Russian conquest of Galicia had apparently succeeded. So euphoric was the mood in Petrograd that Paléologue bet Buchanan £5 "that the war would be over by Christmas."[20]

In Bordeaux (where the French government had relocated as the Germans neared Paris in early September), news of the Russians' successful Galician offensive was received with considerably less pleasure. From the French perspective, Galicia was a sideshow: the German front was all that mattered. And in Eastern Prussia, the news was disastrous. Samsonov had lost nearly his entire Second Army in the soon-to-be-legendary German victory at Tannenberg, which made the reputations of General Erich Ludendorff and, more significantly, Field Marshal Paul von Hindenburg (Prittwitz's successor), the future German president who appointed Adolf Hitler chancellor in 1933. In reality the victory was something of an accidental "miracle": General Hermann von François, commanding two first-line divisions, was ordered by Ludendorff to attack the left flank of

Samsonov's advancing army. Because his men were exhausted, having just been transferred in from the east, and were still awaiting guns, François first refused, then prevaricated for several days. The delay in François's attack allowed his divisions to reach Samsonov's rear, leading to the encirclement of the Russian Second Army in a kind of Cannae.[21] Although the strategic significance of the battle was overrated (the Russians had soon recovered their footing on the German front, and invaded East Prussia again in September), it is easy to see why the French viewed Tannenberg as proof of Russia's misplaced priorities. After receiving the official telegram from Grand Duke Nicholas celebrating the expulsion of the Austrian armies from Eastern Galicia on 12 September 1914, President Poincaré lamented, "This is all very well, and we can warmly applaud the Russian victory, but it appears that in Eastern Prussia the Germans have got their own back again, and that Russia, contrary to our repeated requests, is making her chief effort against Austria, as if the surest way to beat Austria were not to begin by beating Germany."[22] Not for the last time, Russia's uncompromising war aims threatened to gum up the works of the Entente alliance, even in the flush of victory.

It is worthwhile to pause here to examine the Russian approach to occupied Galicia, for it gives us an important window into what the postwar world might have looked like if the European war had ended in fall 1914—just as nearly everyone expected it to. Setting aside, for the purposes of the exercise, the "miracle of Tannenberg," we may propose instead merely an inconclusive series of battles in East Prussia, leading to a tactical retreat of the German Eighth Army behind the lower Vistula (exactly what Prittwitz himself recommended shortly before Tannenberg). Alongside the post-Marne stalemate on the western front, this would have led to some kind of compromise ceasefire, even if a temporary one. The scenario posited here—a significant, though not overwhelming, Russian victory in Austrian Galicia, a partial German abandonment of East Prussia (though with Prittwitz's Eighth Army intact), and a significant (but not overwhelming) Teutonic victory in the west that left part of France under German occupation—is in fact precisely what, all other things being equal, the mobilization line-up in August 1914 would suggest as the most likely outcome. Of course, "other things" are never equal in war. But once again, to understand a country's *true* war aims, it is better to use logically expected outcomes than actual ones.

With the case of Austrian Galicia, we need not even greatly distort what actually happened in August and September 1914 to imagine Russia's desired postwar situation. That the peoples inhabiting this territory were largely Slavic—Poles and Ruthenes (or "Ukrainians")—was a convenient fact for Russian pan-Slavic propaganda both before and during the war, but it mattered little to the generals.[23] In raw strategic terms, the Galician "problem" was as obvious as was its solution: Russia aimed simply to reach her "natural" frontier at the Carpathian Mountains. This she had very nearly done by mid-September 1914. Conrad's armies, reduced by nearly 350,000 men (of which 30,000 were prisoners), had been driven back across the river San, in all some 150 miles from eastern Galicia. This "primordial Russian land" (as Yanushkevitch described it gleefully to Goremykin, the chairman of the Council of Ministers) was now under Russian occupation. The occupation was confirmed in a legal sense by the "Temporary Directive on the Administration of Austro-Hungarian Territories Taken by Right of War" issued by Stavka on 17/30 August 1914. Western Galicia, with its mostly Polish population, had been only partially conquered, but the general Austrian retreat opened the prospect that it, too, would soon be in Russia's hands.

That Russia planned and expected to take all of Galicia from the outset of the war is clear from the "Appeal of the Supreme Commander" to the Polish nation issued in the name of Grand Duke Nicholas, published in Polish newspapers, and placarded around "Congress Poland" on 3/16 August 1914. Drafted under Sazonov's supervision at the Foreign Ministry, the grand duke's proclamation vowed that a self-governing Polish nation "would be reunited under the scepter of the Russian tsar," although leaving unsaid whether this nation would be autonomous or independent (the word used was *samoupravlenie,* literally "self-government," which could be variously translated) and what its future borders would be.[24]

In view of both its vagueness and the fact that it did not bear the tsar's signature, it would be easy to dismiss the importance of the famous Polish manifesto. Intriguingly, the Germans' even vaguer proclamation to the Poles, dropped behind front lines on 7–8 August 1914, which offered them "freedom and independence" from the "Muscovite yoke," likewise did not bear the kaiser's signature. One senses that neither Germany nor Russia was ever operating entirely in good faith when making wartime promises to the Poles. Russia issued other vague "proclamations," all in the name of the grand duke, not the tsar, to other Slavic subjects of the Habsburgs, such as Ruthenes/Ukrainians (named specifically) and (only by implication) the Czechs and Slovaks. Sazonov made other nonbinding territorial promises, in case of pro-Entente intervention or continued neutrality, to Balkan states like Romania (which was offered Habsburg-Hungarian Transylvania), Serbia (offered Bosnia-Herzegovina and Dalmatia), Greece (offered southern Albania), and Bulgaria (offered Serbian Macedonia, which shows how hollow was Russia's espousal of the Serbian cause). Much of this was clearly humbug. Romanian or Greek intervention probably would not have made any more difference in the battles on the eastern front in 1914 than any putative morale problems inside the Habsburg armies caused by the grand duke's vague proclamations of Slavic solidarity. Balkan diplomacy was a notorious backwater of bad faith, as illustrated by Sazonov's territorial bribes to keep the Serbs in the war if they themselves agreed to bribe Bulgaria to stay out. The Central powers were making similar offers to all the Balkan neutrals, and with just as much cynicism.[25]

The Polish issue was of a far more serious nature. The fact that Chorister's Bridge, unlike the Wilhelmstrasse and the Ballplatz, was offering to "reunite" historic Poland at the outset of the war has much to tell us about Russia's war aims. Because so many Poles lived in Austrian Galicia, especially its western half, the grand duke's proclamation in effect committed Russia to a war platform of dismembering Austria-Hungary, rather than merely a defense of Serbia and "Slavic honor" against Teutonic aggression as the war had been originally justified. As Tsar Nicholas II himself pointed out before the State Council on 26 July/8 August 1914, "We are not only defending our honor and dignity on our own land, we are fighting on behalf of our brother Slavs united to us in blood and faith."[26] Translated into foreign policy terms, this meant that Russia would expand the boundaries of "Russian Poland"—that is, of Russia itself—up to the Carpathian Mountains. Although seizing Austrian Galicia was clearly a Russian strategic priority all along, such an annexationist program had never been cleared with the French and British governments. Nor had the grand duke's proclamation itself been cleared with Paris or London, although Sazonov did warn Paléologue (though not, significantly, Buchanan) shortly before it was placarded around Poland.[27]

Because of France's historic ties to Poland, it is not surprising that the French were the first to take alarm at Russia's territorial ambitions in eastern Europe (Sir George Buchanan, as usual, was slow to catch on).[28] Even the exceptionally friendly Paléologue was a bit skeptical at first when Sazonov told him what was brewing, demanding to know why a political manifesto supposedly offering Congress Poland "autonomy" bore the signature of the grand duke, not the sovereign, Tsar Nicholas II.[29] Back in France, President Poincaré was livid that he had not been consulted beforehand about the manifesto, which had thrown up "veiled annexations as to which no agreement has been concluded between Russia and ourselves, which may traverse the whole idea of a defensive war"—this last a loud and persistent theme of British and French war propaganda.[30] Besides, the French statesman remarked sardonically, "I fear that the scepter of the tsar will scarcely suggest itself to the Polish eyes as an emblem of freedom." To put such suspicions to rest, Ambassador Izvolsky summoned Poles resident in Paris (among them Madame Marie Curie, the Nobel Prize–winning physicist) to the Russian Embassy in order to win support for the Russian cause. And yet the Russian ambassador, the Poles reportedly complained, gave them only "an evasive and ambiguous answer" on the question of autonomy for postwar Poland.[31] Making Izvolsky's job difficult, the French papers had translated *samoupravlenie* as "autonomy," which was not what Sazonov, for fear of lending ammunition to Germanophile and conservative critics in Russia, had really meant to offer Poland.[32] Even the mostly favorable publicity the grand duke's proclamation received in the French press was a bit muddled, with the manifesto welcomed not as an endorsement of Polish independence so much as a Russian vow of eternal hostility toward Berlin and Vienna: the idea was that "*For ever* Russia . . . has raised Poland against the two Germanic Powers."[33]

To dispel some of the confusion resulting from the grand duke's proclamation, France's ambassador sought to clear the air with Russia's foreign minister in a historic "tête-à-tête" luncheon on 20 August 1914. After the two men agreed that the conflict at hand would be a "war to the death in which each group of belligerents stakes its very existence," Sazonov came clean for the first time about Russia's real war aims. In order to "destroy German imperialism," Sazonov told Paléologue, "in addition to the restitution of Alsace-Lorraine to France, *Poland must be restored,* Belgium enlarged, Hanover reconstituted, Schleswig returned to Denmark, Bohemia freed and all the German colonies given to France, England, and Belgium, etc." Although Paléologue did not quite endorse this "gigantic programme" of conquest, he made no objections, either.[34]

It was not long before Sazonov's Polish trial balloon had expanded to fill a good deal of eastern Europe. Just as the Germans famously worked out their own wartime program of imperial expansion in September 1914, so did Russia's foreign minister formulate an extensive—and quite explicit—plan of territorial conquest that same month. By the terms of the "London convention" of 4 September 1914, the three Entente powers vowed not to make a separate peace with the Central powers.[35] Ten days later, Sazonov laid out his Polish program before Paléologue while inviting Sir George Buchanan to sit in, too, for the first time. Following the expected victory over the Central powers, Sazonov proposed that Europe be remodeled more or less along ethnic-national lines (at German and Austrian expense, of course), thus with Schleswig-Holstein restored to Denmark, Serbia expanding on the "irredentist" principle to include Bosnia-Herzegovina, Dalmatia, and Northern Albania (though tossing Bulgaria the Serbian-Macedonian fillip to win her neutrality), Habsburg Transylvania turned over to Romania, France taking back Alsace-Lorraine, and so forth. All this was mere prelude to Russia's own ambitions: the tsar would annex outright "the lower course of the Niemen and the eastern part of Galicia." Meanwhile, the "Kingdom of Poland," whether "self-ruling" or "autonomous" (but in either case under Russian suzerainty) would, in Sazonov's scenario, expand beyond the current borders of Russian "Congress Poland" to include also "eastern Posen, Silesia . . and the western part of Galicia." All of this, Sazonov emphasized repeatedly during the audience, was still an "unofficial sketch" of Russia's war aims, but Paléologue was in no doubt that Sazonov was sincere in wishing to "lay down for us his line of thinking" for the postwar world.[36]

Russian Claims on Austrian and German Territory, Fall 1914

To Sazonov's disappointment, neither Paléologue nor Buchanan was quite willing—yet—to sanction Russian territorial ambitions in eastern Europe. It was not that either man objected, on principle, to the Russian plans for expanding the boundaries of postwar (Russian) Poland, but rather that the strategic situation in September was still perilous enough that Russia's entire Galician campaign seemed like a strategic mistake. On the morning of the same day Sazonov serenaded him with visions of remaking Europe wholesale at Germany's expense (14 September 1914), Paléologue had received an urgent plea from Bordeaux that he lean on the Russians to reorient their efforts on the eastern front against Germany. Meeting with Sukhomlinov at the War Ministry shortly before he was summoned by Sazonov, Paléologue lodged a formal protest that Stavka was "neglecting the German front in order to concentrate its efforts on opening the road to Vienna." Mounting what was perhaps not the most convincing defense, Sukhomlinov pointed to Tannenberg, where Russia had "sacrificed 110,000 men" in order to "save the French army." Painfully, Paléologue pointed out that the disaster which befell Samsonov's Second Army "was not our fault." While not quite demanding that Sukhomlinov call a halt to the Galician offensive against Austria, the French ambassador did request that it not be pursued *outre mesure,* and that Sukhomlinov remind Grand Duke Nicholas that "our primordial objective is the destruction of German power."[37] Three days later, the (ever tardy) Buchanan affixed his own signature to a formal aide-mémoire in which the French and British governments requested that Russia recognize that "the triumph of the Russian army in Galicia shows that only a negligible importance should be attached to the armed forces of Austria-Hungary," and that the war could only be won if the three Entente powers "took the war into the heart of Germany itself."[38]

Predictably, the French-English request that the Russians focus on beating the Germans instead of conquering Austrian Galicia went nowhere. While encountering nothing but humiliation in East Prussia, on the southwestern front "we are indisputably the vanquishers," as Prince N. A. Kudashev, director of the Diplomatic Bureau at Stavka, reported gleefully to Sazonov on 18 September 1914.[39] The Russians were hardly going to abandon "primordially Russian" eastern Galicia, where they (as General Ivanov, commander of the southwestern front, promised his men) were the "true liberators of foreign Rus' from the Austrian yoke."[40] Kudashev's deputy Nikolai Bazili added another wrinkle to the imperial argument, informing Grand Duke Nicholas on 29 September 1914 that the "Russian farmers" of Eastern Galicia awaited from Russia not only deliverance from Austrian misrule, but also "liberation from their oppression by the Jews," who, he claimed, had enslaved them financially. So far from having pacified this "primordially Russian" territory, in fact, Bazili thought there was immense work still to be done. The Polish minority of Eastern Galicia was "secretly hostile" to Russia, while the Jews scarcely bothered to hide their hostility to the occupiers. Because the population of (still partly unconquered) Western Galicia was even more heavily Polish and Jewish, it was not surprising that, Bazili had heard, "the mood there was one of open hostility towards us." In Lemberg, the occupying Russians discovered that "several million Kroner" had been raised for volunteer Polish legions against Russia. All in all, Bazili informed the grand duke, the occupation of Galicia would prove "an extremely difficult task," requiring not only able administrators but also "monumental outlays" on food and medicine to win over the wavering population.[41]

Compared to her "historic mission" unfolding in Galicia, Russia's halfhearted invasion of East Prussia was unable to inspire much passion at Stavka. The only thing keeping the Russians from giving up entirely on the northwestern front was that Rennenkampf's retreat threatened to open the Russians' Galician flank to the Germans. Generals Ivanov and his deputy, Alekseev, would have dearly loved to pursue the retreating Austrians beyond the San to Cracow and Budapest, but this objective could not be squared with the unstable situation farther north. Had the Germans pursued Rennenkampf's First Army with any vigor, they may well have threatened Warsaw or Kovno, which would have forced Ivanov, too, to retreat. But the German advance on the northern front bogged down quickly. Rather than pursuing Rennenkampf, the Germans reinforced the Austrians, mounting an offensive on the central Polish front between Cracow and Warsaw, getting within some twelve miles of the latter by mid-October before themselves retreating. The battle of Lodz, engaged between 11 and 23 November, was typical in its indecisiveness, with repeated German attacks failing to pierce Russian lines until the Russians simply abandoned the exposed position in early December. All across the eastern front, the situation remained "confused and bewildering" in October and November, with the ebb and flow of attacks, counterattacks, and retreats leaving the front lines by December 1914 fairly close to where they had been in mid-September, with the Russians holding onto Eastern Galicia and a Polish line just east of Lodz between the rivers Pilitsa and Vistula, but unable yet to penetrate into East Prussia or break through Austrian lines west of the river San in the direction of Cracow. Przemysl, the great Habsburg fortress on the San, held out until March 1915.[42]

Russia's historic mission in Austrian Galicia, however compelling, had proved more difficult to achieve than prewar visionaries had hoped. Even while Sazonov continued pressing Russia's imperial claims in his negotiations with Paléologue, the generals at Stavka had to deal with the organizational headaches of occupation on top of the logistical difficulties of transporting and munitioning the armies. So long as the war continued, under the "Statute of the Field Administration of Troops in Wartime" the actual administration of the front zone (including occupied territories) was the responsibility of Stavka, not the civilian government in Petrograd.[43] And Russia's political objectives in Galicia, Yanushkevitch reported to Goremykin on 2 October 1914, had bogged down just as badly as her armies. To begin with, there were difficulties communicating with the locals, and not only the Poles: what Yanushkevitch called "the so-called Ukrainian language" proved more difficult to harmonize with Russian than hoped. So, too, did the Ruthenian (or Ukrainian) adherents of the Greek Uniate Church stubbornly resist Russification if it meant adopting Russian Orthodoxy. Most of all, there was the "open hostility" of the Jewish population, manifest not least in the numbers who had fled Eastern Galicia in advance of the Russian occupation. Their abandoned property must now be accounted for and somehow fairly administered. Behind the front lines, meanwhile, nearly the entire Pale of Settlement fell within the zone of Russian military rule. "In any case we must realize," Yanushkevitch warned Goremykin only several weeks into the occupation of Galicia, "that a very difficult struggle with Judentum lies in store for us."[44] With these somewhat less than innocuous words began the army's campaign of forced expulsion and/or deportation *(vyselenie)* of "unreliable elements" and "enemy subjects." Between 500,000 and 1 million Jews were expelled from homes in areas under Russian military administration between 1914 and 1917, along with some 250,000 German nationals. Despite evidence of hostility among the Polish population as well, Poles were generally spared this treatment in order to promote the pan-Slavist solidarity implied in the grand duke's proclamation. Many Poles were even encouraged to take over the property of deported Jews.[45]

Predictably, a substantial gap began to open up between the generals fighting Russia's increasingly ugly war and the politicians formulating her war aims. Even as Yanushkevitch sought advice from the chairman of the Council of Ministers on how he might better pacify the little territory Russia had already conquered, Goremykin's colleagues were advancing plans to conquer huge tracts of land elsewhere. In late September, Sazonov and Krivoshein began quietly intriguing with the French and British ambassadors to sign off on Russian ambitions at the Straits and Constantinople in any final peace treaty ending the European war. Although both men admitted there were serious complications ahead—not least that Turkey was not yet at war with the Entente!—Krivoshein, for his part, told Paléologue point-blank "that the Turks must be expelled [from Europe]" *(chto turki dolzhnyi uiti v Aziyu),* and that Constantinople should be made, at worst, a neutral city, with guaranteed Russian naval access to the Bosphorus, the Sea of Marmara, and the Dardanelles—up to and including the installation of coaling stations. Sazonov was tasked with winning over Buchanan to Russia's ambitions at the Straits without provoking the British by mentioning Krivoshein's more ambitious plans for reducing Turkey to an Anatolian rump state. (He assured Buchanan, with suspicious vagueness, that he "was not completely in agreement with Krivoshein's views.")[46] Significantly, Paléologue informed Paris that, unlike in the 1/14 September meeting, this time Sazonov was speaking not "simply of schemes," but rather of policies actually resolved upon *(doveril nam ne prostoi proekt, no svoe reshenie).*[47]

Just as Russia's claims on Galicia had been formulated long before the war of 1914 made them potentially operable, so, too, was the occupation of Constantinople and the Straits a war aim decided upon long before Turkey's actual entry into the war. Improbable as the connection between Galicia and Turkey may seem at first glance, the two were intimately related in the minds of Russian policymakers, and not only in those of neo-Slavists who blustered that "the road to Constantinople runs through

Warsaw." The basic gist of Russia's annexationist war aims for Austrian Galicia and Turkey was broadly shared inside the Russian government. What little criticism there was of the Sazonov-Krivoshein program laid out in September 1914 inside the Council of Ministers came neither from the revolutionary "Left" nor from antiwar Germanophile conservatives on the "Right," but rather from nationalist-imperialist critics who thought the foreign minister too timid. In the first serious memorandum on war aims produced by the "Opposition" that fall, a group headed by Nikolai Maklakov, the reactionary interior minister, proposed instead the "incorporation of Eastern Galicia, Northern Bukovina and Carpathian Ruthenia" into Russia; the outright annexation of Constantinople and the Straits; adjustment of the frontier in both East Prussia and eastern Turkey to Russia's benefit; the "liberation" (in other words, irredentist absorption into Russia) of Slavic subjects of Austria-Hungary, and the unification of Russian Poland "inside the widest possible frontiers."[48]

Sweeping as the Opposition platform was, it was still not sweeping enough for the most important policymaker in Imperial Russia: Tsar Nicholas II. In a remarkable audience with the French ambassador held in November 1914, the emperor laid out his vision for the postwar world, providing a precious glimpse into what Russia's "Little Father" thought his peasant children were fighting, bleeding, and dying for. Apart from the dismemberment of Germany along lines nearly identical to those Sazonov had proposed in September, the tsar envisioned Austria being reduced to the original Habsburg family possessions, Salzburg and the Tyrol (that is, not even including *Vienna*). Austria would be replaced by a ring of friendly Slavic buffer states: an enlarged Romania, including Transylvania; some new Czech or Czechoslovak state; and a much-enlarged Russophile Serbia, which would also incorporate Croatian and Albanian territory. Russia could then attain her natural frontier along the Carpathian Mountains while incorporating East Prussia as far as the Vistula, along with Prussian Posen and part of Silesia, into newly reunited (Russian) Poland. It was in Russia's postwar plans for Turkey, though, that the tsar became most animated. "Should I annex Armenia?" he asked Paléologue rhetorically, before answering that he would only do so if the Armenians asked him to. More important, Russia's sovereign insisted that "the Turks must be expelled from Europe," that Constantinople be made an international city under Russian protection; and that Russia annex European Turkey east of the Enos-Midia line. Asked, by Paléologue, whether he had understood correctly that Russia wished to reduce Turkey to a mere Asian rump "with Ankara or Konya as its capital," Tsar Nicholas II replied, "perfectly so."[49]

One can accuse the Russians of many sins in the European catastrophe of 1914, but a lack of forthrightness in formulating war aims is clearly not one of them. Already Paléologue and (when he paid attention) Buchanan were finding it difficult to conceal their distaste for the crusading imperialism of their slightly embarrassing ally. This distaste was not strong enough, of course, for either France or Britain to cut Russia loose—certainly not while the Germans were dug in fifty miles from Paris. As Sazonov knew only too well, the disposition of the German armies—and the fears in the French high command that Petrograd could cut a separate peace whenever she desired—gave Russia overwhelming diplomatic leverage. Her program of annexing Austrian Galicia, first floated carefully in August, was by September already a diplomatic fait accompli, awaiting only the final rout of the Habsburg armies in the field. Russia's plans for Turkey, first broached by Sazonov and Krivoshein in September, were by November 1914 so confidently held that the tsar himself felt no need to conceal them. France and Britain, it was beginning to appear, had no choice but to swallow whatever war aims Russia force-fed them. To complete Russia's age-old dream of conquering Constantinople and the Straits, only one obstacle remained. Turkey must enter the war.

CHAPTER FOUR

Turkey's Turn

> We need a strong boss ruling over Constantinople, and since we
> cannot let any other power assume this role, we must take her for
> ourselves. For us to accomplish this without waging war on Turkey
> would, of course, be impossible.
>
> —M. N. Girs, October 1914[1]

I N HIS SECOND INAUGURAL ADDRESS, delivered as the American Civil
War entered its final terrible year, U.S. president Abraham Lincoln
said of chattel slavery, "all knew that this interest was, somehow, the cause
of the war." Much the same could be said of the Ottoman Empire and
the First World War. Everyone knows that the July crisis grew out of the
"Sarajevo outrage" of 28 June 1914, which brought to a head the long-
simmering rivalry between Austria and Russia in the Balkans, which was
in turn a product of the decline of Ottoman power in Europe as mani-
fested in the Balkan Wars of 1912–13. The fact that the brunt of the initial
fighting and dying took place in France and Belgium due to the strategic
accident of the Schlieffen Plan has colored popular memory of the conflict and dominated its literature, but not even the most blinkered historians of the western front deny that the war's real causes lie farther east.

There remains considerable confusion, however, about how far east
we should go in explaining the origins of World War I. The dominant
theories of the war's outbreak relate to German imperial ambitions and
fears of the growth of Russian power. The assassination of the archduke,
by this account, functions merely as a kind of "inevitable accident" used
by the Austrians to chastise Serbia and by the Germans as a convenient

excuse for settling accounts with Russia. The outbreak of the world war by this logic was all owing to what Bismarck famously called "some damn fool thing in the Balkans." On this view, the war's proximate origins were essentially meaningless, a mere happenstance pretext for the insatiable ambitions of German *Weltpolitik*.

Like all great historical myths, this one is appealing in its simplicity—and its elegant Bismarckian cynicism. But we must be careful with Bismarck's seductive *bon mots*. The "damn fool thing in the Balkans" line appears to be apocryphal, likely inspired by Bismarck's actual speech to the Reichstag during the Balkan crisis of 1876, when he notoriously said that the Balkans were "not worth the bones of a single Pomeranian grenadier." Except that this is not quite what Bismarck said: in fact he claimed that the entire Ottoman Empire *(den ganzen Orient)* was not worth the life of a Prussian soldier.[2] In this misquote, we can see something of the elision in popular mythology of the true nature of the Eastern Question, which was never really about "the Balkans," as many western (particularly British) observers mistakenly believed, but rather about the entire Ottoman inheritance, up to and including—especially—the Straits.

There are good reasons for this enduring confusion. Sazonov, as we have seen, kept the British deliberately misinformed about Russia's real foreign policy aims in July 1914, using Serbia and "the Balkans" as a brilliant smokescreen to conceal Russia's secret mobilization—and Russian ambitions to dominate Turkey. Russia's designs on the Straits had nearly been a *casus belli* between London and Petersburg in 1878, and might easily have sundered the fragile Anglo-Russian Accord had they emerged into public consciousness that fateful summer. True, the Liberal ascendancy in British politics since 1905 had tipped the balance at Whitehall slightly toward Russophilia and Turcophobia (as against roughly the opposite tendency among old-line Tories). But the new pro-Russian line was fragile, needing constant massaging: thus Sazonov's careful May 1914 instructions that Benckendorff, his ambassador in London, not even use the word "agreement" *(soglashenie)* in his discussions of naval policy with Churchill and Grey.

While French leaders like Poincaré and Viviani had a better idea about the belligerent atmosphere in Petersburg in July 1914, the overriding obsession in Paris with the German threat meant that they, too, failed to perceive Russia's true war aims. In part the diplomatic disconnect between the western and eastern halves of the Entente coalition could be attributed to simple geography: Constantinople and the Straits remained an ever-present concern of Russian foreign policy in a way it had not been for London or Paris since the Crimean War, when, tellingly, the joint object of Britain and France was more to deny them to Russia than to achieve anything in particular for themselves. In the intervening half-century, the primacy of the Porte had been downgraded in both Paris and London. Britain's long-serving ambassador, Lord Stratford Canning de Redcliffe, had been, in his day, arguably the most powerful man in Constantinople; Louis Mallet, in 1914, was an afterthought in the British Foreign Office, and not incidentally the worst-informed ambassador in the Ottoman capital. By contrast, the Porte had long been and remained the most important post in Russian diplomacy, the province of old-line dynasties (like the Girs) who frequently served as foreign ministers. M. N. Girs, ambassador to the Porte during the Balkan wars (when command of the Black Sea fleet had been entrusted to him), was such a crucial figure in Russian foreign policy that he was asked to attend the notorious planning conference of 8/21 February 1914, which produced Russia's historic naval program envisioning conquest of the Straits. Revealingly, the primacy of the Porte had become a truism in German diplomacy as well: Marschall von Bieberstein, the "Giant of the Bosphorus" who served from 1897 to 1912, was a former state secretary; Hans von Wangenheim, his successor, was a confidant of Kaiser Wilhelm II who had ambitions for the Chancellery. Girs and Wangenheim would both have a leg up in reading the tense diplomatic drama at the Porte in fall 1914 because they took the place seriously in a way their British and French counterparts simply no longer did.

It is curious, although hardly surprising, that the downgrading of Turkey's importance by western ambassadors of the time has carried over into the historical literature. In what remains the most influential popular account of Turkey's entry into the war, *A Peace to End All Peace,* David Fromkin notes astutely that the anti-Semitic prejudice of Gerald Fitzmaurice, the embassy dragoman, left London woefully misinformed about the government of the Committee of Union and Progress (CUP), as the ambassadors Fitzmaurice advised, including Mallet, mistakenly believed the

Young Turks to be crypto-Jewish internationalists, rather than adamant Ottoman-Turkish nationalists. So heavily does Fromkin rely on British sources that their dismissive tone toward Turkey seeps subtly into his own account. "Few Europeans of Churchill's generation," he writes with elegant detachment, "knew or cared what went on in the languid empires of the Ottoman Sultan or the Persian Shah . . . there was little in the picture to cause ordinary people living in Paris, London, or New York to believe it affected their lives and interests." Small wonder Fromkin emphasizes the "relative casualness with which the British drifted into the Ottoman war," which was "not a war to which they attached much importance."[3] Much like the Bismarckian view of a world war brought on by some silly Balkan bagatelle, Turkey's entry into the same appears on this view a tragic accident, mere spillover from a basically European conflict the belligerents had been unable to settle on the main battlefields.

Nothing could be further from the truth. Although Fromkin is probably right that few people in France, Britain, or the United States cared overmuch in 1914 about what was happening in Turkey or Persia, these two countries constituted the primary arena of Russian imperial ambition. In Petersburg, Ottoman affairs were deadly serious business in 1914, followed and analyzed with the rapt attention—and nearly unlimited intelligence budget—that Paris then paid to Germany, London to Egypt and India, and Washington to its own strategic backyard in Mexico and South America. French and British diplomats may have been surprised and perturbed when Krivoshein and Sazonov began demanding Constantinople before Turkey had even entered the war, but this was because they had not been paying careful attention. Austrian Galicia, the subject of so much inter-Allied acrimony in fall 1914, clearly mattered to Russia's leaders—but nowhere near as much as the Straits. For Russia, the war of 1914 was always, ultimately, about Turkey.

This essential truth is borne out clearly by the evidence. In the last week of July 1914, as the eyes of most European governments remained focused on Austria's threat to punish Serbia, Russia's own leaders were thinking about Turkey. Yanushkevitch (secretly) mobilized the Caucasian army on the Ottoman frontier as early as 27 July 1914. On the same day, Girs wrote a "top secret" memorandum to Sazonov in which he highlighted the importance of not backing down in the face of the Austro-

German threat because doing so would lead to the "complete ruin of our entire position in the Near East," an outcome which, Girs warned, would force Russia "to take the initiative ourselves in waging war [against Turkey]."[4] Two days later, Yanushkevitch wired Tiflis command to proceed with variant 4 of Russia's general mobilization plan for a European war in which "Turkey does not *at first* take part." On 30 July, as Europeans first awakened to the acute danger posed by Russia's mobilization against Germany and possible German countermeasures, Sazonov issued a little-known yet profoundly revealing directive to his ambassador to London. "In the present crisis," Russia's foreign minister wired urgently to Benckendorff,

> it is a matter of the highest degree of importance that Turkey not receive the two Dreadnoughts "Rio de Janeiro" [aka the Sultan Osman I] and "Reshadieh" [Reshad V] being built for her in England. The construction of these ships is so far advanced, that the first of them could be sent off to Turkey within weeks, and the second within months. Please make the English government aware of the overriding importance of this question for us, and impress upon them energetically that these ships must be retained in England.[5]

Already a vital matter for Russia in May and June, when Sazonov had first authorized Benckendorff to raise the matter with Grey and Churchill as delicately as possible, with a general war on the horizon on 30 July the question had become so urgent that the foreign minister could not afford to pussyfoot around any longer.

As we know now, Sazonov need not have insisted so strongly. Churchill had in fact already resolved to detain the Turkish dreadnoughts in the interest of impressing them into Britain's own navy. That Sazonov *did* take the time to insist that the British government block delivery of these warships to Turkey in such an unequivocal manner—on the very day when Russia's general mobilization against Germany began—gives us a good idea as to just how important the issue of Ottoman naval power was to Russia. Once the world war was on, Russia could not possibly hope to import warships of any kind through the Straits, which, in case Turkey was able to deploy the dreadnoughts on order in England, would leave the Russian Black Sea fleet entirely at Ottoman mercy and close off any possibility of securing control of the Straits. It was a nightmare scenario for Russian foreign policy, avoided only due to Churchill's rash and controversial action.[6]

The nightmare nearly came to pass anyway. Matching Russia's Caucasian mobilization tit for tat, War Minister Ismail Enver Pasha ordered general Turkish mobilization on 2 August 1914, and on the next day "ordered the immediate closure and mining of the southern end of the Dardanelles *(Bahr-i Sefid)* and the northern end of the Bosphorus *(Bahr-i Siyah)*."[7] While a small passage in both the Bosphorus and Dardanelles remained open for "friendly vessels," Said Halim Pasha, the Ottoman grand vizier who played something like "good cop" with the Entente ambassadors to the ostensibly Germanophile "bad cop" Enver, warned Girs on 4 August that any Russian naval provocation in the Black Sea would be met by the complete closure of the Straits to Russian ships of any kind.[8] To show the Turks meant business, Enver then "ordered the requisitioning of foreign, mainly Russian, merchandise docked in Ottoman ports, including Russian oil and foodstuffs." In retaliation, the Russians began detaining Ottoman subjects in Black Sea ports, arresting over a thousand in Batum alone.[9] The Porte (despite signing a secret alliance treaty with Berlin on 2 August 1914) still maintained a posture of neutrality in the European conflict, but Turkey's and Russia's armies and navies were already on a mutual war footing. The only real question regarding an armed clash between these ancient enemies was when, exactly, it would begin.

This question acquired new urgency following the arrival of two German warships, the SMS *Goeben* and *Breslau,* in Beşik Bay at the mouth of the Dardanelles on 10 August 1914. The preceding week had seen furious diplomatic intrigue at the Porte. The grand vizier had negotiated stiff terms for allowing in the German ships, which, if denied entry, would have been blown out of the water by a superior British force in pursuit. These terms, we now know, included Berlin's acceptance of the abrogation of the hated Capitulations, which allowed European subjects a kind of extra-territorial legal status on Ottoman soil, a promise to "procure appropriate reparations" from the Entente powers "to be paid to the Ottoman Empire," along with a German commitment to help Turkey win back

Aegean islands lost to Greece in the Balkan wars and enough Caucasian territory lost to Russia in 1878 so as to give Turkey "direct contact with the Russian Muslims there."[10] The Entente ambassadors, naturally, did everything they could to convince the Turks not to let in the German warships, up to and including—in Russia's case—authorizing the Black Sea fleet to sink them if they did finally arrive in the Bosphorus. Winston Churchill's own angry threat to sink the *Goeben*, issued in conversation with Prime Minister H. H. Asquith on 17 August 1914, a week after the German ships had passed through the Straits, is well known, despite its proving hollow due to strong Cabinet opposition.[11] But the still little-known Russian threat was of a far more serious nature, issued not in passing conversation like Churchill's, but in a formal written directive from Sazonov to his ambassador in Constantinople, who possessed the power to summon the Black Sea fleet. "In case the *Goeben* and *Breslau* come through the Dardanelles," Russia's foreign minister instructed Girs ominously on 9 August 1914 (one day before they actually did come through), "flying the German flag, we will authorize [Black Sea fleet commander] Admiral [Andrei] Eberhart to pursue all measures in his power to prevent them from entering the Black Sea and to annihilate them, even if this means *we must violate Turkish territorial waters.*" Such measures, Sazonov warned Girs, could easily provoke Turkey into declaring war, a possibility he wished his ambassador to do his utmost to prevent, as he believed that "a war with Turkey would not be advantageous [for us] *at the present time.*"[12]

Advantageous timing or not, a new Russo-Turkish war seemed imminent when the *Goeben* and *Breslau* entered the Sea of Marmara on 11 August 1914. Although this event did not quite commit Turkey to enter the war against the Entente powers, the arrival of the two German warships was a clear violation of the laws of neutrality, as protested vigorously by all the Entente ambassadors. Had the ships docked in Constantinople under the German flag, there is every chance Eberhart would have carried out Sazonov's orders to mine the Bosphorus exit to the Black Sea, if not also to venture into the Bosphorus itself to try to catch Admiral Wilhelm Souchon, the commander of the *Goeben*, unaware with a surprise attack. It would have been hard for any Ottoman government to survive such a humiliation without declaring war on Russia, not least because the Germans would have demanded such a declaration as payment for Souchon's sacrifice. Enver, who had been willing to let in the German warships without even a quid pro quo—the terms discussed above were drawn up by Said Halim Pasha—would certainly not have minded such an outcome. But the wily old grand vizier again outsmarted Enver, concocting an ingenious ruse which saw the ships "sold" to Turkey on 11 August to replace the two "stolen" by Churchill: the *Goeben* and *Breslau* were renamed the *Yavuz Sultan Selim* and the *Midilli*, while their German crews famously put on Turkish fezzes and ran up the Ottoman colors (although the Germans were not above periodically teasing Ambassador Girs by donning German caps in full view of the Russian Embassy and singing a few loud bars of "Deutschland über alles" before putting the fezzes back on).[13]

The war scare was over, for now. Paradoxically, the arrival of two German warships in Constantinople—at least after they had been transformed into "Turkish" ships by Said Halim's fictitious sale—likely delayed the onset of hostilities between Turkey and Russia for months. The reason should not be difficult to grasp, when we recall Russia's keen interest in the Turkish dreadnoughts commandeered by Churchill at the end of July. In terms of striking power, *Goeben* and *Breslau* did not truly "replace" the *Sultan Osman I* and the *Reshad V*. The *Breslau* was only a light cruiser, about one-fourth the weight of the *Goeben*, itself just barely dreadnought class. The *Goeben*, though mounting ten 11-inch guns and capable of making twenty-six knots, was itself inferior in firepower to the state-of-the-art British-built *Sultan Osman I* with its 13½-inch guns. But then the *Sultan Osman I*, impressed into the British navy, no longer factored into Russian naval calculations. The *Goeben* did. At a stroke, Russia's Black Sea fleet had lost its supremacy vis-à-vis the Ottoman fleet. Although Russia still floated more warships overall in the Black Sea than did Turkey, she had none in the *Goeben*'s class in terms of either speed (her five pre-dreadnought battleships could make only sixteen knots) or firing range.[14] The arrival of the German dreadnought in Turkish waters rendered Russia's fleet strategically useless. It is not that Russia's surface ships could no longer operate in the Black Sea, but rather that whenever doing so they would be acutely vulnerable to hit-and-run attacks. This made offensive operations supremely difficult, and rendered any kind of amphibious operation in the Bosphorus—the highest operational priority at Black Sea naval headquarters—well-nigh impossible. Had the *Goeben* not made it through the Allied Mediterranean screen against heavy odds—an achievement that owed as much to British naval blundering as to Souchon's irascible will—the Russians might themselves have forced the issue, as suggested by Sazonov's aggressive orders to Girs on 9 August 1914. The Porte's acquisition of the *Goeben* instead forced Russia's Black Sea fleet to play defense while allowing the Turks to play offense. As Wangenheim himself had noted in a 2 August 1914 dispatch to Berlin (when pitching Enver's request that Germany dispatch her Mediterranean warships to Constantinople), "With the *Goeben,* even a landing on Russian territory would be possible."[15] Effectively, this put the power to initiate hostilities in Turkish, not Russian, hands. The war would not begin until the Turks were good and ready.

Meanwhile, the diplomatic battle over Ottoman belligerence was on. Inevitably, a bidding war developed between the two coalitions, with the Turks extracting everything they could from the Central powers for letting in the German warships and promising to attack Russia, even while quietly promising the Entente ambassadors they would remain neutral— but only if the latter offered substantially *more* than the Germans were offering, as the Ottoman finance minister, Djavid Bey, at one point told Russia's ambassador.[16]

It was not a game the Russians could possibly win—nor one they wanted to. Publicly, Girs, along with his British and French counterparts Louis Mallet and Maurice Bompard, made a great show of desiring Ottoman neutrality, but there is little chance the Russian diplomat was ever sincere about this. "There is no doubt," Girs wrote Sazonov as early as 2 August 1914 (without knowing that Turkey and Germany were signing a secret alliance treaty that very day), "that the Turks, knowing of our . . . plans to seize the Straits, desire in their deepest heart the triumph of our enemies."[17] Showing that he was just as capable of operating in bad faith as Russia's ambassador, Enver had launched a trial balloon of breathtaking cynicism with Russia's military attaché, Generalmajor M. N. Leontiev, on 5 August 1914. Just three days after he had engineered a secret alliance with Berlin (and requested that the Germans send him their entire Mediterranean fleet!) Enver told Leontiev that he was willing to pull back the now fully mobilized IX and XI Corps of the Ottoman Third Army from the Caucasian front, so that the Russian army command in Tiflis might choose, if it wished, to send the entire Caucasian army to reinforce the western fronts against Germany and Austria. Turkey and Russia could then reach a sweeping agreement on Balkan issues (by which either western Thrace or several Aegean islands would be returned to the Ottomans, in exchange for Bulgarian, Greek, and Serbian gains at Austro-Hungarian expense) as prelude to an outright defensive alliance to last five or ten years.[18] The very day such a Russo-Ottoman alliance treaty were signed, Enver promised Leontiev, he would expel the Liman von Sanders military mission from Turkey.[19]

Considering the inopportune timing—Germany's warships passed through the Straits less than a week after Enver's improbable démarche—it is not surprising that Petrograd did not ultimately take up his offer. But in fact the Russians rejected Enver's terms on 9 August 1914, a full day before the *Goeben* and *Breslau* reached the mouth of the Dardanelles. The reasons they did so—and the identity of the man who insisted the offer be rejected—are significant. While Girs and Leontiev had both been willing to indulge Enver's alliance offer to see what they might learn from it, Yanushkevich, from Stavka, intervened to cut off further negotiations. One might think that the chief of the General Staff, which was just then entering the final throes of Russia's mobilization against Germany and Austria-Hungary, would have jumped at the chance for reinforcements, not least because of impassioned French insistence that every available resource be directed against the common German enemy. But Yanushkevich was already thinking ahead to Turkey's entry into the war. In strategic terms, he reasoned, the current "dispersal" of Ottoman troops *(razbroski)* was far more advantageous to Russia than would be their concentration *(sosredochennost')* brought about by redeployment of IX and XI Corps elsewhere. More to the immediate point, if word got out that Russia was negotiating for a redeployment of Turkish troops from the Caucasian front, as if Tiflis command was afraid of the Ottoman army, it would be interpreted across the entire Near East "as a sign of our weakness."[20]

Here we have a precious glimpse into Russia's real war aims. Given even the hypothetical chance of a rapprochement with Turkey, which would free up troops from the Caucasus to reinforce the European fronts, the architect of Russia's mobilization on those very fronts said no, absolutely not, because these fronts were no more important than the Caucasian one, even if the latter was still inactive. Sooner or later, Russia and Turkey would be at war, and the last thing Stavka wanted to do was deprive Tiflis command of the troops it needed to fight—or of the fear they inspired on the battlefield.

It was not only Russia's generals who feared losing strategic ground with Turkey. As Girs reported to Sazonov on 12 August, the day after Said Halim's fictitious "sale" had been arranged to great popular fanfare, "from a military standpoint I believe that Turkey's preparedness for war has increased considerably. Also from a political standpoint the [sale of the German warships] has strongly increased the Turks' self-assurance."[21] While not quite expecting the Turks to initiate hostilities, at least not yet, Russian diplomats were now just as anxious about a Turkish sneak naval attack as Ottoman statesmen had previously been about a Russian amphibious strike. In effect, the Russo-Ottoman rivalry had been turned on its head. As even the normally unexcitable Count Benckendorff told His Majesty's Foreign Secretary Edward Grey on 15 August, "the Turks, viewing Russia as their most abiding enemy, may consider the present situation favorable for avoiding the fate by which Russia will put an end to their empire."[22] These fears were reinforced by a report from the Russian Consul at Erzurum of aggressive Ottoman dispositions in eastern Turkey, which Girs and Sazonov forwarded urgently on 22 August to Stavka with the request that reinforcements be sent to Tiflis command.[23] Next day Girs sent an even more alarming report of war preparations underway across Turkey, from shipments of German arms arriving to grain requisitions, the calling up of reserves, and trainloads of troops setting out eastward from Haydarpasha, the German-built station that served as Constantinople's gateway to Asiatic Turkey. "There is a general feeling in the people," Girs wrote Sazonov on 23 August, "particularly among officers involved in the mobilization, that a war against Russia is being prepared."[24]

Good intelligence in wartime is notoriously hard to come by, and so we could easily discount this sort of talk as mere speculation. The curious thing about Russian intelligence on Turkey in 1914, however, is that it was almost uniformly good, and much better than that of any of the other

powers. While the British Admiralty had been caught napping as Souchon raced toward Constantinople, never suspecting his destination or
the political importance of his mission until it was too late, the Russians
knew perfectly well where he was going and why. Lacking the British capacity to screen the Mediterranean with a surface fleet, Russia had no
control over whether or not the *Goeben* and *Breslau* reached Turkish territorial waters, but her admirals and diplomats were under very clear instructions on how to proceed if and once they did so. Had Said Halim
Pasha not cooked up his clever gambit of "buying" the ships from Germany, there is every chance that Eberhart's aggressive maneuvers in the
Bosphorus would have drawn Turkey into the war by the second week of
August.

Likewise, Russia's ambassador remained exceptionally well-informed
about Ottoman Cabinet politics as the diplomatic battle over possible
Turkish belligerence heated up in September and October. Russian cryptographers had broken the Austro-Hungarian codes, which meant that
Girs could read much of the correspondence of Markgraf Johann von Pallavicini, the Habsburg ambassador known as the "Dean of the Diplomatic
Corps" for having served longer than anyone else at the Porte. Reading
his correspondence was nearly as good as reading the German traffic.
The Romanians also frequently passed on intelligence gleaned from the
Germans to the Russians. Sazonov had paid informants attending Ottoman Cabinet meetings.[25]

It was from one of these many intelligence feeds (the ambassador did
not reveal which one) that Girs was able to report to Sazonov on 2 October 1914 that Kaiser Wilhelm II had signed off on Admiral Souchon's acceptance into the Ottoman navy at the rank of vice-admiral, which meant
the German commander could now carry out naval maneuvers in the
Black Sea under the Turkish flag.[26] In another telegram dispatched the
same day, Girs reported that the grand vizier had told his (unnamed)
source that "Turkey was ready to enter the war, but was not certain under
what terms she would do so." In order to make the strongest possible impression on Bulgaria and Romania, Said Halim Pasha told Girs's informant, "the goal of a [naval strike] will be to annihilate Russia's fleet, or at
least, if it survives the battle, to establish Turkish dominance of the Black
Sea *(obez"pecheniem' turetskago gospodstva v Chernom More)*." All that

the Turks were waiting for, the grand vizier continued, was the "most favorable moment."[27]

The full mining and complete closure of the Dardanelles by the Porte on 27 September 1914 effectively cut off Russia's only year-round warm water access to the world. Souchon was authorized to strike at the Turks' command. The countdown to war had begun. October 1914 saw a strange sort of phony war between Turkey and Russia, as the impending Turkish naval "sneak attack" unfolded by precise stages, each one closely anticipated and followed by the Russians. On 3 October, just a day after he had reported on Souchon's commission into the Ottoman navy, Girs reported to Sazonov that "Turkey is being flooded with German officers, enlisted men, guns, and shell": the country was an "armed camp." More important was the psychological transformation wrought by the acquisition of the two German warships, which had "completely gone to the Turks' heads" *(sovershenno vskruzhilo golovu Turkam')*. Combined with the influx of German arms and soldiers, the increasingly belligerent mood in Constantinople meant that a Russo-Turkish war was now "inevitable."[28] Adding credence to his hunch, Girs reported on 4 October that Ahmed Djemal Pasha, the Ottoman naval minister rumored to harbor pro-Entente sympathies, had been won over to Enver's war party exactly one week before the famous "war council" held inside the German Embassy, which Djemal mentions in his own memoirs. (Attending this war council were Enver, Djemal, Interior Minister Talaat, and Halil Bey, president of the Ottoman Chamber of Deputies; the only significant absentees were Djavid Bey and the grand vizier.)[29]

On 11 October 1914—the very day the Ottoman war council convened in the German Embassy—Girs wrote a long memorandum for the Russian Foreign Office that aimed to steel everyone's nerves for the coming clash. Knowing full well that Souchon had already received authorization to carry out a "sneak attack" in the Black Sea, Girs wanted Russians to rise to the challenge.[30] The opportunistic closure of the Dardanelles in late September had proved that the Turks could not be trusted with the task of ensuring free passage. Nor could Balkan states like Bulgaria or Greece, whose loyalty was every bit as unreliable as promises from "slippery Ottoman Ministers." "We need a strong boss ruling over Constantinople," Girs concluded, "and since we cannot let any other power assume this role, we must take her for ourselves." With Russian troops bogged down on the eastern front, defeating Turkey would be difficult; but war was now unavoidable. The time had come for Russia to "settle accounts" with her ancient enemy, so as to "liquidate the Straits question once and for all."[31]

One can fault Girs for his rhetoric, but not for his realism. If he was not quite in control of events at the Porte, he was marching only one step behind the Turkish and German conspirators, who were together stacking the decks for war. The decision to strike had in fact been made by the Ottoman war council the day he wrote his impassioned memorandum, with the caveat that the Turks would not agree to unleash "Ottoman Vice Admiral" Souchon until the second of two German shipments of one million pounds in gold had physically arrived in Constantinople. It took only about a week for Girs's informants to pass on the financial details of the Turco-German deal, which Girs reported to Sazonov on 17 and 19 October 1914.[32] Duly warned, on the 20th—the day before the last trainload of German gold came in—Russia's foreign minister sent a top-secret telegram to the Russian naval command at Sevastopol, telling commanders to expect Souchon's attack as soon as the second gold shipment arrived.[33] Next day, Admiral Ketlinskii reassured Sazonov that the Black Sea fleet was "completely ready."[34] All Russian Black Sea naval and port officers were given special instructions not to fire first if and when they were engaged by Ottoman ships, to ensure that it was clear to any neutral observers that the Turks had taken the initiative themselves.[35] In a final message dispatched on Sunday 25 October, Girs passed on his informant's prediction that Souchon would set out from the Bosphorus that Thursday, October 29.[36]

Russia's clairvoyant ambassador was off by only two days. In fact the Ottoman fleet steamed out into the Black Sea on Tuesday. Then again, as to the date Souchon's naval attack began, Girs had it right on the number: 29 October 1914. That fateful Thursday, in the early morning hours, the Turco-German fleet began shelling Odessa. Souchon, the "Ottoman Vice Admiral," scored direct hits on five Russian warships, sinking one (the *Donetz*) and heavily damaging another, setting five oil tanks ablaze for good measure. At Novorossiisk, the *Breslau* fired off 308 shells, sinking fourteen Russian grain ships and blowing up another fifty petroleum tanks. Other Ottoman ships shelled Feodosia, Kerch, Sevastopol, and Yalta, doing less damage.[37]

A curious Kabuki drama now ensued over a would-be Turkish apology for Souchon's sneak attack. The grand vizier, Said Halim Pasha, pressed hard in the Ottoman Cabinet for a formal note of apology, which was indeed dispatched on 1 November 1914 to Petrograd, with a cynical passage penned by Enver that, absurdly, blamed the Russians for provoking the attack. Sazonov treated the note with the seriousness it deserved, declaring himself perfectly willing to accept Turkey's apology, provided Enver expel, at once, all German military personnel in the Ottoman Empire (who by this point numbered over two thousand). To no one's surprise, this cynical suggestion, too, went nowhere, and Russia duly declared war on the Ottoman Empire on 2 November 1914. The Ottomans followed suit, declaring war on Russia and its French and British allies (along with Belgium, Serbia, and Montenegro) eight days later.[38]

Far from an accidental spillover from the European conflict, as most British and French accounts would have us believe, Turkey's entry into the war was just as inevitable as Girs had foretold, given the presence of the *Goeben* in the Bosphorus. Even absent the German dreadnought, the commanders of Russia's Black Sea fleet would have probably taken the initiative themselves.[39] There is a popular theory that pro-Entente (or at least pro-neutrality) forces in the Ottoman Cabinet, led by Said Halim Pasha and Djavid Bey, could have outmaneuvered Enver and kept Turkey out of the conflict even after the *Goeben* arrived, if only the Entente powers had showed more flexibility on, for example, the Capitulations question.[40] Although it is true that this issue was crucial for nearly everyone in the Turkish government, there is no evidence that any of the Entente ambassadors ever considered accepting their abolition, or that doing so would have strengthened their position anyway. The Russians, in particular, often used the Capitulations to protect their wayward subjects from Ottoman justice; they would not abandon this privilege without a fight.[41] Every single belligerent ambassador at the Porte (and the Italian one, too) joined forces to decry the Turks' abrogation of the Capitulations on 8 September 1914, but none of them gained a thing for their trouble.

The only other scenario which might have led to enduring Ottoman neutrality was the expulsion of Liman's German military mission. Liman's expulsion was demanded repeatedly by the Entente ambassadors, to just as little effect as their protests over the Capitulations. Djavid Bey did attempt to propose such a motion in the 1 November 1914 Cabinet meeting following Souchon's attack, but his proposal was immediately swatted down by both Enver and Djemal on the grounds that "the armed forces could not function without German specialists." Djavid, the most Germanophobic of all Ottoman ministers, was even persuaded not to resign in protest (his resignation was finally accepted on 5 November, three days after Russia had declared war).[42]

As for the grand vizier himself, he was every bit as slippery as Girs had called him. Said Halim Pasha repeatedly promised the British and French ambassadors that he would keep Turkey out of the war, even as he constantly assured Wangenheim and Pallavicini that she would fight. The vizier's theatrical indignation following Souchon's sneak attack was characteristically hollow: he did not even resign from the Cabinet, the only gesture which might have seriously undermined Enver's war party.[43] It was none other than Said Halim Pasha who had gleefully told Girs's informant back on 2 October that Souchon would "annihilate Russia's fleet." Although he did not attend the war council at the German Embassy on 11 October, on the following day the grand vizier had quietly assured Pallavicini that he did not really oppose a naval attack on Russia.[44] Things were never quite what they seemed at the Porte, where diplomatic dissembling had been turned into an art form over the centuries of Ottoman decline. Said Halim Pasha and Djavid Bey may well have been upset by the naval provocation cooked up by Souchon and Enver, but not so upset as to actually do anything about it. When war finally came in November 1914, the Ottoman Cabinet was united in supporting the war against Russia.

The government in Petrograd was no less united: in fact likely even more so. The only criticism of the increasingly acquisitive Krivoshein-Sazonov line on Turkey came from those who thought it not harsh enough. Everyone in the Council of Ministers was agreed that Turkey must be dismembered; the only matter of dispute was over precisely which parts of the Ottoman Empire would be incorporated into Russia. The Russo-Ottoman conflict of 1914 (if not also the British- and French-Ottoman clash) was that rare sort of war, the one that absolutely everyone wanted. If the reasons Berlin and Petrograd had come to blows in August over Austrian bullying in the Balkans remained somewhat murky to most Russians, there was no mystery about what was at stake in November. In the official sovereign declaration of war on the Ottoman Empire signed on 20 October (2 November) 1914, Nicholas II could not conceal a feeling of satisfaction at the wonderfully clarifying turn of events. "It is with complete serenity and faith in the assistance of God," the tsar's proclamation began,

> that Russia takes on the appearance of this new enemy, this ancient oppressor of the Christian faith and of all Slavic nations. It will not be the first time that Russia's valiant arms overcome the Turkish hordes and chastise this insolent enemy of our motherland. Together with all Russian nations we believe without fail that Turkey's reckless intervention in the present conflict will only accelerate her submission to fate and open up Russia's path towards the realization of the historic task of her ancestors along the shores of the Black Sea.[45]

Russia's date with destiny had arrived. The Straits question would be settled at last in the only way it could be: in a struggle to the death between Christianity and Islam.

Sergei D. Sazonov, 1916
(Nikolai Aleksandrovich Bazili Collection, Envelope A,
Hoover Institution Archives)

Vladimir Sukhomlinov,
Russian war minister,
1909–1915

The tsar receives French
president Raymond
Poincaré in Petersburg,
July 1914

Maurice Paléologue, French
ambassador to Imperial
Russia, 1914–1917

Grand Duke Nicholas,
commander-in-chief of
the Russian Imperial
Army, 1914–1915

Personnel of the diplomatic chancellery at Russian military headquarters (Stavka), 1916. Nikolai Bazili, the director, is seated center (Nikolai Aleksandrovich Bazili Collection, Envelope A, Hoover Institution Archives)

Winston Churchill in 1904

Enver Pasha, Ottoman
war minister, 1914–1918

Djemal Pasha, commander of the
Ottoman Fourth Army, 1915

Nikolai Yudenich, chief
of staff of the Russian
Caucasian army

Mikhail Alekseev (Nikolai
Aleksandrovich Bazili
Collection, Envelope A,
Hoover Institution Archives)

Tsar Nicholas II and Tsarevich
Alexei,1915 (Nikolai Aleksandro-
vich Bazili Collection, Envelope A,
Hoover Institution Archives)

CHAPTER FIVE

The Russians and Gallipoli

All solutions [to the Straits question] must remain precarious and incomplete, unless Constantinople, the western bank of the Bosphorus, the Sea of Marmara and the Dardanelles, along with the Thracian plain as far as the Enos-Median lines, are not permanently incorporated into the Russian Empire.

> —Ambassador Maurice Paléologue, March 1915, passing on the
> views of Sazonov and Tsar Nicholas II.[1]

T HERE WAS NO MYSTERY about Russia's war aims against the Ottoman Empire. Not unlike gleeful German geostrategists suddenly freed from the need to conceal their imperial designs by the Guns of August, Russia's leaders felt liberated by Turkey's entry into the conflict. The Straits question, long a delicate business for Russia's diplomats in dealings with her jealous allies, was now fair game. The Bosphorus, Constantinople, and the Dardanelles were nearly in Russia's grasp: the only question was when they would be seized from the Turks, and by whom. Just as the Ottoman war against the Entente was (at German insistence) declared a state jihad by the *Şeykh-ul-Islam,* November 1914 brought a kind of holy war fever to the Russian Foreign Ministry, where once-fanciful plans of imperial conquest were now hashed out in deadly earnest.[2]

Foremost among the Straits planners was Nikolai Bazili, Sazonov's personal liaison at Stavka. Although only thirty-one years old when the war broke out in 1914, Bazili was already an important figure in Russian foreign policy circles, having served as second secretary in the Paris Embassy from 1908 to 1911, during a critical period in the evolution of

Franco-Russian military planning. For this service he was promoted to director of the Chancellery (or political department) of the Ministry of Foreign Affairs, while also being given the rank of emperor's chamberlain. A close confidant of Nicholas II, Bazili would later be named director of the tsar's diplomatic staff when the emperor assumed personal command of the armed forces in August 1915.

If one were to draw up the perfect biography for a Russian strategist tasked with planning the conquest of the "Second Rome," one could not possibly do better than Nikolai Bazili. Bazili's ancestors were Greek Phanariots, those cosmopolitan Hellenic aristocrats who ruled Romania (then known as the Principalities of Wallachia and Moldavia) on behalf of the Ottoman sultan; one branch of the family line owned an estate on Mount Olympus. His aptly named paternal grandfather Constantine was born in Constantinople, the son of a fervent nationalist conspirator, Mikhail Bazili, who was forced to leave the city in the wake of the execution of Orthodox Patriarch Gregory V in 1821. Mikhail and his son then fled to Russia under protection of her ambassador to the Porte, Baron Grigorii Stroganov, who arranged for the boy's Russian education (Bazili *père* was a classmate of Gogol's). Constantine Bazili was Russian naval attaché at the Battle of Navarino in 1827, which destroyed Ottoman naval power in the Mediterranean, thus ensuring Greek independence from Turkey. He would later serve as Russian Imperial Consul in Syria and Palestine, and represent Russia at the Paris conference following the Crimean War. On his mother's side, meanwhile, Nikolai Bazili was descended from Phanariot Greek diplomats who had married into the French aristocracy. His maternal great-grandfather had served on Napoleon's staff.[3]

Phanariot Greek by origin and an avid Francophile (which latter sympathies carried over into sympathy for the Poles, although not, apparently, Jews), Nikolai Bazili was like a fish out of water at Stavka in fall 1914, having no great personal stake in the reduction of Austrian Galicia by Russian arms. Turkey's entry into the war in November proved a golden opportunity for Bazili: his whole life had been preparation for this moment. The old Phanariot poured his soul into a passionate policy paper on the Straits question, outlining the irreducible foreign policy aims that must attend the war against Turkey.

It is worth examining Bazili's November 1914 memorandum at length, for it represents the merging of strategic thinking between the Russian Foreign Ministry and Stavka, which provided him with relief maps of the Straits area. Bazili's key Stavka collaborator on the November memorandum, Quartermaster-General Yuri Danilov, was chief of operations and the principal architect of Plan 19; his key naval adviser, Captain A. V. Nemits, was the Admiralty's leading expert on the Straits. Both Danilov and Nemits had attended the February 1914 planning conference, and they provided Bazili with the best available intelligence on Black Sea trade statistics, Russian and Turkish naval dispositions, the British dreadnoughts-saga, the *Goeben* and *Breslau*—everything.

Much of what Bazili had to say was neither new nor particularly surprising. The necessity of "right of free passage through the Straits" had already become a truism in Russian government circles, along with the more recent corollary that neither Turkey nor any other power could be trusted to provide this to Russia during wartime—as had been proven in the Italian and Balkan wars. Making matters still more disturbing for Russian interests, Turkey was not even a belligerent when she closed the Dardanelles in September 1914: the general atmosphere of war had been a good-enough pretext to sever Russia's economic lifeline to the world. International treaties and conventions guaranteeing access to Russian merchant vessels were useless in any real crisis; in fact they were worse than useless. Since the London convention of 1841, Russia's warships were denied the right of passage, even in peacetime. (So, too, were other powers' warships; but then this cost them only the chance to attack Russia, whereas Russia saw its naval access to the Mediterranean permanently disabled.) During the Russo-Japanese War of 1904–05, Bazili recalled, British pressure on the Porte (ostensibly to uphold the terms of the Berlin Treaty of 1878, but in reality pursuant to London's treaty obligations with Japan) had helped ensure that Russia's Black Sea fleet could not join the Baltic squadron sent to the Straits of Tsushima, with its absence possibly contributing to the great Japanese victory there, or so Izvolsky claimed so as to justify his ill-fated quid pro quo with Aehrenthal of Russian Straits access for Austria's Bosnian annexation in 1908. It is noteworthy that Sir Edward Grey, upon learning about Izvolsky's demand for Russian naval access to the Mediterranean that year, had made a counteroffer that the Straits be opened to warships of *all* countries—a proposal even more "repugnant" to the Russians than maintenance of the status quo, as it would open Russia's southern coastline to attack from any rival naval power. To the unreliability of conventions was thus added the problem of fickle third powers like Britain. If the Turks held onto the Straits after the war, there would always be some European rival keen to bottle up Russia's fleet in the Black Sea or send warships through the Straits to attack and disable it, even if the Porte remained friendly to Petrograd. "Only in the case," Bazili concluded, "that control [of the Straits] is in our hands can we be absolutely certain [of free access]."[4]

Achieving outright control of the Straits must therefore be Russia's first priority. But simply to command the naval passages themselves was not enough. Even if Russia controlled these waters, a hostile power could still bottle up her Black Sea fleet simply by blockading the mouth of the Dardanelles. So, too, could access be denied by shore batteries, if the coastal areas were not also under Russian control. Further, any fleet exiting the Dardanelles must still reckon with naval or shore batteries based on nearby Aegean islands, such as Tenedos, Imbros, Lemnos, and Samothrace. In *Germany and the Next War* (1910), Germany's most famous warmongering strategist, General Friedrich von Bernhardi, had galloped from "The Right to Make War" (chapter 1) to the imperative of "World Power or Downfall" (chapter 5). With something of the same logical mania, Bazili moved from the premise that Russia needed free access to the Mediterranean to the inescapable conclusion that she must therefore annex four Aegean islands, the European and Asian defiles of the Dardanelles and Bosphorus (including the entire Gallipoli Peninsula, and the "Trojan" peninsula as far as Bandırma and Edremit, or roughly halfway to Bursa), and the Thracian plain up to the Enos-Midia line, or, "in the ideal solution . . . all of Thrace up to Adrianople [Edirne]."[5]

Achieving this was, of course, easier said than done. With admirable coolness of head but something less than Germanic thoroughness, Bazili calculated the costs likely attending such a massive program of territorial annexation. Just to garrison the Bosphorus, he estimated, would require "at least two full army corps" and initial fortress construction costs of 150 to 200 million rubles, while the Dardanelles would require at least this much (not bothering to make precise measurements, Bazili simply guessed that garrisoning Gallipoli and Troy would "double" the amount he calculated for the Bosphorus). To his credit, Bazili asked rhetorically "if the value of these territorial acquisitions would justify the sacrifices incurred?" He noted realistically that four army corps could not possibly be spared from either Odessa command (keeping a watchful eye on not only the Austro-Hungarian front but still-neutral Romania as well) or Tiflis, which was, of course, tasked with fighting the Turks on the Caucasian front. And yet it is curious that Bazili hashed out the mathematics of occupying the Straits area *before* considering how much it would cost Russia, or her Allies, in blood and treasure to acquire it. Reasoning back to front, Bazili had already decided Russia needed to annex European Turkey, the Straits, and their Asian shoreline. The question was not whether or not this was a good idea, but rather how it might be done at the least cost to Russia.[6]

There was almost no way the Russians could achieve Bazili's program on their own. Sufficient troops were not, evidently, available—but then sufficient naval striking power was lacking, too. Even before the arrival of the *Goeben* and *Breslau* in the Bosphorus (although happily not also, due to Churchill's improvisation, the *Reshad V* and *Sultan Osman I*), Russia's Black Sea fleet had enjoyed only a precarious supremacy over the Ottomans'. The Russians had five ships of the line, battleships of the predreadnought class, dating from 1893–1910, to the Turks' three; both sides had two cruisers of roughly the *Breslau* class (although older than the German cruiser); the Russians had twenty-two minesweepers to the Turks' ten. The dreadnought-class *Goeben* easily cancelled out Russia's battleship advantage, and the *Breslau* meant Turkey now had one more cruiser. Just barely feasible before, any Russian attack on the Bosphorus would now, barring a fortuitous sinking of the *Goeben*, be virtually impossible.[7]

Bazili, however, was not a strategist easily discouraged. If Russia lacked the means to achieve her foreign policy ends, then other means must be found. For anyone familiar with the great sanguinary tragedy that flowed in its wake, the matter-of-fact casualness with which Russian strategists first conceived the idea of a British-French amphibious assault on the Gallipoli Peninsula—thereafter to be occupied by Russian troops—must seem astonishing. And yet it all made perfect sense to Bazili. "If the establishment of our dominion over the Dardanelles should prove unattainable," he reasoned, "then a compromise by which [they] would be taken in combination . . . [with our allies] would become tempting." Warming to this prospect, Bazili noted that "the enormous sea power which the . . . [Entente] powers disposed of" could allow for "the occupation of the Dardanelles defile by the naval forces of England, France, and Russia." Russian access to the Mediterranean would be secure at last "once the coastlines had been taken by amphibious forces" *(poka eti berega . . . budut zanyatyi desantom)*. Such forces would, of necessity, be mostly British and French, which would leave "the defense of [Russia's] interests in alien hands." But that was a problem for the diplomats.[8]

In this curious way was born the irresistible notion that Russia's age-old dream of conquering the Straits would have to be achieved in the nearest future by her Allies. In late November 1914, Sazonov, who needed little convincing, commissioned a formal legal aide-mémoire to be presented to London and Paris outlining Russia's sovereign claim on the Straits along the lines suggested by Bazili. To his credit, Sazonov does seem to have thought that Russia should contribute at least *some* troops to any operation to force the Straits, in order to justify her postwar claim on them. In December 1914, Sazonov repeatedly asked Yanushkevitch whether Stavka could spare troops for amphibious operations at the Bosphorus: the answer, each time, was no. Bazili asked Danilov the same question and received an even more emphatic answer. (Danilov thought a proper Russian amphibious strike at the Bosphorus would require eight to ten army corps—or nearly 300,000 troops—which was clearly out of the question.)[9]

Far from being discouraged by Stavka's refusal to contribute even to-ken forces to a prospective Allied Dardanelles campaign, Sazonov only redoubled his efforts to win the Straits by means of diplomacy alone. One might think the odds would have been stacked against him. Aside from the odd notion that Frenchmen and Britons should die so as to satisfy Russian imperial ambition, there was also the gross lack of inter-Allied good faith shown by Stavka so far, with Yanushkevitch and Grand Duke Nicholas scarcely bothering to humor French requests that they prioritize the German front over the Austrian. Looking at Russia's demands for the Straits levied on her beleaguered Allies in November 1914 without even the pretense that she would be able to take them herself, one is reminded of Bismarck's line about Austrian diplomats' demand for Bosnia-Herzegovina following Russia's unilateral defeat of Turkey in 1878: "I have heard of people refusing to eat their pigeon unless it was shot and roasted for them, but I have never heard of anyone refusing to eat it unless his jaws were forced open and it was pushed down his throat."[10]

Against all reason, British and French statesmen now began consenting to shoot, roast, and shove Russia's pigeon down her gullet. Agreement on the full Russian menu of demands did not come about at once, of course; it took many months of careful diplomatic manipulation to bring about the Dardanelles campaign, and then British operational blundering to produce the Gallipoli landings themselves. Nonetheless, it is remarkable that a good deal of the basic program was agreed on in November-December 1914, long before any kind of military imperative in the Ottoman theater was apparent.

The Russians had already done much of the diplomatic spadework, introducing Buchanan and Paléologue long before Turkey's entry into the world war to the basic outlines of Russia's program of annexation in the Ottoman Empire. Primed by the Sazonov-Krivoshein good cop/bad cop routine in September, the French ambassador was not even surprised when Nicholas II spoke openly of annexing the Straits, European Thrace, and "Turkish Armenia" on 21 November 1914, although he does seem to have been a bit taken aback when the tsar vowed openly that the postwar Ottoman Empire be confined to an Asian rump centered on Ankara or Konya. With no vital French interests at stake at the Straits, in European Turkey, or in Anatolia, Paléologue had no objections as such to the tsar's program, although he did feel compelled to remind Russia's sovereign that France had "historical, moral, and material interests" in Syria and Palestine which it would be wise for the tsar to consider.[11]

As neither France nor Russia had sufficient means to seize these Ottoman territories themselves, the discussion between Paléologue and the tsar remained essentially abstract, a kind of imperial horse-trading with imaginary horses. With the British, who really did have the naval and amphibious capacity in the Mediterranean that might allow them to force the Straits, Sazonov had to play a more serious game. Russian diplomats needed substantial British military aid to open up the Straits (and ideally, make possible their easy annexation by Russian occupying troops) but had little of substance to offer in exchange. It should have been exceedingly difficult for the Russians to thus gain something for nothing. In the event, it was not difficult at all, as British leaders, for their own possibly misguided strategic purposes, one by one declared themselves willing to accept imaginary horses in exchange for real ones.

The keys to Russia's diplomatic sleight of hand were Persia and Egypt, both infinitely more important to British imperial interests, circa 1914, than Turkey. Russia's land grab in Persian Azerbaijan had greatly disturbed Britain. In a peculiar way, the very obnoxiousness of prewar Russian policy in Persia created the opportunity for wartime "concessions" of great symbolic value to Britain. Stranger still, these concessions, as it turned out, need not even be real; it was enough merely to suggest that Russia would be more forthcoming about its intentions. Persia was the main item on the agenda on 9 November 1914 in the first meeting between Grey and Russia's ambassador, Count Benckendorff, following Turkey's entry into the war. The authorities in British India were deeply concerned, Grey told Benckendorff, that the Russo-Ottoman war might spill over into Persia. While he understood that Turkish troops might violate Persian territory (as they had in fact done repeatedly in the years before 1914), Grey was adamant that Russia not disperse its strength southward: only a direct assault on Turkey from the Caucasus could have any real effect on the world war. All this was sensible enough, and Benckendorff hardly needed to object. Before Grey finished, however, he made a curious linkage that piqued the Russian ambassador's interest. "If and when Germany is crushed," Grey told Benckendorff by way of exhorting Russia not to disperse its efforts from the war's main fronts, "the question of Constantinople and the Straits must be settled in accordance with [your] interests."[12] By a mysterious process of diplomatic osmosis, Russia's ambassador had not even needed to convey to Britain's foreign secretary his innermost desires: Grey had intuited them on his own, and relieved Benckendorff of the need to state them himself.

There must have been something in the air in London that week, because Grey was not the only British statesman to channel Russian imperial ambition. Herbert Asquith, the prime minister, made a speech the very day Grey spoke with Benckendorff in which he vowed that Turkey's entry into the war had "rung the death knell for Ottoman dominion, not only in Europe, but in Asia." No Russian imperialist could have said it better. To be sure, both Grey and Asquith were fairly doctrinaire Liberals who shared, to some extent, Gladstone's old anti-Turkish prejudice. Yet it is telling that the only significant Tory criticism of Asquith's program of dismembering Turkey in the House of Commons came from Sir Mark Sykes, who apparently remained immune to the odd virus sweeping through London that November—at least he would be, until he famously helped Russia carve up the Ottoman Middle East just two years later.[13]

Testing out the limits of Russian imperial ventriloquism, four days later Benckendorff tried the trick on King George V. Granted an audience with the British sovereign ostensibly to discuss the latest Russian troop dispositions in Persia (this remained London's primary concern in bilateral relations with Petrograd), Benckendorff did not even bother to pay lip service to the Persian question before changing the subject to the heroic, terrible British losses at the recent Battle of Ypres, for which the Russian ambassador expressed his wholehearted gratitude. When Benckendorff (presumably with less than great forcefulness) suggested they reorient their amiable discussion toward "the eastern question," King George V immediately volunteered, entirely unprompted, that "as concerns Constantinople, it is clear that it must be yours." Upon being shown the transcript of this conversation by Sazonov, Tsar Nicholas II, not surprisingly, recorded his content: "Wonderful!" *(Znamenatel'no).*[14]

It would not be strictly true to say that London received nothing at all for so unequivocally endorsing Russia's program of dismembering the Ottoman Empire. Sazonov did pass on Grey's request to Stavka that Russian troops not violate Persian territory in pursuit of the Turks (doing so, Grey explained, would be roughly akin to what the Germans had done in Belgium on the way to France). But this was it. In exchange for a nonbinding promise to avoid violating Persian territory, Sazonov received the following pledge from the British Foreign Office: "Sir E. Grey regards the conduct of the Turkish Government as having rendered inevitable a complete settlement of the Turkish question, including that of the Straits and Constantinople, in agreement with Russia. This settlement will of course be reached after the defeat of Germany irrespective of whether Turkish rule is actually overthrown in the course of the hostilities now being conducted."[15] By linking the "complete settlement of the Turkish question" to defeat of Germany in the world war, Grey likely thought he was simply reminding the Russians of what should be their highest military priority. But in doing so he had also curiously de-linked Russia's claims on Ottoman territory from Turkey's defeat in that very war. In effect, Britain's foreign secretary had promised Russia Constantinople and the Straits, whether or not she contributed in any way to a military campaign that might conquer them.

The Egyptian magic trick was almost as easy as the Persian one. Russia had no major interests in Egypt: not financial, nor commercial, nor strategic. Britain, by contrast, had been occupying and administering this nominally Ottoman province since 1882. Following Turkey's entry into the war, it was natural that London seek to clarify Cairo's status, so as to preempt Ottoman claims that might justify a Turco-German invasion. Asked by Grey on 18 November 1914 about Russia's attitude toward the prospective incorporation of Egypt as a formal British protectorate, Sazonov cleverly assented to this, "in view of England, for its part, having given us permission to resolve the question of the Straits and Constantinople."[16] It was an ingenious linkage. Russia would "give" London something it already had (Egypt)—and had acquired over thirty years previously—in exchange for Britain agreeing to give Russia the "great prize" of every tsar's dreams after, as one diplomat put it, "a thousand years of frustration."[17] In this way Sazonov turned Grey's aide-mémoire into a quid pro quo, by which Russia had "paid" for what England was preparing to give her. The pigeon had been caught, the mouth opened. All that was needed was to roast it and shove it down Russia's gullet.

We should pause for a moment here to consider the enormity of the diplomatic revolution wrought by the end of November 1914. In the Crimean War, British troops had bled and died to prevent Russia from dismembering the Ottoman Empire. Following the Russo-Ottoman War of 1877–78, Disraeli's government had dispatched Britain's Mediterranean fleet to deny Constantinople to the Russians, whose troops had advanced to the shores of the Sea of Marmara, provoking the European war scare that led to the first Congress of Berlin. True, Gladstone's return to power on something like an anti-Turkish platform in 1880 had seriously damaged London's relations with the Porte, but the maintenance of some kind of Ottoman buffer against the Russian threat had endured as a cardinal aim of British foreign policy right up to 1914, as illustrated by British fears of Russian incursions into Persia ostensibly justified by the Turkish threat there. And yet here were British statesmen openly advocating the total dismemberment of the Ottoman Empire so that Russia might have naval access to the Mediterranean—the urgent prevention of which had been a full-on British *casus belli* as recently as thirty-six years ago.

Of course, endorsing Russia's postwar claim to Constantinople and the Straits was not the same thing as actively endeavoring to win them for her. But it did not take British policymakers terribly long to move from one idea to the other. Just as Grey, Asquith, and King George V had all intuited Russian diplomatic desires in November without forcing Benckendorff to state them himself, in the last week of December 1914 the British War Cabinet began mulling over the possibility of forcing the Straits to aid Russia without even bothering to consult with Russia's ambassador. There seems to be no better explanation for this new bout of British Russophilia than the national penchant for grand geopolitical scheming, especially in that time of year when people like to take in the big picture. The basic problem of the world war was obvious enough: stalemate on the western front, with no realistic prospect of dislodging the Germans from their secure, elevated positions. What Britain had, if not an army large enough to tip the balance in Europe, was naval striking power: why not use it against Turkey? As Maurice Hankey, secretary of the War Cabinet, proposed in his notorious "Boxing Day Memorandum" on 28 December 1914, "Germany can perhaps be struck most effectively, and with the most lasting results on the peace of the world through her allies, and particularly through Turkey."* Hankey was not committed as to where this attack should be made. The Dardanelles was a strong possibility, but then so, too, would an amphibious landing in Syria "prove a severe blow to Turkey." Winston Churchill, First Lord of the Admiralty, composed a

---

* Technically, "Boxing Day" is December 26—the day after Christmas, when the British traditionally distribute gifts to the less fortunate. Hankey apparently first began composing his memorandum on Boxing Day. Whether or not the title of the memorandum is chronologically accurate, it is diplomatically appropriate: Hankey's idea was to aid the "needy" Russians with a diversionary attack on Turkey.

memorandum the following day proposing a diversionary strike in the Baltic to open up Russian ports before reading Hankey's memorandum and being impressed by it. (Churchill himself had favored a Dardanelles campaign at the outset of the war, only to be overruled.) There remained serious problems to hash out. Should Greek troops be enlisted in the effort? Grey believed, correctly, that the Russians would object. Most crucial, could the Straits be forced with naval power alone? On 2 January 1915, Lord Kitchener, the war minister, at last threw his considerable weight into the debate, ordering Churchill to investigate the possibility of mounting a naval assault on the Dardanelles, to be conducted without the army or ground support, which also meant no Greeks. Churchill did not like the idea: he thought the operation should be combined with amphibious landings by the army. But Kitchener was "adamant" that no troops could be spared from the western front; the navy must attack the Dardanelles alone. Kitchener's own idea was to conduct a mere "demonstration" of British power to impress the Russians. This rather vague proposal was transformed, in an ill-thought-out 3 January communication from Lord Fisher to Churchill, into the idea of "forcing" the Dardanelles, which was a considerably different proposition. Because Fisher, the First Sea Lord and a retired Admiral of the Fleet, technically outranked Churchill, a civilian, Churchill was cornered. How could he oppose both Kitchener and Fisher? After sounding out Admiral Sackville Carden, who commanded the squadron blockading the Dardanelles, Churchill duly informed Stavka on 20 January 1915, by way of Buchanan and Sazonov (again bypassing Benckendorff, who had not once been consulted by the British War Cabinet), that "the British Admiralty" had resolved to "force a passageway through the Dardanelles"—an operation which Churchill estimated would take "3 to 4 weeks," and to which Britain would devote at least twelve battleships ("of the line"), sixteen destroyers, three light cruisers, four submarines, one aircraft carrier platform (this, of a very early iteration, could launch only small hydroplanes), and "a great quantity of minesweepers and other support ships."[18]

We have, unfortunately, no reports on the Russian reaction when this astonishing news was received at Stavka—news that seemed frankly to defy belief. Why had Kitchener, Fisher, and then Churchill resolved in these fateful days of January 1915 to risk so many British lives and naval vessels on a chancy campaign that served almost exclusively Russian interests? So far as we know, Kitchener, who enjoyed unalloyed prestige in the Cabinet thanks to an outsized military reputation dating to the conquest of Khartoum in 1898, had reacted with genuine alarm to a pointed (yet suspiciously vague) request lodged by Grand Duke Nicholas on 31 December 1914, as disturbing news of a Turkish offensive in the Caucasus was filtering in to Stavka, for an Allied diversionary attack elsewhere in the Ottoman Empire.[19]

Russian panic was real. Initial reports sent in to Stavka on 29 December had the Turks taking not only Sarıkamış, the city that would soon give its name to the battle, but the Russian border town of Oltu as well, with a column heading for Ardahan. Tiflis command requested two full army corps be sent from Europe to reinforce the Caucasian front. Next day, Tiflis command reported that the "situation was critical": Sarıkamış had been surrounded and cut off, Ardahan taken, and the Turks were pressing on toward Azerbaijan. Orders were given for the evacuation of the entire Transcaucasus, with Tiflis beginning its own evacuation on 1 January 1915 (at about 3:30PM).[20]

In the event, these measures proved premature and unnecessary. Enver Pasha, who left the capital to command the operation, had not provided his men with adequate gear for a winter offensive; most guns had to be abandoned as they could not be dragged through the deep snow. Three whole divisions of the Ottoman IX and X Corps, outrunning precarious supply lines, were encircled by the Russians. Those Turkish soldiers not killed in battle or succumbing to an outbreak of typhus still had to cope with bitter cold (temperatures dropped at one point to $-40°C$): many fell prey to frostbite. In the end more than 30,000 Turkish troops perished in the snowdrifts of Sarıkamış, with another 7,000 taken prisoner by the Russians. It was a defeat from which the Ottoman Third Army never fully recovered. While news of this great Russian victory filtered out very slowly to the world, the generals at Tiflis command had realized their error as early as 3 January 1915, just two days after they had ordered their own evacuation.[21]

Why, then, did Stavka, or at least Sazonov, not rescind the grand duke's request for an Allied diversionary strike on the Ottoman Empire, now that the immediate danger had so clearly passed? We must recall, first,

that Russia enjoyed far greater leverage than her western alliance partners. Most of Germany's armies remained entrenched deep in France,
while Russia's main cities and agricultural heartland were (at least in the
war's opening stages) under no real strategic threat. For this reason Stavka
had felt free to continue prioritizing Austrian Galicia over the German
front, no matter how many times the French complained. In similar fashion, following Turkey's entry into the war, France's one urgent request
was that Russia's Black Sea fleet cut off the underwater cable from Romania, which (due to Austria's inability to knock out Serbia) was the primary
communications link between Berlin and Constantinople; the Russians
barely bothered to try.[22] Britain's one request was that Russian troops not
violate Persian territory in pursuit of the Turks: the Russians did exactly
this when they chased Ottoman troops from Tabriz on 30 January 1915.[23]
By contrast, the Russians had not even needed to ask the British and
French Mediterranean fleets to shell the outer Dardanelles forts in retaliation for Souchon's sneak attack, as they both did, entirely of their own
volition, on 3 November 1914.[24]

The Dardanelles campaign represented the logical culmination of this
pattern. With both Paris and London on perennial alert that Petrograd
might cut a separate peace with Berlin, a Straits campaign had a compelling strategic logic for the western Allies, even if Petrograd stood to reap
the principal reward. Certainly, the thinking went, the Russians would
not waver in their commitment to the war while her alliance partners were
endeavoring to win her Constantinople. At a minimum, such an ambitious campaign, launched to aid Russia, would improve Russian fighting
morale. If it succeeded, it would open Russia's year-round, warm-water
Black Sea ports for western arms (and maybe also food) shipments. Such
arms shipments, in turn, might prod Stavka into re-evaluating its priorities on the eastern front: focusing at last on the common fight against the
Germans. In this curious way, the innermost desires of Russian policymakers converged with inter-Allied strategy, at least as conceived by
Kitchener and Churchill.

The issue of the Russian home front added another layer of attraction
to an Allied Straits campaign. Although there had been no significant unrest in Petrograd since the start of the war, Buchanan, Paléologue, Poincaré, and Viviani had all witnessed the terrible strikes of July 1914, which

had put both London and Paris on high alert for signs of another outbreak. The Russians knew all about these fears and were not above subtly
exploiting them. In the rambling conversation with Britain's military attaché at Stavka, Major-General Sir John Hanbury-Williams, which was
typed up with such fateful consequences, Grand Duke Nicholas did
not even mention the Dardanelles. The theme that animated Russia's
commander-in-chief, rather, was Russia's fragile domestic morale, which
might be irreparably damaged if she were dealt a series of defeats by Turkey, her old punching bag. Tiflis command, he told Hanbury-Williams,
had been forced to "deprive the Caucasus of the better part of its troops
to meet the common [German] threat as [desired] by our Allies" *(myi
vzyali s Kavkaza bol'shuyu chast' voisk dlya glavnoi tseli, obshei s
soyuznikami).*[25] While true in a literal sense—the Caucasian army disposed of about 350,000 troops when Turkey entered the war in November 1914, as against potentially 800,000 if fully mobilized against Turkey
alone—this was still grossly misleading. Tiflis command had been ordered in July 1914 to mobilize against Turkey, not Germany or Austria,
and in August Yanushkevitch had pointedly refused to consider reinforcing the western front from Tiflis when Enver offered to pull back Turkish
troops. Besides, even at 350,000, Tiflis command still boasted three times
as many men as did the Ottoman Third Army, which could throw only
100,000 effectives into Sarıkamış. In artillery, the Russians enjoyed a superiority of 600 guns to 262.[26]

Grand Duke Nicholas, however, was not bothered by such mundane
details. Because of the denuding of the Caucasian theater of troops, he
told Hanbury-Williams that "we had been expecting these losses on the
Caucasian front even before Turkey entered the war." Here was a double,
or triple, untruth. Not only was it false that the Transcaucasus had been
stripped of its troops, it was also untrue that the Russians had expected
the huge Turkish attack at Sarıkamış, which came as such a shock that
Tiflis command had begun evacuating in panic. Finally, although the
Russians did not know this yet, the "great Turkish victory in the Caucasus" that, the grand duke warned Hanbury-Williams, threatened to tear
asunder Russia's fragile wartime morale, never happened.

After manipulating his sympathetic British listener with this distorted
picture of the Caucasian front, the grand duke slyly suggested that "there

were many places in the Ottoman empire where any force brought to bear could broadly compensate for Turkish victories in the Caucasus, or even wipe out the memory of them, turning the [current] upswing in [Ottoman] morale into panic"—unless, that is, Russia's allies did not wish to help her in her hour of need. With a dose of passive-aggressiveness, the grand duke at last burbled that, if the British and French "believed differently, that the common interest was not imperiled by the Turks' exploitation of their victory in the Caucasus," then, well, *nichego*.[27] Hanbury-Williams, like King George V before him, did not need to be asked twice: he promptly asked Russia's commander-in-chief whether a naval demonstration against the Ottoman Empire would be helpful? Grand Duke Nicholas, Hanbury-Williams reported to London (by way of Buchanan) on 1 January 1915, "jumped at [this idea] gladly." Next day Kitchener made his request to Churchill: the rest is history.[28]

Sazonov, too, helped manipulate the Allies during the Dardanelles campaign, although he spoke with more forthrightness than Grand Duke Nicholas. Whereas the commander-in-chief pleaded impotence to get France and Britain to relieve him, Russia's foreign minister threatened to resign if Paris did not sign off on Russian claims on Constantinople and the Straits—with the implication that he would be immediately replaced by Count Sergei Witte, who everyone knew to be the greatest Germanophile in Petrograd, a man who thought the current war was madness.[29]* Sazonov's unsubtle threat was specifically tailored to French fears that Russia would sign a separate peace with Germany. With Buchanan and Grey, such tactics had not even been necessary; they had given their assent to Russia's postwar claims without prompting. But it will be recalled that Paléologue, despite having expressed sympathy for Russian aspirations to the tsar, had coolly demanded territorial concessions in return— Syria and Lebanon. To put the squeeze on France's ambassador, Sazonov told him, as the Dardanelles campaign heated up in early March, that

---

* "If I had died before the war," Witte reportedly told a conservative colleague, "and they approached my grave and said 'get up, there is a war on,' I would have asked, 'Who is fighting whom?' If they said, 'England and Germany,' I would have said, 'That's understandable.' . . . But if they added, 'and Russia,' I would ask, 'Why?' 'For Poland.' 'To prevent Poland from liberating itself?' 'No, to restore its independence.' Then I would have said, 'Let me stay dead.'"

Russia would accept nothing less than the "permanent incorporation" into its empire of "Constantinople, the western bank of the Bosphorus, the Sea of Marmara and the Dardanelles, along with the Thracian plain as far as the Enos-Median lines." If France did not agree to this, he warned, "the consequences would be incalculable": he would "offer his immediate resignation." Although Sazonov did not say exactly who would replace him, Paléologue was certain, he reported to Paris on 6 March 1915, "that it was Count Witte that Sazonov had in mind."[30]

Unlike Grey or Buchanan, Paléologue was astute (or cynical) enough to see Russian hardball tactics for what they were. So, too, was President Poincaré, who had never had any illusions about Russian foreign policy. As the French president reminded his ambassador on 9 March 1915, Paris had essentially been dragged into the world war over a Balkan issue that "interested Russia much more directly than France." The same process was at work with Constantinople and the Straits, the lust for which in Petrograd had already "distracted Russian opinion from . . . the essential object of the war," defeating Germany. France, as the greatest creditor of the Ottoman Empire, "had no good reason to desire [its] partition," on which her Russian ally was now so flagrantly insisting. But allies were allies. If Turkey was to be torn apart after all, then France must receive its fair share. With an eye on Syria and Lebanon, Poincaré at last instructed Paléologue that "we can agree to the Russian desires only in proportion to the satisfactions that we ourselves receive."[31] In this way, out of Russian diplomatic blackmail, was born the French end of the notorious Sykes-Picot blueprint for carving up the Ottoman Empire.

The British, too, were beginning slowly to wake up to the disturbing behavior of their grasping Russian ally—or at least some of them were. Not everyone in London was such an easy mark as Hanbury-Williams, Kitchener, and Grey. Churchill, for one, sensibly conceived of the Dardanelles campaign as a joint operation in which the Russians would play an active role. His 20 January 1915 directive to Stavka expressly stipulated that Russia must contribute both warships and amphibious landing forces to the campaign. Her Black Sea fleet, Churchill demanded, was to begin shelling the upper Bosphorus defenses "as soon as the outer Dardanelles forts were destroyed" by the Allies (*sleduyushchemu za razrusheniem vneshnikh dardanell'skikh fortov,* as rendered officially into Rus-

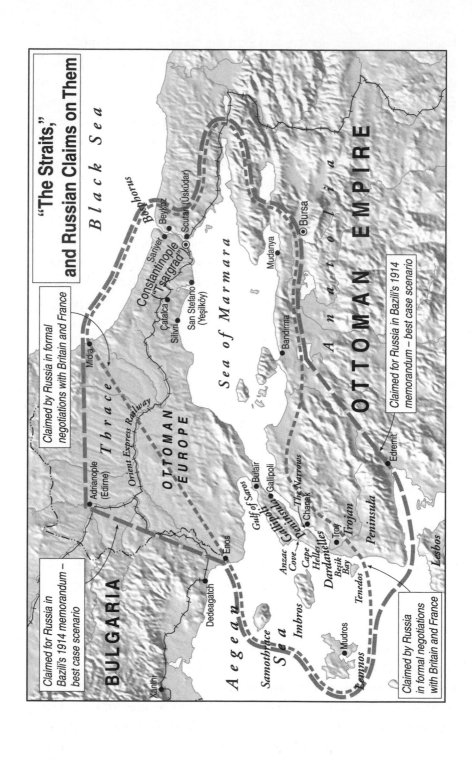

"The Straits," and Russian Claims on Them

Claimed by Russia in formal negotiations with Britain and France

Claimed for Russia in Bazili's 1914 memorandum – best case scenario

Claimed for Russia in Bazili's 1914 memorandum – best case scenario

Claimed by Russia in formal negotiations with Britain and France

Black Sea

Bosphorus

Sariyer
Beykoz
Scutari (Üsküdar)
Constantinople
("Tsargrad")
Çatalca
Silivri
San Stefano
(Yeşilköy)

Midia

Bursa
Mudanya

Sea of Marmara

Bandırma

Anatolija

OTTOMAN EMPIRE

Adrianople
(Edirne)

Orient Express Railway

Thrace

OTTOMAN
EUROPE

Eros

Edremit

BULGARIA

Dedeagatch

Xanthi

Gulf of Saros
Bulair
Gallipoli
Gallipoli Peninsula
The Narrows
Chanak

Anzac Cove
Cape Helles
Dardanelles
Beşik Bay
Troy
Trojan
Peninsula

Tenedos

Aegean Sea

Samothrace

Imbros

Mudros

Lemnos

Lesbos

sian). Contrary to common belief, the Russians *were* supposed to play a significant role in the Gallipoli campaign, as it was originally conceived.[32]

As the Dardanelles campaign drew near in February, British and French requests for Russian collaboration naturally grew more insistent. Strangely, though, specific demands regarding Russia's contribution—numbers of ships, troops, and so on—seem to have been lodged only *after* Admiral Carden's squadron first began shelling the outer forts on 19 February 1915. On 23 February, the day after a British Admiralty communiqué first publicly announced the campaign, Izvolsky passed on to Sazonov France's desire that Russia attack the Bosphorus simultaneously with the Allied assault on the Dardanelles. It was an odd request, considering that the latter attack had begun four days previously, which meant that a simultaneous Russian attack on the Bosphorus was already, *ipso facto,* impossible. Next day, on 25 February, Benckendorff passed on a similar request from Grey, which Sazonov forwarded to Stavka only three days later.[33] Not until the 1st of March, a full nine days after the initial Allied bombardment began, did Sazonov finally instruct Stavka to pass on to Odessa a formal Allied request that Russia contribute 80,000–85,000 troops to combined amphibious operations. Working up belated inspiration, Sazonov told the generals it would be "undesirable that the historic task of banishing the Turks from Tsargrad not occur without our participation."[34]

Inspired or not, Russia's generals saw no reason to risk losing their own sailors and soldiers if the British and French were willing to do this for them. On 24 February, just before receiving the British and French requests, Stavka had proactively informed Sazonov that no more than one corps (or a maximum of about 30,000 or 40,000 troops) could possibly be made available for the Bosphorus that year. As to exactly when they would be available, Russian answers were not immediately forthcoming. The end of February, then March came and went without further report. At last, on 31 March 1915, Sazonov informed Kitchener, by way of Count Benckendorff, that Russia's one amphibious army corps was armed and ready to be dispatched to the Bosphorus.[35]

It was heady news—or at least, it might have been, had the Allies' Dardanelles campaign not reached its tragic climax thirteen days earlier. On 18 March 1915, two British battleships ran over a line of mines in the Narrows and sank, causing consternation in British command circles (the sinking occurred in a previously swept area—unbeknownst to the admirals, a new line of mines had been laid there only ten days previously). A French battleship, the *Bouvet,* ran aground under heavy fire. Winston Churchill wanted dearly to press on with the naval-only operation despite the losses, noting reports of cracking enemy morale and diminishing supplies of ammunition at Turco-German shore batteries. Churchill asked for Admiral John de Robeck, senior commander in theater, to consider "the supreme moral effect of a British fleet with sufficient fuel and ammunition entering the Sea of Marmara." But de Robeck demurred, and his superior naval rank overawed Kitchener and the War Cabinet, which resolved to call off the mine-sweeping campaign until troops could first demolish the forts and shore batteries.[36]

Churchill rued this decision, which led to the tragic saga of Gallipoli, for the rest of his life. And yet, in the celebrated passages in *World Crisis* in which he lamented the dual folly of first refusing to plan a joint army-navy assault on the Straits and then calling off the naval-only campaign just when it seemed to be on the cusp of success, Churchill neglected to note that by the critical day of 18 March 1915 (and for weeks afterward), the Russians, for whose near-exclusive benefit the operation had been organized, had not contributed a single one of the things he had asked them for back in January. Instead Churchill, with that curious historical amnesia that seemed to overcome so many Allied statesmen who pitied Russians after their terrible revolution, spoke years later of how the breaking off of the Dardanelles campaign "dispelled the Russian dream . . . and this while Russia was pouring out her blood as no race had ever done since men waged war." Certainly, Russia's soldiers suffered greatly in 1915, after the German breakthrough at Gorlice-Tarnow led Stavka to order a general retreat on the eastern front that summer, panicked news of which nearly brought down the tsarist regime. But the Germans broke through Russian lines in May—two months after the Dardanelles campaign was over. In regard to the actual events of March 1915, Churchill's remark about "Russia pouring out her blood" was grotesque.[37]

True to form, Russia's Black Sea fleet had been missing in action through the whole Dardanelles drama. Churchill's request that the Russian bombardment of the upper Bosphorus begin as soon as the outer forts were reduced had evidently been lost in translation: those forts had been fully reduced by 25 February, when British marines literally occupied them (the Turkish and German gunners at Cape Helles had fled farther north to man the main defenses at the Narrows, where the famous shore guns of Chanak guarded passage). And yet as February turned to March, and March to April, the Russians were still nowhere to be seen.

In part, the failure of the Black Sea fleet to show up on time was the Brits' own fault for launching the campaign so early and successfully and without properly notifying the Russians in advance. (The timing was tricky, not least because the concentration of such a huge armada in the eastern Mediterranean presented an easy target to German submarines if it remained idle for long.)[38] Manipulated though they had undoubtedly been by Sazonov and Grand Duke Nicholas into a naval campaign so tailored to Russia's interests, British leaders clearly must have felt that it served Britain's interests, too, or else they would not have tried to force the Dardanelles without Russian help. It was not only the prospect of opening Russia's only year-round warm-water ports to arms and ammunition shipments (thereby alleviating the "shell shortage" Stavka was using as an excuse for Russia's poor performance against the Germans), but also the idea that, by knocking Turkey out of the war, the Entente powers would win over wavering neutrals like Greece, Italy, Romania, and maybe even Bulgaria, who, by threatening the Austro-German armies on their southern flanks, might force the Germans to sue for peace. By thus ending the world war in spring 1915, the Straits campaign—as Churchill later lamented—could have saved Europe from the terrible war of attrition in the trenches of the western front from 1915 to 1918, and from every horror that followed in its wake. Churchill may well have been wrong about the real potential of Britain's Straits-Balkans gambit in 1915, just he would later famously exaggerate the importance of Hitler's "soft underbelly" with the Allies' Italian campaign of 1943. Even had the Franco-British fleet, as Churchill urged, pushed on through the Narrows into the Sea of Marmara after the losses of 18 March 1915, with what we know of the Gallipoli battles to come, one can hardly credit the idea that the Turks would then have surrendered Constantinople without waging a bitter fight.[39] Churchill's notion of ending the world war with one decisive blow at the Straits was probably a fantasy. Still, the appeal of the idea was powerful enough to overcome any hesitations the British may have had about launching a campaign to force open Russia's access to the Mediterranean—without bothering to coordinate it with the Russians.

We should not let the Russians entirely off the hook, however. Russian intelligence on Turkey in spring 1915, as in fall 1914, was far superior to British. As early as February 1915, Russian spies had informed Black Sea fleet command that the outer Bosphorus defenses had been heavily fortified with guns stripped from the fortress at Adrianople (Edirne). The Princes' Islands in the Sea of Marmara, from which the Turks and Germans could harass the Russian fleet on the slim chance it had secured the Bosphorus, had been fortified as well. The Russians also knew by early February that the Ottoman army had 70,000 to 80,000 mobile troops in Thrace, along with a "reserve" of 150,000, ready to pounce on any Russian amphibious landing force.[40] Small wonder Stavka and the Russian Admiralty were gun-shy.

The operational disconnect also resulted from poor communications between British and Russian commanders in the field, helped along by Russian guile and procrastination. Sazonov's "urgent" directives at the end of February did coax a vow out of the Russian Admiralty that the Black Sea fleet had been ordered "ready to sail" for the Bosphorus by 1 March 1915.[41] But Russia's admirals were evidently in no rush. Ten days later, Stavka informed London that Russia would begin a "serious Bosphorus attack" not after the reduction of the outer Dardanelles forts as promised (by now completed two weeks earlier) but only after the Allied fleet was through the Narrows—after, that is, it had passed the last serious barrier before the Sea of Marmara, which would basically mean the campaign was over and won. Only then, Admiral Eberhart, commander of Russia's Black Sea fleet, informed Admiral Carden (by way of Kudashev at Stavka, Sazonov in Petrograd, Benckendorff in London, and Churchill at the Admiralty), only "after the annihilation of the Turkish fleet and the union of the Allied fleets in the Black Sea," would Russia be ready to send amphibious forces to secure the Bosphorus coastline.[42]

In view of the failure of his ally to show up for the March battles, Carden understandably requested that Eberhart be submitted to his command to ensure at least minimal compliance with his inter-Allied obligations. Sazonov agreed to this on 29 March 1915—eleven days too late for it to affect the Dardanelles campaign. But even this concession was hollow: a reliable communications link had not been established. In a painful reminder of the strategic disaster of the previous August, on 8 April 1915 Eberhart informed Carden (by way of Odessa, Stavka, Sazonov, and so on) that the *Goeben,* which, along with the *Breslau,* was now cruising menacingly between Odessa and Sevastopol to scare off the easily frightened Russians, was jamming his signal, making it impossible to reach the British commander directly.[43]

Signal or no signal, the breathing space created by calling off the minesweeping campaign should have allowed the Russians to get their act together. Nearly five weeks passed between the great March battle at the Narrows and the Gallipoli landings the last week of April. Or, to put the matter another way, the Franco-British-ANZAC amphibious campaign at the Dardanelles began three months and five days after Churchill had first lodged his request for Russian collaboration. Even Sazonov, no slouch at procrastination himself, was beginning to grow impatient by mid-April. On the 18th, he passed on an urgent message from de Robeck (who now had unfettered command) to Eberhart that the Russians should begin embarking the amphibious corps aboard ships so that "they can be sent to Turkey quickly." Two days later, Sazonov informed the Black Sea command that the Gallipoli landings were slated for 23 April, asking Eberhart to be ready to mount some kind of simultaneous operation. If the Russians were going to show up for their own battle to seize the Straits, it was now or never.[44]

Eberhart's heretofore phantom squadron did make its first appearance on the historic day of (as it turned out) 25 April 1915. But it cannot have had any impact on the Allied landings at Gallipoli. "Projectiles from our ships reached as far as Sariyer and Beykos," Eberhart proudly reported after the day's activities. The shells launched, Eberhart admitted, did not do visible damage to "any populated areas" aside from Akbaba, a small, unfortified town on the Asian Black Sea coast, but then, they had been fired at the Turkish shoreline. It was something.[45]

But it was not very much. While the Russians were firing a few token shells at mostly unpopulated stretches of the Black Sea shoreline,[46] tens of thousands of British, French, and ANZAC troops were rushing ashore and clambering up ridges under heavy fire all over the Gallipoli Peninsula (and, lest we forget, on the Asian "Trojan" shore as well). The men and their officers were too exhausted that night to reckon casualty figures, but both sides must have lost thousands of dead and wounded in some of the most savage fighting of what would become a notoriously bloody campaign. In a scene that eerily foreshadowed the terrible drama of D-Day some thirty years later, hundreds of British troops attempting to land at Cape Helles were butchered alive as they stood, "crowded shoulder to shoulder, without even the grace of an instant of time to raise their rifles." After one sailor managed to "pole his cutter up to the beach," it was said, "when he turned to beckon the passengers to the shore he found they were no longer alive." On the Ottoman side, the 57th regiment of Mustafa (the future Atatürk) Kemal was "almost completely wiped out." But then Kemal's men, unlike the ANZAC troops facing them, were able to hold the heights of Çonk (Chunuk) Bair, which turned out to be the key to the whole peninsula. Although neither side knew it yet, the battle had essentially been won by the Turks on the very day it began.[47]

While their gallant allies bled and died for them, the Russians continued to prevaricate. Not until 3 May 1915, more than a full week after the Gallipoli landings, did Eberhart's real offensive begin, and even then it was a naval-only attack lasting all of "several hours," with not a single soldier landed ashore. This time, unlike on 25 April, a few genuine hits were landed by six-inch Russian naval guns, out of 161 shells fired. At least one visible explosion was scored, at the fortress of Elmaz. This, Eberhart claimed speciously, was a "fantastic" result *(otlichnaia)*. However, most Russian shells launched at the Bosphorus shorelines, he admitted, had detonated "without any result."[48]

So meager were the results of Russia's Bosphorus campaign that Sazonov chastised Stavka and the Admiralty for failing to live up to his promises to Kitchener (although he did not apologize to Kitchener himself). Blaming Stavka and Admiral Eberhart alike, Sazonov lamented that they had not come close to providing the diversionary "help from the Bosphorus that our Allies counted on." The sufferings of Russia's brethren-in-arms on the Gallipoli Peninsula, Sazonov continued, "were greatly exacerbated, because the Turks were able to concentrate against them all of their strength." (And, he might have added, without worrying about the three divisions the Greek government had offered to contribute—only for the Russians to veto the idea.) It would be deeply unfortunate, Sazonov reminded Stavka again, if "Tsargrad, the most valuable prize that we might gain out of the present war, were conquered exclusively by the efforts of our allies, without our participation."[49]

Sazonov was protesting too much.[50] That "Tsargrad" would be conquered without Russia's help was in fact exactly what Russia's generals and admirals wished, and quite literally planned, to happen. In the last operational directive Eberhart shared with Russia's allies in mid-May 1915, he informed them that he had assembled an expeditionary force of some 40,000 men, including cavalry, marines, and medical corps. The British and French commanders should understand, however, that this was only a "symbolic force" put together for the final occupation of "Tsargrad," and that "it could only possibly land once the Allies had arrived in Constantinople and the Turkish fleet had been destroyed." If the great battle of the Straits was won by Britain and France, that is, Russia would be happy to claim her prize. (Amphibious operational planning in Odessa, including the purchase of transport ships from still-neutral Italy, Romania, and Bulgaria, continued on well into summer 1915).[51] Alas, Eberhart was not sure he would get his chance. "This moment," he predicted so as to excuse in advance his refusal to show up at any future point in the Gallipoli campaign, "will not likely occur in the near future."[52]

Here, in the painfully honest remarks from the Russian commander who failed to appear at the battle, was the essential tragedy of Gallipoli. By the end of this illogical and ultimately futile campaign, Britain, France, and the ANZAC countries had sacrificed nearly 50,000 dead and another 100,000 wounded men to achieve "every tsar's dream for a thousand years," while the Turks themselves lost still more than this: 56,000 killed, 97,000 wounded, and 11,000 missing.[53] Russia itself had contributed so little to a campaign devoted to winning her the greatest prize of the First World War that no one bothered to count up her casualties. Had Constantinople been conquered, one can only imagine the scenes of jubilation that would have ensued among the Russian occupying troops—jubilation which surely would have grated severely on the nerves of the British, French, and ANZAC troops who had actually won the city. Meanwhile, as they continued dreaming the old dream through their Allies' long slog at Gallipoli that terrible spring and summer, Russia's diplomats, pleased with the favorable calculus of inter-Allied strategy in the Ottoman theater, set out to repeat the Gallipoli trick with Ottoman Armenians.

CHAPTER SIX

Russia and the Armenians

In the case war breaks out [between Russia and Turkey], the Armenians and Assyrian Christians may be of great help to us. We should therefore pursue friendly relations with them, but we must absolutely insist that they not undertake anything without our instructions. If they launched an uprising that was not supported by us, this would inflict an irreparable blow to our prestige.

—S. D. Sazonov, August 1914[1]

T HE LONG-FORGOTTEN STORY of Russia's role in the Gallipoli campaign provides a case study in selective historical memory. Misdirected pity born of the Russian Revolution has militated against condemnations of Russian opportunism and passivity by most French and British authors. Then, too, naval commanders such as Carden and de Robeck seem scarcely to have noticed, much less later remembered, Eberhart's nonappearances at the Bosphorus. What little concern they expressed about Russia's minimal contribution to the Gallipoli landings was largely drowned out by the terrible trench war of attrition that followed. While the battle raged on, there was little time to point fingers of blame. When it was over, the British were more than happy to blame themselves (or more precisely, Kitchener and Churchill, who took the lion's share of the scapegoating). Aside from passing on a general sense that the campaign had aimed to open up Russia's warm-water access to the Mediterranean (and noting that the Allies' failure to do so was part of the economic back story of the revolutions of 1917), most historians of Gallipoli hardly mention Russia at all. But then why would they? If Winston Churchill, the man unjustly blamed for the disaster, who had personally formulated Russia's inter-Allied obligations in the Dardanelles campaign, could not himself recall that these were never fulfilled, one can hardly fault others for missing the story, too.[2]

In the case of Russia's role in the Armenian tragedy of 1915—a story that not only occurred in uncannily precise chronological parallel with Gallipoli, but was directly intertwined with it at its most critical stage—historians' neglect, while understandable, is less innocent. Because the still-raging controversy over the Armenian massacres of that year (or "genocide," as many now call it) has entered the arena of parliamentary debate and international law, it is a far more serious distortion of the truth to tell the story of the Armenian tragedy of 1915 without reference (or with only passing reference) to Russia.[3]

The story of 1915 usually begins with the Armenian uprisings and massacres of 1894–1896. Although Armenian and Turkish historians naturally differ on interpretation of the key events, there is broad agreement that these years brought about a serious escalation in antipathy between Armenians and Ottoman Muslims, who had until then lived in relative harmony (relative, at least, to what was about to transpire). There were many causes for the upsurge in tensions, from the general decline in Ottoman authority and prestige over the past century to the organization of Armenian revolutionary groups like the *Dashnaktsutyun* (or "Dashnaks") and the Hunchakian Revolutionary Party (the "Hunchaks"). Inspired in part by the spread of Social Democratic parties in Europe and Russia in the late nineteenth century, after 1900 the Armenian organizations also learned from the success of Balkan politico-terrorist organizations like the Internal Macedonian Revolutionary Organization (IMRO) in staging anti-Ottoman provocations which came to the notice of the great powers. (The IMRO was the model for the Black Hand, responsible for the assassination of Archduke Ferdinand.) The Armenian groups maintained a façade of legality in Constantinople and through European committees-in-exile, even as their provincial Turkish branches advocated open resistance against the Ottoman government in the name of winning "freedom" (the Dashnaks) or "independence" (the Hunchaks) for Armenians, the aim being to facilitate intervention by outside powers. Beginning around

1890, a series of violent incidents occurred, mostly attempts on the lives of Ottoman officials, that appeared to have been worked up by Armenian revolutionaries or guerrilla bands, the latter operating from Russian or Persian territory near the nebulous borders of eastern and southeastern Turkey. Not unnaturally, the Ottoman government inaugurated repressive measures against what it saw as a dangerous rebel movement. These measures included the organization by Sultan Abdul Hamid II of an irregular police militia of Kurdish tribesmen, the soon-to-be-notorious "Hamidiye" regiments, in 1891. Each Armenian attack led to predictably savage reprisals by these "licensed oppressors," as one British consul called the Hamidiye, feeding a classic escalatory spiral.[4]

In 1894 the slow-burning civil war in Turkey's eastern provinces came to the notice of Europeans when a series of clashes between Armenians and Turkish troops (backed by Hamidiye regiments) in Sassun province, in the plains west of Muş and Lake Van, grew so violent—some 265 Armenians were reportedly killed—that the Ottoman government set up a commission of inquiry. As seems often to happen in such cases, a government's efforts to quiet outside criticism by investigating its own actions succeeded instead in directing unprecedented outside attention toward those actions. A great hue and cry arose in the western press, which had been primed by William Ewart Gladstone's famous pamphlet, *The Bulgarian Horrors and the Question of the East* (1876), leading it to indulge in another round of ritualistic indignation against the Turks. Riding the public wave of western condemnation, the British, French, and Russian ambassadors to the Ottoman Empire teamed up in July 1895 to demand political reforms for the six "Armenian" provinces of eastern Turkey, using as a pretext Article LXI of the Treaty of Berlin of 1878, which stipulated that the Porte "realize . . . ameliorations and reforms demanded [by]" and "guarantee the security" of Armenians in these provinces, and "periodically render account of the measures taken with this intent to the Powers, who will supervise them."[5]

The crisis had thus already taken on the ominous air of irredentist rebellion and anti-Ottoman diplomatic encirclement that had preceded the Russian invasion of 1877, when a new wave of Armenian sedition led the sultan to initiate violent countermeasures. Concurrent to and following the European diplomatic intervention, there were violent incidents in Bitlis, Van, Zeytun (north of Aleppo), Erzurum, Trabzon, and even the capital itself, where some sixty Armenian protesters were killed on 30 September 1895 along with about fifteen Ottoman policemen, which suggests the demonstrators were well-armed. The burgeoning crisis reached its climax on 26 August 1896 when armed Armenian revolutionaries seized control of the Imperial Ottoman Bank and threatened to blow it up if reforms for the six eastern provinces were not granted; they also demanded that Armenian political prisoners be freed. Despite its great drama, the bank seizure seems to have caught no one by surprise. It is said that Muslim mobs had been preorganized to take revenge, as they soon did, beating, looting, and killing Armenians throughout the city. Reportedly, many Armenians had fled the capital, expecting this would happen. Further reprisals were carried out elsewhere in Turkey. No one knows exactly how many Armenians perished in 1894–1896 in popular massacres, both spontaneous and organized, but it is probably somewhere between the official Ottoman estimate of 13,432 and contemporary European estimates of 50,000 to 80,000.[6]

All these facts are known, even if there remains considerable dispute over interpretation and casualty figures. There remains, however, a huge gap in understanding about the international context. Most commentators concede that Armenian revolutionary groups deliberately aimed to enlist outside powers in their cause by staging provocations such as the bank heist, and that outside powers did indeed take the Armenian side in 1895–96, even if none intervened in any effective way. But the privileging of French, German, and especially English-language sources on the Armenian question has distorted understanding of *which* power the Armenians were trying, primarily, to influence by staging provocations. The same historiographical distortion can be observed in the Balkan crisis of 1875–1878, when, to judge by the vast literature on the subject, the primary actors were a pamphleteering British politician (Gladstone), his cynical Tory punching bag (Benjamin Disraeli), and an even more cynical statesman (Otto von Bismarck) who helped defuse the crisis. After reading about Gladstone's invention of Liberal moralizing in foreign policy with the *Bulgarian Horrors* and the Midlothian campaign of 1880, one may need to be reminded that it was Russia, not Britain, that actually invaded Turkey in 1877 to "liberate" the Bulgarians.[7]

Gladstone was, in this sense, the first and greatest British ventriloquist for Russian imperial designs on Ottoman Turkey—foiled in his (perhaps unintentional) promotion of Russia's conquest of the Balkans only by Bismarck and the Tory team of Disraeli and Lord Salisbury.[8] He would not be the last. Because Salisbury and the still generally Russophobic Tories were in power from 1895–1896, London was quieter than it otherwise might have been in demanding justice then for the Armenians; but British diplomats in the Ottoman Empire, along with their French counterparts, were increasingly falling in behind the moralistic Gladstone line. What few of these consuls understood was that public campaigning for greater Armenian autonomy on grounds of Ottoman oppression, like Gladstone's pamphleteering, ultimately served Russian interests far more than British or French. It was not only that the Armenian revolutionary movement received most of its arms from Russia and aimed above all to provoke armed intervention from the same. What made the "Armenian reform" movement particularly dangerous to the European equilibrium was that the Russians themselves believed they had the Armenians in their pocket and aimed unambiguously to exploit them. Whereas most British, French, and American observers were genuinely shocked by interethnic violence in Turkey and wished to ameliorate it, their Russian counterparts, as we shall see, sought intentionally to exacerbate ethnic tensions as a prelude to invasion.

This essential truth about Russian Imperial foreign policy should not be surprising, considering the evidence of the Russo-Ottoman War of 1877–78 and the First World War. However, the same policy was consistently followed in the peacetime years in between these conflicts, with predictable—and revealing—upswings in the intensity of military planning during each successive Armenian crisis. It was precisely in order to piggyback on the Armenian uprisings of 1895–96 that Russia first began serious logistical research into the possibility of staging an amphibious operation at the Bosphorus. After a comparatively calm period in Turkish-Armenian relations, the Young Turk Revolution of 1908 (and even more so the short-lived Hamidian counterrevolution of 13 April 1909) produced another outbreak of religious violence, centered in Cilicia and particularly in Adana, where thousands of Armenians were killed by Muslim mobs. Once again, in the wake of internal Ottoman turmoil with unruly Christian minorities, Russian operational planning for seizing Constantinople was accelerated. These plans expressly specified that "agents from the Christian population" would cut off rail lines to Constantinople (Macedonians and Bulgarians in Europe, Greeks and Armenians in Anatolia), whereupon native Christians would "burn down all the wooden bridges spanning the Golden Horn and set fire to Stambul." A more explicit blueprint for using Armenians (and other Ottoman Christians) as a fifth column for an invading Russian army could scarcely be imagined.

The period of the Italian and Balkan wars of 1911–1913 saw another surge in interethnic and interfaith violence in the Ottoman Empire, and another predictable round of Russian opportunism. These wars, in fact, were arguably not so much the cause of the explosion in ethno-religious tensions in Turkey as part of the same general phenomenon brought on by the hemorrhaging of Ottoman prestige following the Young Turk Revolution. Austria-Hungary, famously, had exploited the turmoil in Turkey to annex Bosnia-Herzegovina in October 1908, an annexation that Russia (in Izvolsky's ill-fated deal with Aehrenthal) had even used as pretext to make a claim on the Straits. Bulgaria had declared independence that same month, shortly before Crete, still nominally Ottoman, had announced its union with Greece. By the time Italy and the Balkan jackal states pounced in 1911–12, the empire's days seemed to be numbered. Everyone wanted a piece of the Ottoman carcass, while there were still pieces to be eaten.

While Ottoman Europe was being carved up by the Greeks, Serbs, and Bulgarians, in eastern Turkey the melting away of Ottoman authority gave broad license to tribal marauders and to the Russian consuls in the area who alone seemed to have the authority to protect villagers and townsmen against them. Although the Armenian question dominated high-level diplomacy regarding the volatile areas of Turkey bordering the Caucasus and northwestern Persia, nomadic Kurdish tribesmen were arguably the prime movers in the region. They wrought havoc on the settled population, whether they were Ottoman or Persian government officials, or the bewildering mix of Armenian, Assyrian, and Syriac Christians who dominated trade and worked the land.*

In a real sense, the whole disputed area of eastern Anatolia (or Turkish Armenia, as many Armenians and Europeans then, somewhat optimistically, called the region),[9] where the Ottoman and Russian empires intersected with Persia, was on a permanent war footing long before 1914. Most Kurdish tribal chiefs were exceedingly well-armed and virtually sovereign in the areas they roamed. Like nearly everyone else, they bought primarily Russian weapons. Christian townsmen, too, bought arms from the Russians, although rarely in enough quantity to scare off Kurdish marauders if they really meant business. The great Kurdish tribal chiefs, like Sheikh Tagi (who roamed mostly in the Urmia province of northwestern Persia), Sheikh Mahmud (from northern Mesopotamia, near Mosul), and Mullah Selim (of southeastern Turkey, in the area around Bitlis and Van) generally had the rule of the roost, unless they were directly confronted by Ottoman or Russian troops, in which case they would simply flee to friendlier marauding pastures.

The story of eastern Anatolia in this tense and dangerous time, then, was about far more than Turks and Armenians. One could claim that Kurdish nomads were consistently hostile to the Christian population, but further generalizations about which groups were on which "side" are hazardous. Many Kurds did join the Hamidiye regiments, which implies a kind of solidarity between them and the government, but then others fought frequently with Ottoman gendarmes or troops: it was usually in pursuit of rebellious Kurdish tribes that the Turks violated the Persian border. Armenian organizations, too, although generally consistent in their hostility to nomadic Kurdish marauders, were not uniformly antagonistic to the Ottoman government, especially those revolutionary branches that aimed to topple the Russian tsar. Surprising as it seems in retrospect, before the world war the Porte even offered financial, legal,

---

* To be fair to the Kurds, not all of their tribes were nomadic, nor were all nomads marauders. Those few Kurdish farmers who resided permanently on the land were just as vulnerable to nomadic raids as were settled Christians, Turks, and Persians. Still, if it was true that not all Kurds were nomads, it was no less true that virtually all nomads in the region were Kurdish.

and occasionally armed support to the Dashnaks, so long as their activities were directed against the Russians (as they tended to be in northern Persia). At one point early in 1912, nearly seventy anti-Russian activists, the bulk of them Armenian revolutionaries, were holed up in the Ottoman consulate in Tabriz, fearing extradition to Petersburg.[10] At times, armed Armenian groups inside the Ottoman Empire might even join forces with Turkish troops to pursue Kurdish chieftains who had wronged their people.[11]

Complicating the regional picture immeasurably were the opportunistic Russians, willing to work with anyone who might extend their influence. In classic divide-and-conquer style, Chorister's Bridge cultivated close relations with Kurdish tribal chiefs and their Christian victims alike. Both groups were often at loggerheads with the Ottoman government, Russia's primary antagonist. This made them desirable friends, even if they saw each other as enemies. Kurdish depredations, because indiscriminate, accomplished two things for Petersburg at once: they tied down Ottoman troops in counterinsurgency operations, and they gave Armenians cause to demand Russian protection. By thus promoting general mayhem, Kurdish nomads were the ideal imperial tool. And the Russians were not loath to use them, sending arms, money, and even trade missions to Ottoman and Persian Kurds. So serious was Russia's commitment that Kurdish language institutes were founded in Petersburg.[12]

When the First Balkan War seemed to herald the final end to Ottoman rule, the Russians swung into action. In a 28 November 1912 directive, Sazonov instructed Russian consuls in eastern Turkey to work toward a unification of the Kurdish tribes against the beleaguered Ottomans.[13] Tiflis command also took a hand, sending four Russian military officers, disguised as nomadic tribesmen, across the Turkish border to incite the Kurds against the government.[14] Although the task of unifying often mutually hostile tribes ultimately proved beyond Russia's ken, many individual Kurdish tribal chiefs, believing the Turks to be finished, responded positively to Russian initiatives. Sheikh Tagi, of Urmia province in northern Persia, pledged loyalty to Imperial Russia in December 1912.[15] Sheikh Mahmud, who roamed northern Mesopotamia, "placed himself and [his] Kurds at Russia's disposition" in February 1913.[16] Abdurrezak Bey, a Kurd from the prestigious Bedirhan clan who had served as an Ottoman diplomat in St. Petersburg, made a vow of fidelity to the Russian consul in Bitlis in early March.[17] Not wishing to be outdone, Mahmud went further still that month, promising N. M. Kirsanov, the Russian vice-consul at Mosul, that his Kurds were "ready to give Russia every possible assistance she might ask of them, up to and including an armed uprising against the Turkish government." The sheikh promised that he could put 50,000 men into battle. Kirsanov, impressed, informed Petersburg that a serious Kurdish uprising, during a war between Russia and Turkey, could possibly tie down two whole Ottoman army corps.[18]

Although doubtless pleased by these avowals of unconditional loyalty, Russian diplomats had to be careful with the Kurds. Periodic tribal skirmishes with Ottoman troops were one thing: summoning armies of 50,000 men was something else entirely, not least because their first target after routing Ottoman troops would almost certainly be Armenians and other Russia-friendly Christians. It would hardly redound to Russia's benefit if one or another uppity Kurdish tribe grew powerful enough for its chieftain to entertain ideas of self-rule, or of replacing the Ottoman sultan. The ideal scenario was simply to promote enough regional chaos to give Russia a pretext for intervening, with no single ethnic or religious group emerging to dominate the others.

Fortunately for St. Petersburg, the Kurds were not the only group in eastern Turkey keen on enlisting Russia's help to overthrow the tottering Ottoman Empire. Armenian revolutionaries, it is true, had once had high hopes for the Young Turks, with whose European branches their own exile committees had worked closely in the years before 1908 as both schemed to topple the regime of Abdul Hamid II. Religious equality, despite being contrary to the Sharia, had even been part of the original CUP platform, although since April 1909 it had been honored mostly in the breach. Then, too, most Ottoman Armenians remained suspicious of the reactionary tsarist regime, which spied on the Dashnaks and Hunchaks just as it spied on all other avowed revolutionaries, and for good reason. By 1914 Dashnak and Hunchak branches in eastern Turkey had evolved into IMRO-style paramilitary organizations that devoted their primary energies to weapons smuggling, as an Okhrana agent attending a Dashnak conference in Berlin reported to the tsar.[19] In general, Armenian socialists, like their European counterparts, were ideological opponents of "imperialism" of whatever stripe, as Dashnak headman Aram Pasha reminded Russian Vice-Consul Olferiev in March 1913.[20]

For Armenian revolutionaries in eastern Turkey, however, not all imperialists were the same—not when the Ottoman Empire seemed ripe to fall at any minute. As Olferiev informed Sazonov, the arms the Porte had been furnishing anti-Russian Dashnak rebels in northern Persia could just as well be used against the Ottoman government, which was now reeling under the assault of the Balkan coalition. Where before these rebels had smuggled weapons across the Persian frontier into Russia, now they were smuggling them right back. For this reason Olferiev recommended that Russian border guards continue looking the other way when Dashnak guerrillas slipped into Persia, en route for eastern Turkey (despite official requests from Teheran, lodged on behalf of the Porte, that such rebels be disarmed).[21] As Olferiev gleefully reported to Girs and Sazonov, the "mood of Armenians" throughout the vilayet of Van, previously somewhat ambiguous, was now "one of complete Russophilia . . . the Dashnaks are completely on our side."[22] Using the Persian route, the Dashnaks were now smuggling huge numbers of weapons into the Ottoman Empire. By April 1913, Olferiev reported, Van had turned into "an armed camp": "all the Armenian merchants are stockpiling guns in their stores."[23] Encouraged by the ongoing collapse of Ottoman authority, overcome by "Russophilia," the Dashnaks seemed poised to strike a blow for Russia.

It did not turn out quite that way. The primary enemy of the Armenians of Van—at least in spring 1913—turned out to be Kurdish tribesmen even more eager than they to overthrow the Ottoman government. So severe had Kurdish depredations become that Sazonov (instructed by Olferiev and Girs) formally demanded, on 29 May, that the Porte dispatch regular troops to protect them. When the Ottoman army arrived in force in Van vilayet some ten days later (this was during Turkey's brief respite in between the First and Second Balkan Wars), Vice-Consul Olferiev was treated to the sublime spectacle of watching nearly 500 heavily armed Armenian Dashnaks, under the command of Aram Pasha, pursue fleeing Kurdish nomads—alongside Ottoman troops.[24]

It is important to emphasize what was happening on the ground in eastern Anatolia in early June 1913, for it was at precisely this time that

Russia inaugurated the famous Armenian reform campaign, which cast such a long shadow over the First World War. Just as in 1895, St. Petersburg seized on burgeoning ethnic unrest in eastern Anatolia as both pretext for the campaign (the idea being that Armenians were in danger) and, of course, to hammer the Ottomans when they felt most vulnerable. The initial volley in the Armenian reform campaign was fired by A. A. Neratov, Russia's vice-minister for foreign affairs, on 2 June 1913, three days after Sazonov had demanded that the Porte send troops to Van and nine days before the Kurds were put to flight by the Dashnaks and Ottoman troops. This stunningly successful joint operation, one might well suppose, had obviated the need for the great powers to put the squeeze on. Using the Van crisis as a pretext (but neglecting to draw conclusions from actual events there), Neratov proposed to Girs in Constantinople, Izvolsky in Paris, and Benckendorff in London that they push a new Entente campaign "according to the 1895 draft."[25]

Although the diplomatic campaign itself is well known and is featured in most books on both the First World War and the Armenian tragedy of 1915, it is not generally appreciated how exclusively Russian the campaign was. In a way the Armenian reform project was a dry run for the diplomacy of the world war itself, with Russia manipulating its allies into supporting its own imperial goals while provoking hostile German countermeasures. Predictably, Germany's ambassador to the Porte, Hans von Wangenheim, emerged as the most powerful opponent of the Russian "reform" plan—acting "against the code of the Therapia Embassies," as Sazonov complained in a circular sent to all major European ambassadors on 12 June 1913.[26] Wangenheim was prevailed upon by his superiors in Berlin to work with the Russian draft in the interest of cooling tensions, but he still demanded that Russia's ambassador, Girs, insist that the grand vizier, Said Halim Pasha, agree to controversial points, such as the appointment of European inspectors in the six eastern "Armenian" provinces, so that the Germans could escape Turkish opprobrium. As Girs complained to Wangenheim on 17 October 1913, "it would be dangerous if we alone had to make this demand, as then all of Turkey's exasperation would fall exclusively on us [Russians]."[27] Although the agreement ratified on 8 February 1914 did provide for two European inspectors, German persistence ultimately allowed the Turks to wiggle out of the most offensive clauses. The final version (signed exclusively by the Russians, on behalf of the powers) did not even mention "Armenians" or "Armenian" provinces.[28] Still, to ensure that the watered-down agreement was accompanied by the proper hint of menace, Sazonov warned Turhan Pasha, the Ottoman ambassador to St. Petersburg, several times: if another Armenian "massacre" occurred in eastern Turkey, Russia would intervene.[29]

Bracketing the campaign on both ends were ominous developments in eastern Anatolia, which confirmed for the Porte that the whole Armenian reform issue was just a Trojan horse for Russian imperialism. Although Van was relatively quiet in the months following the Ottoman-Dashnak offensive of June 1913, the nearby province of Bitlis had turned into a veritable battlefield by February-March 1914, just after the Russians put the final turn of the screw on the Porte to sign the Armenian reform agreement. Bitlis had never really been "quiet," but a series of incidents over the preceding months seemed to portend trouble. Seven Armenians had been killed there in May 1913.[30] Kurdish tribesmen had also attacked Turkish troops garrisoned outside Bitlis in October 1913.[31] This may have been a trial probing of government defenses, for a general Kurdish uprising was apparently in preparation all winter. Having assembled actionable intelligence on Kurdish plans, the Ottoman authorities arrested the ringleader, Mullah Selim, in the nearby district of Hizan on 8 March 1914, only for him to be freed by an armed force of 200 Kurds within hours as he was being transported to Bitlis, which rather proved the government's point. Regrouping at the Kurdish stronghold at Kumich, two hours' ride from Bitlis, Mullah Selim proclaimed a general Kurdish rebellion against the "impious" CUP government, the idea being to restore Sharia law (there were also complaints about a new cattle tax). Within two days, nearly 300 Kurdish tribal leaders had rallied under his banner, mustering a force of 8,000 armed men ready to strike against Bitlis. Although Mullah Selim had expressly promised not to harm Christians, most Armenians, understandably due to past precedent, refused to believe him. Not unreasonably, Armenian leaders in Bitlis asked the government to provide them with arms, so that they might "defend the constitution" against the bloodthirsty, Sharia-spouting mullah.[32]

While superficially similar to the saga in Van the previous spring that had given Russia the pretext for the Armenian reform campaign, the Bitlis battle of March 1914 ended very differently. Because the government had refused to arm them, local Christians were unable to fight back against the marauding Kurds, who seized a nearby Armenian monastery on 13 March (although the government did send a small detachment there), nor against the larger Kurdish force that entered Bitlis proper on 2 April 1914. Helpless, most local Armenians sought refuge in the Russian consulate, as did Mullah Selim himself, along with several key conspirators, on 5 April, after government forces had put his tribesmen to flight—to the presumably unpleasant surprise of the Armenians who had holed up there to escape him and his conspirators. Amazingly, Mullah Selim was still hiding in the Russian Consulate when the world war broke out in August. Nor had he left the building complex by November, a full six months later, when Turkey entered the conflict.[33]

The lesson for Ottoman Armenians was clear. Whether because of resentment at officious Russian diplomatic interference on their behalf or out of simple, long-simmering spite, the Turkish government had pointedly refused to work together with the Armenians of Bitlis against the common Kurdish threat. True, Russia's own behavior—the sheltering of Mullah Selim—was not entirely reassuring, either. But even this episode provided yet more confirmation that Ottoman power was in decline, and that Russia was the only reliable protector of the Christian population. This was believed even by American Christians, now numerous in the Protestant missions sprouting up in eastern Anatolia. Dr. G. C. Reynolds, secretary of the American Mission Board in Turkey, had formally "arranged with the Russian government," via Consul Olferiev in Van, "to assume a general protectorate of American interests in eastern Turkey."[34]

With the outbreak of the world war in August, the death knell for Ottoman rule in eastern Anatolia seemed finally to have sounded. It is true that the Armenian Revolutionary Federation, at its annual congress at Erzurum in August 1914, publicly vowed support for the Porte in case of war with Russia.[35] The Erzurum Dashnak Committee, along with that in Muş, even sent a delegation to Tiflis to discourage the enrollment of Armenian volunteers in the Russian army.[36] Still, there was little question where the loyalty of most Armenians lay worldwide. The Russian Diplomatic Archives bulge with letters of support for the tsar sent in by Armenian leaders after the outbreak of the war in August, which all say more or less the same thing: "we pray with all our hearts for the victory of your arms, which will liberate Christians suffering under the Muslim yoke." (This particular letter was posted from four Armenian clerics in Paris on 29 August 1914—two months before there were any Muslim powers at war with Russia.)[37]

Ottoman Armenians, of course, had to be far more circumspect if they sympathized with the Russian cause. This was only true, however, as long as they remained inside the empire. For this reason, thousands of Armenians, mostly Ottoman army deserters, began crossing over to Russian lines in August 1914, aided by Dashnak guerrillas familiar with the border areas. The Erzurum garrison alone hemorrhaged more than 50,000 deserters before Turkey even entered the war, most (but not all) of them Armenians, in part because soldiers had not been issued warm clothing (the first snows that year fell in September, foreshadowing the bitter winter to come).[38] While no strictly accurate count could possibly have been kept, the Russian Foreign Ministry estimated that "about 200,000 Armenians" crossed over to Russian lines in the first twelve months after Turkey entered the world war, although the vast majority of these likely crossed over after the serious violence and deportations began in spring 1915, making the humanitarian situation for Armenians in eastern Turkey insupportable.[39]

For Tiflis command, it was an embarrassment of riches. Caucasian Armenians had already established a central recruitment bureau in the Georgian capital to enlist Ottoman Armenian volunteers in the Russian army. Its leading lights were Hampartsum Arakelyan, editor of *Mshak,* the leading Armenian-language newspaper in the Caucasus, and General Andranik Toros Ozanian, a veteran of countless skirmishes with the Turks who had also fought in the Bulgarian army during the Balkan wars. Andranik arrived in Tiflis, by way of Varna and Odessa, on 2 August 1914.[40] Before long, there were so many Armenians volunteering that the Russians could not find enough small arms to equip them. On 31 August 1914—two full months before the Porte declared belligerency—Lieutenant-General Yudenich, chief of staff of the Caucasian army, asked Yanushkevitch at Stavka for an extra 25,000 rifles and 12 million rounds of ammunition to arm the Armenian guerrilla bands being organized

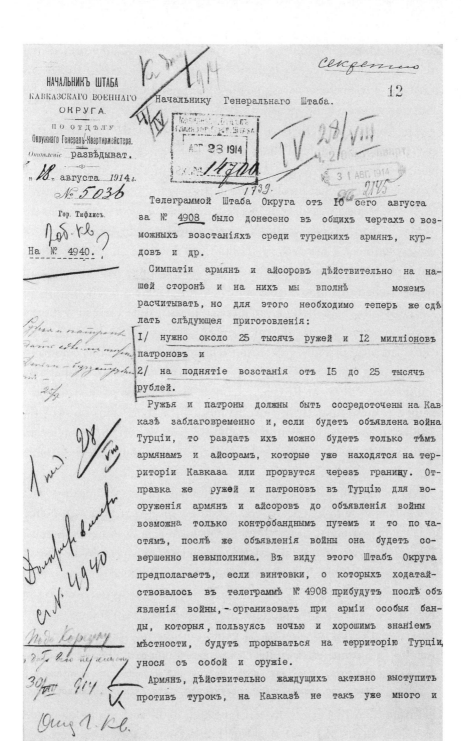

НАЧАЛЬНИКЪ ШТАБА
КАВКАЗСКАГО ВОЕННАГО
ОКРУГА.

ПО ОТДѢЛУ
Окружнаго Генералъ-Квартирмейстера.

Отдѣленіе *развѣдыват.*

„ *18* „ августа 1914 г.

№ *5036*

Гор. Тифлисъ.

На № 4940.

Начальнику Генеральнаго Штаба.

секретно

АВГ 28 1914

IV 28/VIII

31 АВГ 1914

1739.

Телеграммой Штаба Округа отъ 10 сего августа за № 4908 было донесено въ общихъ чертахъ о возможныхъ возстаніяхъ среди турецкихъ армянъ, курдовъ и др.

Симпатіи армянъ и айсоровъ дѣйствительно на нашей сторонѣ и на нихъ мы вполнѣ можемъ расчитывать, но для этого необходимо теперь же сдѣлать слѣдующія приготовленія:

1/ нужно около 25 тысячъ ружей и 12 милліоновъ патроновъ и

2/ на поднятіе возстанія отъ 15 до 25 тысячъ рублей.

Ружья и патроны должны быть сосредоточены на Кавказѣ заблаговременно и, если будетъ объявлена война Турціи, то раздать ихъ можно будетъ только тѣмъ армянамъ и айсорамъ, которые уже находятся на территоріи Кавказа или прорвутся черезъ границу. Отправка же ружей и патроновъ въ Турцію для вооруженія армянъ и айсоровъ до объявленія войны возможна только контрабаннымъ путемъ и то по частямъ, послѣ же объявленія войны она будетъ совершенно невыполнима. Въ виду этого Штабъ Округа предполагаетъ, если винтовки, о которыхъ ходатайствовалось въ телеграммѣ № 4908 прибудутъ послѣ объявленія войны, — организовать при арміи особыя банды, которыя, пользуясь ночью и хорошимъ знаніемъ мѣстности, будутъ прорываться на территорію Турціи, унося съ собой и оружіе.

Армянъ, дѣйствительно жаждущихъ активно выступить противъ турокъ, на Кавказѣ не такъ уже много и

Yudenich requests arms from Stavka for Armenians, 31 August 1914 (RGVIA)

along the Ottoman frontier. In fact, Yudenich expressly demanded that these arms (and money to pay the warriors) be shipped *before* Turkey entered the war, as those few smuggling routes still open would likely be shut down once that happened.[41]

The Russian army, then, actively sought to arm Ottoman Armenians even before Turkey entered the war, with the full cooperation of the Dashnaks, General Andranik, and Armenian leaders in Tiflis. So, too, was the Russian Foreign Office involved, and at the very highest level. Yudenich's 31 August request was just one in a series lodged in accordance with a directive he had received from Chorister's Bridge to investigate ways of arming Ottoman Christians (including also Assyrian and Syriac Christians) to take up arms against their Ottoman oppressors. Sazonov had first broached this idea in general terms with General Sukhomlinov on 5 August 1914.[42] After some preliminary investigation (and in response to the burgeoning flood of Armenian refugees across the border), three weeks later Russia's foreign minister recommended that Tiflis command begin arming Ottoman "Armenians and Assyrian Christians" so that they could strike a blow for Russia as soon as Turkey entered the war. Crucially, Sazonov stipulated that Yudenich tell the Armenians not to "undertake anything without our instructions," because "if they launched an uprising that was not supported by us, this would inflict an irreparable blow to our prestige."[43]

The parallel to Gallipoli in Sazonov's thought process is uncanny. The Armenians were to be encouraged to achieve an essential foreign policy goal for Petrograd: the overthrow of Ottoman rule of eastern Anatolia. The Russians would offer all assistance to the Armenians in this endeavor, just as they had initially promised Churchill operational support at the Dardanelles and then at Gallipoli; but they would do so only so long as the latter parties acted in full obeisance to Russia's instructions, so that Russia could reap the strategic benefit. Considering the human consequences in both cases, Sazonov's carelessness about ends and means is almost breathtaking.

To his credit, Yudenich saw through Sazonov's elision of moral responsibility. With a front-row seat for much of the recent ethnic turmoil in eastern Turkey, the chief of staff at Tiflis command was almost as concerned about the well-being of Ottoman Armenians as he was about Russia's own interests in the region. In response to Sazonov's directive,

О СНАБЖЕНІИ ОРУЖІЕМЪ ТУРЕЦКИХЪ АРМЯНЪ.

Возможное участіе Турціи въ войнѣ можетъ отразиться плачевнымъ образомъ на ея армянахъ.

Представленіе турокъ объ армянахъ, какъ объ элементѣ, мѣшающему туркамъ осуществить ихъ мечту о сліяніи турко-татаръ въ одно цѣлое, способствовало тому, что ниодно конституціонное правительство Турціи не упраздняло гамидовскаго лозунга-" уничтожить армянъ".Тотъ же лозунгъ приняла и Германія, которая усиленно поощряетъ турокъ въ этомъ, ибо ей выгодна на югѣ Россіи сплошная турко-татарская стѣна.

Отвлеченіе вниманія Россіи на западъ войной отозвалось на армянахъ репрессіями турокъ и фактическимъ упраздненіемъ русско-турецкаго соглашенія отъ 26 января с.г. о реформахъ въ Арменіи.

Лишившись поддержки Россіи, армяне принуждены отстаивать себя исключительно собственными силами.

Турція будетъ тѣснить и насиловать армянъ и въ случаѣ побѣды и и въ случаѣ пораженія.

Въ I-мъ случаѣ - мусульмане, отступая, будутъ изъ мести вырѣзывать армянъ.

Въ 2-мъ случаѣ - т.е. наступая на Россію, они будутъ уничтожать армянъ, дабы легче достичь завѣтной цѣли. Опытъ Во время Балканской войны и послѣ нея доказалъ всю практичность и безнаказанность подобныхъ пріемовъ.

Потери армянъ отъ насилій можно было бы довести до замѣтнаго минимума при условіи широкой самозащиты населенія оружіемъ. Опытъ показалъ, что мусульманскія банды и курдскія шайки не производятъ серьезныхъ опустошеній и даже не нападаютъ, если у обороняющихся крестьянъ есть достаточно оружія.

У армянъ, конечно есть оружіе, но его не достаточно, чтобы спасти населеніе отъ разгрома.

Благодаря системѣ управленія турокъ въ отношеніи христіанъ, армянамъ съ неимовѣрнымъ трудомъ удается доставать оружіе у себя на мѣстахъ.

Это затрудненіе могла бы облегчить Россія.

The Yudenich report of 29 August 1914, "On the Arming of Ottoman Armenians" (RGVIA)

Yudenich composed a long and thoughtful memorandum on 29 August 1914, "On the Arming of Ottoman Armenians," which outlined the painful dilemma he was facing. The Russian commander, already overwhelmed by Ottoman Armenian volunteers itching to settle accounts with the Turks, had no doubt that a day of reckoning for their beleaguered compatriots had arrived. "Deprived of Russian support" due to the army's concentration on the western front, he wrote, "the Armenians will be compelled to defend themselves exclusively under their own power." Based on the recent form of the Russo-Ottoman and Balkan wars, Turkey would probably "suppress and brutalize the Armenians in the case of [Russian] victory or defeat": the first case would see "retreating Muslims slaughtering Armenians in their path"; in the second, the flush of victory over Russia would make it easier for Turks "to carry out their cherished goal of annihilating the Armenians." With the inexorable logic of the self-fulfilling prophecy, Yudenich therefore proposed to prevent the "annihilation" of Ottoman Armenians as a fifth column by smuggling "at least 20,000 rifles and accompanying ammunition" into Turkey to allow them to defend themselves. This would have to be done "in strictest secrecy," by the establishment of covert weapons depots along the Caucasian-Persian border (the north Persian smuggling route had been used by the Dashnaks for years), and the selection of trustworthy Armenian couriers to accompany the weapons and account for their delivery.[44]

This remarkable document can be read in two ways. On the one hand, Armenians could easily claim Yudenich as a prophetic ally, who foresaw the "genocide" of 1915 and sought to arm them so as to prevent it. But it is just as easy to read the Yudenich report as damning evidence of intent, as Russia's long dalliance with Ottoman Armenians crossed the Rubicon into outright wartime treachery. The formation of Armenian volunteer "bands" in the Transcaucasus was long underway when Yudenich first proposed smuggling weapons across the Ottoman frontier. This development had reached maturity by the end of August 1914, a full two months before Souchon's sneak attack ostensibly gave Russia its *casus belli* against the Ottoman Empire, and not incidentally alongside the (almost certainly disingenuous) declaration of loyalty to the Porte at the congress of the Armenian Revolutionary Federation at Erzurum that same month. One could see evidence of Russian arming of volunteer Armenian legions as sufficient cause for Turkey to declare war on Russia. Ottoman military surveillance of Russian activities was just as thorough as Russian intelligence on Turkey. The Turkish Consulate in Kars, for example, reported as early as July 1913 that Russian agents were smuggling weapons to Armenian rebels inside Turkey.[45]

However, the Porte did not mention Russian mobilization of anti-Ottoman partisans in outlining its *casus belli* in November 1914. It is not hard to see why. The Turks had been no less active than the Russians in covert operations. Enver's notorious paramilitary-espionage organization, the *Teşkilat-i-Mahsûsa,* had been hard at work enlisting Azeris, Circassians, Tatars, and other Caucasian Muslim volunteers in anti-Russian partisan bands even as the Russians were mobilizing the Armenians.[46] Both powers deliberately drew in thousands of deserters and malcontents from the other side, as they had in the 1877 war. Neither wished to publicize such successes, as the whole ugly process of ethno-religious sorting (disloyal Christians fleeing to Russia, as Muslims to Turkey) offended western sensibilities of the time, just as it does now.

In the sense that both empires played the same game, one cannot fault the Russians for trying. The root of the Armenian catastrophe lies not so much in the fact of treachery and collaboration, which was rampant among other groups on both sides, but rather in the gap between Russia's enormous imperial ambitions and her limited means for achieving them. The reform campaign of 1913–14 had left little doubt at the Porte that Russia aimed to annex Turkey's six eastern provinces over which she had essentially declared proprietary interest, if not (yet) a formal protectorate. Likewise, the Dardanelles campaign and the diplomacy surrounding it— if not also the previous 500 years of history—made perfectly clear that Russia aimed to conquer Constantinople and the Straits. Any group inside Turkey rumored to be aiding and abetting the Russians near either of these fronts would not simply be suspected of disloyalty, but likely relocated for reasons of urgent military necessity, as were Ottoman Greeks from the Gallipoli Peninsula in April-May 1915. (Contrary to what one might expect, there was a good deal more anti-Greek sentiment than anti-Armenian rhetoric in the Turkish press that fateful year.)[47] That Armenians were eventually targeted in the same way is not the least bit surprising, considering how much the Ottomans stood to lose from defeat to the Russians.

The Russians, by contrast, did not stand to lose quite so much if Turkey won the war—but they still had plenty of reason to worry about the loyalty of Caucasian Muslims. Despite gossip about Enver's supposed pan-Turanianism—the idea that all "Turkic" nations be united in a single empire, which implied an imperial claim on much of Russia's Central Asian steppe—there is little evidence that realistic Ottoman war aims went beyond reconquering recently lost territories, especially the Aegean islands forfeited in the Balkan wars and *Elviye-i Selâse,* the three provinces lost to Russia in the 1877 war—Kars, Ardahan, and Batum. Even so, Enver's Sarıkamış offensive was threatening enough to produce a panicked wave of anti-Muslim violence in Ardahan and Kars provinces. Ottoman sources reported some 30,000 Muslim civilians killed. Traveling the Ardahan-Merdenek road in Ardahan province in early January 1915, an Azeri Duma deputy, Mahmud Yusuf Dzhafarov, witnessed "mass graves of unarmed Muslims on both sides of the road." Whatever the exact number of victims, the wave of Christian vengeance killings against Caucasian Muslims was serious enough that the long-serving viceroy of the Caucasus, Count I. I. Vorontsov-Dashkov, issued a series of decrees forbidding further atrocities while also ordering the deportation of about 10,000 Muslims from sensitive areas near the front lines to the Russian interior. A prison island in the Caspian Sea was established to warehouse Caucasian Muslim deportees, with the first group of about 5,000 arriving there by the end of January 1915.[48]

Had Enver's offensive pushed on to Kars and beyond, producing the very collapse of Russian morale Grand Duke Nicholas had predicted by way of goading Britain into the Gallipoli campaign, historians may well have argued ever since over the scope and intent of the Muslim deportations and Russo-Armenian atrocities against Muslims in the Caucasus during Russia's terrible revolution—of 1915. Instead, the catastrophe suffered by the Ottoman Third Army at Sarıkamış in January, followed the next month by the Allies' crushing Dardanelles offensive, turned the strategic momentum entirely around, relaxing Russian fears about Caucasian Muslims and producing the prickly Ottoman defensiveness which lay behind the atrocities to come. Contrary to Yudenich's assertion about the Turks' indiscriminately murderous intentions in case of either victory or defeat, it simply defies belief that anything quite like the Armenian tragedy of 1915 would have transpired had the Turks been victorious at

Sarıkamış, routing the Russians, or had the Allies not undertaken the Dardanelles and then the Gallipoli campaign. The fortunes of war are fickle, and no outcome is ever determined in advance.

This is true not only in the counterfactual case of Turkish victory in January 1915, but also in the diametrically opposite scenario—that of a dynamic Russian victory that would have seen the Caucasian army rout and pursue the retreating Turks westward toward Ankara, rather than (as in fact) merely surrounding its shattered remnants left behind in the snowdrifts of Sarıkamış. The muddled yet clearly pro-Russian outcome of the battle produced the worst of all worlds, with the Turks desperate and on the run (but not yet beaten), the Russians overconfident yet cautious, and, most important, Armenian revolutionaries expecting a full-on Ottoman collapse at any minute and counting on substantial Russian aid to help bring this about—preparing, basically, for Armageddon.

Russian operational planning for a general Armenian uprising in eastern Anatolia was underway long before Sarıkamış—before, indeed, Turkey's actual entry into the war. In accordance with Sazonov's directive that nothing be undertaken "without our instructions," Tiflis command, together with Viceroy Vorontsov-Dashkov, worked out a careful step-by-step strategy in September 1914 that aimed to give the Russians as much control as possible over events. Small Armenian guerrilla cells (less than 100 men each) would be created in frontier towns on the Russian side of the border, including Oltu, Sarıkamış, Gizman (Kâğızman), and Igdyr (Iğdır). In addition to one rifle with corresponding ammunition per man, each cell would also receive 250 surplus weapons to be smuggled across the border into Turkey. Similar guerrilla bands would be formed at Hoy and Dilman in northwestern Persia. These, because the smuggling routes there were easier, would each receive an extra 2,000 rifles destined for Armenian cells inside Turkey. In both cases, the weapons would be disbursed as soon as Turkey declared war, along with the first stash of cash. In all, the viceroy estimated it would cost Russia 100,000 rubles per month to run Armenian sabotage operations in Turkey. These subsidies would be drawn from the Persian occupation budget, so as to camouflage them.[49]

Russia continued planning for an armed Armenian uprising all through fall 1914, although with the same air of confident lassitude that character-

шизаться во всѣ дѣла, касавшіяся арміи и обслуживавшихъ ее частей,
до интенданства и военно-санитарнаго вѣдомства включительно. Это
обстоятельство сразу пришлось не по душѣ многимъ турецкимъ офицерамъ, которыхъ вскорѣ же еще болѣе возстановили противъ германска-
го Паши и его свиты заносчивость и грубость нѣмцевъ, нестѣснявшихся
дѣлать турецкимъ офицерамъ, въ присутствіи ихъ подчиненныхъ, выго-
воры и замѣчанія въ самой рѣзкой и оскорбительной формѣ. Еще сильнѣ
отшатнуло отъ Германцевъ нетактично высказанное Поссельдъ Пашою
недовѣріе къ турецкимъ крѣпостнымъ офицерамъ, которыхъ онъ отнялъ
завѣдываніе крѣпостными пороховыми складами и зарядными магазинами
, отдавъ таковые въ управленіе своимъ нѣмцамъ.

Отношеніе къ войнѣ въ Россіей! I/ Турецкихъ военныхъ кру-
говъ.

Въ самомъ Эрзерумѣ далеко не всё Турецкое   Офицерство
могло считаться сторонникомъ войны съ Россіей : если безусые подпоручики
ручки и вообще молодежь рвалась, такъ сказать въ бой , то среди
штабъ-офицеровъ многіе вовсе не раздѣляли этого пыла и при всякомъ
удобномъ случаѣ, высказывали опасенія   за окончательную судьбу
Турціи. Въ Эрзинджанѣ то же самое приходилось слышать отъ капитана
пулеметной команды, Нузхетъ бея, конвоировавшаго меня съ чинами
Генеральнаго Консульства отъ Мамахатуна до Эрзинджана, причемъ изъ
его словъ можно было понять, что значительная часть мѣстнаго
офицерства считала безумной затѣю Энвера Паши, котораго недоволь-
ные называютъ почему то " нашимъ Наполеономъ ". По разсказамъ
Настоятельницы католическихъ сестеръ въ Сивасѣ, одинъ ея знакомый
офицеръ просилъ назвать его лгуномъ , если онъ не приведетъ въ
Сивасъ Русскихъ солдатъ, чтобы положить конецъ позорной комедіи
происходящей нынѣ въ Оттоманской Имперіи, подъ видомъ младо-турец-
каго управленія.

2/Арминъ.

Армянское населеніе не только Эрзерума, но и всѣхъ посѣщен-
ныхъ нами городовъ, какъ то Мамахатуна, Эрзинджана, Сиваса и Кайса-
ріэ, не говоря уже о деревенскихъ жителяхъ и сельчанахъ, ждетъ
не дождется прибытія Русскихъ войскъ и освобожденія ихъ отъ вѣкового

Report of A. A. Adamov, Russia's consul in Erzurum, on the military
readiness of Armenian partisans in eastern Turkey on the eve
of war, 1 November 1914 (RGVIA)

го Турецкаго гнета. Сами они врядъ ли рискнутъ произвести возстан-
ніе раньше, чѣмъ Русскія войска будутъ у порога ихъ жилища,
опасаясь, что малѣйшее опоздание Русской помощи можетъ повести къ
окончательному ихъ истребленію, ибо, хотя они и имѣютъ еще скрытое
въ различныхъ тайникахъ оружіе, но не посмѣютъ взяться за него
вслѣдствіе объявленнаго въ странѣ военнаго положенія и угрозы
немедленной рѣзней. Даже Дашнакцаканы Эрзерума , всегда отрица-
тельно относившіеся къ Россіи и за время пребыванія тамъ Герман-
скаго Консула, Андерса, начавшіе съ нимъ заигрывать, отказались
въ концѣ концовъ отъ своей оппозиціи и перешли на сторону
руссофиловъ, особенно послѣ провала проекта реформъ въ Арменіи,
при содѣйствіи европейскихъ инспекторовъ.

3/ Турецкое население.

Население Эрзерумскаго вилайета, какъ городское, такъ и
сельское, въ конецъ разоренное еще до войны общей Турецкой моби-
лизаціей, когда Т   военныя власти, для удовлетворенія своихъ потреб-
ностей, реквизировало все, начиная со съѣстныхъ припасовъ и това-
ровъ и кончая тюфяками, котлами, ложками, смотритъ на войну какъ
на новое бѣдствіе, посланное Аллахомъ. Если горожане особенно
чувствительно пострадали отъ реквизицій, вслѣдствіе болѣе высокой
цѣнности, забраннаго у нихъ имущества и особенно скота, которымъ въ
Эрзерумѣ владѣютъ и торгуютъ преимущественно мусульмане, то сельчане, вслѣдствіе распредѣленія войскъ по деревнямъ для прокормленія
ихъ за счетъ мѣстнаго населенія, обречены на полное почти обнища-
ніе. Немудрено поэтому, что многіе эрзерумцы неоднократно выра-
жали Нештатному Драгоману Генеральнаго Консульства пожеланія о
скоромъ переходѣ въ русское подданство, которое дастъ имъ наконецъ
возможность одтохнуть отъ поборовъ и вымогательствъ нынѣшнихъ
турецкихъ заправилъ. Сельчане же высказываются въ томъ смыслѣ,
что Турецкое Правительство повидимому, заранѣе отказалось отъ
надежды сохранить за собою Эрзерумскій вилаетъ и потому, до
перехода его подъ владычество русскихъ старается выжать изъ населенія всѣ соки. Даже въ Сивасскомъ вилаетѣ менѣе пострадавшемъ
отъ реквизицій, приходилось слышать отъ сельчанъ и горожанъ не-
лов

ized her Gallipoli campaign. A. A. Adamov, the Russian consul at Erzurum (where, significantly, the headquarters of the Ottoman Third Army
was located), wrote a long analysis of the Armenian situation as he left
Turkey following the onset of hostilities, which is almost as damning as
the earlier Yudenich memorandum. The Adamov report of 1 November
1914, because it represented the latest information from inside eastern
Turkey on the eve of war, was forwarded immediately by Sazonov to
Stavka. "It is not only the Armenian population of Erzurum," Adamov
informed Russia's generals, "but also in all cities surrounding it, including Erzincan, Sivas, Mana Hatun and Kayseri, not to mention in the villages and rural areas, who are awaiting with impatience the arrival of
Russian troops who will free them from the Turkish yoke." Even the
Dashnaks of Erzurum, he reported, who had always been wary of Russia
and had cultivated strong ties with the German consul, had, following the
Armenian reform agreement saga, "finally given up all opposition and
turned fully Russophile." Not being suicidal, the Erzurum Dashnaks and
other Armenian partisans in the region, Adamov promised, "will not
likely risk launching the uprising until the Russians are right on their
doorstep" *(sami oni vryad' li risknuyut' proizvesti vozstanie ran'she, chem'
Russkiya voiska budut' u poroga ikh' zhilishcha).* Although the rebels had
carefully "hidden their weapons in secret storage caches," they "would
not dare to take them up" in a country under martial law, fearing immediate reprisals. For this reason "the slightest Russian delay," Adamov
warned ominously, "in coming to aid [the Armenians] could lead to their
complete destruction."[50]

Unfortunately for Ottoman Armenians, delay was in the operational
DNA of the Russian army. Vorontsov-Dashkov's September plan was nowhere near being fulfilled when Turkey entered the war in November. By
14 December 1914, the Armenian bands in northwestern Persia, at least,
were "ready for partisan operations," as P. P. Vvedenskii, the vice-consul
in Urmia, reported to Tiflis.[51] Things were moving more slowly on the
Turkish Caucasian front, but Yudenich received a small fillip on 18 December, when the Hunchak leader Yakob Turabian arrived in Tiflis, by
way of London and Copenhagen, to help organize Armenian bands
on the border. Armenian volunteers were enlisting in the cause all over
Europe, and in America, too—although aside from the odd notable like

Turabian, it was difficult for most of them to get to the Caucasus.[52] With words straight out of the Gallipoli playbook, Sazonov instructed his western diplomats to inform would-be Armenian guerrilla warriors that they would be welcome to fight for Russia—if they paid their own travel expenses and purchased their own arms.[53]

Sazonov's fingerprints were all over Russia's reckless, self-serving Armenian gambit. If it were up to the military men alone, Tiflis command might have worked more exclusively with the Kurds, who were ideally suited to guerrilla warfare and much more mobile than the Armenians.[54] But Sazonov repeatedly insisted that Tiflis command arm Armenians: Russia's claim to be the protector of Ottoman Christians was the whole point of the war with Turkey.[55] Above all, the Armenians must realize who their patron was. On 17 December 1914, just as the Armenian bands on the Turkish border were finally readying for action, Sazonov's deputy K. N. Gulkevich sent a directive to Yudenich reaffirming Sazonov's stipulation that "any order for an Armenian uprising must only be given after receiving prior agreement with the Foreign Ministry."[56] Based on the heavy chatter on the subject at Tiflis command at this time, there is every reason to believe this order would have been given in the next few weeks —only for the idea to be rendered moot by the Turkish offensive at Sarıkamış in late December 1914.

To sum up Sazonov's position on a possible Armenian uprising in eastern Turkey on the eve of Sarıkamış: Russia must not be seen recruiting (or funding) Armenian revolutionaries in Europe or America, so as to have plausible deniability in case they ultimately got into trouble. Russia must have veto power and full operational control over Armenian partisan activities in Turkey. And finally, the Armenians, if successful in overthrowing Ottoman authority, must give thanks to Russia—whose armies would then occupy all territories thus liberated.

To some extent, the Russians were less sanguine about the prospects for an Armenian uprising after Sarıkamış. A deputation of Ottoman Armenian rebel leaders from Zeytun, in the highlands north of Aleppo, reached Tiflis in mid-February 1915, claiming that they had 15,000 men ready to "pounce on Turkish [army] communications" if they received Russian arms and ammunition. (Zeytun sat astride one of the principal southern supply routes for the Ottoman Third Army.) Vorontsov-

Dashkov, although intrigued, promised nothing, claiming that Tiflis command had no way of getting weapons that far inside Turkey. Not wishing to send the Zeytun Armenians away empty-handed, however, the viceroy made an "offer" reminiscent of Bazili's Straits memorandum: perhaps the French or English could arrange a covert weapons dump for Cilician Armenians along the Mediterranean coast.[57]

Simply by meeting with the Zeytun Armenians—who must have received substantial Russian aid and encouragement to make it all the way from Ottoman Cilicia to Tiflis (presumably by way of northern Persia) —Vorontsov-Dashkov had committed a deeply provocative act. By then tossing the hot potato (by way of Sazonov) over to London and Paris, where it was kicked around all through February and March at the height of the Dardanelles campaign threatening the Ottoman capital, the viceroy created an enormous paper trail, with the inevitable rumors following in its wake. It did not take long for Ottoman authorities to pick up the threads of the conspiracy, with portentous consequences after Armenian rebels attacked an Ottoman weapons convoy and an army barracks in Zeytun in early April 1915, killing some five hundred Turkish soldiers before they (along with 20,000 Armenian civilians from Zeytun) were forced to flee into the mountains.[58]

While it is true that the British and French ultimately balked at sending arms to the Armenians of Zeytun, there is no way the Ottomans could have known this for sure. And the Zeytun conspiracy was only the tip of the iceberg. A delegation of Hunchaks reported to Tiflis command the first week of April 1915 that Armenian partisans were ready to rise "all over Cilicia" *(vo vsei Kilikii)*. No less than 3,000 armed revolutionary cells, the Armenians claimed, had been created across this mountainous Ottoman region, from Adana to Aleppo, including Sis, Hacin, and Furnuz, near Zeytun, which was the epicenter of resistance, along with Dörtyol, along the coast near the railway chokepoint of Ceyhan (where Armenian agents were witnessed coming ashore in early March 1915, presumably having been carried on British warships from Cairo).[59]

The Hunchaks were not exaggerating about the extent of rebel activity in Turkey. By April 1915, Russian military intelligence was gleefully passing on reports of a "general uprising in Cilicia," of "bloody clashes" between Armenians and the government in Bitlis, Van, and Muş, and of

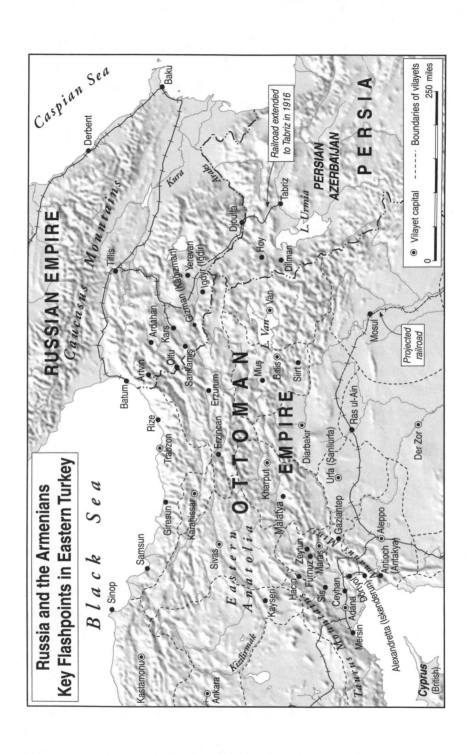

Russia and the Armenians
Key Flashpoints in Eastern Turkey

Caspian Sea

Black Sea

RUSSIAN EMPIRE

Caucasus Mountains

PERSIA

PERSIAN AZERBAIJAN

O T T O M A N   E M P I R E

Eastern Anatolia

Railroad extended to Tabriz in 1916

Projected railroad

⊙ Vilayet capital
----- Boundaries of vilayets

0   250 miles

Baku
Derbent
Kura
Aras
Tabriz
Djoulfa
Hoy
Dilman
L. Urmia
Tiflis
Yerevan
Igdir (Iğdır)
Gizman (Kağızman)
Van
L. Van
Ardahan
Kars
Oltu
Sarıkamış
Artvin
Erzurum
Muş
Bitlis
Siirt
Batum
Erzincan
Rize
Trabzon
Diarbakir
Ras ul-Ain
Giresun
Karahissar
Kharput
Urfa (Şanlıurfa)
Der Zor
Mosul
Samsun
Sivas
Malatya
Gaziantep
Aleppo
Sinop
Kayseri
Zeytun
Furnuz
Hacin
Maraş
Sis
Dört Yol
Ceyhan
Adana
Antioch (Antakya)
Mersin
Alexandretta (İskenderun)
Kastamonu
Ankara
Kızılırmak
Taurus Mountains
Amanus Mountains

Cyprus
(British)

"systematic slaughter in Erzurum . . . Zeytun and environs."[60] Ottoman
sources, too, confirm an escalation of counterinsurgency operations that
same month, both in Van vilayet, in Bitlis province, and in Cilicia, near
Ceyhan/Dörtyol (where fifty kilos of dynamite were discovered), Zeytun,
and the Hatay between Alexandretta (Iskenderun) and Aleppo, an area
astride supply lines to Damascus, which saw "armed attacks by Armenian
guerrillas using guns and bombs in the rear area of the [Ottoman] 4th
Army."[61]

Where was the Russian Caucasian army when the long-awaited Armenian uprising against Ottoman authority at last began spreading across
Cilicia and eastern Anatolia in April 1915? Having failed to get serious
quantities of arms to the rebels at Zeytun or Van, much less as far as Erzurum, Erzincan, Sivas, Kayseri, or other cities targeted in the Adamov
report, Tiflis command found itself in roughly the same place as Eberhart's Black Sea fleet vis-à-vis the Allied amphibious landings later that
month: watching with keen interest from a safe distance. Turkey's Armenians, like the ANZAC, British, and French troops wading ashore at Gallipoli, would now pay in blood for Russia's unwillingness (or inability) to
fight for its own interests.

The rebellion at Van provides a perfect illustration of the Armenian
tragedy. Local Dashnaks had been in close contact with the Russians ever
since the Kurdish depredations of the previous spring. Violent clashes
between the Dashnaks and government forces in Van were reported as
early as September 1914. On 24 September 1914, the Ottoman Third
Army reported evidence that the Russians were smuggling weapons and
ammunition across the border, and warned that anyone caught aiding this
traffic "shall be immediately executed."[62] All winter, the frontier areas
buzzed with activity, as Armenian deserters, fleeing Van, crossed over
to the Russians, while others were witnessed coming back into Turkey.
By early 1915, the Ottoman Third Army had assembled actionable—and
mostly accurate—intelligence on the "Armenian gangs" Tiflis command
had "set up in Oltu, Sarıkamış, Kağızman—whom the Russians equipped
with machine guns and artillery."[63] February and March 1915 saw the first
reports of significant rebel activity near Van, Bitlis, and Erzurum, including the cutting of telegraph wires, the detonation of bombs, attacks on
Turkish army and police barracks, and, if we are to believe the rather pur-

plish account of Ottoman army intelligence, the "pillaging and destroying [of] Muslim villages," as Armenian rebels "massacred even the babies in their cradles." Whether or not these Armenian partisan activities had been pre-approved by the Russian Foreign Ministry, as Sazonov had stipulated, they certainly looked Russian-inspired to Ottoman Third Army command, which was beginning to fear a "catastrophe of unimaginable proportions."[64]

On or about 13–14 April 1915, the Turks' worst nightmare came to pass, when partisans expelled government forces from Van and erected barricades around the city. No one knows exactly how many men the Armenians were able to put under arms at Van, but it must have been a significant number, as they ultimately held the city for more than four weeks against three full Ottoman Jandarma (police) battalions, the First Expeditionary Force sent by the Third Army, and untold Kurdish Hamidiye militiamen. The fighting was merciless, with Armenians dispatching Muslims caught inside the town even while the Turks and Kurds were massacring Armenian civilians outside its walls. Although initial Ottoman claims that more than 100,000 Muslims were slain at Van are surely wildly overblown, it is abundantly clear that terrible atrocities were committed by both sides. As a Russian Cossack observed, "the Turks and Kurds took no Armenian prisoners, and the Armenians took no Kurds or Turks prisoners."[65]

Armenian historians tend to describe the Van rebellion as a kind of preventive "Warsaw uprising" against Turkish plans for mass expulsions (rather than, as the Turks claim, the event that justified the "relocation" of Armenians from frontline areas), but this is certainly not how it was seen at the time. Tiflis command received messages from Van on two separate occasions in early May 1915 (sewn into the lining of the messengers' clothing) while the Armenians still held the city, which suggests that, despite telegraphic communications having been cut, the Dashnaks still believed themselves to be aiding the Russian army, and vice-versa: the Armenians, as the second message specified, "were expecting Russian help every day."[66] *Mshak,* the Armenian newspaper in Tiflis, openly boasted that Armenian partisans had delivered Van to the Russians—with reason for pride, as its editors had been directly involved in the organization of partisan bands in border areas.[67] According to a proud telegram sent from "the Armenians of Van" to Vorontsov-Dashkov on 20 May 1915, after the city had fallen to the Russians (who had evidently restored the outgoing cable line), at least 3,000 Armenian "volunteers" had accompanied the Cossacks on their triumphant ride into Van, which suggests that the recruiting by Tiflis command had not been in vain after all.[68]

The story of the Armenians of Van, however, does not have a happy ending. While the uprising almost certainly contributed to the fall of the city to Russian arms, the Russians, as usual, arrived late in the game. Had Russian troops reached the city by early or mid-April in coordination with the partisan rebellion, the lives of thousands of innocent Armenians living outside the town walls could have been saved—along with those of the unfortunate Muslims trapped inside the city during its terrible month-long siege. Instead, the first advance guard of Cossacks rode into town on 18 May 1915—almost five weeks after the rebellion began. By this time, the city was in ruins, with its Armenian quarter bombed out by Ottoman artillery and the Muslim neighborhoods razed to the ground by Armenian partisans. Tens of thousands of Armenians, Kurds, and Turks alike had perished, the vast majority of them civilians. If not before, Van was an Armenian town now, with most of its few surviving Muslims having fled, even while Armenian refugees from miles around had poured into the city. Scarcely had the town's reconstruction under Russian occupation begun before it was retaken by the Ottoman army in August 1915—with predictably dire consequences for its now almost exclusively Armenian population, of which some 50,000, Vahakn Dadrian claims, were summarily massacred in retaliation for having helped deliver the city to the Russians in May.[69] Taner Akçam goes still further, claiming that the Turks, upon retaking Van, "killed the city's entire Armenian population."[70]

The short-lived and ultimately futile Armenian rebellion at Van, meanwhile, had set in motion that whole terrible series of events about which historians still argue today. The traditional narrative of the "Armenian genocide" claims that it was set in motion on 24 April 1915, with the arrest of some 240 Armenian notables in Constantinople. However, new research in now-open Ottoman archives, mostly carried out by Turkish scholars, demonstrates that several deportation orders actually preceded this date, including a small-scale "relocation" decree applying only to

Zeytun and Dörtyol that was issued by Talaat Bey, the interior minister, in early March 1915. A similar order pertaining to Maraş was issued early in April.[71] It was only after the Cilician and especially the Van rebellions had gotten serious, however, that the deportation campaign became semiofficial—or moved from a "strategic" to a "genocidal" rationale, as Taner Akçam would have it.[72] The first major Ottoman "relocation" decree was issued on the crucial day of 24 April 1915, not by Talaat Bey, the interior minister, whom most Armenians have blamed principally for the excesses of the deportation campaign, but by Enver Pasha, the war minister (although he prepared the decree on Talaat's rather vague instructions).[73] In this document, issued against the backdrop of the burgeoning Van and Cilician rebellions and just as the Allied armada was assembling to strike at Gallipoli, Enver ordered that the Armenian population in rebellious areas close to the front lines be reduced to less than 10 percent. In a series of follow-up decrees, Enver further ordered the relocation of Armenian political leaders and recommended to Talaat's Interior Ministry that Armenian "rebels" be removed from border areas, which should thereafter be resettled with Muslims.[74] Not until 31 May 1915, nearly five weeks later (and not incidentally after the government had learned all about the bloodbath in Van), did Talaat issue his infamous decree on the coercive political circumstances necessitating the relocation and transfer of the Armenians, which applied to the six eastern provinces.[75] The final, terrible escalation occurred in July 1915, when a new series of armed uprisings in Gaziantep, Antioch (Antakya), Maraş, Urfa, and Zeytun—Armenian partisan activity was by then substantial enough to tie down three whole Ottoman army divisions—gave Talaat a pretext to extend the deportation campaign for the first time to Anatolian areas well behind the front lines, such as Samsun, Sivas, Trabzon, Urfa, Mersin, and Adana. The Armenian deportation decrees were never universally applied in Turkey. There were exemptions, in theory at least, for Armenian Catholics and Protestants, women, children, the elderly, soldiers and their families, and certain irreplaceable artisans (such as those working on the Baghdad railway). But these exemptions were often willfully disregarded, and there is no question that by summer 1915 the Armenian deportations had gone well beyond any putative strategic rationale, turning into a generalized campaign of ethnic cleansing. Many though not all Armenians were deported even from Ankara, Smyrna, and Constantinople, miles away from any active military front.[76]

The human consequences of the Armenian deportation campaign were devastating. Almost all of those "relocated" lost their homes and whatever personal property they could not carry with them—compensation for which was, in theory, going to be given by the government, but which, in practice, never came. Among the hundreds of thousands who perished in 1915, doubtless many died at the hands of Turkish and Kurdish execution squads, just as Armenian authors insist. But the vast majority likely succumbed to starvation or thirst along the "route of horrors" in the Syrian desert, if not along the mountain passes of the Taurus and Amanus long before—often, cruelly, within sight of the Baghdad railway on which most were denied passage.[77] Although scholars differ on the figures, even most Turkish authors today will concede that about 500,000 Armenians died during the deportation campaign (although some claim that nearly as many Muslim civilians died at Armenian or Russian hands in eastern Turkey and the Caucasus during the First World War); Armenian authors have estimated that as many as 1.5 or 2 million died in a deliberate campaign of extermination. Based on the latest demographic research on the Armenian population before and after the deportations, Fuat Dündar, a rare Turkish historian who credits Armenian claims about the premeditated expulsion (if not the deliberate extermination) of the Armenian population of Anatolia, recently arrived at a plausible death toll of 664,000.[78]

It is a terrible, terrible story, and one that has been told many times before. But in all the political and scholarly acrimony over "genocidal intent," the true scale of the Armenian security threat, and casualty figures, there remains one conspicuously unasked—and unanswered—question. Where were the Russians? Having helped summon into being the Armenian uprisings of 1915 through years of diplomatic bullying, covert meetings inside Turkey with Armenian revolutionaries, the funding and arming of partisan bands, and countless promises of imminent military intervention, why did the Russians stand by and watch as these Russophile partisans were crushed by the Ottoman army and Kurdish militiamen, and their fellow Armenians were deported *en masse?*

In Russia's defense, the moment of reckoning for her Armenian clients occurred against the backdrop of her own "Great Retreat" of summer 1915, as first Western Galicia, then much of Poland and the Baltic area, fell to the enemy. Compelling as the Armenian problem had seemed to Sazonov during the Reform campaign of 1913–14, and to Yudenich as he plotted the course of Russia's war against Turkey in fall 1914, after Gorlice-Tarnow, the great German breakthrough that occurred on 2 May 1915 at the height of the Armenian rebellion at Van, and just as the Ottoman deportation campaign began, there was simply no way Stavka could have spared arms, ammunition, or troops to reinforce the Turkish Caucasian front. It was the wretched luck of Turkey's Armenians that the wrath of the Ottoman government descended upon them at exactly the same time as Russia's own moment of truth against the German armies.

The Armenians were not the only victims of Russian strategic impotence in 1915. More than 500,000 Jews were also expelled from frontline areas before the east European retreat began, and they were the lucky ones, as many who remained behind were targeted in anti-Semitic pogroms.[79] In all, Russia's retreat "produced an exodus of almost two million civilian refugees."[80] On 4 August, just as the last Armenian uprisings were being snuffed out in eastern Turkey, Warsaw was taken by the Germans. By September, Baranovichi itself fell, forcing Stavka to retreat east. The only thing which slowed down the German advance guard was the inability of supply units to keep up as they entered the barren lands of the north European plain, made still more barren by the Russians' "scorched earth" policy.[81] Although it would later emerge that the retreat, conducted in fair order, had saved the army, at the time panic in Petrograd was so great that the government nearly fell. Famously, Tsar Nicholas II took over the army command in September 1915 to rally the public—foolishly, as he would thereafter be the principal scapegoat for Russia's faltering war effort (aside from the Jews, that is). Amid an ongoing strategic (not to say moral) meltdown that nearly brought down the tsarist regime, it is hardly surprising that the Caucasian army failed to hold onto Van that August, or to protect Armenians further inside Turkey.

Seen in inter-Allied context, however, the story of the great retreat illustrates yet again Russia's perennial opportunism and tardiness. The best time to beat the Germans, as the French had told Stavka repeatedly, was August 1914, when East Prussia had been left wide open due to the imperatives of the Schlieffen Plan. By the following spring, Germany had recovered her strategic maneuverability, and it was far too late to deliver against her anything like the crushing blow France had asked for. The Russian contribution to Gallipoli, such little as it was, came at least three months too late to make the slightest bit of difference to her allies. Likewise, the time to invade eastern Turkey in coordination with an Armenian uprising was November 1914, before the Ottoman Third Army could get its act together—or, at the very latest, March-April 1915, when most Armenian rebels had grown tired of waiting for the Russians and decided to force the action themselves. By 18 May 1915, when the first advance Cossack regiments of the Caucasian army finally made it as far as Van, Ottoman Armenians had already begun dying in droves for Russia's hollow promises—as they would in even greater numbers after her half-hearted invasion of eastern Turkey swung into reverse that summer. One can hardly blame the Dashnaks and Hunchaks for arming themselves in self-defense. Their error lay in expecting the Russian cavalry to arrive in time to protect them once the inevitably brutal counterattack against their rebellion commenced. These revolutionaries, and the Ottoman Armenian civilians they claimed to represent, fell victim to Russia's peculiar mixture of imperial greed and impotence, as the would-be liberatees of an army unable—or unwilling—to liberate them. A mere twelve months into the world war, Russia had failed on every important front but the diplomatic. To stiffen wavering public morale, some at Stavka now improbably concluded, it was time to open a new one.

CHAPTER SEVEN

The Russians in Persia

All Persia had been cleared of the enemy . . . the Transcaucasian
Front and the rail connection with Russia through Baku into Persia
was secure . . . at last, the entire Russian sphere of influence in Persia
was entirely in our hands.

—N. N. Baratov, early 1917[1]

PERSIA WAS THE FESTERING SORE of the Entente alliance. In a literal sense, the Triple Entente was born out of an agreement over the
country: the Anglo-Russian Accord of 1907 had been negotiated and
signed between London and St. Petersburg due largely to French insistence. France was the fulcrum of the alliance, both in that her own defensive agreements with Russia (1894) and England (1904) predated the accord between the other two powers, and in the more basic sense that,
since 1871, her enmity with Imperial Germany was the fundamental constant of European diplomacy. That France and Germany would fight each
other in any major power conflict was a given. The Austrian-Russian enmity born of the Crimean War and reinforced by each successive Balkan crisis was nearly as certain, making clear to everyone the basic power
blocks of a general European war which would inevitably pit Germany
and Austria-Hungary, as the "Central powers," against the Franco-
Russian partners that enveloped them. As Sazonov and his French co-
conspirators had so brilliantly grasped in July 1914, the great strategic
question was what Britain would do in such a conflict. Had there been a
real diplomatic flare-up that month between London and St. Petersburg
—as quite nearly occurred over Russia's aggressive "forward policy" in

northern Persia, despite frantic French efforts to douse tensions—the Triple Entente may never have coalesced on the battlefield.[2]

Once Britain entered the war alongside Russia, the Persian question naturally lost its urgency for Paris. But the fundamentals of diplomacy do not suddenly change merely because two countries take up a temporary brotherhood-in-arms. As Arthur Reade, a British expatriate, reported confidentially to the Foreign Office on 17 December 1914, "already in Petrograd it is being said that 'in a few years' we shall be at war with England."[3] This was assumed on the English side as well. A good deal of Britain's Middle Eastern policy during the war was predicated on the idea that Russia would reemerge as Britain's primary enemy as soon as Germany was beaten. Kitchener's notoriously misguided idea of installing a Mecca-based caliph, first mooted in December 1914, was mostly intended to keep the Russians from "inheriting" the Ottoman caliphate along with Constantinople, the idea being that they might "use" it to stir up Islamic unrest against the British Raj in India. Likewise, the whole ill-fated gambit of promising Syria and Lebanon to the French was conceived in order to create a buffer zone between Britain's own Arab sphere of influence and the Russians (with these promises predictably broken after Russia dropped out of the war in 1917).[4]

While there was an air of the fanciful about Kitchener's preoccupations with the postwar future of the Caliphate, Britain's abiding concern about Russian territorial encroachment on its southern neighbors rested on much firmer ground. Although Turkey was more central to Russia's own war aims, it was Persia, the crucial land bridge to Afghanistan and India, that figured so prominently in Great Game intrigue dating back to the time of Napoleon, and that remained the primary irritant in Anglo-Russian relations for London. Buchanan, Britain's ambassador to Russia who was so amenable (or indifferent) to Russian policy on matters such as Poland, had always taken a much tougher line on Persia, despite the inherent weakness of Britain's position. As Grey had written Buchanan back in March 1914, the essence of the problem was simple: "The Russians are prepared to occupy Persia, and we are not." Before the world war began, Russia already had something like 12,000 troops in northern Persia, making her obvious yet still undeclared intention of annexing Persian Azerbaijan nearly a fait accompli.[5]

Following Turkey's entry into the war Grey was adamant that Britain would not tolerate further Russian meddling in "neutral" Persia. The problem went deeper than simple concern over the Gulf region and communications with India. Persia was a predominantly Muslim country. As Britain's Ambassador Buchanan warned Sazonov in an official British aide-mémoire on 2 November 1914—the very day Russia declared war on Turkey—any Russian-inspired perturbations in Islamic affairs, whether taking place in Turkey or Persia, might gravely prejudice "Muslim opinion in Egypt and India." For this reason Grey had enjoined Buchanan to "make clear to Sazonov just how colossally important it is to inculcate in Russia's Persian consuls and personnel the necessity of maintaining friendly and conciliatory relations with Persia."[6] A week later, Grey made the first, and curious, linkage between Russian good behavior in Persia and the Straits issue.[7] On 13 and 14 November, Benckendorff (after reporting on the remarkable, unprompted promise of Constantinople to Russia by King George V, who seems to have forgotten his briefing on the Persian issue) passed on a series of official communiqués from Sir Edward Grey that outlined Britain's policy: any violation of Persian territory by the Caucasian army must be avoided at all costs, so as not to damage the standing of the Entente among neutrals: the Russians would be doing just what the Germans had done in Belgium.[8]

As with the Straits issue, however, the British position on the Russians in Persia softened almost immediately. With the same forgetfulness that overcame Britons during the Dardanelles campaign, Grey abandoned his Persian quid pro quo almost as soon as he offered it. Whereas, in November 1914, British policy was that Constantinople would be given to the Russians at the end of the war so long as they refrained from (further) meddling in Persia, by 22 December, Grey's stated position was that Russia could, if presenting good cause, send more troops into Persia than she already had there, and still have Constantinople after the war.[9] As modified by Kitchener in early January 1915, British policy was that Russia could not only have the Straits and the Ottoman capital regardless of her behavior in Persia: the western Allies would endeavor to win them for her.[10]

What accounts for this British propensity for giving Russia its every diplomatic desire before the Russians themselves bother to ask for it? In the case of Persia, if not Gallipoli, an explanation is readily available. Grey's reversal on the issue of Russian troops in Persia came after he received disturbing intelligence reports of enemy maneuvers there—disturbing because they related to that very issue of "Muslim opinion" about which he had warned Sazonov. Following the proclamation of Islamic holy war against the Entente powers in November 1914 by the Ottoman sultan (sanctioned by the *Şeykh-ul-Islam*), jihad agents from both Germany and Turkey had begun flooding Persia with propaganda, weapons, and gold, even while regular Turkish troops continued violating the border with impunity. By 22 December, Grey told Benckendorff, the situation in Persia had grown "thorny." Thus far a serious outbreak of "pan-Islamic sentiment" in the region had been avoided, but any "provocation" might now set one off. One might think this would militate against the dispatch of more Russian troops, just as Grey had suggested back in November. But the danger now was that the Persian government itself might fall, bringing forth some new Germanophile Islamic regime that might declare war on British India. It was in order to give Teheran "the means to defend itself" that Grey first declared himself willing to allow in more Russian forces.[11]

For neither the first nor the last time, German overreaching had caused London to abandon a solid pillar of traditional British foreign policy. Not surprisingly, there was resistance inside the diplomatic establishment to Grey's policy shift. Sir Walter Townley, His Majesty's Consul in Teheran, had to listen daily to Persian complaints about the depredations of Russian troops—complaints that long pre-dated Turkey's entry into the war. As Townley reported to Grey as early as 8 October 1914, the Persians "merely sought to prevent, if possible, [Persian] Azerbaijan from becoming a theater of war between Russia and Turkey . . . they profess to believe that friction likely to lead to hostilities, sooner or later, might have been avoided had Russia consented to withdraw her troops, but think war was unavoidable now that she has refused to do so . . . there can be but small doubt that all Persia would dearly love to seize the opportunity to have a shot at the hated Russians."[12]

Like most British officers and diplomats in the field, Townley found it difficult to see why he should sign off on Russian imperial aims he had spent so many years combating. Channeling the thoughts and fears of

Persian officials about Russian intentions came naturally to him: so naturally that he had a difficult time getting on with his Russian counterpart, V. O. Korostovets. On 9 December 1914, the Russian consul in Teheran complained to Sazonov that Townley was in "solidarity with the Persians on the question of the withdrawal of Russian forces" from Azerbaijan, the Anglo-Persian idea being that such a gesture would placate public opinion in Teheran, deeply suspicious of Russian intentions, and "work against the growth of Islamism."[13] This was, indeed, the position Grey had elaborated in November. Little did Townley know that Grey had flatly changed his mind on the matter. For his dutiful efforts to carry out what he believed to be the policy of His Majesty's Government, Townley was now denounced as a "Russophobe" by Korostovets, with this accusation being repeated by Benckendorff, to Grey, on 23 December.[14] By early January 1915, Sazonov was insisting on Townley's removal from his post at Teheran on grounds of Russophobia—while conceding, somewhat rudely, that it was possible the consul, a "man of weak will," was merely the tool of true British Russophobes—like Winston Churchill![15]

What had poor Townley done to deserve this abuse? While it is unclear exactly which remark or report set Sazonov off, his outburst likely had something to do with miscommunication relating to the explosive events at Sarıkamış. It will be recalled that the Ottoman offensive there, launched on 28–29 December 1914, produced sufficient panic on the Russian side that Tiflis command ordered the evacuation of the entire Transcaucasus. Significantly, these orders extended to Russian troops in northern Persia—including all of Urmia province, Tabriz, Kazvin, and Enzeli, on the Caspian coast.[16] As if innocently, on 1 January 1915 Townley passed on to Grey Korostovets's report that "Russian troops would be withdrawn from Azerbaijan for strategical reasons." Adding his own two cents on the matter, Townley opined that there was indeed "absolutely no necessity for Russian troops at Kazvin, Meshed or Mazanderan."[17] Two days later, after hearing from Korostovets that Kazvin, too, was being abandoned, Townley told Grey that he thought the Russians should withdraw all remaining troops from Persia—not under Turkish pressure but as a political gesture to show the Persians who their real enemy was (that is, the Turks, not the Russians), and thus improve Britain's precarious standing. "We are rapidly coming to be considered as false friend," Townley explained, "who is no more than an accomplice of Russian spoliator in disguise."[18] Considering that the Russians were then faced with serious Ottoman offensives on two fronts—at Sarıkamış and in Persian Azerbaijan, where the Turks were nearing Tabriz—it is little wonder Sazonov took umbrage at Townley's request for a blanket withdrawal of Russian forces.

Sarıkamış panic notwithstanding, the Russians were not about to abandon their hard-won position in northern Persia. While Tabriz was indeed evacuated before the onrushing enemy, substantial Russian garrisons remained entirely unmolested at Kazvin, less than 100 miles from Teheran, and at Resht and Enzeli on the Caspian.[19] This was not even to count the guerrilla bands of Christians and Kurds Tiflis command had been arming since summer 1914, mostly in the Lake Urmia area around Hoy and Dilman.[20] Grey's strategic nightmare, that the Russo-Turkish War would spill across the Persian border, was fully realized by January 1915. The Turks took Tabriz on 10 January (although it fell again to the Russians three weeks later). Dilman, epicenter of the Kurdish-Christian anti-Ottoman guerrilla movement in Urmia province, fell briefly to Ottoman troops in January, only to be retaken later that month by the Russians before it fell again to the Turks in April. The Russo-Ottoman skirmishes in northern Persia in 1915 were fairly small in scale compared to the fighting at Sarıkamış (much less that on the European fronts), mostly involving flanking maneuvers by forces numbering less than 5,000. Nevertheless, it was real war, and Persia had walked right into the middle of it.[21]

To their credit, most British diplomats figured this out fairly quickly. At least in winter 1914–15, it was mostly the Turks who were creating havoc in Persian Azerbaijan, looting and burning down villages, while the Russians were simply reacting to Ottoman aggression. The Porte's position, expressed repeatedly to Teheran all during the winter battles, was that Turkish troops would leave the country as soon as the Russians did. By the end of January, if not at the beginning, the "Russophobe" Townley was sounding like a veritable Russophile, telling Grey that "the sooner Russian troops drive Turks out of Azerbaijan the better," before reporting proudly that he had just admonished the Persian *chef de cabinet* that he "had more faith in a crushing Russian victory to restore Persians to their senses [to dissuade them from endorsing the Turco-German jihad] than in assurances of a Turkish Grand Vizier."[22]

In Petrograd, Ambassador Buchanan, sensitive as ever to the issue of not disturbing Russia's fighting morale, had taken the Russian position even before being prompted by Grey or Townley. On 5 January 1915, while the struggle for Tabriz was heating up, Buchanan insisted to Grey that "we cannot reasonably expect Russia to recall her troops, and a very bad impression will be made here if it becomes known that we are urging her to do so." Sazonov had already spoken of reinforcing Persian Azerbaijan by as much as a full army division (although as it turned out, Tiflis command was not yet ready to spare this much), and Buchanan expressed no objection. Intriguingly, Townley tried to reconcile himself—and Grey —to the eventuality of a full-on Russian occupation of northern Persia by predicting that, "if Russian troops were to be recalled a situation would be created that would in the end force Russia to annex Azerbaijan, which was a thing he wished to avoid."[23]

Once more Russian diplomacy had pulled off the unthinkable. In barely two months, British policy on Persia had gone from adamant insistence that Russia not intervene there and, ideally, withdraw; to acquiescence in the maintenance of troop levels in Persia; to endorsement of the dispatch of as much as a full army division, with Russian annexation of Persian Azerbaijan spoken of by the British ambassador in Petrograd, in a sort of dangling participle. True, Grey did stiffen up enough this same month (March 1915) to demand that Russia accept the expansion of the British "sphere of influence" in Persia northward into the neutral zone— this had been the goal pursued by Townley and Buchanan before the war, back when Britain was seeking to counter Russia's aggressive "forward policy" in Persian Azerbaijan.[24] However, at Russian insistence, an enlarged British zone in Persia was negotiated as a direct quid pro quo for Britain's acceptance of Russia's claim on the Straits. The Russians, as always, got something large and tangible (a sovereign claim on Constantinople, the Bosphorus and Dardanelles defiles) in exchange for a vague promise to respect a "zone of influence." And even this nonbinding pledge Sazonov gave only with conditions: that Russia sign off on any British railways to be built in the formerly neutral zone; that the area around Isfahan and Yezd, in the same zone, be "reserved for Russia," and not least that Britain recognize Russia's "complete freedom of action" in her own zone—which would now soon, thanks to Britain's climb-down, be blanketed with Russian troops.[25]

Meanwhile, the reeducation of Britain's consul in Teheran continued apace. Where before he had channeled Persian fears out of what Korostovets called "Russophobic solidarity," by 23 March 1915 Townley was chastising Persian officials, who (having evidently not undergone the Russophilic mind-melding the British experienced) were still stubbornly insisting that Russia recall its occupying forces from Ardebil and Kazvin, at least. "I replied," Townley reported to Grey, "that there could be no question of any such thing at the present moment." In a meeting at the French Legation, the three Entente consuls had in fact just "unanimously agreed that the Russian force at Kazvin should be increased rather than diminished."[26] By late spring, Townley's even more Russophilic successor, Charles Marling (Sazonov's express choice for the post),[27] was recommending troop levels for a Russian expeditionary force: first "2,000 or 3,000" to be landed at Enzeli (12 May 1915), then "6,000 at least" (20 May).[28] With British opposition having vanished into the ether, the only thing that now stood in the way of a Russian invasion of Persia was the Russians' own tardiness in mounting it.

In defense of British diplomats, it was not simply spinelessness that accounted for their stunning climb-down on the issue of Russian boots on the ground in Persia. The Turkish danger was real. Omer Fevzi Bey, who commanded the Ottoman force that had occupied Tabriz, at one point threatened to march all the way to Teheran if the Russians did not withdraw their forces from Persia. Turkish soldiers (or Kurdish irregulars) burned down the Russian bank in Tabriz, putting nearly the entire European population of the city to flight.[29] A detachment of troops from the Ottoman Sixth Army, under its commander Rauf Bey (Orbay), sacked the border towns of Hanekin and Kasri-Shirin in March with such relish that their German allies lodged a formal complaint. The brutal behavior of Rauf's men, his German liaison officer reported to Berlin, "had destroyed the sympathies of Persians for Turks, such little as they were."[30] The Germans, too, were rumored to be behind outrages of all kinds, from Robin Hood–style heists of Entente money caravans to the murder of a

Russian bank manager in Isfahan the night of 19–20 May 1915. This last incident caused outrage in Entente circles, particularly after the Russians claimed that the assassins had taken refuge in the German Consulate. A political assassination like this, Marling reported to Grey, offered a "plausible excuse for the dispatch" of Russian troops (this is when he upped his request to "6,000 or more").[31]

Still, there was a revealing difference in inter-Allied diplomacy as practiced on the two sides. Just as the Germans had been able, in August 1914, to force the Austrians to wheel around their Second Army from Serbia to face the Russians, so did they now prevail upon the Porte to call off the invasion of Persia and even sack Rauf Bey from his Sixth Army command in September 1915.[32] By contrast, in fall 1914 the Russians had disregarded Franco-British requests to concentrate their strength on the Germans, just as they later ignored Britain's repeated demands to withdraw troops from Persia—until Britain simply stopped making them, and then began requesting exactly the opposite. Russian diplomacy had worked its magic again.

It is worth examining the thought processes of British and Russian diplomats on the ground closely, for they reveal deep-seated cultural differences and even bring to light the reason the Russians kept winning. Constantly running afoul of his Russian counterpart, accused of Russophobia by Sazonov, Sir Walter Townley had every reason to resign in protest. A gesture like this might have awakened Grey and the British War Cabinet to the grasping nature of Russia's wartime diplomacy. Instead, he genuinely came over to the Russian point of view to the extent that he began making Russia's arguments to Persian government officials, rather than the other way around. With his talk of "faith in a crushing Russian victory to restore Persians to their senses," Townley had fully absorbed the Sazonov-Korostovets worldview, in which Russian prestige in the Orient trumps all other questions, and made it his own. One is reminded here of John Buchan's famous line from his novel *Greenmantle* that "we" —the British—"are the only race on earth that can produce men capable of getting inside the skin of remote peoples."[33] Townley may not have spoken enough Russian to pass for one. But he could certainly, now, think like one.

Townley's Russian counterpart, by contrast, showed no inclination

to think like a Briton. And why would he? Although Tiflis command
had begun evacuating some troops from northern Persia in the wake of
Sarıkamış (only to call off the withdrawal nearly as soon as it began), Korostovets himself had never entertained the idea seriously, no matter how
many times Townley had suggested it. Even when requests came from the
top of the British foreign policy establishment, Korostovets calmly swatted them down without blinking. Sir Edward Grey, for example, floated
the trial balloon of a tactical Russian withdrawal on a number of occasions in the first war winter, the idea being to convince Persia to declare
war on Turkey, as the only power truly threatening Teheran. If a Muslim
power could be won over to active belligerence on the Entente side, Grey
explained to the Russians, it would destroy the key premise of the Turco-
German holy war: that the Islamic world was united behind the Central
powers. (This was much the same idea that lay behind Kitchener's simultaneous courting of the Sherif of Mecca.)[34] Predictably, Grey got nowhere
with the idea, although Sazonov did at one point suggest, in true Gallipoli
style, that the Persians might be induced to fight Turkey if the Entente
powers promised them the holy Shia cities of Najaf and Karbala (which
sacred ground, lying in southern Mesopotamia, it would naturally be up
to the British to conquer!).[35]

It was not that the Russians did not *understand* British concerns about
Muslim opinion in Egypt and the Indian subcontinent. They just did not
care. In a lengthy memorandum on the Persian situation sent to Sazonov
in February 1915, Korostovets laid out a fairly accurate version of the British case for Persian belligerence against Turkey, which might exercise
"moral influence on India, Afghanistan, and generally on Muslims, even
possibly on the Arab tribes in the south [of Persia], with whom the English, I have heard, have already begun fighting." All this was understood.
But none of it was in Russia's interest. Russia's own Muslims, Korostovets
explained to Sazonov, were indifferent as to whether or not Persia fought
in the war. Their view was eminently sensible: Persia did not, after all,
have an army. Moreover, he continued, the "fighting quality of her tribes
is doubtful, with exception of the Bakhtiaris," who roamed mostly in the
British zone of southern Persia, making them, again, largely irrelevant to
Russia. More to the diplomatic point, for Persia to be enlisted as co-
belligerent would compromise Russian claims on its territory after the

war, particularly relating to "the introduction of a new regime in Azerbai-jan together with a revision of the Anglo-Russian Accord [of 1907]." Un-like their British counterparts, Korostovets and Sazonov kept their eyes fixed clearly on their objective: sovereign control of northern Persia. The rest—exaggerated panic over Turco-German intrigues, the issue of win-ning over to belligerence a country (Persia) without an army, pan-Islam and global Muslim opinion—was just background noise, best ignored. It was all well and good to understand the sometimes silly views of one's ally, but this did not mean one needed seriously to indulge them.[36]

Having thus helped to open Pandora's box, the British would soon see Russia's occupation of northern Persia spread well beyond anything Grey, Townley, or even Marling had envisioned. Sazonov could barely conceal his glee in passing on Britain's request for 6,000 reinforcements for the Kazvin garrison, though he noted that he was not sure Tiflis com-mand could spare this many troops. In any case, it was clear that Russia had the green light. Having enlisted Stavka's help in leaning on Tiflis command, orders had been sent to Baku to ready as many as 10,000 troops to be sent to Kazvin.[37]

Although the usual delays intervened, by late summer 1915 the Rus-sians were preparing to make a show of force. At first, this entailed the Kazvin garrison staging threatening maneuvers on the Teheran road, as ordered by Lieutenant-Colonel Belomnestov on 6 August. Warsaw had fallen two days before, producing panic at Stavka, and so these maneu-vers were called off absent further reinforcements from Baku.[38] In mid-September, another 1,000 Russian troops landed at Enzeli, making a "fa-vorable impression" on the Entente legations in Teheran.[39] The arrival of Grand Duke Nicholas in Tiflis on 24 September 1915, who after being re-placed by the tsar as commander-in-chief was given the Caucasian com-mand, seemed to suggest the Russians were getting more serious in the theater. But it was hard for even a man of the grand duke's rank and pres-tige to countenance sending troops to a front of secondary importance like Persia while the German armies were galumphing through Russian Poland. Only in early November, after Russia's "great retreat" had at last stabilized the east European front, did the grand duke and his chief of staff, General Yudenich, feel they could spare more men (about 6,000 in-fantry and 8,000 mounted cavalry), horses, and mobile artillery (about thirty guns, including two 4.8-inch howitzers) for the Persian theater. After months of skirmishing, the real Persian war was about to begin.

Because there are so few good sources on the world war in Persia, it is difficult to disentangle the real balance of forces during the crucial days of November 1915 when the issue was decided. By this time rumors were swirling through Teheran that Ahmad Shah, the eighteen-year-old nominal ruler of the country, was about to throw in with the Germans and declare holy war on Britain and Russia. The idea was for the shah to perform a *hejira,* or exodus, from Teheran to the holy city of Qom, just as Muhammad had tactically abandoned Mecca for Medina. Against the temptation of pan-Islamic solidarity (even if most Persians were Shia Muslims, not Sunnis like the Turks) and German bribe money, the shah had to calculate the strength of Entente forces on the ground. An "east Persian cordon" had been set up on the frontier to prevent a German jihad mission led by Oskar von Niedermayer from reaching Afghanistan, but this was thinly garrisoned along a stretch of nearly 1,000 miles from the Russian north to the British south—so thinly garrisoned that Niedermayer's men made it through unscathed. Near the Persian Gulf coastline, the British had occupied Bushire, but this was a matter of just a few battalions, hundreds of miles from Teheran.

The Russians, by contrast, were now assembling a proper army in northern Persia, the size of which Ahmad Shah could only guess at. Under the command of Major-General N. N. Baratov, the main Caucasian expeditionary force of 6,000 infantry (mostly Cossacks) and 8,000 cavalrymen, after embarking on a veritable armada of Volga-Caspian steamers and barges, began landing at Enzeli (modern Pahlavi) on 7 November 1915. Considering that the Russians had told their allies in September that they already had 5,000 troops in Kazvin, this suggests that, by mid-November 1915, the Russians had—potentially at least—20,000 troops along the main communications route from Enzeli-Kazvin-Teheran, within easy marching distance of the capital. On Persia's northwest frontier, facing Van, General T. G. Chernozubov disposed of an entire Caucasian Cossack Division (the 4th), two brigades of Transbaikal Cossacks, and four bands of Armenian irregulars *(druzhiny).* As many as 5,000 Russian-commanded troops and agents were also operating in Urmia province, according to the German guerrilla commander in the area. At

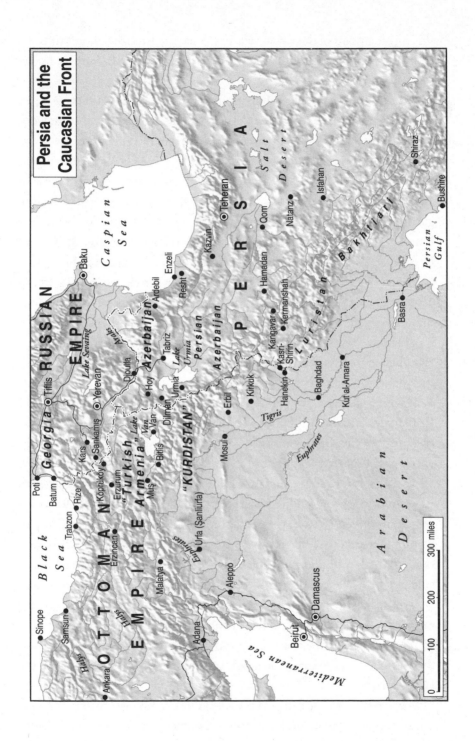

Persia and the Caucasian Front

Black Sea

Sinope
Samsun
Halys
Ankara

OTTOMAN EMPIRE

Adana

Aleppo

Mediterranean Sea

Beirut
Damascus

Arabian Desert

Trabzon
Rize
Poti
Batum
Kars
Erzincan
Erzurum
Köprüköy
Sarıkamış
Malatya
Muş
Bitlis
"Turkish Armenia"
Euphrates
Urfa (Şanlıurfa)

Georgia
RUSSIAN EMPIRE
Tiflis
Yerevan
Lake Sevang
Araks
Djoulfa
Djoulfa
Hoy
Van
Lake Van
Dilman
Urmia
"KURDISTAN"

Baku
Caspian Sea

Ardebil
Enzeli
Resht
Azerbaijan
Tabriz
Lake Urmia
Persian Azerbaijan
Erbil
Mosul
Tigris

Kazvin
Teheran
Qom
Hamadan
Kangavar
Kasri-Shirin
Hanekin
Kirkuk
Baghdad
Kut al-Amara

PERSIA

Salt Desert

Natanz
Isfahan
Kermanshah
Luristan
Bakhtiari

Shiraz
Bushire
Persian Gulf

Basra
Euphrates

Scale:
0   100   200   300 miles

this turning point of the world war in Persia, the Russians thus had some 25,000 or 30,000 boots on the ground (or in stirrups), with more on the way.[40]

Baratov's orders from Tiflis command were unambiguous: to seize and then reinforce and hold the Persian capital. It took him about a week to get his forces in order, but uncertainty in Teheran about the size of the force Baratov commanded worked to his advantage. As it turned out, marching a token force on Teheran was sufficient to produce an impression of menace. On Baratov's orders, an "advance guard" of the Kazvin garrison, consisting of about 700 cavalrymen, 300 infantrymen, and just four howitzers and two machine guns, set out for Teheran on 15 November 1915. This force, Korostovets assured Ahmad Shah, was being dispatched toward Teheran only as a precautionary measure and would not actually enter the capital unless it proved necessary for the maintenance of public order. As if to reassure the shah (while also perhaps not wishing him to know how small Baratov's "advance guard" actually was), the Russians halted their march about thirty kilometers north of Teheran to allow the young sovereign to mull over his options.[41]

Having evidently given up on winning over Persia to the Entente, the British now laid down the law to Ahmad Shah—the law of Russian imperialism. "We gave him to understand in unmistakable language," the British consul reported to London of his conversation with Ahmad Shah, "that if the Persian government did not act against the Germans, then Russian troops would undertake the task, and that if Persia allowed herself to be driven to war against us, the results to Persia and to himself would be disastrous."[42] With the British happily serving as the battering ram of Russian diplomacy, Ahmad Shah had no recourse other than to surrender to (what appeared to be) superior force, as he did on 15 November 1915. Having already sent along their own stores of rifles, bombs, machine guns, and ammunition to Isfahan (stores that were considerably larger than those of the small Kazvin advance guard marching on the city), the German and Austrian ambassadors in Teheran now took refuge in the U.S. Embassy.[43]

With even nominal Persian opposition to becoming a Russian protectorate now abandoned, Russian troops fanned out across northern Persia, "securing" the country at last from ongoing Turco-German depredations.

From their base of operations at Kazvin, Baratov's men took Hamadan and Qom in December 1915, Kangavar in January 1916, and Kermanshah in February 1916, just 120 miles from the Ottoman Mesopotamian border. Isfahan, epicenter of German jihadist propaganda and arms stores in Persia, fell on 20 March. "After a series of short, resolute blows," the Russians had "cleared Persia of the Germano-Persian armed forces, and had occupied a vast territory spreading 800 versts long in front and 800 versts broad" (a verst is roughly equal to one kilometer, or about six tenths of a mile).[44] With the equivalent of about half of a single army corps (though with a particularly strong cavalry component), Baratov had achieved the long-standing Russian goal of occupying Persian Azerbaijan. "At last," he later boasted, the "Russian sphere of influence in Persia was entirely in our hands."[45]

The Baratov expedition to Persia remains largely a blank page in the history of the First World War. There is a very good Russian study of the subject, published only in 2002, after military history had at last come back into fashion following the collapse of Communism.[46] British accounts of the Persian affair of November 1915 make vague mention of "the Cossacks" as the saviors of the Entente position, although often without so much as naming the commander of the Russian expeditionary force.[47] At least here there were grounds for gratitude, as the Russians really had taken many Entente consular officials and civilians under protection at Teheran, Kazvin, and Kermanshah. For once Britain's ally had not left it wholly in the lurch: the Allies had well and truly dodged the bullet of Persian belligerence, such possibly imaginary bullet as it was.

If we look more closely at the operational history of the Baratov expeditionary corps, however, a plausible reason for British selective amnesia emerges. Compared to the main battlefields in the Ottoman theater at the time, the Russian deployment in Persia was a sideshow at best, an inopportune distraction at worst. While Baratov was mopping up what little armed opposition there was in northern Persia,[48] scarcely a hundred miles away a British-Indian expeditionary force under General Townshend, advancing on Baghdad, had met a devastating counterattack by the Ottoman Sixth Army under Nurettin Pasha near the ancient ruins of Ctesiphon (Selman Pak, as the battle is known to the Turks) on 22–25 November 1915. Although Turkish losses were heavy (6,000 killed and wounded), Townshend lost yet more men, and his losses were harder to make good. The British commander retreated back down the Tigris to Kut-al-Amara pursued by the Sixth Army, command of which had been turned over to the German field marshal Colmar von der Goltz Pasha. By 7 December 1915, Townshend's troops were surrounded at Kut-al-Amara, where they would remain under siege for the next five months. As most British First World War buffs know, two separate relief missions were dispatched up the Tigris from Basra, first 20,000 troops under General Fenton John Aylmer in January 1916, then another 10,000 under General George Frederick Gorringe in March—both to no avail.

What most Britons do not know is that a Russian force was available just on the other side of the Persian border, less than 150 miles away—closer than Basra. On Townshend's request, General Baratov was ordered by Tiflis command in January 1916 to relieve the British garrison by staging a diversionary strike via the Persian border town of Hanekin (eighty miles from Baghdad, and not much farther from Kut-al-Amara). So obvious was Townshend's need for Russian relief that the Ottoman Sixth Army moved four whole battalions and twelve heavy guns from Baghdad toward the Persian frontier to face the Russians. So dangerous was the Russian threat, as seen from Baghdad, that von der Goltz Pasha gave this command to a German, Major Bopp, rather than a Turk.[49]

In a pattern that would have been painfully familiar to the British naval commanders at Gallipoli (had they paid closer attention), Baratov began looking for excuses almost immediately. Upon receiving his orders, he told Grand Duke Nicholas that he would not be able to march on Baghdad unless he was granted "time, means, and men"—only for Nicholas to reply that he "had none of these at his disposal." Baratov therefore chose to assemble his relief expedition out of "what forces and means I had"—mainly time, which Russian commanders always had in abundance. After prevaricating for three months, Baratov's men finally marched out of Kermanshah en route for Hanekin, which they reached on 25 April 1916. The Russian expeditionary force in Persia was now "only five days' march from Baghdad," which meant that the diversionary relief the British had requested could now materialize, just possibly, by about 30 April. Alas, this was not in time for poor Townshend or his starving men, who had surrendered to Halil "Kut" Pasha (von der Goltz having succumbed to typhus) the day before Baratov promised to reach Baghdad, 29 April 1916.[50]

In a cruel replay of the Gallipoli campaign, the Russians had arrived late to the British funeral again. Except that they did not, in fact, arrive at all: Baratov, having learned of Townshend's surrender by radio, feared that his horses would not find forage in Mesopotamia and that his Cossacks would not be able to handle the heat (some 500 had died on the march from Kermanshah to Hanekin). He decided not to march on Baghdad after all.* Under pressure from the British to help salvage something from the wreckage of Kut, in late May 1916 Stavka ordered Baratov, once again, to push on into Mesopotamia, toward Mosul, to "[relieve] the English, operating along the Tigris river below Kut-al-Amara." Citing, again, issues of climate and morale—malaria and cholera were sapping the strength of his evidently not-so-hardy Cossacks—Baratov again disobeyed his orders and chose to retreat into the cooler mountains of Luristan.

In Baratov's defense, he did engage the Turks while withdrawing from the border town of Hanekin, claiming (somewhat speciously) that his forces had seen off "four Ottoman infantry divisions" and "slaughter[ed] a whole battalion" before conducting a methodical tactical retreat. By the end of June, Baratov had established a Russian defensive line centered on Hamadan, guarding all the approaches to Kazvin and Teheran. He was able to accomplish this, he later boasted, despite "not receiving a single man of reinforcements" from Tiflis command. Having evidently forgotten (or forgiven) Baratov's insubordination, which had anyhow only harmed the British, Grand Duke Nicholas even sent him a congratulatory telegram in July 1916, saluting Baratov's expeditionary force for the "supreme valor" it had displayed *(sverkhdoblestnyimi)*.[51]

Just as at Gallipoli, Russia's diversionary "contribution" did not amount to much. The reason Grand Duke Nicholas was unable to send Baratov the reinforcements that—the latter claimed—he would have

---

* Baratov may have had another reason for holding back. Yudenich had recently informed him that, following the British withdrawal from Gallipoli in January, the Germans had transferred every officer they had to Baghdad, along with "150 machine-guns of the latest type." It is little wonder that Baratov was so reluctant to relieve the British forces.

needed to properly relieve Townshend was that Tiflis command had decided to mount a major operation in eastern Turkey instead, to which it devoted 200,000 men and most of its mobile artillery. Under General Nikolai Yudenich (who commanded under Grand Duke Nicholas), a furious Russian offensive began on 10 January 1916 that breached the Turks' defensive "Köprüköy" lines a week later. The Russians then laid siege to Erzurum, headquarters of the Ottoman Third Army. This imposing fortress city fell on 16 February. The retreating Turkish forces, under Mahmut Kamil Pasha, just barely escaped encirclement. Farther north, the Russians advanced along the Black Sea, capturing Rize in March and on 16 April the crucial port city of Trabzon, whence the Ottoman Third Army's seaborne supplies came. Erzincan fell on 25 July 1916. By the time the dust settled in autumn, the Russians were encamped at Erzincan, Muş, and Bitlis, threatening Sivas and the main road to Ankara. The Ottoman Third Army was "all but destroyed" by the Caucasian army in 1916, losing some 100,000 men and most of its guns.[52]

The Russians had thus mounted their long-awaited Turkish offensive in January 1916—the very month Britain requested that Baratov relieve Townshend at Kut-al-Amara. Baratov himself claimed that such a relief mission was impossible because Grand Duke Nicholas had told him Tiflis command could not spare troops, evidently because of the ongoing eastern Turkish offensive. It is curious that the fall of Erzurum, because dramatized in Buchan's novel *Greenmantle,* is the only significant military development on the Russo-Ottoman front of the First World War with which most English-speakers are familiar. Buchan's readers, however, remain just as unenlightened about the impact of the Erzurum offensive on the simultaneous siege of Kut-al-Amara as most Gallipoli buffs are about the Russian no-show at the Bosphorus. The parallel runs deeper still. Just as Eberhart had promised to send his men to occupy Constantinople as soon as the British and French had won it for him, so would Baratov, having cut off his half-hearted diversionary offensive on Baghdad after hearing of Townshend's surrender on 29 April 1916, later resume his aborted march into Mesopotamia—not in January-February 1917, when the British requested it, but only at the end of March, after Baghdad had fallen to the British.[53]

When it came to inter-Allied obligations (and those to beleaguered enemy minorities like the Armenians), timing was not Russia's strong suit. The crushing Caucasian offensive of 1916 would have greatly pleased the British, had it been mounted in November 1914 (as per Grey's request that the Russians focus their fire on eastern Turkey, rather than being drawn into Persia) or still more in spring 1915, when it could have taken pressure off the French and British during the Dardanelles and Gallipoli offensives. It would have pleased Ottoman Armenians still more, had it been launched at any time before the insurrections of March-April 1915 had pried loose the genie of minority sedition in eastern Turkey, with such fateful consequences.

Instead the Russians launched their Erzurum offensive only in January 1916, after hundreds of thousands of Ottoman Armenians had perished. The timing, vis-à-vis Gallipoli, is more shocking still: the great Russian offensive began on 10 January 1916, the day after the last British soldier left Cape Helles. Having twiddled their thumbs for fourteen months, the Russians suddenly did not wish to wait any longer, hoping to capture Erzurum before the Turks could route reinforcements from Gallipoli.

Despite his poor timing, Baratov had played no small role in the turn-around of Entente fortunes in the world war. With the rout of the Germans and Turks in Persia, land bridge to India, any lingering fantasies German pan-Islamists still entertained about unleashing a holy war from Afghanistan against the British Raj were put to rest. Niedermayer and his fellow German jihadists were rounded up one by one in 1916, most of them on Persian soil, as tribesmen sensed which way the wind was blowing in the world war.[54] The humiliating Allied withdrawal from Gallipoli in January 1916, along with Townshend's wretched surrender at Kut-al-Amara in April, both dealt serious blows to British prestige in the Near East—but this would soon be countered by the surge in Russian prestige following the fall of "impregnable" Erzurum, along with Erzincan and Trabzon. It was likely a matter of indifference to Sazonov, Yudenich, and Baratov, if not also the sentimental Grand Duke Nicholas, whether Britain would recover its regional footing. With or without British help, and whether or not there would be any Ottoman Christians left alive to welcome them, the age-old Russian dream of carving up Asiatic Turkey was finally coming into focus. It was time to draw up a blueprint of the postwar world.

CHAPTER EIGHT

Partitioning the Ottoman Empire

The entire territory between the Black Sea and a line beginning at
Urmia province . . . below Van, through Bitlis, Muş and Kharput
(Elâzığ), up to the mountain range of Tavra and Antitavra [near
Sivas]—must be placed at Russia's disposal in order to demarcate
the [borders] with the future Turkish Sultan of Anatolia.
—S. D. Sazonov, March 1916[1]

S ERGEI SAZONOV HAD NEVER been particularly shy about Russia's
desire to dismember Turkey. Although at times delegating the "bad
cop" role to Krivoshein, who had more of a reputation for bellicosity,
Russia's foreign minister had been fairly up front as early as August 1914
about the war aim of seizing the Straits. Tsar Nicholas II's formal sovereign demand for postwar control of Constantinople and the Straits (along
with Imbros and Tenedos, Asiatic Turkey up to the Sakarya River, and
European Thrace up to the Enos-Midia lines), delivered by Sazonov to
his ambassadors on 4 March 1915, should not therefore have come as a
great surprise to anyone in Paris or London.[2]

Sazonov's historic aide-mémoire does, however, seem to have offended
French and British sensibilities in its deeply inappropriate timing. It was
issued at the height of the increasingly bloody Dardanelles campaign, to
which Russia had not yet contributed a thing. Even the cynical Paléologue was taken aback, especially after Sazonov issued his threat on 5
March 1915, the day after lodging the tsar's demand, that if the Allies did
not agree he would resign and bring the Germanophile Sergei Witte into
the government in order to cut a separate peace with Germany.[3] Sir Ed-

ward Grey, too, was perturbed by the timing of Sazonov's demand (the gist of which the French had passed on to London), but in the by-now-familiar pattern of British ventriloquism, instead of standing firm he took on Sazonov's view as his own. As Grey later recalled the argument he put to the Cabinet, if Britain did not accede to Russia's demands, then Germanophile conservatives like Witte would persuade the tsar that "It had always been British policy to keep Russia out of Constantinople and the Straits . . . of course it was our policy still."[4] On this curious logic the British Cabinet, on 12 March 1915, adopted the position of endorsing Russia's every imperial claim on Constantinople and the Straits, despite her having done nothing to acquire them, in order to deprive a phantom would-be government in Russia of the argument that Britain would not, in fact, give them to her. When it came to Russia's wartime diplomacy, the old canard was true: truth was stranger than fiction.

The French, as usual, drove a harder bargain. Paléologue, in the face of Sazonov's threat to resign, issued his own aide-mémoire on 8 March 1915 endorsing Russia's claims on Constantinople and the Straits in principle. But he stopped short of formally endorsing Sazonov's 4 March memorandum as a matter of official French policy, linking Russian demands to British and French claims in the Levant, all of which must equally await "the conclusion of a final peace treaty."[5] In view of France's dominant financial position in Turkey, on 12 March 1915 Paléologue also made his own demands on Constantinople (insisting strongly against blanket Russian usurpations of property), taking care to include British interests as well. Each of the three Allied powers, France's ambassador insisted, would have its own "high commissioner" in the occupied capital, divided into zones of occupation. In part because he had anticipated French resistance, Sazonov had already drawn up a partition plan for Constantinople, which he now modified to meet Paléologue's criteria. The idea was for the British to occupy the Asian side of the city ("Scutari," or modern Üsküdar), and the French the old European quarter of Pera (modern Beyoğlu, from Karaköy through Galata and Taksim, up to Ortaköy on the Bosphorus coast). In addition to the Straits, Russia would content herself with "only" Stambul—that is, the ancient city of Byzantium, from Topkapı palace to the walls of Theodosius, an area that housed all the important Orthodox religious sites, from the Chora church to the Orthodox Patriarchate and the Hagia Sofia.[6] Having held out long enough to squeeze these concessions from Sazonov (along with Russia's acceptance of French claims on Syria, the Hatay, and much of Ottoman Cilicia, granted by the tsar on 16 March 1915), Paléologue at last endorsed the original 4 March Sazonov aide-mémoire on the Straits and Constantinople in a "Note Verbale" dated 10 April 1915, having defended British interests more ably than had the British themselves.[7]

In spite of a bit of French resistance, Russian diplomatic bullying had paid off again. Still, even Sazonov had the sense to tone things down once the souring of the Gallipoli campaign in summer 1915 had made it clear that the Straits, much less Constantinople, European Thrace, and Asiatic Turkey, were not about to be conquered in the near future. With Russia's postwar claims to these territories already secured in writing, there was no need to press for more—nor, evidently, to put up any effort to actually secure them while her Allies were making such a heroic effort to do the job. Besides, for the Russians to demand yet more Turkish territory even while Stavka was conducting its "great retreat" in eastern Europe, very nearly losing the war to Germany, would have been a step too far even for Sazonov. On the Ottoman front, meanwhile, 1915 had begun promisingly enough for the Entente with Sarıkamış and the Dardanelles campaign, but by year's end the Turks had mostly turned the tables. With Serbia overwhelmed by the combined forces of Austria-Hungary, Germany, and (after it entered the war on their side in October) Bulgaria, an uninterrupted rail and communications link was opened up between Berlin and Constantinople for the first time, which effectively sealed the doom of the Allied armies at Gallipoli, just as Townshend's men were being surrounded at Kut.

Despite Britain's continued difficulties in the East, however, in Russia's own war against Turkey the prospects began to look brighter than ever before with the Erzurum offensive. This strategic fact bears emphasis, for the "Sykes-Picot Agreement" was in fact drawn up against the backdrop of Russia's victories in Turkey in spring 1916.[8] Indeed, the story of the diplomatic partition of the Ottoman Empire would make little sense otherwise, as the period of the principal inter-Allied negotiations (January-April 1916) coincided with Britain's two greatest humiliations of the world war, the withdrawals from Gallipoli and Kut, the latter witnessing "the largest mass surrender of [British] troops between Yorktown in 1783 and Singapore in 1942"—both suffered at the hands of Turkey.[9] On what logical grounds would Sykes (representing a power losing on all fronts in the Ottoman theater) and Picot (a power engaged in a limited supporting role in Gallipoli, until that campaign ended in disgrace) have decided that this—winter 1916—was the time to partition the Ottoman Empire?

The real inspiration for the Sykes-Picot Agreement, at least from the English end, was Kitchener's fear that Russia would reemerge as Britain's primary antagonist after the world war was over, the idea being to create a French buffer zone in between the old Great Game antagonists. In the original Sykes-Picot draft, ratified bilaterally on 10 February 1916, Britain agreed to "give" France Syria, Lebanon, and Cilicia (extending all the way from the Taurus mountains, through northern Mesopotamia up to the Persian border) in exchange for French recognition of British primacy in Mesopotamia south of Mosul, the "Palestinian" ports of Acre and Haifa, and (through Arab proxies) Arabia—despite France not being expected to conquer its own share. Just as with Kitchener's "offer" of the Caliphate to Hussein of Mecca, the British were bequeathing things that did not belong to them, rather as Paléologue and Tsar Nicholas II had traded imaginary horses back in November 1914.[10]

At least at this initial stage, the dynamics of the Sykes-Picot Agreement represented an intriguing reversal of Dardanelles diplomacy. True, the French were playing essentially the same game both times, demanding Cilicia, Lebanon, and Syria even while promising to contribute virtually nothing to any campaign that might conquer them. But with Britain and Russia, the diplomatic poles had reversed, with the former foisting far-reaching claims on Ottoman territory while the latter was actually doing the heavy lifting in the theater. Had the reverse Gallipoli parallel continued on like this, the negotiations over Sykes-Picot in spring 1916 would have seen Russia continue to do the hard work of destroying Ottoman power on the battlefield while France and Britain jockeyed to claim the choicest morsels of Turkish territory, offering the Russians only her token occupation zone of Constantinople (Stambul and environs).

The Russians, however, were not as easy to manipulate during their own offensive as the British had been at the Dardanelles. Sazonov was ready to pounce when Sykes and Picot arrived in Petrograd in March 1916, having prepared even more thoroughly than usual for the meeting. To see where the Russians were coming from, we must pause here to examine the well-known but little-understood "Djemal peace offer" of winter 1915–16, which ran parallel to the Sykes-Picot negotiations and, in a sense, overlay them. According to a well-varnished legend, Djemal Pasha, who, as commander of the Ottoman Fourth Army in Damascus, was the virtual dictator of Syria, Lebanon, and Palestine during the First World War, offered in December 1915 to "take measures for the safety of Armenians" if the Allies would help him march on Constantinople and depose the CUP government, thus creating a new hereditary sultanate for Djemal and his sons. Giving this claim at least superficial plausibility, Djemal's message was supposedly delivered to the Russian Foreign Ministry by Dr. Hakob Zavriev, an Ottoman Armenian originally hailing from Muş who was now holed up in Bucharest. Zavriev had close ties to the Dashnaks and claimed to speak on behalf of "Armenian circles in Constantinople." The idea promoted by Zavriev, who had written to Petrograd by way of the Russian minister in Bucharest, was to give Djemal enough arms to enable him to seize Constantinople by force. In exchange for Allied help in winning Djemal a restored empire, Djemal would grant autonomy to Turkish Armenia and cede Constantinople and the Straits to Russia. Alas, as the story usually goes, the Djemal-Zavriev peace initiative broke down on the shoals of French stubbornness: Paris would not agree to give up its claims on Cilicia and Syria.[11]

Intriguing though it is, there was always something fishy about the whole story. To date no one has unearthed the slightest bit of evidence that Zavriev spoke on Djemal's authority, a notion Turkish historians treat as too incredible to be indulged seriously. To begin with, it defies belief that a would-be Turkish sultan would willingly forfeit the Ottoman capital to the *Russians*. Despite a certain reputation for Francophilia (he did speak passable French), Djemal had in fact turned sharply in the other direction after he discovered documents in the French consulate in Damascus (sacked following Turkey's entry into the war in November 1914) linking Paris to Arab nationalist rebels. Djemal had no great love for the English, either: in December 1914 he was even rebuked by Talaat, the interior minister, for using British civilians in Damascus as human shields against a naval attack on the Lebanese coastline. As Colonel Kress, Djemal's German liaison officer, wrote after working closely with him for nearly the entire duration of the First World War, Djemal was "neither pro-German nor pro-Entente, rather he was a Turk, filled with a burning sense of Turkish patriotism."[12] As for the Russians to whom Djemal supposedly wished to give Constantinople and the Straits, meanwhile, there has never been any evidence that Djemal viewed them with the slightest sympathy.

When we look more closely at the messenger(s) Djemal supposedly used, the story grows less plausible still. Why, if Djemal wished to pass such a sensitive message on to the Allies—a message he surely would have wished dearly to conceal from the CUP government in the capital—would he have transmitted it through "Armenian circles in Constantinople," who in turn forwarded it to Zavriev, in Bucharest, of all places? It would have been far simpler for Djemal to submit his ostensible peace offer directly by courier to the Russian Tiflis command, which would have been much faster and infinitely harder for the Ottoman government to intercept than routing it through "Armenian circles" in the capital via Romania. Particularly when we recall that Armenian rebels from Van and Zeytun had no difficulty getting secret messages of all kinds to the Russian Caucasian command, it would hardly have been difficult for Djemal, the most powerful man in Ottoman Syria, to pull off the same feat.

The available evidence gives us no reason to believe that Djemal was an active party in the December 1915 peace parley. The only documents in the Russian Foreign Ministry archives relating to the affair bear not Djemal's signature (original or reproduced) but rather that of Dr. Zavriev, who turns out on closer inspection to have been more a habitué of the Russian Foreign Ministry (he was a graduate at the Russian Army Medical Academy in St. Petersburg) than a spokesman for anyone inside Turkey. Dr. Zavriev was a classic wartime intriguer-opportunist, who had begun waving schemes for Armenian autonomy before the Russians in March 1915, at which time he was still in Petrograd.[13] Seeing a possible use for the Armenian conspirator in winning concessions over "Turkish Armenia" from the western Allies, Sazonov's deputy A. A. Neratov had dispatched Zavriev to London and Paris in April 1915.[14] In June 1915, Zavriev teamed up with Boghos Nubar Pasha, the Egyptian-born head of the "Armenian National Delegation," which functioned as a kind of semiofficial Armenian liaison to the western governments, only for the two to run afoul of Paris over claims for an independent Cilicia (which territory the French government wished to rule itself).[15] For the next six months, Dr. Zavriev dropped off the diplomatic radar, only to emerge mysteriously at the Russian Legation in Bucharest in December, bearing his astonishing offer from Djemal.

There was a curious discrepancy in the new proposal, however, which should have given the game away. Why was "Djemal"—said Zavriev—willing to utterly renounce any future Ottoman claim on the Straits and Constantinople, but not on Cilicia, Lebanon, Syria, Mesopotamia, or Arabia? Why was this new offer, that is, so perfectly tailored to *Russian*, but not British and French, territorial ambitions? One explanation is that Djemal had grown accustomed to ruling Syria, and aimed to make Damascus his capital. But if this were true, then why was "Djemal" asking for guns, artillery, and ammunition so that he could march all the way from Damascus to Constantinople—after which time he would supposedly hand over the conquered capital to the Russians?

The entire Djemal Pasha scheme was clearly a concoction of the Russian Foreign Ministry—of, it appears, Sazonov himself. With mischievous timing, Sazonov sent Djemal's mythical peace offer to his ambassadors in Paris and London on 25 December 1915 (according to the Gregorian calendar used in the West, not the Julian one used in Orthodox Russia), hoping, evidently, that the British and French might not wish to look a Christmas gift horse too closely in the mouth.[16]

Sazonov's motive should not be hard to fathom. From Zavriev's prior initiatives, the Russians had learned that the French were probably going to stand firm on Cilicia. Sazonov's "Djemal" trial balloon appears as a feint, designed to tease out French and British intentions toward partitioning Turkey—or more likely, to drive a wedge between Paris and London over these plans. Sazonov knew that the negotiations in Paris between Sykes and Picot had bogged down earlier in December; his Christmas Day offer was issued while Sykes was back in London, receiving further instructions.[17] To a considerable extent Sazonov succeeded, as serious negotiations over the (in fact mythical) Djemal peace deal continued for weeks. The British Foreign Office did not finally rule out the idea of cutting a deal with Djemal (on the grounds that doing so might compromise obligations undertaken to the Arabs) until 23 January 1916, in the process delaying the ratification of the bilateral Sykes-Picot Agreement for at least a month.[18] The French, by contrast, had ruled out a peace deal at the end of December 1915, going along with the idea of initiating talks with Djemal mostly to humor the English, who were, as always, the last to cotton to the game.[19]

Sazonov, it is true, was unable to manipulate France's Foreign Ministry into forfeiting its claims on Cilicia, which must have been the ultimate goal of the Djemal feint. Even the English had showed some backbone in the end—although it took them, characteristically, almost four weeks longer to do so than the French. Still, if nothing else, the various Russian "Zavriev" and "Djemal" trial balloons had put French greed and stubbornness over Cilicia on display for months—not least to the English, whom Sazonov had set up as a perfect diplomatic foil.

Just as we would expect, Picot found a much cooler reception in Petrograd than did Sykes. The Russian Foreign Ministry journal entry (or "diary," literally) for the initial tripartite meeting held on 9 March 1916 notes that "Sir Mark Sykes, with his openness of character, his thorough knowledge and his clearly favorable disposition towards Russia has made the best possible impression on the Foreign Minister. But we cannot say the same for M. Picot, who demonstrated to Sazonov, in the narrowness of his outlook, shades of a certain clericalism." This, moreover, was the diary record of Sazonov's reactions merely after the men had exchanged pleasantries. Sazonov liked Picot even less after the actual business at hand was discussed, contrasting the "extremely favorable impression" Sykes made with his presentation to the "vague account Picot gave of himself," which left "frankly the opposite impression."[20]

In the rarified world of Old World diplomacy, this was virtually a declaration of war. Picot, naturally, brought in reinforcements, calling in Paléologue and Buchanan to sit in on the meetings held the next day, 10 March 1916. A diplomatic struggle of excruciating precision now ensued, with Picot and Paléologue insisting that any bilateral agreements ratified between Sykes and Picot were "like a done deal" which could not now be altered (*comme une chose faite,* or in Russian, *kak delo reshennoe*) or, if the Russians and English preferred, merely "a completed arrangement"

(*arrangement fait,* or in Russian, *zaklyuchennom soglashenii*). Buchanan now chimed in with his own formulation, that of a "decided on affair" (*affaire faite* or, in Russian, *reshennomu delu*)—before noting that, even to this, he was not authorized by London to stipulate.[21]

With the wedge between Sykes and Picot now firmly in place, Sazonov was ready to strike. Showing that he was a professional where the over-matched Briton was an amateur, Sazonov actually *ordered* Sykes to draw up a new map meeting Russia's key demands, including the incorporation of "Turkish Armenia" (or "Kurdistan," depending on demographic taste) as far south as the Bitlis passes in the Taurus mountains and as far east as Lake Urmia, which area had, in the 10 February draft, been placed in the French "blue" zone. Sykes did as he was told, drawing up a new map submitted to Sazonov in the presence of Sir George Buchanan on 11 March 1916 with the "blue" area erased and with a new eastern boundary of the French zone at the Tigris River. As a sop to Paris, the Sivas area, including a triangle formed by Sivas-Kharput-Kayseri, was now colored blue, in a curious and possibly cynical cartographical non sequitur, as it would bring the French zone so far north that it would envelop the new Russian provinces of eastern Anatolia. Meekly, Sykes told Sazonov that he "hoped that all such changes would be acceptable to France, because of his previous discussions with Picot." But neither Picot nor Paléologue, crucially, had been allowed in the room as all this took place. Not unlike Korostovets working over Townley in Teheran, Sazonov had forced Sykes to think like a Russian: he would now present Russia's own arguments to the French.[22] Or as Sazonov himself gloated to his aides after watching Sykes draw up Russia's own desired map of conquest, following his "conversations with Buchanan and Sykes [he] had the distinct impression, that the English government on its part does not look sympathetically on too deep a French penetration into Asia Minor."[23]

Sazonov's chief point of contention with the French was over "Turkish Armenia," or, to put it another way, those few areas of eastern Turkey that Russia had not yet conquered. The Erzurum offensive was at this stage (in March 1916) pitched mostly to the north, with the Russians advancing along the Black Sea coast towards Rize and Trabzon. Not until the latter fell, cutting off the main seaborne supply route for the Ottoman Third Army, did the Russians wheel south to take Erzincan, Muş, and Bitlis.

Sazonov did not need to ask for British or French permission to annex northeastern Anatolia: most of it was already under Russian military occupation. What concerned him was the "Armenian" area abutting northern Mesopotamia and Persia, which Sykes (channeling Kitchener's desire for a strong buffer zone, and also the strong current of Armenophilia in France) had apportioned to the French zone of influence.

The issue of who "protected" the Armenians of Cilicia was essentially academic to the British, who viewed the whole matter with something of the sentimental abstraction that later characterized the Balfour Declaration. For the Russians, and only slightly less so for the French, the Armenian question was deadly serious business, because it touched on sovereign claims over territory, in the former case encompassing nearly all of eastern Turkey, in the latter case Ottoman Cilicia (control over which would allow France to dominate the entire eastern Mediterranean littoral above Palestine—or ideally, if Britain would budge on the latter, all the way down to Egypt). So far from realizing the serious imperial stakes he was playing with, Sykes tried to get the Russians to sign off on a French protectorate over the "historical Armenian cities" of Zeytun and Diarbakır on the grounds that the last Armenian king had died in Paris in 1393.[24]

As if his amateurish approach to the Armenian question was not enough, Sykes now introduced the classic wartime British red herring into the discussion of partitioning Turkey: Palestine and the Jews. For reasons best known to themselves, a growing number of British leaders became convinced in 1916–17 that an endorsement of Zionism by His Majesty's Government could have a material impact on the world war by winning over world Jewry to the Entente side. Sykes's own interest was apparently piqued (in characteristically haphazard fashion) by a single conversation with Captain William Reginald Hall on the subject shortly before he set out for Petrograd. Although he had not spoken of Zionism in the first discussions at the Russian Foreign Ministry, on 13 March 1916 Sykes and Buchanan received instructions from Sir Edward Grey to raise the issue with the Russians, Grey himself having been induced to do this after he received a pleading letter from a Jewish journalist, Lucien Wolf. Wolf, perhaps unbeknownst to Grey, Buchanan, and Sykes, was known to most English Jews as "Public Enemy Number One of the Tsarist Government." Grey's instructions were predictably vague: Buchanan and Sykes were to "demand that the Russian government take a serious approach to this question and favor [us] if possible in the near future with a statement of the Russian point of view."[25]

To demonstrate Russia's good faith, all Sazonov was required to do was "take a serious approach to the question" and give Sykes and Buchanan his "point of view." Taking his most obliging tone, Sazonov promptly reported that "the Russian government would agree to any plan" for Palestine, so long as Russia's traditional "rights and privileges" pertaining to Orthodox holy sites there were protected. (Sykes may not have known that "rights and privileges" was a loaded phrase—used by the French to justify their claims on Lebanon and Syria, just as Napoleon III had once asserted similar "rights and privileges" over Levantine "holy places," sparking the Crimean War.) Just as a gentle reminder, Sazonov linked even this conditional and possibly loaded pledge of support for British (or French) claims on Palestine to "the fulfillment of the agreement made by France and England relating to Constantinople and the Straits."[26]

Having given the British the minimal cooperation they had asked for, Sazonov now named his price. Sykes was summoned to the Foreign Ministry several days later (on 17 March 1916) and asked, apropos of nothing in particular, what his view would be if someone (Sazonov did not say who) would build a strategic railway between Trabzon and Ankara, passing through "the territorial area between Sivas, Kharput, and Kayseri." This area, assuming Sykes had not forgotten, the Russians had supposedly agreed to cede to France. Apparently without giving the matter any thought, Sykes assented immediately *(otvetil utverditel'no)*.[27]

With the Caucasian army advancing along the Black Sea coast, the Russians, unbeknownst to either Picot or Sykes, were planning to incorporate the entire northeastern quadrant of Asia Minor into the empire—and wanted to see what objections Britain or France might raise. At a secret high-level meeting reminiscent of the famous February 1914 planning conference, on 30 March 1916 Sazonov summoned to the Foreign Ministry I. K. Grigorevich, the naval minister; from Stavka, General Beliaev and Generalmajor Leontiev (the former military attaché in Turkey); and the new chairman of the Council of Ministers, Boris Stürmer. Together with the Foreign Ministry's own Ottoman and Persian experts, these men now drew up Russia's strategic blueprint for the postwar occupation of Asiatic Turkey.

All in attendance were agreed that the original Sykes-Picot draft could not stand. While willing to concede English pretensions about a new "Arab caliphate," Zionism, and to cede Palestine to French or English control (with protections for traditional Russian prerogatives over Orthodox holy sites), Russia's leaders agreed unanimously that the French zone must not include Urmia province or the Taurus mountains. Sazonov would not sign any agreement that did not "give to Russia possession of the important [mountain] passes and crossings." As for the north and western boundaries of Russia's Turkish annexations, Grigorevich was adamant that Russia extend control of the Black Sea littoral past Trabzon (which fell just two weeks after this meeting) and Samsun, all the way to Sinop, the city that marks roughly the Anatolian halfway point between Batum and Constantinople, north-northwest of Ankara. Sinop was important not only strategically, as a kind of peninsular outcropping that dominated a large swathe of the Black Sea in both directions, but also historically, as the scene of major naval battles—most recently in 1853, when the Russians had destroyed the Ottoman Black Sea fleet there at the onset of the Crimean War. (More recently, Sinop was an important listening post for American intelligence on the USSR during the Cold War.) Above all, Grigorevich emphasized, Sinop provided the "best natural harbor" along the Anatolian Black Sea coast and was located on almost exactly the same north-south meridian as Sevastopol, just 180 miles away. With Sinop in the Russian sphere, the Russian fleet would dispose of the impregnable strategic triangle of Sevastopol-Constantinople-Sinop, which would scare off any future Romanian or Bulgarian naval threat to Russia's domination of the Black Sea.[28]

Convincing as Grigorevich was on the strategic point about Sinop, Sazonov saw political problems. Whatever rump version of the Ottoman Empire emerged out of the wreckage of the war, after all, would have to be put *somewhere*. If the Russians took over Sinop and its hinterland, Sazonov warned in a revealing turn of phrase, it would effectively be "seizing from neighboring Turkey a province with a native Ottoman population" (in other words, of Turkish Muslims), which would "of course

ROMANIA
Bucharest
Constanta
Danube
Varna
Sevastopol
proposed lines of Russian naval communications

Black Sea

BULGARIA

Adrianople (Edirne)
Midia

GREECE
Enos

R

Constantinople
Izmit
Bursa
Edremit

Kastamonu
Sinop
Samsun
planned French railway Diarbakır – Sivas – Samsun
Giresun

planned Russian railway Trabzon–Sivas–Ankara

Aegean Sea

Sakarya
Eskişehir
Ankara
Kızılırmak
Sivas

Smyrna (Izmir)
Afyon

OTTOMAN EMPIRE
Konya
Kayseri
Malatya

F1

Zeytun
Maraş
CILICIA
Adana

Taurus Mountains

Alexandretta

Amanus Mtns.

Aleppo

SYRIA

Cyprus (British)

Mediterranean Sea

Beirut
Damascus

C

Alexandria
Gaza
Jerusalem

EGYPT
(under Direct British rule)
Cairo

B1	Red Zone: Area of direct British Control
B2	"B" Zone: Area of indirect British Control
F1	Blue Zone: Area of direct French Control
F2	"A" Zone: Area of indirect French Control
R	Areas of direct Russian Control

0   250 miles

The Partition of the Ottoman Empire by Sazonov, Sykes, and Picot, 1916

RUSSIAN EMPIRE

Caucasus Mountains

Caspian Sea

Batum
Rize
Trabzon
Artvin
Ardahan
Olty
Sarıkamış
Kars
Gizman (Kâğızman)
Yerevan
Igdyr (Iğdir)
Tiflis
Baku
Kura
Araks

Erzincan
Erzurum
"TURKISH ARMENIA"

R

Muş
L. Van
Van
Hoy
Kharput
Bitlis
Siirt
"KURDISTAN"
Dilman
Tabriz
L. Urmia
PERSIAN AZERBAIJAN
Diarbakır
Urfa
Ras ul-Ain

Mosul

Tehran

Der Zor

F2

Tigris
Euphrates

P E R S I A

B2

MESOPOTAMIA
Baghdad
Isfahan

B1

Basrah
Persian Gulf

become the cause of endless misunderstandings and tensions."[29] It was a curious point to make, considering that neither Sazonov nor anyone else in Petrograd had seen the sentiments of the "native population" as a problem regarding Russia's proposed seizure of Constantinople, Thrace, the "Trojan" peninsula opposite Gallipoli, Imbros, Tenedos, Van, Bitlis, Erzurum, Trabzon, Erzincan, and so on. Still, one must grant the foreign minister at least this small dose of realism in constraining Russia's ambitions in partitioning Turkey.

One should not go too far, however, in crediting Sazonov with newfound concern for the views of the people of the country Russia was conquering. His primary worry remained the clash with France over territorial claims and concessions. Demanding Sinop would be a diplomatic step too far, which would make it harder to get France to sign off on Russia's claims over Urmia and the Taurus mountain passes, not to mention the Russian line from Trabzon to Ankara, which might compete with the planned French railway from Diarbakır to Samsun via Sivas.[30] After hearing out the military men, Sazonov wrote up a "compromise" proposal to Paléologue on 26 April 1916, declaring that "Russia will annex the provinces of Erzurum, Trabzon, Van and Bitlis up to a point along the Black Sea coast to the west of Trabzon." In addition, Sazonov laid claim to what he called "the province of Kurdistan, lying south of Van and Bitlis, between Muş, Siirt, the course of the Tigris . . . and the line of the [Taurus] mountains," while conceding France the territory southwest of this, along the ragged line of the Taurus mountains from Aladağ through Akdağ (in Afyon province) to Kayseri and Sivas via Kharput (Elâzığ).[31]

While Sazonov's final proposal to the French represented a (slight) retreat from the more extreme positions advanced by Grigorevich at the planning conference, in fact he held firm to his own position, elucidated in an aide-mémoire signed by the tsar on 14 March 1916, that "the entire territory between the Black Sea and a line beginning at Urmia province, through . . . Van . . . Bitlis, Muş and Kharput (Elâzığ), up to the mountain range of Tavra and Antitavra (near Sivas)—must be placed at Russia's disposal."[32] The manipulation of Sykes in March, and the good cop/bad cop act over Sinop, had thrown a good deal of diplomatic smoke in the air, rather as the "Djemal peace offer" had done in December and January. But in the end, the Russian position had not budged one bit.

The French nonetheless put up a good fight. In principle Picot had agreed to go along with ceding "Kurdistan" to Russia in exchange for Kayseri-Sivas, but Sazonov had held out, going so far as to leak news of the "Sinop" discussions of 30 March 1916 to Paléologue to see if Paris would budge still further.[33] The French, too, were standing tough, insisting on linking the Turkish partition agreement to a Russian endorsement of Polish autonomy, an issue that was a personal obsession of Aristide Briand, who had taken over the government as both premier and foreign minister in October 1915. Reprising his tack of March 1915, when he had threatened to resign in favor of Witte if he did not get his way on Constantinople and the Straits, Sazonov warned Paléologue on 18 April 1916 that he was "going down a perilous path" in raising the Polish question. Napoleon III, he reminded the French ambassador, had done exactly the same thing in 1863, and this Polish flirtation had led inexorably to the "rupture of friendly relations between Russia and France" and, not incidentally, to the Franco-Prussian War and the French humiliation at Sedan.[34]

Browbeaten by Russian threats and isolated due to the British failure to fully underwrite the Sykes-Picot Agreement, the French finally gave in. On 26 April 1916, in a diplomatic "Note" reminiscent in tone of his reluctant acquiescence to Russia's claim on Constantinople and the Straits almost exactly one year earlier—in similar circumstances of Russian quasi-blackmail—Paléologue agreed to the terms of Sazonov's Ottoman partition plan. The French ambassador attached only the conditions that a "border commission" be appointed to work out the exact frontiers between the Russian and French zones in the Taurus mountains, and that Russia honor all French debt and other concessions entered into by the Ottoman government, including the proposed Diarbakır-Sivas-Samsun railway. Sazonov inserted a clever open-ended condition at this point, stipulating that, if Russia might later "express the desire that [such railway concessions] be later changed . . . this change will take place only in agreement with [France]." Significantly, there was no mention of the Russians' own Trabzon-Ankara railway. The Russians apparently planned to inform the French of their own railway plans at some later date—presumably after the line was already a fait accompli. With Sykes already won over to whatever Sazonov wanted, up to and including vague, unspecified

Russian strategic railway plans, the final Sykes-Picot (or, more accurately, "Sykes-Picot-Sazonov") Agreement partitioning Asiatic Turkey was ratified in Paris and London on 15–16 May 1916.[35]

In this way the three Entente powers, famously, divided up the Ottoman Empire among themselves, from the desert sands of Arabia to the Thracian plain guarding the European approaches to "Tsargrad." It goes without saying that the people living in the areas divvied up had no say in the agreement, aside from some ambiguous promises the British had made (through questionable intermediaries) to Sherif Hussein in case he launched an "Arab revolt" against the Ottoman Empire, and the even more ambiguous promises made thus far to Zionists regarding Palestine. Still, despite all the bad faith involved in dealings between Cairo, London, and the Hashemites of Mecca—and the even greater bad faith surrounding the Balfour Declaration of 1917—one must concede that the British at least *pretended* to care about the opinions and aspirations of the peoples of Arabia and Palestine (if not also Mesopotamia), whose territories London proposed to administer after the war. As for the French, it is an open question whether or not men like Picot sincerely believed, as they professed to, that the inhabitants of Syria, Palestine, and Cilicia were "unanimous" in desiring to be ruled from Paris. At least in the abstract, the French believed in popular sovereignty. While these territories remained under Ottoman control—as most of them would until 1918—how could Paris have canvassed the people to ascertain which ruler they preferred, anyway?[36]

The Russians did not have the excuse of ignorance. It is true that Kurdish and Armenian leaders had been petitioning the tsarist regime for years for help in overthrowing the Ottomans. Many Kurdish tribal chieftains had vowed fidelity to tsarist rule during the Balkan wars: so they could hardly complain now that Russia was asserting suzerainty over their lands. In the case of the Armenians, however, it was clear that they wanted the Russians to grant them autonomy, not subjugation to Russian rule. Dr. Zavriev, the semiofficial Armenian intriguer of the Russian Foreign Ministry, had, despite all his Russophilia, been consistent about this, even in the mythical "Djemal" deal Sazonov had concocted in his name. As for Boghos Nubar Pasha, he was adamant that any agreement between the Entente governments not violate the key principle of Armenian autonomy, as Izvolsky warned Petrograd from Paris on 1 May 1916—just four days after Sazonov and Paléologue had secretly conspired to do precisely that.[37]

The Russians, however, were not about to back down in the flush of diplomatic—and military—victory. With Caucasian army units advancing along the Black Sea coast all spring, even as the main thrust from Erzurum to Erzincan resumed in June, the military imperative argued against further indulgence of Armenian pretensions. On 18 June 1916, the Caucasian army wrote up a set of "Rules for the Temporary Administration of Turkish Areas occupied by the Right of War," a document reminiscent of the similar decree on occupied Galicia and just as dismissive of Armenian aspirations as the Galician one was of the Jews'. Painfully, considering all that Armenian revolutionaries and helpless civilians had risked and suffered during the world war, neither the term "Armenia" nor "Armenians" was mentioned, even once, in the rules.[38]

This was not the only bitter pill the Armenians were asked to swallow. Armenian partisans, despite playing a certain useful role for the Russians at Van and Bitlis in 1915, had long since worn out their welcome at Tiflis command, which kept hearing about the atrocities they were committing against Muslims. "The Armenians," General Pechkov wrote on 29 June 1916, "have shown themselves to be a very cruel people. It appears they have massacred the Kurds without pity."[39] Other reports spoke of rampant "lawlessness and looting" by Armenian volunteer units, which were now disbanded by direct order of Grand Duke Nicholas himself. Another decree from Tiflis command imposed "strict censorship on all Armenian publications." Adding insult to these measures, Russian commanders began turning away returning Armenian refugees if these did not have "valid property deeds," which few of them, driven from their homes in 1915 under conditions of acute duress, possessed.[40] In September 1916, an Armenian hailing from Van—the city that had shed so much blood on Russia's behalf in 1915—complained to Philips Price, the famous *Manchester Guardian* reporter who would later serve as Trotsky's channel for revealing Russia's darkest diplomatic secrets to the West, that the Russians were openly "scheming to colonize the most fertile plains of Alashkerd, Erzerum, Mush & c. in Turkish Armenia by Russian labour battalions and Cossacks."[41]

The cause of Armenian autonomy did have sympathizers in Petrograd (if not also in Tiflis). Pavel Miliukov, for one, founder of the Kadet Party, accused Yanushkevitch and Grand Duke Nicholas on the floor of the Duma of having proved "more friendly to [Kurds] than to our old friends [the Armenians]." (Miliukov likely did not know that the Caucasian army had been just as "friendly" to the Kurds as to Armenians).[42] Because Miliukov spoke for the increasingly influential Liberal bloc, Russia's foreign minister was willing to discuss Armenian complaints of bias and mistreatment, but only up to a point. In a letter dispatched to Tiflis on 27 June 1916, Sazonov reminded Grand Duke Nicholas that Russia had pushed for greater Armenian autonomy—under Ottoman rule—during the reform campaign of 1913–14. But now that the Armenians were under Russian suzerainty, things looked different. Making an argument conspicuously absent from prewar Russian diplomacy, Sazonov noted that "the Armenians nowhere constitute a majority" in the area he called "Greater Armenia"—particularly after the deportations of 1915. Armenians now comprised, even in the areas of their greatest concentration, at most 25 percent of the population. In view of this fact, for Russia to grant Armenian autonomy "would mean unjustly enslaving the majority to the minority." Tensions between Christians and Muslims would explode yet again, this time in Russia's face instead of Turkey's. An enduring peace would only be possible, Sazonov argued, if the tsarist government could rule "on the basis of its own laws, its own system of justice, and with complete impartiality towards all national elements in the land." Russia must treat everyone equally, without "offering exclusive patronage to one or another ethnic group at the expense of another" *(ne okazyivaya isklyuchitel'nogo pokrovitel'stva odnoi kakoi-libo narodnosti v ushcherb drogoi)*. The only concession Russia's foreign minister was willing to grant Armenians was to allow them to use their own language and to run their own churches and schools. However, other ethnic groups, too, would be given these rights "in accordance with their level of cultural development"—meaning that here, too, the Armenians were not supposed to be given special treatment.[43]

Grand Duke Nicholas agreed to all these stipulations. To show that he was not hostile to the Armenians as a people, he did tell Sazonov that the army was trying to streamline the process of resettling Armenian deportees, if only to improve agricultural productivity (as it was, the occupying army of Anatolia was struggling mightily to meet its requisitions needs).

So far, most of the land had been occupied instead by "unauthorized" colonists from Russia, the flow of which the commander wished to "dam up," as it was interfering with army logistics. Having thus adjudicated to the best of his abilities this still evidently smoldering issue, Grand Duke Nicholas told Sazonov that "It is my profound conviction that, within the bounds of the present Russian empire, *there is absolutely no Armenian question,* nor should mention of such a question even be permitted, for the Armenian subjects within the Viceroyalty are equally Russian subjects as are the Muslims, Georgians, and Russians."[44]

It was quite a fall. The Armenians of eastern Turkey, Sazonov's favorite political football in 1913-14, the key strategic ally for the Caucasian command at the onset of the war against Turkey in 1914-15, were now no more or less important to Tiflis command than were Georgians, who had ceased being a major foreign policy concern after their kingdom was incorporated into the tsarist empire in 1801. As Sazonov confessed in a follow-up letter to the grand duke, Russia's aim in "supporting the Armenians" all along had been simply "the weakening of Turkey" *(oslableniya Turtsii).*[45] As the Caucasian army raced victoriously ahead toward Erzincan, Sivas, and Ankara, even as the simultaneous Brusilov offensive of June 1916 in Galicia nearly broke the back of Austria-Hungary, the Armenian question that had obsessed Russia's diplomats and Caucasian generals for decades was squarely in the rearview mirror.

Of course, Russia's great offensives of 1916, perhaps inevitably in a war in which defenders were always at an advantage, had largely petered out by the end of the summer. By August the Austrians had been saved, again, by German reinforcements,[46] even as a reconstituted Ottoman Second Army, headquartered at Diarbakır, was able to relieve pressure on Sivas with a counterattack on the Russians' southern flank in August-September. Still, with the Ottoman Third Army a shell of its former self after its crushing losses in 1916, the road to Ankara would likely be opened as soon as Russia's spring offensive commenced. From there, the Caucasian army could simply hop on the German-built railhead to Constantinople, less than a day's journey away. It looked like only a matter of time before Turkey gave up the ghost and "Tsargrad" was conquered at long last. Little did the Russians know that, with a historic victory squarely in sight, the ground was beginning to shake beneath their feet.

CHAPTER NINE

1917

The Tsarist Empire at Its Zenith

[It would be] absurd and criminal to renounce the biggest prize of the war . . . in the name of some humanitarian and cosmopolitan idea of international socialism.

—Pavel Miliukov, March 1917[1]

Until the end of my days I will hold sacred in the depths of my heart and soul the memory of all of you who stood by my side, as, with the will of Divine Providence, with success, honor, and glory, we carried out our predetermined Great Power mission in the name of Great Russia in the historical path of Alexander the Great.

—Cavalry-General N. N. Baratov, June 1918[2]

FOR THE WESTERN ALLIES, 1916 had not been a terribly happy year. Millions of young Britons and Frenchmen were mired for much of the year in two of the most colossal—and colossally wasteful—trench campaigns of all time, at Verdun (February to December) and the Somme (July to November). That the first of these terrible battles of attrition was occasioned by a German offensive and the second by a Franco-British one mattered less than that both of them were equally futile and destructive of human life. Future generations would marvel at the way wave after wave of men was ordered to advance against murderous machine-gun fire, all to gain a few square yards of what was now little more than a muddy, barbed wire–strewn wasteland. Making matters still worse, the damage to Allied shipping wrought by German submarine torpedoes was eating into civilian morale in England and France, even as the British blockade was at last beginning to put the squeeze on the Central powers' food imports, leading to the terrible German "turnip winter" of 1916-17. In such unpromising circumstances, scapegoats were inevitably sought out and punished. On the German General Staff, Erich von Falkenhayn was forced to make way for Hindenburg (in reality, Erich Ludendorff), while on the Allied side, civilian politicians took most of the heat. The prevaricating Liberal Herbert Asquith made way for the ruthless pragmatist Lloyd George in December 1916, while the French, after a series of Cabinet reshuffles, settled on the Radical "Tiger," Georges Clemenceau, to pursue the war with principle and rigor.

If there was a single belligerent spared the worst horrors of 1916, it was surely Russia. Where the western powers had gained scarcely a scrap of defensible territory all year with their bloody offensives, the Russians, after an initial disaster at Lake Narotch in March,[3] had won victory after victory in the East, from Brusilov's numerous (albeit tactical) breakthroughs in Galicia to northeastern Turkey, where the Caucasian army was carrying all before it. True, Romania's entry into the war in August 1916 had not gone well. The fertile plains of Wallachia, including Bucharest and the oil fields of Ploesti, had fallen to the Central powers by December. But then this had been foreseen by Russia's generals, who viewed the Romanians with contempt and had tried to convince the French not to push them into the war.

Congress Poland, too, remained lost to the Russians, despite all Brusilov's heroics in Galicia. And yet the loss of Poland in 1915, despite the initial panic it caused, had not been an unmitigated disaster for Russia. If it had been, Sazonov and the tsar would surely have responded more positively to the peace feelers German diplomats sent out that fall—the Germans' idea being to cut a separate peace on the grounds of some kind of Polish partition.[4] In the political sense, the Polish question opened up by Grand Duke Nicholas's manifesto of August 1914 had been nothing but a headache, giving Witte and the conservative "Germanophile" opposition a cudgel with which to browbeat Sazonov and the government. There had been more serious opposition in Petrograd to the platform of expanding Congress Poland at the expense of Austria-Hungary than to any other war aim. The annexations program for Turkey, by contrast, was one on which all politicians agreed. Even before the Germans occupied Warsaw in August 1915, Sazonov had cooled down considerably in his rhetoric. Disappointing Polish nationalists who viewed him as an ally, Sazonov emphasized that Eastern Galicia would never be included in any future Polish kingdom.[5]

As for the enthusiastically pro-Polish French, Sazonov had held firm in the final throes of negotiations over Sykes-Picot. (The British, meanwhile, continued to maintain a posture of "complete indifference" on the Polish question, to Paléologue's consternation.) Not even in April 1916, by which time Congress Poland had essentially become a German rather than a Russian problem, was Sazonov willing to "internationalize" the Polish issue so as to help the cause of Entente propaganda, as Paléologue complained to Briand. With little to lose by making another proclamation to the Poles now that most of them were (unlike in August 1914) subjects of the enemy coalition, Sazonov still insisted unequivocally that "the relations between the Tsar and his Polish subjects comprise a subject of internal politics [only]." Despite the promising Duma speech on Poland given by Goremykin on 1 August 1915, when the chairman of the Council of Ministers had used the term autonomy *(avtonomiya)* for the first time (as opposed to the original proclamation of August 1914, which had only suggested *samoupravlenie,* or self-government), Sazonov made clear to Paléologue that no new proclamation of Polish "autonomy" would be issued—certainly not by the tsar, and certainly not as part of some quid pro quo over the partition of Turkey. In Paléologue's view, there was little to distinguish Sazonov's position from that of Germanophiles, so ephemeral had been the former's embrace of the Polish cause in 1914. "Among all Russians," Paléologue concluded sadly, "the maintenance of the Polish state under the scepter of the Romanovs is a fundamental axiom, a national dogma. The resurrection of an independent Poland could only possibly come about through violence."[6]

Whether Poland would be ruled by Petrograd or Berlin was, it seemed, less important to Russia's war aims than the "fundamental axiom" that postwar Poland not be independent. It is true that Baron Boris Nolde, working on behalf of Sazonov, drew up a Polish autonomy plan in April 1916, under which "Poland would have her own Council of Ministers and Ministries and a *Sejm,* consisting of a Senate and a Chamber of Deputies," with only a personal viceroy of the tsar to exercise oversight from Petrograd. But Sazonov, fearing fierce opposition from the Germanophiles, kept these plans "in cold storage," not even mentioning them to Paléologue, much less the tsar. Only after the Brusilov offensive of June 1916 restored Russian prestige on the eastern front did Sazonov, ever so carefully, broach the matter with Mikhail Alekseev, who as chief of staff under Tsar Nicholas II was now the real commander of Russia's armies, at Stavka. Alekseev, keen for any gesture that might improve morale at the front, responded positively, as did the tsar, after he heard out Sazonov and Alekseev. But even Nicholas II himself was afraid to authorize a proclamation of Polish autonomy without clearing it first with the politicians in Petrograd. In the end the tsar backed down under pressure from Tsarina Alexandra, who (on Rasputin's advice) convinced him to sack Sazonov on 23 July 1916 to make way for the reputed "Germanophile" Boris Stürmer.[7]

To the exasperation of her Allies, Russia simply would not issue any proclamation of Polish autonomy bearing the tsar's signature during the war—certainly not after Stürmer took over the Foreign Ministry from Sazonov expressly in order to scotch a Polish autonomy proclamation. Remarkably, in light of the fact that most of Poland had, by fall 1915, already come under German military administration—meaning that the tsar and the Russian Foreign Ministry could have made any phantom promises they wished, as they were unlikely to have to honor them—Berlin and Vienna actually outbid Petrograd in idealistic promises to the Poles, issuing on 5 November 1916 a "Proclamation of the Two Emperors," which promised Poland "independence." (This independence was just as vague as that promised by Grand Duke Nicholas's *samoupravlenie* in August 1914; the idea was that "independent" Poland would be part of a German customs union, with its army subject to German command.[8]) In the face of this propaganda coup, Stürmer, despite his reputed Germanophilia and hostility to the Poles, at last readied to make Russia's long-delayed announcement on Polish autonomy before the Duma on 1/14 November 1916 only to lose his nerve at the last moment, literally walking out of the chamber (followed by a disappointed Paléologue and Buchanan). Stürmer's departure may have been a simple matter of stage fright, but this hardly helped to dampen the suspicions of pan-Slavists and liberal imperialists. It was in response to Stürmer's cowardly exit from the chamber that Miliukov launched into his famous "Is it stupidity or is it treason?" Duma speech, castigating Stürmer for the latter's (in fact much exaggerated) Germanophilia.[9]

Miliukov's incendiary rhetoric aside, the lack of urgency with which Russian leaders like Sazonov and Stürmer approached the once-explosive Polish question owed much to the fact that, by 1916, Russia's defensive lines in Europe had largely stabilized, with most of Poland clearly in the Austro-German sphere. The loss of Warsaw and, more recently, Bucharest was unfortunate, but in strategic terms these "plains" cities had been well-nigh indefensible. (The oilfields of Ploesti, meanwhile, had been mostly torched by a team of British engineers, so as not to benefit Germany unduly.) So quiet was the eastern front that there would be little fighting of any kind there in 1917—until the Russians themselves broke the peace with a renewed Galician offensive in June-July. Both sides were reasonably secure in their current positions. The Germano-Bulgarian advance in Romania had bogged down at the Siret river, on the border of present-day Moldovo, where the Russians (and those Romanians able to escape encirclement) firmly controlled the bridgeheads. Russia still held much of eastern Galicia. Control of this "primordial Russian land" had been her primary European strategic objective all along. Further north the Polish salient had, despite all the diplomatic sound and fury over the matter, in effect been tactically abandoned by Stavka as indefensible, just as Sukhomlinov had always recommended. Whether Alekseev chose to go back on the offensive against the Austrians and Germans, or merely to hold the line in eastern Europe so as to better reinforce the Caucasian army as it subdued Turkey and Persia, Russian prospects looked bright. On the western and eastern fronts alike the Entente powers now enjoyed "superiority of at least sixty per cent in men and guns," while in Anatolia the Russian advantage was more like two to one. Little wonder that, at the inter-Allied conference at Petrograd in February 1917, "Russia's generals were full of fight."[10]

Even on the home front, the Russians looked to have weathered the worst of the storm. The notorious (and much exaggerated) "shell shortage" of 1915 had been brilliantly overcome, in part through ramped-up domestic production of weapons and ammunition, and also by a growing

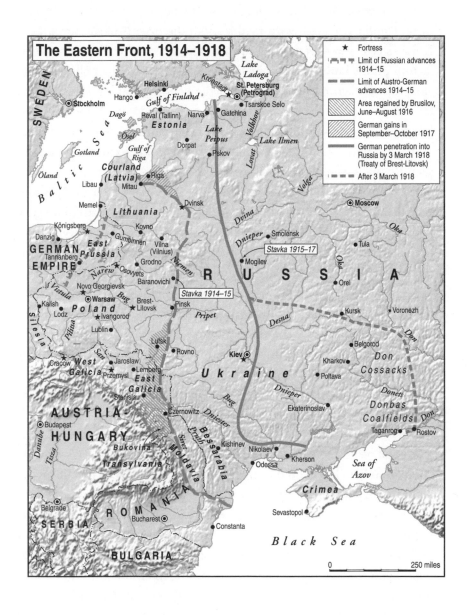

The Eastern Front, 1914–1918

★ Fortress

Limit of Russian advances 1914–15

Limit of Austro-German advances 1914–15

Area regained by Brusilov, June–August 1916

German gains in September–October 1917

German penetration into Russia by 3 March 1918 (Treaty of Brest-Litovsk)

After 3 March 1918

SWEDEN

Stockholm

Öland

Gotland

Baltic Sea

Dagö

Ösel

Memel

Königsberg

Danzig

GERMAN

Tannenberg

EMPIRE

Kalish

Lodz

Silesia

Cracow

Przemysl

Jaroslaw

West Galicia

AUSTRIA-HUNGARY

Budapest

Belgrade

SERBIA

BULGARIA

Helsinki

Hango

Gulf of Finland

Reval (Tallinn)

Narva

Estonia

Dorpat

Gulf of Riga

Courland (Latvia)

Libau

Riga

Mitau

Lithuania

Kovno

Vilna (Vilnius)

Grodno

Osovyets

Narew

Novo Georgievsk

Vistula

Warsaw

Ivangorod

Poland

Lublin

Pilitsa

East Galicia

Stanislau

Czernowitz

Bukovina

Transylvania

ROMANIA

Bucharest

Constanta

Lake Ladoga

Kronstadt

St. Petersburg (Petrograd)

Tsarskoe Selo

Gatchina

Lake Peipus

Pskov

Volkhov

Lake Ilmen

Lovat

Dvinsk

Dvina

Smolensk

Dnieper

Mogilev

Stavka 1915–17

Stavka 1914–15

Baranovichi

Brest-Litovsk

Pinsk

Pripet

Desna

Lutsk

Rovno

Kiev

Ukraine

Dnieper

Bug

Dniester

Bessarabia

Moldova

Prut

Seret

Kishinev

Nikolaev

Odessa

Kherson

Moscow

Oka

Tula

Oka

Orel

Kursk

Voronezh

Belgorod

Kharkov

Poltava

Don

Don Cossacks

Ekaterinoslav

Donets

Donbas Coalfields

Taganrog

Rostov

Don

Sea of Azov

Crimea

Sevastopol

Black Sea

RUSSIA

Gumbinnen

East Prussia

Memen

0   250 miles

stream of gold-financed imports from the West. Russia produced four times as much shell as Austria-Hungary in 1916 and nearly as much as Germany, which was still sending most of its own output to the western front. Contrary to well-worn myths about the origins of the revolution, Russia's economy was thriving in 1916–17, with employment figures and factory profits both rising dramatically. There was even a bull market in stocks, as foreign capital flowed into the country, reaping huge returns from the war production boom. True, in part due to the Allies' failure to break through at Gallipoli in 1915, there were shortages of bread and fuel in the northern cities, and the winter of 1916–17 bit hard in Petrograd; but then Russians were inured to the cold. Judging by the material and military situation, wartime morale should have been far better in Russia in 1917 than in beleaguered Turkey, starving Germany, or Austria-Hungary with its perennial crises of command, logistics, and ethnic loyalty—better even than in reasonably stable democratic Britain and France, the governments of which were lurching from one political crisis to another.

On strategic grounds, there was every reason for the Russians to fight on. The full particulars of the Sykes-Picot-Sazonov agreement remained secret, but not the basic gist of the thing. A. F. Trepov, Stürmer's successor as chairman of the Council of Ministers, upon being confronted by the usual mob of hecklers in his inaugural address to the Duma on 2 December 1916 (a mob led by Alexander Kerensky), had revealed publicly for the first time that Britain and France had promised Russia Constantinople and the Straits.[11] As Trepov's desperate revelation suggests, "Tsargrad" still resonated with the Russian public. According to Paléologue, a common refrain heard on the streets of Petrograd at about this time was: "what is the point of this war if it will not give us Constantinople?"[12]

The war with Turkey was popular in no small part because it was going so well. Grand Duke Nicholas may have failed to spearhead Russia's armies to victory over Germany in 1914–15, but in Tiflis his name had become synonymous with triumph (even if Yudenich was the real mastermind of the Anatolian campaign of 1916). Although the Caucasian winter of 1916–17 was brutal, after the spring snowmelt the Russians were ideally positioned to resume their westward march on Sivas and Ankara, well supplied not only overland from Tiflis and Erzurum but now by sea as well, via Trabzon. The Russians were building a new rail line parallel to the Black Sea coast, too, from Batum to Trabzon, turning the latter, formerly Turkish port city into an important Russian forward base. The new commander of the Black Sea fleet, Admiral A. V. Kolchak, was busy all fall and winter assembling transport ships (including river barges) and supplies all along the Black Sea littorals, from Trabzon and Batum to Sevastopol, Odessa, and Romania (with its substantial, and now mostly idle, Danube River fleet). On 30 November 1916 Russia's Black Sea fleet finally launched its first completed dreadnought, the *Empress Catherine II* —named, ominously, after the great empress who had first broached the idea of the conquest of Constantinople back in Russia's glory days in the eighteenth century. Four weeks later, on 24 December 1916, Tsar Nicholas II issued the order forming a special "Black Sea division" targeting the Ottoman capital, styling its first regiment the "Tsargradskii" (this was apparently Kolchak's idea).[13]

The augurs for an amphibious strike were, unlike in 1914–15, favorable. November 1916 had seen not only the launching of Russia's long-awaited Black Sea dreadnought, but the first major setbacks for the enemy fleet: three German submarines had run over Russian mines off the Bulgarian coastline, near Varna. Far more significantly, both the dreadnought *Goeben* and the cruiser *Breslau*, scourges of Russia's Black Sea fleet ever since they had broken through the British Mediterranean screen in August 1914, were down for serious, long-term repairs—so serious that most of their guns had been stripped and re-mounted on shore batteries at the Bosphorus and Gallipoli.[14] So weak was Turkish morale that neither the Ottoman Second nor Third Army conducted a single offensive operation in 1917, as they had managed to do even in the dire strategic circumstances of summer 1916. Meanwhile, the British, having recovered from the disaster at Kut the year before, were storming up the Tigris, taking Baghdad on 11 March 1917 after the Ottoman Sixth Army had evacuated the city three days earlier. After lingering for a century at death's door, the "Sick Man of Europe" was keeling over, making possible the realization of the Russian "dream for a thousand years": a triumphant march into Tsargrad, led by Kolchak's "Tsargradskii" regiment.

Across the Persian border, meanwhile, the Russian expeditionary force was poised for a breakthrough. Baratov could claim at least some credit for the fall of Baghdad. After the British forces, under General Maude, had retaken Kut-al-Amara on 22 February, Baratov had resumed a three-pronged offensive into Mesopotamia by way of Hamadan, Bidjar-Senneh (modern Sanandaj), and Dawlatabad. By March 1917, the campaign in Mesopotamia was turning into a rout. Halil "Kut" Pasha, who commanded what remained of the Ottoman Sixth Army after the death of von der Goltz Pasha in April 1916, was down to about 30,000 men, "spread out over a front of about three hundred kilometers," between Ramadiye, on the Euphrates, and the Russian front near the Persian border.[15] Turkish headquarters was now at Mosul, right in the Russian path of advance from Persia. As Baratov later recalled the euphoria of the moment, "My dear, gallant Kuban and Terek Cossacks, horsemen and gunners of my kindred 1st Caucasian Cossack Division, together with our new fighting companions, brave young mounted Georgians and valiant Siberians which joined them, by their energy, labours and [the shedding of] their blood as [we] pursued the enemy falling back from Baghdad, proved to be worthy descendants of their glorious fathers and grandfathers." Waxing more grandiloquent still, upon resigning his command in June 1918 Baratov profusely thanked these courageous heroes of Slavdom for "standing by his side" as he led "Russia in the historical path of Alexander the Great."[16]

Baratov, alas, never did get to march into Mosul as Russian conqueror of Mesopotamia. For reasons deeply mysterious to the Turks at the time, his relentless advance stopped suddenly in April 1917, as if the Russians had simply changed their minds about conquering Ottoman Mesopotamia. The British general, Frederick Stanley Maude, too, decided to hunker down in Baghdad all summer, in part because Baratov had halted his own offensive, awaiting reinforcements that, fortuitously for his Turkish enemy, were denied him.[17]

Even more mysterious, the long-expected Russian offensive against Sivas and Ankara never did materialize in 1917. After being arguably the most eventful theater of the entire world war in 1916, the Caucasian front was so quiet in 1917 that to this day scarcely anything is known about it. Those few books that treat this relatively obscure front at all tend to devote a page or two, at most, to military developments for the entirety of 1917. As the leading western historian of Turkey's war sums up the year curiously, "during 1917 the Turkish Second and Third Armies enjoyed a much-needed respite from over two years of continuous and brutal combat."[18]

What on earth had happened to the Russians? Had Alekseev,* Baratov, Yudenich, the Grand Duke Nicholas, and Tsar Nicholas II suddenly developed a guilty conscience about conquering Turkey?[19] Had the Russians, discouraged by the Allied debacle at Gallipoli, given up on seizing Constantinople and the Straits? Was Russia, then, happy with its gains at Turkish expense so far, angling for a separate peace with the Central powers in order to leave the French dangling, unable to claim their own share from the Sykes-Picot-Sazonov agreement, as they had no troops in the theater? Or was the strategic pause of spring 1917 merely a feint?

Strange as all these scenarios seem in light of Russia's diplomatic behavior from 1914 to 1917, the truth was stranger still. In fact Russia's war aims, as formulated by the same generals and diplomatic professionals, on behalf of the same basic government, remained unaltered in spring 1917, even as all hell broke loose in Petrograd and morale in the armies began slowly to crack. These aims may be summed up in a single phrase: control of Constantinople and the Straits, an axiom of Russian foreign policy held so deeply that not even the world-historical February Revolution could dislodge it. As Nikolai Bazili reported from Stavka on 6 April 1917 to Miliukov, now foreign minister of the new provisional government, preparations by the Black Sea fleet for an amphibious landing at the Bosphorus, led by the impassioned Admiral Kolchak, had been underway since 1 August 1916. Although Alekseev, at Stavka, had initially dragged his heels on diverting troops from the European front, by May two full army divisions, Bazili promised Miliukov, would be ready to sail from Odessa and Sevastopol, although ideally the operation would take place in high summer, between 1/14 June and 1/14 August 1917, to ensure the best odds of favorable weather conditions. The *Goeben* and *Breslau* were still down for repairs, meaning the Russian Black Sea fleet, led by the brand-new dreadnought *Empress Catherine II*, would encounter little se-

---

* At least in Alekseev's case, something of the sort could be said. Following the fall of Erzurum in February 1916, Russia's chief of staff had proposed to Sazonov that Russia, flush with victory, offer a separate peace to the Young Turks that would allow them to remain in power. Sazonov, coveting Constantinople, refused to parley.

rious opposition and be able to shell the Bosphorus defenses with impunity. Russian intelligence on Ottoman army deployments suggested—correctly—that European Thrace and Constantinople were being denuded
of troops, as the Turks sought to shore up an increasingly desperate position in Anatolia, Mesopotamia, and Palestine. Already weak now—only
two Ottoman army divisions guarded the capital—the Bosphorus defenses would be weaker still "in two months' time," that is, in June 1917,
when Russia's long-awaited amphibious descent on Tsargrad, weather
permitting, would commence.[20]

Bazili's latest Straits memorandum was no idle communication. The
Tsargrad offensive was the highest strategic priority in Petrograd in spring
1917, and it was approved at the highest levels of both the "Old Regime"
and the provisional government. Sazonov and Stürmer, though no longer
in office, had each given their imprimatur behind the scenes.[21] Miliukov
had personally visited Stavka to discuss the Straits operation with Bazili
in late March.[22] Alexander Guchkov, head of the Military-Industrial Committee formed in 1915 to coordinate war production, one of the founders
of the Progressive Bloc, and now, in March-April 1917, Russia's minister
of defense, was on board. Guchkov was using his industrial contacts to
procure coal and civilian vessels for the operation.[23] So, too, was Alekseev, the commander-in-chief, and Anton Denikin, Alekseev's chief of
staff.[24] And of course Admiral Kolchak, the creator of the "Tsargradskii"
advance guard regiment, was as eager for action as a naval commander
could be—no Eberhart was he.

Not incidentally, many of these men had played a role in the abdication
of Nicholas II on 15 March 1917. Guchkov had been deputized by the
Provisional Committee in Petrograd to travel to Mogilev (the post-1915
location of Stavka) to demand the sovereign step down to save Russia—
although, unbeknownst to him, General Alekseev had already convinced
the tsar to do so without Guchkov's help.[25] As for Bazili, then the tsar's
diplomatic aide-de-camp, he personally composed the text of Nicholas
II's abdication statement, submitting it to Alekseev for approval before
the tsar was allowed to see it.[26] Alongside these conspirators, General
V. N. Klembovskii, too, a confidant of Alexander Kerensky, helped plan
the Straits operation, his own brief being commandeering Romanian
ships from the Danube River fleet.[27] Led into battle by Admiral Kolchak,

these proud Russian patriots, having safeguarded the national interest, as they saw it, through the turmoil of the February Revolution, would now help Russia carry out her historic mission of seizing Tsargrad.

With benefit of hindsight, there is an air of "Nero fiddling while Rome burns" about this, as if Sazonov, Alekseev, Guchkov, Kolchak, Miliukov, and Bazili did not realize their country was falling apart around them even as they were planning for further conquests. Miliukov, famously, got into hot water shortly after he had met with Bazili at Stavka, precisely because his adherence to the policy of annexing Constantinople and the Straits, announced at a press conference on 4 April 1917, was publicly repudiated by the Petrograd Soviet (*Ispolkom*). The Straits policy of Guchkov and Miliukov even played a role in inspiring the first (failed) Bolshevik coup, judging by Lenin's speech denouncing the provisional government as "thoroughly imperialist" at an emergency Central Committee session that preceded the Bolshevik-manipulated street riots on 3 May 1917.[28] Lenin was more right than he knew. Seizing Constantinople and the Straits was not merely a by-now-publicly-avowed aim of the Russian government and its foreign minister in April-May 1917 but a matter of imminent operational priority at Stavka and Black Sea command.

Tempting as it is to judge these men harshly for their stubborn failure to abandon the quixotic dream of conquering Tsargrad at a time of historic political upheaval, we should be very careful about this sort of anachronistic judgment. Far from representing an upwelling of "antiimperialist" pacifism, careful historical scholarship has established that most of the popular antitsarist rhetoric of winter 1916–17, especially that targeting the tsarina and her beloved Rasputin, was that the depraved monarchy was in cahoots with the hated Germans.[29] This had been the theme of Miliukov's famous speech accusing Stürmer of treason: the sin of the so-called "conservatives" was not their imperialism, but that they were not prosecuting the war vigorously enough. Even Kerensky, in his more hysterical speech in the same Duma session attacking the Cabinet as "hired killers" ruling Russia, had accused these men not of imperialistic greed but of "treason"—they were "fratricides and cowards."[30] The same theme had animated the hecklers of Trepov when he had offered them the rhetorical bone of Constantinople and the Straits. The renewed drive for the Straits in summer 1917 had in fact initially been conceived by Sazonov, Stürmer, and Bazili at a secret meeting on 25–26 February (March 10–11)—during the worst chaos of the February Revolution—precisely as a means of "calming public opinion in Russia," as Bazili put it in language uncannily similar to Sazonov's own exhortation to the service chiefs, in November 1912, that the conquest of Constantinople would "bring healing to our internal life."[31] One can hardly blame Miliukov for misreading shifts in a patriotic popular mood he had personally done so much to shape. As Miliukov told a friend, it would be "absurd and criminal to renounce the biggest prize of the war . . . in the name of some humanitarian and cosmopolitan idea of international socialism."[32] Why, if the crowds had been all against pro-German treason, cowardice, and weakness in November 1916; why, when everyone all along said that Constantinople was the only prize that made the war worth winning, was the mob (at least as channeled by revolutionary politicians) suddenly now opposed to Russia fighting for her most essential interest?

From the point of view of Stavka, the war was still going undeniably well in spring 1917. Whatever disconnect had opened up between the Guchkov-Miliukov crowd of "bourgeois" liberal patriots and the increasingly strident revolutionaries at Ispolkom was dwarfed by the disconnect between Petrograd and the front lines. In Persia, the notorious "Order No. 1" of 1/14 March 1917, which abolished most elements of officer control in the armed forces and mandated the election of "soldier soviets," was received by Baratov as if had been sent from outer space. It was not that Order No. 1 was not followed in Persia—as on other fronts the men immediately began holding "endless meetings" discussing "not only matters of supply" but what Baratov euphemistically called "issues of a most general character." In this case, as in so many others, the February Revolution redounded to the benefit of the Central powers, as the politicking mandated by Order No. 1 distracted the Russian expeditionary forces just enough to cause Baratov to call off the Mosul offensive in late March, saving the Ottoman Sixth Army to fight another day. Still, important as this strategic pause was, it should be emphasized that morale did *not* break down in Baratov's expeditionary force, which continued to hold its position in Ottoman Mesopotamia all through 1917, even mounting a small offensive in early 1918 at Kara-Tepe, in northeastern Mesopotamia (although this gesture predictably fell far short of what the British had asked

Baratov for in October 1917, namely a frontal assault on Mosul).[33] In Baratov's elegiac paeans to his loyal Cossacks after the Bolsheviks finally
forced him to withdraw in June 1918, one hears the siren song of lost im-
mortality, as he wonders what might have been. Absent the Russian Revolution of 1917, his name might redound today like that of Colonel Lawrence "of Arabia," as the legendary conqueror of Persia and northern
Mesopotamia, the man who had carried out Russia's historic mission
to expand southward all the way to the Persian Gulf—even as Alekseev,
Kolchak, or Yudenich would have been immortalized as the conqueror of
Constantinople, who after centuries of frustration had opened Russia's
warm-water access from the Black Sea to the Mediterranean.[34]

While we have no similarly lyrical first-hand report as to how Order
No. 1 was received by the Russian occupying troops in Anatolia, the available evidence suggests that its effect was just as minimal as in Persia.
While Grand Duke Nicholas was forced out at Tiflis command, his post
was assumed fairly smoothly by General Yudenich, who had really been
running things all along. As Yudenich himself reported following the
imposition of Order No. 1 in March 1917, "the membership of the [sol-
diers'] committees is generally favorable in the sense of the inclination to
strengthen law and order and to conduct the war to a victorious end." At
a soldiers' soviet congress held in Tiflis that April—the Caucasian equivalent of Ispolkom—a ranking general was elected chairman, suggesting
that there was virtually no mutinous sentiment in the Caucasus. In this
theater of the war the Russians had, after all, won a crushing series of victories the previous year, and were poised to reap still more if the Caucasian army was given its head again.*[35] A leading historian notes in *The
End of the Russian Imperial Army* that "in most armies only one or two
major operations resulted in disbanding [in other words, the disintegration of one or more military units], and on the Romanian and Caucasian
fronts, none at all."[36]

There was a mutiny, of sorts, in the Black Sea fleet at Sevastopol in
March. Significantly, nearly all of the naval officers shot by their men had
German names—meaning they were presumed to be "traitors" to the war

---

* Muş was evacuated on Yudenich's orders in May, but this was mostly for political reasons,
unrelated to anything the Ottoman Third Army did or did not do.

effort, not to lower-class sailors. By early April 1917, Admiral Kolchak had reestablished "firm control" over the Black Sea fleet, which would, after 1918, offer aid and succor to the Whites in the Russian Civil War (notably in the evacuation of Denikin's Volunteer Army from Novorossiisk in 1919, and then Wrangel's men from Sevastopol in 1920).[37] That Kolchak, architect and leading advocate of the plans to conquer Constantinople in 1916–17, the future "Supreme Commander" of the White armies, was able to secure the loyalty of the sailors in Sevastopol, just as Yudenich, future commander of the Whites' Northwestern Army, was able to do with the Caucasian army, suggests that the "Tsargrad" dream still resonated with Russian sailors and soldiers on the Turkish fronts even after the February Revolution.

By contrast, morale was breaking down on the European fronts, as revealed by the disastrous Galician offensive launched on 29 June 1917. The so-called "Kerensky offensive" is usually discussed against the backdrop of the Russian Revolution as the moment when the war minister, seeking to demonstrate the new regime's *bona fides* with the western Allies, pushed the army a step too far and lost control of public opinion. But the story has equally much to tell us about the ironclad consistency of Russia's war aims. What, after all, was Kerensky, member of Ispolkom, effective leader of a government dominated by socialists, doing carrying out an offensive targeting Lemberg (Lvov), capital of Austrian Galicia? Was this not just the sort of benighted "imperialism" against which the Bolsheviks were thundering in the soviets? Despite all his incendiary anti-Romanov rhetoric and revolutionary idealism, it was hard not to conclude, as so many in Petrograd did, that Kerensky remained a slave to the amoral foreign policy dogmas of the Old Regime.

In Galicia in June-July 1917, if not at Tannenberg in August 1914, we can finally see Russia "falling on its sword" for the western Allies. It is hard not to sympathize with Kerensky's dilemma, compelled as he was by inter-Allied treaty obligations, and the moral-material factor of imported war supplies pouring into Murmansk, into doing *something* to relieve the terrible pressure on the western front (where the French army had been rocked by the so-called Chemin-des-Dames "mutinies" of May 1917, when soldiers began refusing orders to go on suicidal offensives against fortified German trench lines). Kerensky did his best to explain to Russia's enlisted men why they should continue the common fight against the Germans, delivering such "stirring patriotic speeches" at the front that one eyewitness compared him to "a volcano hurling forth sheaves of all-consuming fire."[38] But all the oratory in the world was not enough to steel the men as soon as the inevitable German reinforcements arrived on 6 July, pitching the Russians immediately into "headlong flight." There is a famous picture of Russian soldiers fleeing the Germans on the Galician front in July 1917. It captures better than any other the breakdown of morale in the Russian armies that terrible year.

Still, despite the Galician meltdown, army morale remained relatively strong in Turkey and Persia, where the Russians were having their way against overmatched enemies. One might object here that Persians and Turks were enemies of a different caliber than Germans. It was almost as if Baratov and Yudenich were fighting nineteenth-century style colonial wars, while poor Kerensky was forced to fight the last, terrible battle of a twentieth-century conflict for which Imperial Russia had shown itself to be woefully underprepared. But then no one *forced* Kerensky to attack in Galicia, rather than in Turkey or Persia. Kerensky's mistake, in this sense, was not so much in choosing to wage an offensive to demonstrate continued good faith to Russia's western allies, but rather in choosing the wrong

Russian soldiers fleeing Germans on the Galician front, July 1917, *Daily Mirror*

theater for the offensive. To put the matter bluntly: as a wide-eyed idealist new to the cutthroat world of geopolitics, Kerensky had swallowed whole French and British pleas to relieve them. Had they still been running things, Sazonov, Sukhomlinov, and Yanushkevitch might well have lightly deflected these requests as they had all through 1914 and 1915. Stavka then might have held precariously onto faltering morale on the east European front by not wasting Russian lives in more futile offensives. Meanwhile the generals might have concentrated instead on the amphibious operation against Constantinople planned for summer 1917.

With hard-line "bourgeois" politicians like Miliukov and Guchkov out of the picture by May, and the Bolsheviks having made clear their own opposition to pursuing the war any further, Kerensky was forced to take full responsibility for the failure of the Galician offensive. In his naiveté— judging by his famous speeches at the front—Kerensky had truly imagined that staging a diversionary strike against the Austro-German armies in Galicia served the cause of Russian democracy, the Allies, and so on.* Kerensky believed that justice had a place in foreign policy, which had for so long been dominated by amoral, cynical Old World realists. One can see this idealism at work in a tortured policy memorandum of 28 May 1917 on the Armenian question, in which the post-Miliukov Foreign Ministry tried to square the circle of Russian imperialism with the western-style human rights rhetoric of Ispolkom's "peace without annexations" declaration of 9 April. Showing that old habits died hard, the document referred to "provinces of Asiatic Turkey taken by right of war" before asserting, in the name of the provisional government, that the former Ottoman vilayets of Van, Bitlis, and Erzurum would be "forever Armenian." Confusingly, however, the document still implied (but did not explicitly state) that these three provinces would be administered by Russia, which would help repatriate Armenian, Kurdish, and Turkish refugees, and would pay for the reconstruction of battered areas.[39]

Admirable as these sentiments are, they do not add up to statesman-

---

* There is a scene in the David Lean epic *Doctor Zhivago* where a Kerensky-like commissar, lecturing soldiers on their patriotic duty while standing on a beer barrel, whips the men into a martial frenzy—until the barrelhead gives way and he falls ridiculously into the beer. The men laugh; the commissar is shot.

ship. Either these eastern Turkish provinces would be administered by Russia without any group receiving favorable status, as Sazonov and Grand Duke Nicholas had determined in 1916, or they would be "Armenian," that is, autonomous: the two scenarios were mutually exclusive. Kerensky's Galician offensive was, likewise, a fundamental mistake, not so much because it failed, but rather because, for all his speechifying, he had failed to make clear what strategic purpose it served. Sukhomlinov had ordered the invasion of Austrian Galicia in 1914 to consolidate the defensive lines of European Russia. Brusilov had invaded the same territory in 1916 to break Austria-Hungary. Neither man had succeeded, but at least they knew what they were trying to do. Kerensky did not.

The Bolsheviks, by contrast, knew fundamentally what they stood for. "We don't want the Dardanelles!" one of their popular antiwar slogans, was not merely a rhetorical flourish meant to provoke the government. The Bolsheviks knew exactly what they were doing when they helped break Miliukov over his refusal to disavow Russia's claims on "Tsargrad" and the Straits. At this crucial moment of the Russian Revolution, the Bolsheviks, like mad political savants, laid bare the essential truth about the world war. Miliukov, Guchkov, and the generals and admirals wanted Russian *muzhiks* to die so that the tsar—or whichever Russian government emerged from the war—could rule Constantinople. The Bolsheviks did not. Kerensky, with his ill-fated Galician offensive, was trying to cloud this basic issue by implying that there were other, vaguer reasons to fight—for love of country, democracy, honor, the Allies, whatever. Judging from the breakdown of morale in Galicia, Russia's soldiers, at least those facing Germans, were not buying it.

Of course, the Bolsheviks themselves were hardly pacifists. It was not that they did not want Russia's enlisted men to fight and die; they wanted them to fight and die for different things: to butcher their superior officers; destroy the tsarist order; expropriate the propertied classes; and so on. In the sense that the Bolsheviks (or Lenin, at least, who was clear on the matter) wished for Russia to surrender the war to the Central powers and abandon "imperialist" claims on other countries' territories, one could say, in effect, that the Bolsheviks wished for the war casualties of 1914–1917 to have died for nothing. One can therefore appreciate the bitterness of generals like Baratov, Denikin, and Yudenich, not to mention

Admiral Kolchak, who saw the hard-won triumphs of their beloved brethren-in-arms and all the preparation that had gone into planning the storming of Tsargrad ground into dust as the Bolsheviks set about dissolving the Imperial Army and surrendering the world war to Russia's enemies. Little wonder that Denikin, Yudenich, and Kolchak would spearhead the White resistance to Bolshevik rule in the Civil War.[40]

For all the nihilistic destruction wrought by their policies, it cannot be denied that the Bolsheviks had grasped a fundamental truth about the war of 1914. The rigid Marxist-Leninist theory of "imperialist war" may not have been universally applicable, and it may not have accurately described the motivations of Russia's western allies, who, conspiracy theories about Sykes-Picot notwithstanding, had not really gone to war in 1914 in order to conquer Palestine and Syria. All the evidence suggests that French statesmen were obsessed that year with avenging the Franco-Prussian war and seizing Alsace-Lorraine, while the British fretted over Belgian neutrality and the German threat to London's global position. But in Russia's own case, the accusation hit close to the mark—as it did for Imperial Germany, where the Marxist Social Democratic Party (SPD) literally cleaved in two in 1917 over the same issue of "imperialist" war aims that divided Miliukov and Guchkov from Ispolkom in Petrograd. The Germans really were planning to annex huge swathes of formerly Russian territory in eastern Europe, as the Brest-Litovsk Treaty of March 1918 made clear, along with much of Belgium, Luxembourg, and the French industrial basin surrounding the Longwy-Briey iron-ore field— and most of these war aims dated all the way back to the "September Program" of 1914. Likewise, Alekseev, Guchkov, and Miliukov, as the Bolsheviks suspected, were indeed plotting to conquer Constantinople in April 1917, just as Sazonov and his colleagues were doing in 1914—just as every Russian government had done since 1895 and had done, in the more fundamental sense, since the beginning of the Romanov dynasty.

Here, at the end of Russia's war, we may finally understand its beginning. Public rhetoric aside, Serbia and "Slavic honor" had nothing to do with it. It was not over these phantom issues that Russia had gone to war in 1914, nor did they play the slightest role in the world-historic political tremors of 1917. For Russia, if not for her allies, the war of 1914 was always principally about the Ottoman inheritance: about Constantinople and the

Straits. In pursuit of this great strategic prize, at a moment that seemed uniquely propitious for enlisting British and French power to neutralize the mounting German threat to Russia's ambitions, Sazonov and the generals at Stavka had plunged Europe into the greatest catastrophe of modern times.

The October Revolution and
Historical Amnesia

The state which possesses the Straits will hold in its hands not only the key of the Black Sea and Mediterranean, but also that of penetration into Asia Minor and the sure means of hegemony in the Balkans . . . on current form, from 1914–16 the Turkish fleet will be superior to ours in the Black Sea.

—S. D. Sazonov to Tsar Nicholas II, 6 December 1913[1]

If, at this critical juncture, the Serbs were abandoned to their fate, Russian prestige . . . would collapse utterly.

—S. D. Sazonov in the Council of Ministers, 24 July 1914[2]

There was no trace in St. Petersburg of the existence of any party which desired war . . . [Amphibious plans targeting Constantinople] were wholly defensive . . . of a peaceful character . . . The Tsar was silent . . . neither he nor his Government desired the war. Both he and they had done everything possible to avoid it and were prepared to sacrifice a great deal of our national pride.

—S. D. Sazonov in *Fateful Years*, 1927[3]

As all the world knows, Lenin and the Bolsheviks seized power in Petrograd on the night of 7–8 November 1917 (new calendar), following which "October Revolution" they set about remaking tsarist Russia along Communist lines. In foreign policy terms, the revolution was at least as dramatic as the Bolshevik abolition of private property was inside the country, as the new regime immediately petitioned for and was granted an armistice by the Central powers, even while repudiating its obligations to its Allies. Trotsky's leaking of the "secret treaties" (especially the terms of Sykes-Picot-Sazonov) to the *Manchester Guardian* later in November 1917 was the most famous instance of this, but this was arguably less important in the long run than the Bolsheviks' repudiation of all tsarist-era bonds, both public and private, which was publicly announced to the world in February 1918. By thus declaring null and void, in nihilistic "year zero" style, all binding contracts and agreements of any kind undertaken under the previous regime, the Bolsheviks burned the bridges linking Russia to the global economy: in some ways the country has still not recovered the wealth it lost to this day.[4]

The western Allies responded in kind. In retaliation for the Bolshevik repudiation of tsarist bond holdings, Britain and France froze tsarist assets and denied credit to the Bolsheviks. Lenin's unilateral request for a ceasefire, sent *en clair* (without encryption) and without precondition to German military headquarters on 25 November 1917, simply confirmed the belief held by western Allied leaders that his was a German puppet regime. In light of what we know today about how much money Berlin invested in Bolshevik propaganda (at least 40 million German marks in gold), along with continuing revelations about the Stockholm banking connection the Germans used to lubricate the Bolshevik regime, this was not an unreasonable presumption.[5] In diplomatic practice, this meant two things. One, the British and French refused to participate in the peace negotiations between Russia and the Central powers at Brest-Litovsk (January-March 1918), which agreement was therefore never ratified or recognized in the West. Two, following Germany's own request for an armistice in October 1918, accepted on 11 November, the western Allies, along with (after April 1917) the United States as an "associated power," formulated their peace terms entirely without reference to the Bolsheviks—such that Russia was denied any share in the (short-lived) British-Italian-French partition of the Ottoman Empire agreed on at Sèvres (August 1920), receiving no "League of Nations" mandates, no occupation zones, and not a single quarter of Constantinople.

One can hardly blame the Allies for this manner of dealing with a treacherous ally that had betrayed the Allied cause. It was not simply that the Bolsheviks had emphatically broken the terms of the London Convention of September 1914, cutting a separate peace deal at Brest-Litovsk with the Germans (among the terms of which was that Russia would supply the Central powers with Caspian oil while also turning over to Berlin 6 billion marks worth of gold), nor that they had impoverished millions of French and British investors by "annihilating" (this was the Bolsheviks' own word) their bond holdings. In a more literal sense, the Bolsheviks had broken off legal connection to the old regime when they murdered Tsar Nicholas II and his family, in cold blood, in July 1918. Russia had entered into its inter-Allied agreements—as it had, indeed, all pre-1917 conventions and treaties—in the name of the tsar. Those agreements were now just as dead as the unfortunate Nicholas and Alexandra Romanov.

The "year zero" effect of the October Revolution reverberated further still. Although happy to publish incriminating documents from the tsarist archives to impugn the reputation of the previous regime, Soviet scholars were understandably reluctant to examine too deeply the reasons the Bolsheviks surrendered the First World War to Russia's enemies. So awkward was the subject in the Soviet times that no official history of Russia's military performance in the First World War was ever published—nor has it been even today, although military history is at last coming back into fashion in Russia.[6]

Russia's war of 1914, to the extent it has been written about at all, has tended to remain the province of disinterested Britons like Churchill, whose lyrical account of the eastern front in *The Unknown War* has much to recommend it—except for its total lack of Russian sources. Norman Stone, in *The Eastern Front* (1975), went deeper, especially into Russia's war economy: but then he, too, relied primarily on German and Austro-Hungarian sources.

Still, sources (or the lack of them) are not sufficient to explain the peculiar historical amnesia that now surrounds Russia's war of 1914. Churchill, like so many historians sympathetic to the Entente cause, spared Russia his usually sharp judgment largely out of sympathy following her terrible revolution. If we look closer at the concluding chapter of his volume on 1915, we see that same kind of ventriloquism that overcame British diplomats during the war, as Churchill takes an imaginary Russian point of view as his own. "In her darkest hours," he writes, "Russia had cheered herself by dwelling on the great prize of Constantinople." Following the British withdrawal from Cape Helles, however, Churchill writes with his characteristically unsourced empathy,

> A profound chill spread through all ranks of the Russian people, and with it came suspicion no less deep-seated. England had not really tried to force the Straits. From the moment when she had conceded the Russian claim to Constantinople, she had not been single-hearted, she had lost her interest in the enterprise. Her infirm action and divided counsels arose from secret motives hidden in the bosom of the State. And this while Russia was pouring out her own blood as no race had ever done since men waged war. Such were the whispers which, winged by successful German propaganda, spread far and wide through the Tsar's dominions, and in their wake every subversive influence gained in power.[7]

Here, surely, is empathy carried too far. In his zeal to impugn the short-sighted British statesmen who insisted on withdrawing, Churchill takes on the paranoid style of Russian conspiracy theorists. It may indeed have been true that many Russians, manipulated by German propaganda and their own yellow press, came to believe that the British had only pretended to promise Russia Constantinople and the Straits—and that (to take the idea to its logical conclusion) they had only pretended to sacrifice a hundred thousand men to win them for her ally. But why was this frankly insane view one that Churchill thought worth indulging, rather than refuting with passion and prejudice? Why did he not denounce Sazonov for failing to live up to his myriad promises during the Dardanelles and Gallipoli campaigns, not to mention the Russian propagandists who lied incessantly to their own people about the true facts of the business? How could the idea even occur to Churchill that Russia was a victim of Gallipoli—a campaign to which she contributed nothing and from which she would have gained everything?

There is much to be said for Churchill's gallantry in both human and literary terms. But in terms of historical understanding, he has done us a grave disservice. Few better than he could have laid down the real facts of the Gallipoli campaign, in which Russia's opportunism and tardiness were so manifest. Likewise, Churchill should have known better than to indulge the hoary "Russia fell on its sword for France" myth about the eastern European campaign of August 1914. By stamping these strangely illogical views with his insider's authority, Churchill set the tone for nearly all books to follow on Russia's war—not only those by fellow conservatives and anti-Communists but, in an odd way, those by historians friendlier to Communism too. When they are not dismissing Russia's entire pre-1917 era as essentially irrelevant back story to the glorious revolution,[8] such historians tend to adopt a version of the Marxist line on the world war's origins in "imperialism as the highest stage of capitalism." In this theory, "backward" Russia was conscripted into imperial rivalries between more advanced powers. As an inferior capital investor in the Ottoman Empire Russia could thus play, at most, a passive and reactive role in the outbreak of the First World War, and of course in such events as Gallipoli and Sykes-Picot.[9]

With Soviet scholars neglecting the subject for decades, and most western historians failing to attack it head-on for the reasons outlined above, the Russian statesmen who helped plunge Europe into war have entirely escaped the opprobrium which has been showered on their German counterparts ever since 1918. Moltke the Younger is fingered in a recent book as the "modest, unexceptional, and indeed rather ordinary career army officer [who] started the Great War."[10] Sazonov, by contrast, Moltke's counterpart on the Russian side, the man who told Germany's ambassador that Russia's mobilization could not be stopped; the man who decided to "partially mobilize" Russia's army before consulting the Council of Ministers on 24 July 1914, a full week before the Germans did the same, and in full knowledge of the probable consequences; a man whose own deeply dishonest memoirs display none of the candor of Moltke's—Sazonov has never, to this day, received similar treatment. Russia's foreign minister must now stand in the dock of historical judgment, along with Sukhomlinov, Yanushkevitch, and of course Tsar Nicholas II himself. These men (with the partial exception of the tsar, who, despite having final veto authority, did not initiate the key policies) chose consciously to mobilize Russia's colossal armies in full knowledge that they were risking war with Germany by doing so, while Sazonov himself deliberately concealed all this from London. We should also spare a critical thought for Ambassador Paléologue and French liaison General Laguiche, who each, with or without formal authorization from Poincaré and Viviani, gave France's imprimatur for Russia's secret mobilization against Germany. Convincing as it is on its own terms, even a watered-down version of the Fischer thesis, set against what we now know about Russia's early mobilization and French collusion in helping Sazonov dupe the British, can stand no more. There were at least as many men in St. Petersburg who wanted war in 1914 as there were in Berlin—and the men in Petersburg mobilized first.

The reason the Russians chose war in July 1914 is just as damning as the timing of their secret mobilization. Russia's war, it should by now be abundantly clear, was fought not for Serbia, but to achieve control of Constantinople and the Straits. Contingent peculiarities of the Sarajevo outrage aside, control of the Straits was Russia's first strategic priority at the time of the Bosnian crisis of 1908–1909, the First Balkan War in 1912, the Second Balkan War in 1913, the Liman affair of winter 1913–14, the diplomatic crisis over the British-Turkish dreadnoughts in April-June 1914, the diplomatic battles over Turkish belligerence from August-November 1914, the Dardanelles and Gallipoli campaigns of winter-spring 1915, the Sykes-Picot drama of spring 1916, the renewed Russian drive for an amphibious Bosphorus strike in winter 1916–17, and even after the February Revolution of 1917. The idea that Serbia acquired outsized prominence as a Russian *casus belli* in July 1914, only to vanish off the strategic map again in August, defies belief. The assassination of Archduke Ferdinand may well have been that "damn fool thing in the Balkans" Bismarck had warned about, a pretext for men bent upon war for other reasons—but if so it was pretext as much for the Russians as for the Germans. For good and for considerable ill, Sazonov and Sukhomlinov chose to go to war in 1914 for the Straits and Constantinople—as would Miliukov and Guchkov in 1917.[11] To achieve this ambition, Russians indeed paid a terrible price, as Churchill lamented: but then so did millions of other Europeans and Ottoman subjects who, unlike the Russians, had no interest in tsarist control of Constantinople.

For all the horrors that ensued in its wake, there is much to learn from the obsessive consistency of tsarist foreign policy. Through the turmoil of the war years, all the inter-Allied acrimony over war aims, Russia's claims on Constantinople and the Straits, not to mention on Thrace, Gallipoli, the "Trojan" peninsula, Imbros, Tenedos, "Turkish Armenia" and "Kurdistan," along with Persian Azerbaijan, remained unaltered. Even on the question of Polish autonomy, which could have turned into a merely symbolic issue for Russia following the fall of most of Congress Poland to the enemy, the Russians displayed rock-solid stubbornness, refusing to so much as humor powerful political sensibilities in France, supposedly Russia's closest ally. London's concerns about Russian ambitions in Persia received even shorter shrift.

The contrast to British foreign policy during the war could not be starker. From an ostensible *casus belli* to do with restoring Belgian territorial integrity and reversing German aggression, London veered from one priority to another between 1914 and 1918, from promises to protect Ottoman territory if Turkey stayed out of the war to a policy of dismembering the Ottoman Empire, from staking everything on a bloody battle to conquer Constantinople by the shortest route and thus restore Russia's seagoing access to the Mediterranean, to a methodical campaign to conquer Asiatic Turkey in slow motion, one desert oasis at a time. In politico-religious terms, British policies were more bewildering still, veering from a flirtation with remaking the Caliphate at Mecca, to a dalliance with (theoretically) secular Arab nationalism, to Sykes's discovery of the Jews of Palestine, the subsequent ideological-cum-sentimental embrace of Zionism by Lloyd George, and the Balfour Declaration.

To some extent, we can chalk up British inconsistency to the perennial dilemmas of making foreign policy in a liberal democracy, where countless ethno-political interest groups vie for attention and patronage. Asquith, Grey, and Lloyd George simply could not display the same insouciant indifference to public opinion as did tsarist statesmen in formulating foreign policy. It was, paradoxically, the very freedom of maneuver enjoyed by policymakers in Russia's autocracy that allowed them to pursue policies with such ruthless consistency, unconstrained (at least until the upheavals of 1917) by any need to placate domestic interest groups. To give one example among many: had Sazonov, Sukhomlinov, or Yanush-kevitch cared a whit about Muslim opinion in the Caucasus, they would never have sanctioned Russia's reckless Armenian gambit of 1913–1915, nor, of course, the mass deportations of Muslim subjects from frontline areas. Likewise, so little did Russian policymakers worry about offending what was arguably Russia's most important minority population that Stavka felt perfectly free to deport nearly a million Jews from frontline areas during the war, despite the fact that more than 400,000 Jews were serving loyally in the Russian army.[12] Tsarist Russia was a state in which leaders felt no need to listen to even the most influential domestic critics, much less the concerns of restless minorities. Such states are free to pursue ruthless *Realpolitik* in a way democratic powers will never be.

If we cannot necessarily fault British policymakers for inconsistency, however, it is still fair to ask why they so readily volunteered to serve the interests of an autocratic power with values so different from their own. The Russians had been right to be concerned about English public opinion, both in May-June 1914, when Benckendorff so delicately broached the issue of the dreadnoughts being built for Turkey, and during the July crisis, when keeping London in the dark was Sazonov's first priority. What is surprising is that so few British statesmen cared to inquire as to why Russia was so concerned about Ottoman dreadnoughts in 1914, why Sazonov was lying about her mobilization the last week of July, and not least, why the Russians were so keen on Britain forcing the Dardanelles in 1915. "Anti-interventionist" British historians, like John Charmley and Niall Ferguson, have argued that preventing German hegemony in Europe was not a sufficient reason for Britain to risk its empire by going to war in 1914.[13] They might instead have asked why Britain risked its empire and a generation of its young men to satisfy Russian imperial ambitions—ambitions that the British public had viewed with considerable distaste and alarm for over a century.

The bamboozlement of the British by clever Russian diplomats like Sazonov has much relevance for our own age. The cardinal weakness of a democratic power in the international arena is not so much inconsistency as naiveté. Without the luxury of public disinterest (or at least indifference) to the fine print of diplomacy, the British of 1914–1918, like Americans today, were compelled to explain what they were doing to the public in something like altruistic terms. It may not really be true that the United States went to war in Iraq in 1991 to restore Kuwaiti territorial integrity, any more than that Britain fought in 1914 to preserve Belgium—or at Gallipoli to open up Russian access to the Mediterranean and thus serve the common Allied cause (rather than, as many Russians suspected, to conquer Constantinople themselves). In the case of Zionism, at least, Britain's policy may well have been just as transparently idealistic as London professed, but then this is hardly an argument in favor of its strategic sense. The Balfour Declaration is a perfect example of the way in which the need of democratic countries to justify policies in altruistic terms leads to imprecision, if not outright confusion, of a country's real national interest. Had the British public been told in 1914 that, in effect, they were being asked to bleed and die in order to fulfill Russia's age-old ambition to control Constantinople and the Straits, they would have rioted in the streets. And yet this is exactly the policy that Asquith, Grey, Churchill, and Kitchener, carefully manipulated by the Russians, actually pursued in 1915. So brilliant was Russian ventriloquism during the First World War that Churchill and the British scarcely remembered that it happened.

The same sleight-of-hand was repeated with Ottoman Armenians. So thoroughly did the Russians pull wool over the eyes of her western allies regarding her dangerous gambit with an enemy fifth column that, even today, few people realize the Armenian victims of 1915 were pawns in a ruthless game of empire, in which their own revolutionary "spokesmen" were heavily implicated. Nothing that the Russians, Dashnaks, or Hunchaks did that terrible year, of course, justifies the inhumane treatment of Armenian civilians by the Ottoman authorities and (perhaps even more so) by Kurdish tribesmen. The notorious article 301 of the Turkish penal code, which has been applied against several Turkish citizens who used the word "genocide" to describe the events of 1915, is rightly an affront to all historians who seek to investigate the past impartially. But then so are the "Armenian genocide denial" laws on the books in France and Switzerland, which are just as clearly meant to stifle free historical inquiry on this explosive subject. Historians may never agree on the issue of genocidal "intent," or on how many Armenian—and Muslim—civilians were killed in Turkey and the Caucasus during the war. But we may at least ask them to tell the tragic story of 1915 in its proper historical context, in which Russia's colossal role is no longer ignored.

Nearly a century has passed since the guns fell silent—at least in the European theater—in November 1918. In the lands of the former Ottoman Empire, the First World War smolders still, as Sunnis and Shiites, Arabs and Jews, and other regional antagonists continue fighting each other (and the great power patrons of their opponents) over the last scraps of the Ottoman inheritance. For decades, historians, politicians, and armchair strategists have focused their fire on Imperial Germany as the primary instigator of the European conflict, even while anti-imperialist and Islamic writers have impugned the Franco-British perfidy of Sykes-Picot in dismembering Turkey and destroying the Ottoman Empire. It is high time that Russia, too, receive its fair share of scrutiny for its role in unleashing the terrible European war of 1914, and for helping spread this war into the Middle East. Neither a deliberate German plot nor an avoidable accident, the First World War was the inexorable culmination of a burgeoning imperial rivalry between Wilhelmine Germany and tsarist Russia in the Near East, each lured in its own way down the dangerous path of expansionist war by the decline of Ottoman power. In the end the war destroyed both regimes, although this was little consolation to the millions who died in it—or the millions more who perished in the Russian Revolution, the Second World War, and other conflicts born out of the wreckage of the First. To tell the truth about the origins of the war of 1914 is the least we can do to honor its victims.

Notes

1. For notable recent restatements of the general consensus about German fears of Russia leading to the fateful decisions made in Berlin, see David Stevenson, *Cataclysm* (2004), chap. 1; Hew Strachan, *The First World War* (2004), "To Arms" (which, somewhat unusually, shifts significant blame to Vienna as against Berlin); Norman Stone, *World War One* (2008), intro. and chap. 1; and particularly David Fromkin, *Europe's Last Summer* (2004), which presents the "state of the scholarly art" case against Germany in the manner of a legal brief. Since Fritz Fischer more or less outdueled the mostly German critics of the thesis he presented in *Germany's Aims in the First World War* (orig. *Griff nach der Weltmacht,* 1961) in a roughly decade-long debate, there have been few attempts in English or any other language to debunk the overall line, even if few any longer accept in its entirety Fischer's argument about premeditated German imperial war aims. As Holger Herwig puts it colorfully in a recent volume he co-edited, *The Origins of World War I,* ed. Hamilton and Herwig (2003), the German decision for war was not quite Fischer's "bid for world power" but rather "a nervous, indeed panicked 'leap into the dark' to secure the Reich's position of semihegemony on the Continent." Herwig, like Strachan and other leading World War I historians today, certainly takes Russia's own strategic dilemmas of July 1914 into account. Still, these authors reject the notion that Russian actions brought about the war; rather, Russia was important insofar as it factored into German or Austrian thinking. As Herwig argues typically (pp. 454–457), any effort to pin blame on Russian leaders for their own provocative actions in July "would be mistaken, as it ignores the outlooks and choices of Germany's leaders," who had "decided for war, 'now or never,' in any case."

In *The Pity of War* (1998), Niall Ferguson does present a kind of devil's-advocate case against the notion of German war guilt, but his concern is mostly to critique England's own decision to intervene, not really to re-examine the July crisis itself. (And when Ferguson does at last discuss the specific issue of war guilt, on pp. 149–154, he follows the anti-German line fairly closely, conceding only that the Germans were thinking in terms of a "military 'first strike,' designed to pre-empt a deterioration in Germany's military position.")

A notable statement of the more balanced, pre-Fischer understanding of "war guilt" responsibility in the July crisis is that of Luigi Albertini, *The Origins of the War of 1914*, 3 vols. (1953–1957). It is no coincidence that Albertini is the only one of the historians mentioned here to have examined Russian sources in some depth.

As for Russian specialists who look into Russia's role in the outbreak of war in 1914, most ape the basic Fischer line on German war guilt, seeing Russia's decision to go to war as deeply reluctant, a kind of honorable-yet-foolish "falling on the sword" for France. In this vein, see particularly Dietrich Geyer, *Russian Imperialism: The Interaction of Domestic and Foreign Policy 1860–1914* (orig. *Der russische Imperialismus*, 1977). "The Russian political elite," Geyer concludes (p. 312), "had no reason to desire a great war in July 1914." A subtler version of this line, which takes into account currents of bellicosity coursing through the Council of Ministers in 1914 (particularly in the person of A. V. Krivoshein, the Agriculture Minister), is proposed by D. C. B. Lieven in *Russia and the Origins of the First World War* (1983), which endures as the standard book-length work on the subject until now. Lieven's conclusions, for example, were adopted with only minor reservations by David McDonald in his widely respected study, *United Government and Foreign Policy in Russia 1900–1914* (1992), in his chapter, "The Decision to Go to War" (pp. 199–207). Although Lieven's argument is more subtle than Geyer's or Fischer's, he still takes German guilt as a proven matter, not needing further elucidation, much less a substantial critique. Lieven is reportedly at work on a new history of Russia in the First World War; it will be fascinating to see if he has revised his reviews in light of a recent explosion in research on the subject. Keith Neilson, in the article on "Russia" in Keith Wilson, ed., *Decisions for War* (1995), goes so far as to declare (p. 112) that "the Russian government was prepared . . . to risk a conflict rather than abdicate its position as a Great Power," but waters down this conclusion with the condition that Russian leaders were still "far from willing war to occur." David Alan Rich, in the "Russia" article in Hamilton and Herwig's 2003 volume, *Origins of World War I*, goes a bit further still in pinpointing Russia's responsibility, attributing it to its controversial early "partial mobilization." But he fails to press the point. (And even his half-hearted attempt to pin some blame on Russia is swatted down by Herwig, the volume's Germanist editor, in the passage cited above.)

2. These works tended to appear at times of intensive Soviet military concern over this or that matter; thus there was a spate of general staff studies of First World War field operations between 1936 and 1940. Curiously, there are several good studies by "civilian" Soviet historians of the Caucasian front, in particular—N. G. Korsun, *Alashkertskaia i Khamadanskaia operatsii na Kavkazskom fronte mirovoi voiny* (1940), and Arutiunian, *Kavkazskii front* (1971). But these are the exceptions which prove the rule. Military histories of the First World War produced in the Soviet era can practically be counted on one hand, whereas they number in the thousands in all western countries. Ideology is the obvious explanation.

3. The essential work remains Norman Stone's *Eastern Front 1914–1917*, first published in 1975. In recent years, due in part to increased access to Russian archives, there has been a boom in research on the Russian army—its command structure, logistics and supply, the education of officers and institutional culture, strategic doctrine and efforts to update it, and so

on. Scholars such as William C. Fuller, *Civil-Military Conflict in Imperial Russia 1880–1914* (1985) and *Strategy and Power* (1992); Bruce Menning, *Bayonets before Bullets* (1992); and John W. Steinberg, most recently *All the Tsar's Men: Russia's General Staff,* have performed yeoman's work in opening up this field to English-language readers. Nevertheless, as to the course of the war itself, Stone's book still, somewhat improbably, commands the field. As Stone himself is fond of remarking, "someone should have made my book obsolete long ago." To date no one has.

4. As noted, Albertini's magisterial work on the origins of the war, published 1953–1956, makes extensive use of the Soviet documentary collections. So too does C. Jay Smith, Jr., in *The Russian Struggle for Power, 1914–1917* (1956), a very thorough study of Russia's war aims. Yet, for all its perspicacity, Smith's book appears to have fallen through the cracks in the Fritz Fischer years; it is not generally cited today, except by Russian specialists. The only major English-language historian employing the Russian documentary collections to tackle the "Germanocentric" theory of the war's origins head-on during what we might call the high Fritz Fischer era was L. C. F. Turner, in "The Russian Mobilization in 1914," published in the *Journal of Contemporary History* in 1968, an argument he later expanded out to book length in *The Origins of the First World War* (1970). But Turner's work was shouted down almost immediately, making scarcely a dent in the emerging modified-Fischer consensus.

In the years since, a few diplomatic historians have kept the flame flickering. Alan Bodger, in "Russia and the End of the Ottoman Empire" (1984), takes Russia's expansionist war aims seriously, but he expressly denies that these aims had anything to do with the outbreak of war in 1914. Horst Gunther Linke's *Zaristische Russland und der Erste Weltkrieg* (1982) harks back to an older, pre-Fischer tradition: German scholars were after all the first, back in the 1920s when they were trying to counter the Versailles war guilt clause, to make wide use of the Soviet documentary collections, and this tradition will likely endure. Perhaps believing Germans to be irretrievably biased, most English-language First World War historians continue to take little note of such books. (Fischer and his disciples are, presumably, given a pass in this regard, as "anti-German" Germans.)

A number of Soviet scholars did examine Russia's war aims (especially towards Turkey and the Straits), in part because they dovetailed nicely with Marxist-Leninist ideas about capitalism and imperialism. In this tradition, see especially K. F. Shatsillo, *Russkii imperialism i razvitie flota nakanune pervoi mirovoi voiny* (1968). After the fall of Communism in 1991, Oleg Airapetov took up the tradition, and in a much more serious (and less ideological) fashion—his long article "Na Vostochnom napravlenii. Sud'ba Bosforskoi ekspeditsii v pravlenie imperatora Nikolaia II," in *Poslednaia voina imperatorskoi Rossii: sbornik statei* (2002), is by far the most thorough study to date of Russian Straits policy. But these works, never translated into English, have had little to no impact on general English-language scholarship on the First World War.

A recent work in English in the same area, Ronald Bobroff's *Roads to Glory: Late Imperial Russia and the Turkish Straits* (2006), may yet succeed in having an impact on the broader English-language narrative about the war, although to date his study remains little known outside Russian-specialist circles (and Bobroff, like most others before him, denies that Russia's Straits ambitions played any role in the outbreak of the First World War, despite the importance of these ambitions for wartime diplomacy). What we might call the landward side of Russia's imperial ambitions in Turkey has also been examined in tremendous depth by Mike

Reynolds, in *Shattering Empires: The Clash and Collapse of the Ottoman and Russian Empires* (2011). Perhaps these works, along with my own, may at last tip the balance in historical understanding of the First World War eastward, allowing Russia its fair share in the story.

5. It is not that tsarist Russia is never *mentioned* in such books: even the most antiwestern authors admit that Britain and France had some help in putting together the Sykes-Picot Agreement and subsequent partition of Asiatic Turkey. But the very fact that "Sykes-Picot" (without also the name of the Russian signatory to the agreements, Sazonov) is now universal shorthand for the thing shows that Russia's role is assumed to be secondary. A good recent example of this is Rashid Khalidi's recent anti-imperialist polemic, *Resurrecting Empire: Western Footprints and America's Perilous Path in the Middle East* (2004), in which Russia's imperial "footprints" in the Middle East are so tiny as to be virtually invisible. There is a brief mention of Russian ambitions in Persia (pp. 18, 80), and an even briefer mention of Russian interest in the Straits (p. 79), but otherwise tsarist Russia is confined to its usual supporting role as a kind of bit player in the "Sykes-Picot accords," which "became the basis for the postwar division of the Middle East into spheres of influence between Britain and France" (p. 32 and *passim*).

In a recent work from what we might call the opposite point of view (that is, anti-anti-imperialist, debunking the more fashionable antiwestern line), *Empires of the Sand* (1999), Efraim Karsh does a much better job describing Russia's intimate involvement in wartime diplomacy. He even uses several Russian documents from the German translation of the Soviet "secret" collections. Nevertheless, Karsh relies so heavily on English sources that he grossly misreads Russian policy regarding the Ottoman Empire in 1914, assuming that St. Petersburg was just as reluctant to go to war with Turkey in October–November 1914 as was London. Even after the Turco-German naval attack of October 1914, Karsh writes, "The Entente *still* hoped that war was avoidable." Many British and French leaders had such hopes, maybe, but not the Russians, who not only knew the attack was coming but also welcomed it, for all the reasons outlined in the present narrative.

6. "Russia's Great War and Revolution, 1914–1922: The Centenary Reappraisal," editors John Steinberg and Anthony Heywood. The approach of Steinberg and Heywood towards what they call "Russia's 'Continuum of Crisis' during the years 1914–1922" is clearly inspired by Peter Holquist's influential study *Making War, Forging Revolution: Russia's Continuum of Crisis, 1914–1921*. To date 220 chapter proposals have been submitted to the editors of the project, on a wide range of themes.

7. A notable exception in this regard is David Fromkin, in *A Peace to End All Peace* (1989). Fromkin goes so far as to state in his introduction that he aims to restore Russia to "a central role in the story" of the creation of the modern Middle East out of the wreckage of the Great War. In many ways Fromkin succeeds admirably in his task, situating the events of the war in the broader narrative of "Great Game" geopolitics (he even insists on calling the 1916 partition accords the "Sykes-Picot-Sazonov" agreement). My own work is largely inspired by Fromkin's global approach. Nevertheless, it remains true that, like most First World War generalists, Fromkin did not use published Russian documentary collections, let alone primary materials, in his groundbreaking study.

8. Unlike the official Imperial German series of documents carefully selected to counter the Versailles accusation of war guilt *(Die Grosse Politik der Europäischen Kabinette, 1871–1914),* the collections published by Soviet archivists in the 1920s were conceived in much the

opposite spirit, as a way of discrediting pre-Communist "imperialism." The most important of these, *Razdel aziatskoi Turtsii. Po sekretnyim dokumentam b. Ministerstva inostrannyikh del* [The Partition of Asiatic Turkey, According to Secret Documents from the Former Ministry of Foreign Affairs] (1924), and the massive two-volume exposé of Russian Straits planning and policy, *Konstantinopol' i prolivy* (1925–1926), were both edited by E. A. Adamov. Other, somewhat better known collections include *Mezhdunarodnye otnosheniia v epoku imperializma* (ed. M. N. Pokrovskii, 1931–), also published in a more widely available German-language edition as *Internationale Beziehungen im Zeitalter des Imperialismus,* and the massive *Krasnyi Arkhiv* (1922–1941).

Of course, there is no guarantee of the authenticity of the documents in question. From my investigation of the original files at the Archive of the Foreign Policy of the Russian Empire (AVPRI), however, I can confirm that every Russian-language original so far (of which I have found more than a hundred matches) checks out perfectly with its transcription in Adamov's volumes. Those documents originally written in French and English, too, check out, although of course with certain discrepancies in translation.

As for documents used in this study from the Imperial Russian military archives (RGVIA), none of these have ever been published until now. Like those at AVPRI, they are open to researchers with very few restrictions, and have been for years.

1. THE STRATEGIC IMPERATIVE IN 1914

1. Cited in Spring, "Russia and the Coming of War," p. 85. Spring's translation.

2. Cited in Mankoff, "Russia and the Polish Question, 1908–1917," p. 90. Mankoff's translation.

3. Cited in Airapetov, "Sud'ba Bosforskoi ekspeditsii," p. 175.

4. Menning, *Bayonets before Bullets,* p. 227.

5. Fifteen days for the initial (not full) concentration on the eastern front was what the Russians were promising the French, in staff conversations before the war; the idea was to force the Germans to be ready to meet the Russians in force by M + 15, even if the Russians themselves weren't quite ready. Bruce Menning, who has examined the Russian military archives more thoroughly, doubts these figures: he thinks that realistically a "complete mobilization of troops in European Russia" in 1914 required something like twenty-six days. Menning, "The Offensive Revisited," p. 224.

6. Stone, *Eastern Front 1914–1917,* p. 17. On the Great Program, and particularly its hidden defects, see also Menning, *Bayonets before Bullets,* pp. 233–234.

7. As one learns from Paul Kennedy, in *The Rise and Fall of the Great Powers.*

8. Fuller, *Strategy and Power in Russia 1600–1914,* pp. 295–296.

9. Lieven, *Russia and the Origins of the First World War,* pp. 8–9.

10. As Bethmann Hollweg complained to the Russian foreign minister, Sergei Sazonov. Sazonov, *Fateful Years,* p. 41.

11. For a basic summary of these ambitions, see Fischer, *Germany's Aims in the First World War,* chapter 1. See also McMeekin, *The Berlin-Baghdad Express.*

12. Spring, "Russian Imperialism in Asia in 1914," p. 305. For more on the subject see also Geyer, *Russian Imperialism,* chapter 14.

13. See Quai d'Orsay memorandum labeled "Russie-Angleterre. Juillet 1914," in QO Russie Politique Etrangère, vol. 50. The Russians were particularly active in Urmia province, where Vice-Consuls Vvedenskii and Gulubinov were active in everything from processing land grants to arming Kurds and Christian minorities. Their field correspondence is preserved in RGVIA, fond 2000, opis' 1, del' 3851; and AVPRI, fond 180, opis' 517/2, del' 3573.

14. "Russie-Angleterre. Juillet 1914." Jennifer Siegel, in her acclaimed recent study *Endgame: Britain, Russia and the Final Struggle for Central Asia,* argues (p. 193) that by 1914, Russia's "forward policy" in northern Persia, and British moves to counter it, meant that "the 1907 Anglo-Russian agreement, guaranteeing the status quo in Persia, Afghanistan, and Tibet, was dead." *Dead* may be too strong a word, but Siegel is right in the sense that negotiations to update the accord in spring 1914 had broken down in mutual acrimony, leaving Anglo-Russian relations in Asia in a kind of dangerous limbo. She is also right that the 1907 agreement was never a real Entente in the way that the Anglo-French agreement of 1904 was. Still, that some kind of working accord over Persia still existed is attested by the fact that British and Russian diplomats continued negotiating on the basis of the 1907 agreement during the First World War (trying to revise it of course, but still using 1907 as a starting point). See chapter 7 below.

15. Lord Durham, British ambassador to St. Petersburg, in March 1836. Cited in Hopkirk, *The Great Game,* p. 162. The Buchanan and Nicolson quotes footnoted are cited in Spring, "Russia and the Coming of War," p. 76.

16. Fuller, *Strategy and Power,* p. 290.

17. See British Embassy aide-mémoire, 30 November 1910, in QO Russie Politique Etrangère, vol. 50. For a typical report on Turkish-Russian-Persian border skirmishing from this era, see "Turkey and Persia. The Prospects of War," in *Times of India,* 19 March 1908.

18. "Russie-Angleterre. Juillet 1914." On the Baghdad Railway in the prewar era see also McMeekin, *Berlin-Baghdad Express,* chapters 2 and 14.

19. Fuller, *Strategy and Power,* p. 430.

20. Sazonov, *Fateful Years,* p. 33.

21. It was actually Austria's ambassador to France, Baron Khevenhüller-Metsch, who first revealed the quid pro quo. But Aehrenthal himself later confirmed it. See Rauchensteiner, *Der Tod des Doppeladlers,* p. 18.

22. From the protocol of the meeting of the Council of Ministers held on 21 January/3 February 1908, reproduced (in German translation) in Pokrovskii, ed., *Drei Konferenzen,* pp. 25, 30. On Palitsyn's order, see Fuller, *Strategy and Power,* p. 411. Fuller claims Palitsyn's decision was taken "without notifying the Council of State Defence," but in light of the very explicit discussions in St. Petersburg that February, it is likely at least some of the principals then present (including Stolypin, then-Finance Minister Kokovtsev, Foreign Minister Izvolsky, and Sukhomlinov's deputy, Polivanov) were in the loop.

23. "Dessantnaya ekspeditsiya k Bosforu." Russian General Staff Doklad, 20 September/3 October 1910, in RGVIA, fond 2000, opis' 1, del' 2219.

24. On Danilov's motivation for reorienting Russia's army concentration east so as to save the army from the Germans, see Menning, *Bayonets before Bullets,* pp. 240–241. Menning also provides excellent "before and after" maps of the 1910 deployment.

25. Fuller, *Strategy and Power,* pp. 296, 425–438.

26. Ibid., pp. 439–440. For an example of French critical thinking on Russia's 1910 mobi-

lization plan, see Lt. Colonel Janin's skeptical memorandum "Au sujet de la valeur de la co-opération russe," December 1911, in the French military archives at Vincennes, box 7 N 1538 (Attachés militaires Russie). Janin's conclusion was that Russia would, on then current form, not be able to undertake "serious" action against the Germans until M + 30, which was "far too late" to offer France any serious assistance.

27. On this point, see especially Stone, *Eastern Front 1914–1917,* pp. 30–31.

28. The "Ruthenian" issue of nomenclature is extremely complex, and controversial. For the most part, the present narrative concerns the "Ruthenians" of Austrian Galicia, most of them belonging to the Greek Uniate Church, who spoke a dialect of "Ukrainian" and yet, confusingly, called themselves *Rusiny* until the convulsions of the First World War, after which most adopted the term "Ukrainian."

29. "Mémoire sur la question polonaise," clipped and translated from "Kurjer Warszaw-ski," 5 December 1913, in QO Russie Politique Intérieure, vol. 4. In a similar vein, see also "La chaine teutonique, la Russie, la France, et la question polonaise," from *Dzien,* 9 January 1914, in QO Russie Politique Intérieure, vol. 4.

30. Cited in Mankoff, "Russia and the Polish Question, 1907–1917," p. 90.

31. Doulcet to Doumergue, 14 March 1914, in QO Russie Politique Etrangère, vol. 45.

32. Cited in Komarnicki, *Rebirth of the Polish Republic,* pp. 5–6.

33. Sazonov, *Fateful Years,* p. 78.

34. "Démembrement de l'Autriche," from *Kurjer Warszawski,* 17 April 1914, a critical commentary on the recent series on Galicia in *Novoe Vremya.*

35. Menning, *Bayonets before Bullets,* pp. 246–247.

36. Paléologue to Doumergue, 3 May 1914, in QO Russie Politique Etrangère, vol. 46.

37. On the various "syndromes" which haunted Russian strategic thinking, see Fuller, *Strategy and Power,* chapters 7, 8, and 9.

38. Turner, *Origins of the First World War,* pp. 41–46.

39. There is a theory, advanced by Fritz Fischer in *Krieg der Illusionen* (1969) that the Germans held their own "war council" on 8 December 1912, at which the kaiser and the generals, warned by Admiral Tirpitz that the navy was not yet ready, decided to delay war until some time in 1914; the obvious implication was that the war of 1914 was premeditated. This is one of those Fischer theories which appears to have taken on a life of its own in the hands of Fischer's critics, such that Fischer himself later intervened to deny holding it. "I never claimed," Fischer wrote in 1988, "that the war was planned for a long time . . . not even by the 'War Council' of Wilhelm II on 8 December 1912." Fischer, "Twenty-Five Years Later: Look-ing Back at the 'Fischer Controversy' and its Consequences," pp. 214–215.

40. Grigorevich telegram no. 320, to Tsar Nicholas II, dispatched at 1:30 am on the night of 25–26 October 1912, and the tsar's reply ("Soglasen. Nikolai."), reproduced in KA, vol. 6, pp. 51–52. For the bit about Ferdinand's Byzantine regalia, see Barbara Tuchman, *Guns of August,* p. 16.

41. Cited in Bobroff, *Roads to Glory,* p. 55. Bobroff's translation.

42. Airapetov, "Sud'ba Bosforskoi ekspeditsii."

43. In this vein, see Sazonov to Grigorevich, 25 November 1912; Sazonov to Girs, 15 March 1913; Sazonov memorandum on the Straits, 18 April 1913, all excerpted in "Konstanti-nopol i prolivyi," in KA 6 (1924), pp. 51–63; and also Sazonov's 23 November/6 December

1913 policy memorandum addressed to Tsar Nicholas II, signed off on by the latter at Livadia, 27 November/9 December 1913, in AVPRI, in fond 138, opis' 467, del' 461, list' 24–29 (and backs).

44. See "Colonel Sirmanov's Scheme," in folder marked "1912. Concentation russe," in VSHD, box 7 N 1487.

45. In this vein, see especially Sazonov to the tsar, 23 November/6 December 1913, AVPRI, fond 138, opis' 467, del' 461.

46. Rauchensteiner, *Tod des Doppeladlers,* p. 19.

47. On the Albanian question in 1914, see Weber, *Eagles on the Crescent,* pp. 47, 54–55.

48. Komarnicki, *Rebirth of the Polish Republic,* p. 8.

49. According to Austrian sources, Izvolsky assured the Ballhausplatz in 1908 that Russia would intervene on behalf of Serbia only if and when Austria staged a "military parade" in Belgrade. Rauchensteiner, *Tod des Doppeladlers,* p. 19.

50. Peter Gatrell gives a good average estimate of 43 percent for the period 1909–1913. Gatrell, *Government, Industry and Rearmament in Russia, 1900–1914,* p. 300.

51. British Foreign Office study of the "Russian Financial Situation," 25 July 1914, in PRO, FO 371/2094.

52. Figures in Miller, *The Economic Development of Russia 1905–1914,* p. 61. While economists might object that it would be fine for Russia to run a current account deficit by importing capital, the fact is that Russia was doing both things at once: importing capital (mostly by selling bonds in Paris and London) and running a trade surplus. In a technical sense, then, the trade "surplus" was fictional; still it was better for Russia's economy to export more than she imported, much as Japan does today (even while running huge government deficits). While the edifice all came crashing down after 1917, in 1914 Russia was still getting the best of both worlds, accumulating huge gold reserves as she bought gold with the revenue from bond sales while paying for imports largely through export revenue.

53. On Krivoshein, see especially K. A. Krivoshein *fils* on *A. V. Krivoshein (1857–1921 g.) Ego znachenie v istorii Rossii nachala XX veka.* I have also drawn on the backgrounder on "Principaux Personnages Politiques Russes" prepared for President Raymond Poincaré's visit, 12 July 1914, in QO, Russie. Politique Intérieure, vol. 4.

On the grain question generally and the threat posed by German imports, see Berghahn, *Germany and the Approach of War in 1914,* pp. 182–183.

54. For a typical discussion, which relies on the correspondence reproduced in *Grosse Politik der Europäischen Kabinette* and on Sazonov's own memoirs (*Fateful Years,* pp. 124–125), see Albertini, *The Origins of the Great War of 1914,* vol. 2, pp. 540–550. Albertini faults Sazonov for his impatience and lack of "cool-headedness."

55. Girs to Sazonov, 14/27 November 1913, in AVPRI, fond 172, opis' 514/2, del' 633, list' 128–130.

56. Charikov to Sazonov, "top secret" memorandum, 9/22 February 1912, in AVPRI, fond 138, opis' 467, del' 461/480, list' 1 (and back), 2.

57. Girs to Sazonov, 14/27 November 1913, in AVPRI, fond 172, opis' 514/2, del' 633, list' 128–130.

58. Sazonov to Tsar Nicholas II, 23 November/6 December 1913, in AVPRI, fond 138, opis' 467, del' 461/480.

59. Sazonov to Tsar Nicholas II, 6 January 1914, reproduced in the *Krasnyi Arkhiv,* v. 6, p. 41 and *passim.*

60. Pokrovskii, *Drei Konferenzen,* pp. 40–42. For Delcassé's promise to Sazonov, see Turner, *Origins of the First World War,* pp. 58–59. For the bit about Sazonov pressuring Serbia to cede Macedonian territory to Bulgaria, see Komarnicki, *Rebirth of the Polish Republic,* p. 8.

61. On the German side of the press war, see especially Berghahn, *Germany and the Approach of War in 1914,* pp. 179–181. On the Russian side, see Spring, "Russia and the Coming of War," p. 79 and *passim.*

62. Fuller, *Strategy and Power,* p. 438.

63. Sazonov, *Fateful Years,* pp. 126–127. The February 1914 planning conference, as Ronald Bobroff has recently noted, was originally scheduled for late December 1913, that is, while the Liman crisis was still at its height, only to be postponed due to the illness of Admiral A. A. Lieven, a former chief of Naval Staff, who was still too ill in February to attend. Curiously, despite devoting a great deal of attention to his illustrious ancestor's role in Russian naval policy while he was chief of Naval Staff, D. C. B. Lieven, in *Russia and the Origins of the First World War,* does not mention the February 1914 conference at all. (Lieven does cite the transcript of the February conference published by the Bolsheviks, but in the course of a massive endnote, no. 111 on p. 184, where it is only one of about a dozen sources cited. For whatever reason, he apparently did not think this conference worthy of special comment.)

64. Sazonov, *Fateful Years,* pp. 126–127. A notable example of a historian misled by Sazonov's line on Russia's weakness is Geyer, who emphasizes in *Russian Imperialism* (pp. 342–343) "how poorly prepared the Russian Government was to accomplish its 'historic mission' in the Near East. Nowhere was Russian weakness clearer than when it came to influencing the affairs of the Ottoman Empire . . . St Petersburg still had good reason to avoid war." Because of Russian financial dependence on France, Geyer argues, "in the Near East the best Russia could hope to do was tag along limply behind her French ally." This may have been true of Russian banking syndicates, but Geyer's dismissal of Russian agency in Near Eastern policy would have astonished Imperial Russia's admirals and generals, who were by 1914 hard at work planning the conquest of the Ottoman Empire entirely without reference to French policy.

65. In fact Bosphorus-seizure planning discussions dated to 1885, the context then being a "Great Game" war scare with Britain. But the first serious technical studies were not begun until the mid-1890s. So in this sense, Sazonov was correct. See Airapetov, "Sud'ba Bosforskoi ekspeditsii," p. 158.

66. Sazonov to Tsar Nicholas II, 23 November/6 December 1913, in AVPRI, fond 138, opis' 467, del' 461/480.

67. "Desantnaia Ekspeditsiia," prepared for the General Staff by the Naval Staff, 28 August/10 September 1913, in RGVIA, fond 2000, opis' 1, del' 2220, list' 2–7.

68. According to Grigorevich, as reported to the 8/21 February 1914 planning conference, in AVPRI, fond 138, opis' 467, del' 462/481, list' 16.

69. Airapetov, in "Sud'ba Bosforskoi ekspeditsii" (pp. 174–175), notes that Danilov and Zhilinskii remained opposed to mounting a Bosphorus strike, as they worried about denuding the European front of troops. But Airapetov admits that the tsar lined up behind Sazonov—as did Grigorevich, the chief of Naval Staff.

70. Grigorevich to Sazonov, 20 December 1913/2 January 1914, in AVPRI, fond 138, opis' 467, del' 461/480, list' 30–33.

71. Attending were: Sazonov (chairing); Zhilinskii, head of the General Staff; Grigorevich,

chief of the Naval Staff; M. N. Girs, Russia's ambassador to Constantinople; Anatolii Neratov, Sazonov's assistant at the Foreign Office; Yuri Danilov, "quartermaster-general" at the General Staff (and confidant of Sukhomlinov, the war minister); Count Trubetskoi, head of the Foreign Ministry's Near Eastern Affairs Department; and Captain Nemits, one of Russia's leading naval strategists.

72. Resolutions 1 through 6 of the original 8/21 February 1914 conference transcript, in AVPRI, fond 138, opis' 467, del' 462 list' 23 (and back). This folder at AVPRI contains an entire series of annotated transcripts *(Zhurnalyi)* of this historic planning meeting, including the final version that was approved and signed by Tsar Nicholas II at Tsarskoe Selo on 23 March/4 April 1914. The final transcript is also reproduced (in German translation), with reasonable accuracy, in Pokrovskii, *Drei Konferenzen,* pp. 46–67. On the Kars-Sarakamış line, see also the German intelligence report from Tiflis, "Eisenbahnen in Russland," 25 December 1913, in PAAA, R 11011.

73. It is noteworthy that most historians who have examined the February 1914 planning conference (or those, like Geoffrey Miller, who have analyzed the *Straits* question without using Russian sources) come to very different conclusions about the nature of Russia's intentions. Alan Bodger, for example, writes in "Russia and the End of the Ottoman Empire" (p. 95) that "the mood at the conference was wholly defensive"—citing for this assertion Sazonov's wholly unreliable memoirs. Ronald Bobroff, unlike Bodger, has seen the original transcripts of the meeting, and notes such measures taken as the expansion of the size of the amphibious force in both men and artillery, the acceleration of construction of the Black Sea dreadnoughts, extension of the Caucasian rail lines, and so on. Still, Bobroff, like Bodger, is convinced that the goals outlined in the February conference envisioned only a long-term scenario, that is, of postponing war until Russia's Black Sea dreadnoughts were ready. (Lieven, too, in *Russia and the Origins of the First World War,* agrees with this line in general terms on pp. 107–109, although without so much as mentioning the February planning conference.) Until that was achieved, Bobroff writes, Russia "must avoid continental war" and meanwhile "prevent naval forces in the Black Sea from shifting too far in Turkey's favor." This analysis is sensible, so far as it goes. Yet by neglecting to note the crucial crisis heading-question under which the conference was originally convened—"the possibility of the Straits question being opened, even quite possibly in the near future" *(byit' mozhet' dazhe v blizkom budushchem)*— Bobroff fails to detect the note of urgency. Nor does he contrast the long-term dreadnought-construction measure (which was hardly new) with the five immediate, short-term mobilization measures against Turkey—which *were* new. Nor does he notice the crucial bit about speeding up "zero hour"—the time troops would be landed at the Bosphorus—from M + 10 to M + 5.

Airapetov, whose study of "Sud'ba Bosforskoi ekspeditsii" is the most thorough to date, gives a much better idea of the atmosphere of the meeting, noting the opposition of Danilov and Zhilinskii to the amphibious strike idea—but also that they were ultimately outnumbered and outvoted by Grigorevich, Sazonov, Girs, and the tsar.

74. Ottoman navy instruction manual, translated into Russian, dated 5/18 December 1911, in AVPRI, fond 138, opis' 467, del' 461/480, list' 4 (and back), 5.

75. Grigorevich to Sazonov, 6/19 January 1914, in AVPRI, fond 138, opis' 467, del' 462/481, 2–4 (and backs). Bodger notes (p. 89) that, "at the outbreak of war [in 1914] *Empress Maria* was only 65 per cent ready, and [the] two other dreadnoughts 53 and 33 per cent ready."

76. Fromkin, *Peace to End All Peace,* p. 55.

77. Girs to Sazonov, 14/27 November 1913, in AVPRI, fond 172, opis' 514/2, del' 633, list' 128–130; Girs to Sazonov, 19 April/2 May 1914, in AVPRI, fond 138, opis' 467, del' 462, list' 104.

78. Headline in *Le Matin,* 29 April 1914, clipped (with alarm) by Izvolsky's embassy staff for the Russian Foreign Ministry, in AVPRI, fond 138, opis' 467, del' 462, list' 115.

79. See Buchanan's secret letter to Grey, 3 April 1914, document no. 537 in BD, v. 10, pp. 780–782, and particularly the postscript on p. 782.

80. Buchanan to Nicolson, 16 April 1914, document 538 in BD, v. 10, pp. 784–785. According to Buchanan, Grigorevich told him Russia wanted these "Chilean" dreadnoughts for her Baltic navy. This was almost certainly untrue. Russia had floated four Baltic dreadnoughts of her own 23,360 ton "Gangut" class in 1911. She needed the Armstrong dreadnoughts urgently not to oppose the Germans in the Baltic (an extra two there would give her a maximum of six, to oppose Germany's *fifteen*), but rather for her still dreadnought-less Black Sea fleet.

Of course, Russia may not have been able to import the "Chilean" Armstrong-built dreadnoughts through the Straits without risking war. Grigorevich's real goal, in making a claim on the Armstrong warships, was probably to deny them to Turkey, or at least delay their arrival through legal subterfuge. On Russia's Baltic Sea dreadnoughts, see Sondhaus, *Naval Warfare, 1815–1914,* pp. 213–214.

81. Sazonov (from Yalta) to Benckendorff, 25 April/8 May 1914; Benckendorff to Sazonov, 25 April/8 May, 2/15 May, 6/19 May, 10/23 May, 20 May/2 June 1914, and 30 May/12 June 1914, and Girs to Sazonov, 8/21 May 1914, all in AVPRI, fond 138, opis' 467, del' 462, list' 111 (and back), 112, 113 (and back), 114, 121–123, 124 (and back), 125.

82. Fromkin, *Peace to End All Peace,* p. 55.

83. Benckendorff to Sazonov, 13/26 June 1914, in which he recounts his and Grey's efforts to reassure Prince Lichnowsky, Germany's ambassador to London, that no such naval convention had been concluded—and alludes to the German press campaign which had just been launched denouncing this (in fact imaginary) convention. In AVPRI, fond 138, opis' 467, del' 462, list' 126. Britain's ambassador to Germany, Sir Edward Goschen, also took note of the press campaign against the prospective Anglo-Russian Naval Convention, launched initially in the *Berliner Tageblatt.* See Goschen to Grey from Berlin, 23 May 1914, document 544 in BD, v. 10, p. 791.

84. Fischer, *World Power or Decline,* pp. 26–28.

85. Benckendorff to Sazonov, 30 May/12 June 1914, in AVPRI, fond 138, opis' 467, del' 462, list' 125.

86. The citation in the footnote is from Berghahn, *Germany and the Approach of War in 1914,* p. 180.

2. IT TAKES TWO TO TANGO

1. Cited in Turner, *Origins of the First World War,* p. 69.

2. Pourtalès to Bethmann Hollweg, 30 July 1914, 4:39 am, in PAAA, R 19873.

3. The original source of this famous quote is Moltke's own memoirs. This translation is Barbara Tuchman's, from *Guns of August,* p. 99.

4. The most thorough examination of the evidence surrounding the Sarajevo conspiracy available in English is that of Albertini, who actually interviewed many of the Serbian principals involved, in *The Origins of the War of 1914,* vol. 2, chapter 2. Most recent accounts, such as that of Stevenson in *Cataclysm* (p. 10), still adopt Albertini's basic conclusions, without going into anywhere near the level of detail. Recent Austrian accounts taking all of the latest evidence include Fritz Würthle, *Die Spur führt nach Belgrad;* and Rauchensteiner, *Tod des Doppeladlers,* chapter 3 ("Blutige Sonntage").

5. There is still some controversy over the authenticity of the Riezler diaries, as the edited collection published in 1972 by Karl Dietrich Erdmann *(Kurt Riezler: Tagebücher, Aufsätze, Dokumente)* was marked by considerable gaps for the period from 1907–1914, "while some pages were cut out of volumes which survived." Moreover, as several scholars discovered, "for the most important times, July and August 1914, the diary was not kept in its usual format in small exercise books, but was available only as loose pages, which differed in style from the rest of the diaries." Riezler may, therefore, have rewritten or at least "tampered with" the diaries after they were originally composed. For a recent summary of the controversy, see Mombauer, *The Origins of the First World War,* pp. 157–159. For discussion, see also Jarausch, "The Illusion of Limited War"; and Fischer, *World Power or Decline,* "Thesis Two."

Nevertheless, there is little reason to doubt the basic gist of Bethmann's remarks about "Russia's growing military might," in which he foretold that "after the completion of their strategic railroads in Poland our position will become untenable." The growth of Russian power was something of a cliché in German official circles by 1914, and a notable bugaboo of Moltke the Younger in particular.

6. Fromkin, *Europe's Last Summer,* p. 286.

7. Cited in Berghahn, in "The July Crisis of 1914," in *Germany and the Approach of War in 1914,* p. 190. Berghahn is particularly good on Bethmann Hollweg's "fait accompli" strategy and the reasons for its failure.

8. Cited in ibid., p. 198.

9. Ibid., p. 201 and *passim.* On Bethmann Hollweg's "strategy of bluff," and the issue of timing the ultimatum vis-à-vis the French presidential visit, see also Rauchensteiner, *Tod des Doppeladlers,* pp. 72–73, 82–83.

10. See editor's note in DDF, v. 10 (1936), pp. vi–vii.

11. For Paléologue's brief and (as Albertini describes it) "laconic" reports on Sazonov and the news from Sarajevo, see his 6 July 1914 telegram to Viviani, no. 477 in DDF, v. 10, pp. 686–687. There is one other, extremely brief post-Sarajevo Paléologue telegram dating to 30 June (no. 459), but it does not discuss any official response from the Russian foreign ministry. As for the dispatches relating to micromanaging the presidential remarks to the tsar, see Paléologue telegrams numbered 491, 497, 503, 505, 506, 513, 531, and 533, dispatched between 10 and 19 July 1914, all in DDF, v. 10.

The author's own searching at the Quai d'Orsay archives (now housed at Courneuve, in the northern Paris suburbs) turned up virtually no Paléologue telegrams in the "Russia" correspondence for June and July 1914. Intriguingly, some have been moved to the Autriche-Hongrie correspondence, in the section on "Conflit austro-serbe," which begins in volume 31—this may account for their having lain mostly undiscovered until now—but even here the rule is for Paléologue's remarks to be mentioned only secondhand, as in an 8 July 1914 dispatch from M. Descos, the French consul at Belgrade which gives the best summary I can find of Paléologue's read on the official Russian reaction to Sarajevo—but the original is missing. Clearly, someone in Paris has expunged some of the Paléologue correspondence of July 1914 from the official record.

Interestingly, Paléologue was far more candid in his memoirs about what was said and done during the July crisis than he was in his own dispatches to Paris—those we have, at least. This is not to say that the dated "diary entries" which make up Paléologue's published memoirs (which were presumably touched up a bit after the fact) are necessarily accurate. But they do give a much more thorough glimpse into Franco-Russian thinking in July 1914 than Paléologue's actual contemporary time-dated reports from Petersburg, simply because so few of the latter have survived.

12. Cited in Albertini, *Origins of the War of 1914,* vol. 2, p. 196.

13. See AVPRI, fond 172, opis' 514/2, del' 632 ("Serbiya"), gap between list' 93 (24 June 1914) and list' 94 (9 July 1914).

14. Aside from the well known correspondence reproduced in *Mezhdunarodnyie Otnoshenie,* there were also the volumes edited by E. A. Abramov, *Konstantinopl i Prolivyi* and *Razdel Aziatskoi Turtsii.*

15. Sazonov, *Fateful Years,* p. 176.

16. Certainly not all historians have been fooled by Sazonov's protestations. Albertini was not. Holger Herwig, likewise, notes in *Decisions for War, 1914–1917,* ed. Hamilton and Herwig (p. 106) that "during the twenty-four hours preceding Austria's demarche, Sazonov had received six warning indicators about the turn Austrian policy was about to take." It would be surprising if Sazonov had not received such warnings, considering that the Russian foreign ministry's *camera noir* cryptographers had broken most of the codes used by the Austrians.

Nevertheless, Sazonov's "stunned ignorance" act has taken in a surprising number of historians, particularly those who tell the story from the Entente perspective. In *France and the Origins of the First World War,* for example, John F. V. Keiger writes that "Sazonov had learnt of the content of the Austrian note on the morning of 24 July."

17. Albertini, *Origins of the War of 1914,* vol. 2, pp. 82–86; and Turner, *Origins of the First World War,* p. 81. Russia's leading diplomatic historian, D. C. B. Lieven, thinks these tentative conclusions unlikely, because Artamonov and Hartwig were hostile to the aims of the Black Hand. Nevertheless, even Lieven concedes (p. 139), in an intriguing double negative, that "Russian documents published by the Soviet government do not prove that Hartwig and Artamonov knew nothing of the conspiracy." The Russians must have known that something was afoot, although this does not mean they were *complicit* in the plot.

18. See, for example, consul reports from Belgrade (29 June 1914) and Sinaia (5 July 1914), in HHSA, P. A. I. Liasse Krieg, Karton 810.

19. Ritter (von Storck) from Belgrade, passing on report from his Italian counterpart, 6 July 1914, in HHSA, P. A. I. Liasse Krieg, Karton 810.

20. Baron von Giesl from Belgrade on the "Haltung der hiesigen russischen Gesandtschaft anläßlich der Sarajevoer Ereignisse," 13 July 1914, in HHSA, P. A. I. Liasse Krieg, Karton 810.

21. Ritter from Belgrade, 4 July 1914, in HHSA, P. A. I. Liasse Krieg, Karton 810. For the evidence regarding Artamonov's possible collusion in the Sarajevo plot, see Albertini, *Origins of the War of 1914,* vol. 2, pp. 82–86.

22. Baron von Giesl from Belgrade on the "Haltung der hiesigen russischen Gesandtschaft anläßlich der Sarajevoer Ereignisse," 13 July 1914, in HHSA, P. A. I. Liasse Krieg, Karton 810.

23. Remarks circa December 1913 as reproduced in an 11 July 1914 memorandum on "Relations de l'Autriche-Hongrie et de la Russie," prepared by Bruno Jacquin de Margerie, the political director at the French foreign ministry, for the presidential summit. In DDF, v. 10, document 500 (p. 723).

24. I have followed Albertini's narrative of the dramatic evening of 10 July 1914, in *Origins of the War of 1914,* vol. 2, pp. 276–277.

25. Paléologue to Viviani, 6 July 1914, in DDF, v. 10, document 477 (pp. 686–687).

26. Szecsen to Berchtold, 4 July 1914, in HHSA, P. A. I. Liasse Krieg, Karton 810.

27. Bizarrely, the Austrians focused the brunt of their accusations against *Narodna Odbrana,* on the logic that it was a more respectably "mainstream" Serbian political organization than the Black Hand, despite possessing good intelligence on the latter. It has never been satisfactorily been explained why Vienna made this tactical error, which undoubtedly cost the Austrians much sympathy in Paris and London (if not in Petersburg), where credible evidence pointing the finger at the Black Hand—which really *was* guilty of organizing the Sarajevo murders—might have been given credence.

28. Pourtalès to Bethmann Hollweg, 21 July 1914, in PAAA, R 19867.

29. Cited in Albertini, *Origins of the War of 1914,* vol. 2, pp. 183–184.

30. Pourtalès to Bethmann Hollweg, 21 March 1914, in PAAA, R 10898.

31. See reports from Klageneck, the German military attaché in Vienna, 4 and 17 March 1914, in PAAA, R 10898.

32. Kaiser Wilhelm from Achilleion to Bethmann Hollweg (addressed via the Wilhelmstrasse), 4 April 1914, in PAAA, R10898. The kaiser may have had in mind the famous 2 March 1914 article in *Kölnische Zeitung* usually credited with kicking off the Russo-German "press war," in which the author, Richard Ullrich, warned that General Pavel Rennenkampf, who commanded the Russian army facing East Prussia, planned to unleash his "pillaging horsemen" against "the prosperous German country on the other side of the border."

33. Shebeko from Vienna to Sazonov, 3/16 July 1914, document 247 in IBZI, vol. 4, pp. 227–228.

34. Entry for 3/16 July 1914, in Schilling, *How the War Began,* p. 25.

35. Entry for 5/18 July 1914, in ibid., pp. 26–27.

36. Buchanan to Grey, 18 July 1914, 8:50 pm, document 60 in BD, v. 11, p. 47.

37. See, for example, Berchtold to Czernin, 14 July 1914, document 218 and accompanying footnotes, in IBZI, v. 4, p. 197.

38. Pourtalès to Bethmann Hollweg (a letter sent by special courier), 21 July 1914, in PAAA, R 19867. Emphasis added.

39. See Albertini, *Origins of the War of 1914,* vol. 2, pp. 188–189.

40. Cited in Turner, *Origins of the First World War,* p. 89. Turner's translation; emphasis added.

41. Entry for 5/18 July 1914, in Schilling, *How the War Began,* p. 27.

42. Paléologue, *An Ambassador's Memoirs,* entry for 21 July 1914, vol. 1, pp. 18–19.

43. Cited in Albertini, *Origins of the War of 1914,* vol. 2, p. 194. Szápáry, incidentally, was less "mild" in his political outlook than his manners. As Rauchensteiner has pointed out in *Tod des Doppeladlers* (pp. 20, 47), the Hungarian count generally took Count Franz Conrad's side in disputes with Aehrenthal, then Berchtold—that is, Szápáry was generally favorable to

the "war party" against Serbia. Apparently, this is not how he was perceived by Sazonov or Paléologue.

44. Sazonov to Shebeko, 22 July 1914, document 322 in IBZI, v. 4, pp. 292–293.

45. Berchtold's secretary brushed off the Russian chargé d'affaires when he visited the Austrian foreign ministry sometime between 3 and 4PM on 23 July, saying that Berchtold was busy. The timing is interesting: according to Rauchensteiner, the ultimatum had actually been dispatched from Vienna to Belgrade around noon, with instructions that Giesl was not to open it until late afternoon, the idea being to give it to the Serbian government at 6PM. The Russians were thus about three hours late—although of course Berchtold may have brushed off the Russian delegate even if he had not already dispatched the Serbian ultimatum. Rauchensteiner, *Tod des Doppeladlers,* p. 82.

46. Viviani to Dumaine (in Vienna), by way of Bienvenu-Martin (in Paris), 24 July 1914, in QO Autriche-Hongrie, vol. 32.

47. Paléologue, *An Ambassador's Memoirs,* entry for 23 July 1914, vol. 1, p. 23.

48. Ibid., pp. 22–23.

49. The grand duchess's influence extended even beyond her husband. Anastasia Nicolaievna and her sister "Militiza," the two "Montenegrin princesses" of the Russian court, had famously and fatefully introduced the Empress Alexandra to Rasputin. So their influence over the tsar was considerable.

50. From the minutes of the Russian foreign ministry for 24 July 1914, document 25 in IBZI, v. 5, p. 31. The remark is also transcribed identically in the entry for 11/24 July 1914 in Schilling, *How the War Began,* pp. 28–29.

51. Buchanan to Grey, 18 July 1914, 8:50 pm, document 60 in BD, v. 11, p. 47.

52. Dobrorolskii, *Die Mobilmachung der russischen Armee,* pp. 17–18; see also Albertini, who gives a masterful narrative of these events, in *Origins of the War of 1914,* vol. 2, pp. 292–293.

53. Dobrorolskii, *Die Mobilmachung der russischen Armee,* pp. 17–19.

54. Albertini, *Origins of the War of 1914,* vol. 2, p. 294.

55. Turner, *Origins of the First World War,* p. 93. On the Austrian mobilization dilemma, see also Rauchensteiner, *Tod des Doppeladlers,* pp. 54–55.

56. Kokovtsev, *Out of My Past,* pp. 346–347. Emphasis added.

57. PBM, box 1, chapter 7, pp. 5–7. Emphasis added. Compare to this passage, from Norman Stone's recent *World War One* (pp. 20–21): "Bethmann Hollweg went several times to Berlin, during the ostensible holiday . . . back and forth he went, organizing the country's finances . . . the likelihood of war, with debts to collect and bonds discreetly to sell or buy. The Warburgs in Hamburg were being told, by special courier, what to do. Berlin meant war."

58. See McDonald, *Government and Foreign Policy in Russia 1900–1914,* pp. 184–186; and Neilson, "Russia," pp. 110–111.

59. PBM, box 1, chapter 7, pp. 9–10 and *passim.* It is noteworthy that, unlike with the meetings in January and February 1914 discussed in chapter 1, there appear to be no surviving "minutes" for the 11/24 July 1914 meeting of the Council of Ministers. Bark does give a reasonably detailed blow-by-blow of who said what. Doubtless certain remarks have been omitted (or misremembered), but the Bark memoirs are better than nothing.

60. Ibid., pp. 15–21 and *passim.*

61. The resolutions of the 11/24 July meeting are reproduced in (among many other places), "Special Journal of the Russian Council of Ministers," 24 July 1914, in Hoover Institution Archives, collection "Russia. Soviet Ministrov." See also Geiss, ed., *July 1914: The Outbreak of the First World War: Selected Documents,* pp. 186–187.

62. Fay, *Origins of the First World War,* vol. 2, pp. 310–311.

63. Journal of the Committee of the Russian General Staff, night of 12/25 July 1914, document 79 in IBZI, v. 5, pp. 67–68.

64. Ibid., footnote 1, which references Yanushkevitch's order no. 1575, time-dated 3:26ᴀᴍ of 26 July 1914. The original, along that of the Dobrorolskii telegram from 4ᴘᴍ on 25 July and the 1ᴀᴍ and 3:26ᴀᴍ orders from Yanushkevitch to Warsaw, were captured by the Germans after they occupied Warsaw in 1915. They are reproduced in full, in German translation, in Hoeniger, *Russlands Vorbereitung zum Weltkrieg* (1919), p. 81.

65. Turner, "The Russian Mobilization in 1914," p. 76.

66. Stone, *Eastern Front,* p. 41.

67. Yanushkevitch to Yudenich at Tiflis command, 14/27 July 1914, in RGVIA, fond 2000, opis' 1, del' 3796, list' 13. A copy of this dispatch is also reproduced as document 156 in IBZI, v. 5, p. 127.

68. Stone, "Moltke-Conrad," p. 216, footnote 39.

69. Rauchensteiner, *Tod des Doppeladlers,* p. 160.

70. Cited in Fay, *The Origins of the First World War,* p. 308. Emphasis added.

71. Ibid., pp. 317–318.

72. Paléologue, *An Ambassador's Memoirs,* entry for 25 July 1914, vol. 1, pp. 35–36. Emphasis added.

73. Cited in Turner, *Origins of the First World War,* p. 101.

74. Von Haydin from Moscow, 27 July 1914 (5ᴘᴍ); Paumgartner from Odessa, 27 July 1914; Baron Hein from Kiev, 27 July 1914 (3ᴘᴍ); Andrian from Szczakowa, 27 July 1914, 10:50ᴘᴍ, all in HHSA, P. A. I Liasse Krieg, Karton 812.

75. Moscow Consul to Bethmann Hollweg, by courier, 27 July 1914, in PAAA, R 19871.

76. Pourtalès from Petersburg, 7:45ᴘᴍ and 8:17ᴘᴍ on 27 July 1914, passing on Riga and Kiev; Brück from Warsaw, 3:45ᴘᴍ, 27 July 1914, in PAAA, R 19871.

77. Von Chelius to Berlin from Tsarskoe Selo, 13/26 July 1914, in PAAA, R 19871. Emphasis added.

78. The claim that Russian mobilization did not mean war is, of course, crucial to any argument of war responsibility. But the matter is by no means as cut and dry as it often appears in the literature. In his article on "Russia" in the recent Hamilton and Herwig volume on the *Origins of World War I,* David Alan Rich has a long footnote, on p. 223, on this issue. To verify his claim that Russian mobilization did not mean war, Rich cites Sazonov's own protestations to the German ambassador; Danilov's postwar memoirs *Russland im Weltkriege* (1925); and Lieven's book on *Russia and the Origins of the First World War.* Rich cites, that is, only *Russian* sources, the first two self-interested, and the third a historian making an argument exonerating Russia for any responsibility in the outbreak of the war, himself using mostly Russian sources. Surely we should at least *consider* the German point of view regarding whether or not a Russian mobilization directed against Berlin "meant war."

79. Menning, *Bayonets before Bullets,* p. 252.

80. Herwig, "Germany," in *Origins of World War I,* ed. Hamilton and Herwig, p. 153.

81. Fay, *Origins of the World War,* pp. 320–321.

82. Pourtalès from Petersburg, 9:30 pm, 26 July 1914, in PAAA, R 19871.

83. Cited in Turner, *Origins of the First World War,* p. 101.

84. See, for example, Pourtalès from Petersburg, 26 July 1914, on the subject of Russian labor unrest and morale in Moscow, and particularly 25 July 1914, in which he reports the rumor that the Crown council that morning had discussed the problem in detail, both in PAAA, R 19869.

The secondary literature is rich on the subject of the Germans' doubting Russian resolve due to labor unrest; it is taken as more or less given in most popular histories of Russia in the war, such as (among many others) Robert Massie's *Nicholas and Alexandra,* which relies on Bernard Pares's *Fall of the Russian Monarchy.*

85. In Fischer, *Weltmacht oder Niedergang,* cited (and refuted) by Turner, in *Origins of the First World War,* p. 95.

86. Pourtalès letter to Bethmann Hollweg from Petersburg by courier, 27 July 1914; and Pourtalès telegram, 28 July 1914, both in PAAA, R 19869.

87. Dobrorolskii, *Die Mobilmachung der russischen Armee 1914,* pp. 21–22. I have used L. C. F. Turner's smooth translation of this remark, in "The Russian Mobilization in 1914," p. 77.

88. Fischer, *Germany's Aims in the First World War,* pp. 85–86.

89. Herwig did find, in the former East German archives, a diary entry by Falkenhayn from 27 July, which suggests that some German premobilization preparations—troops being confined to barracks, large grain purchases—began that day, even if Bethmann Hollweg was still trying to "manage the crisis" short of war. Exciting as such an archival discovery is, it does not actually tell us very much. Herwig admits that the *Kriegsgefahrzustand*—the "Imminent Danger of War," akin to Russia's Period Preparatory to War, which also required the approval of the kaiser, Moltke, and Bethmann, was decided upon only on 29 July, to be activated on 31 July, just as Geiss says. Herwig, "Germany," in *Origins of World War I,* ed. Hamilton and Herwig, pp. 178–179.

90. Geiss, *July 1914,* argument on pp. 265–268, and accompanying annotated documents (particularly nos. 114, 116, and 118). In a similar vein, see also Geiss's more precise summary of the argument in *Der lange Weg in die Katastrophe,* pp. 318–321.

91. Herwig, despite paying more attention to the Russian situation than did Fischer and Geiss, nonetheless makes exactly the same mistake. "On 28 July," he writes, "Austria-Hungary commenced military operations against Serbia, whereupon Russia moved toward partial mobilization." Herwig, "Germany," in *Origins of World War I,* ed. Hamilton and Herwig, p. 179. For an otherwise authoritative historian, this is a howler: he is off by three whole days—or more accurately, four, if we count the decision made by Sazonov, Yanushkevitch, and the Council of Ministers on 24 July 1914 to "move towards partial mobilization." One possible reason for Herwig's confusion is the discrepancy between the Julian and Gregorian calendars. When responding in his capacity as editor, in the same volume (p. 455), to the essay by the Russianist (David Alan Rich), Herwig alludes vaguely to remarks Sazonov made before the Council of Ministers "as early as 11 July"—by which he actually means 24 July.

92. Cited in Turner, "The Russian Mobilization in 1914," p. 77. Emphasis added.

93. Brück from Warsaw to Bethmann Hollweg, 29 July 1914, in PAAA, R 19873.

94. John F. V. Keiger, a leading authority on the French diplomatic side of the outbreak of

the First World War, writes that Paléologue "can certainly be criticised for what he did not do later that day [25 July]—telegraph to Paris the Council of Ministers' decision in principle to call a partial mobilisation, of which Sazonov had informed him." Keiger, *France and the Origins of the First World War,* p. 155. In fact Paléologue reported much more than this. Keiger has written further on France's role in the July crisis, in his article on "France" in *Decisions for War,* ed. Wilson (1995), and in his biography of *Raymond Poincaré* (1997). But Keiger's view of France's role in the outbreak of war remains unaltered; in fact he has grown less critical of Paléologue over time (having never been very critical of Poincaré). In his 1995 article, Keiger skips over the entire period between 23 and 29 July, his idea apparently being that France's president was at sea during this time, and so nothing important happened. Keiger's basic view, as he writes in *Raymond Poincaré* (p. 163), remains that France was "the most passive of the great powers" during the July crisis.

Stefan Schmidt has just published, in German, a lengthy critique of the consensus view associated with Keiger: *Frankreichs Aussenpolitik in der Julikrise 1914: Ein Beitrag zur Geschichte des Ausbruchs des Ersten Weltkrieges* (2009). Although Schmidt works more with French than Russian sources, his incisive analysis of French strategic thinking in 1914 leads him to conclusions about French responsibility for encouraging the Russians during and after the Petersburg summit which are very close to my own.

95. Paléologue from Petersburg, 25 July 1914, 6:22PM (received in Paris 7:35PM), in QO Autriche-Hongrie, vol. 32. L. C. F. Turner is, to my knowledge, the only historian to mention this document (although strangely he does not cite it directly, citing instead the Laguiche report directly following). Turner, *Origins of the First World War,* p. 96. Interestingly, Eugenia Kiesling, in her essay on "France" in the recent Hamilton and Herwig volume on the *Origins of World War I,* mentions (p. 248) a fairly innocuous Paléologue dispatch dated 24 July 1914—but not the far more significant 25 July 1914 report on Russia's secret mobilization. Nor does David Alan Rich, in the article on "Russia" in the same volume. At least until Schmidt's book on *Frankreichs Aussenpolitik,* recent scholarship has consistently maintained the notion of France's essential passivity.

96. Jules Cambon from Berlin, 25 July 1914, 1:15AM, received Paris 2:50AM, in QO Autriche-Hongrie, vol. 32. Cambon informed the Russians, too, of Jagow's remarks. See Bronevskii to Sazonov, 14/27 July 1914, in AVPRI, fond 172, opis' 514/2, del' 636, list' 92.

97. Paléologue from Petersburg, passing on Laguiche, 26 July 1914, 1:55PM (received 4PM), in QO Autriche-Hongrie, vol. 32. At least one French newspaper, *Le Temps,* let the cat out of the bag a bit early, reporting with from Petersburg on the night of 28–29 July that "troop transport trains were setting off every fifteen minutes for Warsaw. Mobilization [has been declared] in Kiev, Vilna, Odessa, Warsaw, and even Petersburg." Report datelined 29 July 1914, 3:20AM, clipped in QO Autriche-Hongrie, vol. 32.

98. Buchanan to Grey, 26 July 1914, 8PM (received 11PM), in BD, v. 11, no 155, p. 107.

99. Grey reporting on his conversation with the German ambassador, 26 July 1914, document 146 in BD, v. 11, p. 103.

100. Buchanan to Grey, 28 July 1914, 8:45PM (received 10:45PM), document 234 in BD, v. 11, p. 155.

101. Buchanan, *My Mission to Russia,* p. 197.

102. Sazonov to Bronevskii in Berlin, telegram no. 1539, 15/28 July 1914, document 168 in IBZI, v. 5, p. 135; Benckendorff to Nicolson, 29 July 1914, and enclosure (i.e., Sazonov's mes-

sage), together comprising document 258 in BD, v. 11, pp. 168–169. Although the exact time of Benckendorff's dispatch to Nicolson is not given, it follows a number of telegrams received between 12 and 12:30PM; thus early afternoon on the 29th is a good guess.

103. Grey reporting on his conversation with the German ambassador, 26 July 1914, document 146 in BD, v. 11, p. 103.

104. Turner, *Origins of the First World* War, pp. 99–100.

105. Paléologue, *An Ambassador's Memoirs,* vol. 1, p. 39. Emphasis added. Buchanan recalls the conversation almost identically, with only slightly different phrasing, in *My Mission to Russia,* p. 199.

106. And possibly over those of Poincaré, too, if we can believe the president's protestations of ignorance of the Russian mobilization measures—and of Paléologue's innocence, too. See *The Memoirs of Raymond Poincaré,* vol. 1, pp. 185–186. Since Poincaré was at sea on 25 July, when Paléologue first informed Paris of the Russian premobilization, it is of course possible that he really did not know. One suspects, however, that the president, too, was in on the secret (or was let in on it upon returning to Paris). In any case, Poincaré clearly had no motive to reveal knowledge of Russia's early mobilization in his memoirs, even if he did know.

107. Churchill, *World Crisis,* vol. 2, p. 6.

108. Cited in Albertini, *Origins of the War of 1914,* vol. 2, p. 545.

109. Yanushkevitch to Yudenich, 16/29 July 1914, in RGVIA, fond 2000, opis' 1, del' 3796, list' 19.

110. Cited in Hoeniger, *Russlands Vorbereitung zum Weltkrieg,* p. 99.

111. Cited in Albertini, *Origins of the War of 1914,* vol. 2, p. 560.

112. Cited in ibid., vol. 3, p. 2.

113. Albertini, for example, says that "Wilhelm wrongly jumped to the conclusion that the mobilization had begun five days earlier." While true in the most literal sense, that Russia had not yet announced general mobilization, the kaiser was correct in the spirit, both in the scale of premobilization inaugurated on 25 July (which was, admittedly, four not five days earlier) and in the more specific sense that Russian *general* mobilization had already been ordered by the time Nicholas told him this.

114. From the diary of the Russian foreign ministry (Schilling, *How the War Began in 1914*), pp. 49–50; also reproduced as document 224 in IBZI, v. 5, pp. 161–162. See also Turner, "The Russian Mobilization in 1914," p. 86.

115. Pourtalès to Bethmann Hollweg, 30 July 1914, 4:39AM, in PAAA, R 19873.

3. RUSSIA'S WAR

1. Yanushkevitch to Ivanov, 10/23 August 1914, in HS, box 1, folder 1.

2. Stone, *Eastern Front,* pp. 37–38.

3. As D. C. B. Lieven points out, in *Nicholas II,* p. 204.

4. See the *Novoe Vremya* article from early August 1914, cited in chapter 2 above, from Hoeniger, *Russlands Vorbereitung zum Weltkrieg,* p. 99.

5. The remark which gave birth to the legend was supposedly uttered by Grand Duke Nicholas to the French military attaché General Laguiche after Tannenberg: "Nous sommes heureux de faire de telles sacrifices pour nos alliés." Significantly, Winston Churchill offered

an elegant version of the "falling on the sword" story in *The Unknown War* (p. 143), declaiming with his usual grandeur that "history will recognize the intense loyal efforts made by the Czar and his generals to make their onfall [in Germany] with the greatest possible strength at the same time [as the clash of arms began in the West]."

So overwhelming was the mood of retrospective gratitude for the (in fact minimal) Russian contribution to the Allied victory at the Marne after Russia's postwar tragedy that authors like Churchill failed to account for Russian behavior at all. Had the Russians really wished to relieve pressure on the western front, they would have sent the bulk of their forces into East Prussia against the Germans, rather than (as in reality) sending twice as many troops against the much weaker Austro-Hungarian army.

Even Norman Stone's *Eastern Front 1914–1917* (1975), while based on far deeper research than Churchill's account, takes the basic scenario as given. One of Stone's key arguments is that Russia's alleged lack of "readiness" for war in 1914 was "at bottom, a hard-luck story," that is, an excuse for Tannenberg discovered after the event. He is doubtless right about this, but it is interesting that he assumes his readers think that Russia plunged into the war on the eastern front "before she was ready," at the behest of her French ally. This erroneous assumption had, by 1975, lodged so deeply in the framework of popular understanding of the First World War that Stone did not even bother explaining where it came from.

More recent scholarship has produced a subtler and richer understanding of the strategic thinking at Stavka in 1914, as, for example, in Hew Strachan's masterful synthesis *The First World War*. Strachan notes, for example (p. 308), that the real significance of the French alliance for Russia was "its ability to confer an offensive option on the Austrian front," something about which the French were "undeniably worried." Strachan notes further that, in part due to the revelations from Colonel Redl, the Russians saw the Austrians as "beatable." It is interesting, though, that even with his updated bibliography (circa 2001), which incorporates much of the recent work of Bruce Menning and William Fuller on Russia's prewar planning, Strachan must still rely on Churchill and Stone once it comes to the actual course of battles after the war began. In this vein see Strachan, *The First World War,* p. 316, fn. 69.

6. Strachan, *The First World War,* p. 290 (for the quote) and p. 316 (for the figures).

7. Kennan, *Fateful Alliance,* pp. 180–181, 252; and Obruchev to Foreign Minister N. K. Giers (with annotations from the tsar), appendix II, p. 268.

8. According to Danilov's later recollection, the Russian general staff did at least "entertain the possibility of a German eastern option" before 1914. Still, this seems to have been more a matter of covering all possible scenarios than serious operational planning. Russia's own offensive plans were so heavily Austria-focused that it would have taken a truly shocking reversal of German strategic doctrine to dislodge them. On all this see Fuller, *Strategy and Power,* pp. 441–443; Menning, *Bayonets before Bullets,* pp. 242–248; and Strachan, *First World War,* p. 309 and *passim*.

9. "At the staff conversations of 1912 and 1913," writes Fuller, "the Russians tried to buy French goodwill by promising to attack Germany with 800,000 men by the fifteenth day after the declaration of mobilization." Whether or not the promise was sincere, it was not fulfilled in August 1914. Fuller, *Strategy and Power in Russia,* p. 439. See also Menning, *Bayonets before Bullets,* p. 245; and Stone, *Eastern Front,* p. 55.

10. Yanushkevitch to Zhilinskii, 28 July/10 August 1914, in HS (the "Hoover Stavka" files), box 1, folder 1.

11. Strachan, *First World War,* p. 316; and Stone, *Eastern Front,* pp. 49–55.

12. Cited in Fuller, *Strategy and Power,* p. 450.

13. Yanushkevitch to Ivanov, 10/23 August 1914, in HS, box 1, folder 1.

14. Stone, *Eastern Front,* pp. 77–80; see also his *World War One,* p. 43.

15. See Yanushkevitch to Grigorevich, passing on Zhilinskii, 28 July/10 August 1914, in HS, box 1, folder 1.

16. Stone, *Eastern Front,* pp. 55, 59, 84. Interestingly, on 15 August 1914 Sukhomlinov informed Paléologue that a third army engaged on the northwestern front against Germany (presumably the newly formed Ninth) "has already struck west from Warsaw." This would have been very good news for France—if it were true, which it was not. Paléologue, *An Ambassador's Memoirs,* v. 1, p. 83.

17. Stone, *Eastern Front,* p. 84; Strachan, *First World War,* p. 347.

18. Rauchensteiner, *Tod des Doppeladlers,* pp. 160–161.

19. Strachan, *The First World War,* p. 347.

20. Buchanan, *My Mission to Russia,* p. 218.

21. I have followed Stone's account, in *Eastern Front,* pp. 63–67. There are more recent scholarly accounts of Tannenberg, but there seems to be little variation on the key events (e.g., François's insubordination and its significance, when coupled with Samsonov's pressing on in the center; the notion that the Germans achieved a "Cannae"). For a nice synthesis of the state of the art, see Strachan, *First World War,* pp. 325–333.

22. *Memoirs of Raymond Poincaré,* v. 2, p. 159.

23. On the politics of ethnicity/religion and the Galician question, see, for the Russian perspective, Bakhturina, *Politika Rossiiskoi Imperii v vostochnoi Galitsii v godyi pervoi mirovoi voinyi,* and also her *Okrainyi Rossiiskoi Imperii,* pp. 117–155; and for the Austrian, Klaus Bachmann, *Ein Herd der Feindschaft gegen Russland,* esp. pp. 259–270; and Wendland, *Die Russophilen in Galizien.*

24. Citations in Mankoff, "Russia and the Polish Question," pp. 154, 183, 185.

25. On the grand duke's various proclamations, and the general cynicism of Entente Balkan diplomacy in 1914, see Smith, *Russian Struggle for Power, 1914–1917,* pp. 8–41.

26. Cited in Mankoff, "Russia and the Polish Question," p. 160.

27. Komarnicki, *Rebirth of the Polish Republic,* p. 38. See also Paléologue, *An Ambassador's Memoirs,* v. 1, p. 81.

28. With characteristic obtuseness, Buchanan does not even mention the Polish question in his memoirs. Nor is there any record of protest or undue concern in his diplomatic correspondence in fall 1914, as we shall see (although Buchanan did take a keen interest in Russia's territorial ambitions in Persia and Turkey).

29. Paléologue, *An Ambassador's Memoirs,* v. 1, p. 81.

30. "Diary entry" for 15 August 1914, *Memoirs of Raymond Poincaré,* p. 50.

31. "Diary entry" for 16 August 1914, in ibid., p. 55.

32. Mankoff, "Russia and the Polish Question," p. 161.

33. Cited in Komarnicki, *Rebirth of the Polish Republic,* p. 37.

34. Paléologue, *An Ambassador's Memoirs,* v. 1, p. 96.

35. Among many other locations, the 4 September 1914 London protocol is reproduced as document 218 in IBZI, v. 6, p. 165.

36. Paléologue to Delcassé, 1/14 September 1914, document 256 in IBZI, v. 6, pp. 193–194.

37. "Diary entry" for 1/14 September 1914, in Paléologue, *La Russie des Tsars,* v. 1, pp. 128–130.

38. Paléologue/Buchanan aide-mémoire, addressed to Sazonov, 4/17 September 1914, document 267 in IBZI, v. 6, pp. 203–204.

39. Kudashev to Sazonov, 5/18 September 1914, document 277 in IBZI, v. 6, pp. 244–245.

40. Cited in Mankoff, "Russia and the Polish Question," p. 178.

41. Basily to Grand Duke Nicholas (and attachment), 16/29 September 1914, with the grand duke's (mostly affirmative) marginalia, document 338 in IBZI, v. 6, pp. 259–263.

42. Stone, *Eastern Front,* pp. 92–107, 114–116.

43. Mankoff, "Russia and the Polish Question," p. 178.

44. Yanushkevitch to Goremykin, 19 September/2 October 1914, document 349 in IBZI, v. 6, pp. 270–272.

45. Lohr, "The Russian Army and the Jews." On tsarist Russian wartime ethnic deportations generally, see Von Hagen, "The Great War and the Mobilization of Ethnicity in the Russian Empire"; and Lohr, *Nationalizing the Russian Empire.*

46. As we shall see below, Sazonov, despite sounding some constructive criticism of Krivoshein here, would soon prove willing to go even further than his colleague in his territorial ambitions for Russia in Turkey. For the time being, it paid for him to play "good cop" to Krivoshein's grasping imperialist, to allay British suspicions about Russian designs on Constantinople—which had, after all, nearly provoked a war between London and Petersburg in 1878.

47. Paléologue to Delcassé, 26 September 1914, in KP, v. 1, pp. 221–223. The letter is also reproduced as document 320 in IBZI, v. 6, pp. 245–246.

48. Cited in Komarnicki, *Rebirth of the Polish Republic,* pp. 40–41. The other "dissenting Ministers" included Shcheglevitev, the justice minister; and Kasso, minister of public education.

49. Paléologue "diary entry" for 21 November 1914, in *La Russie des Tsars,* v. 1, pp. 198–200.

4. TURKEY'S TURN

1. Girs to G. N. Trubetskoi, 28 September/11 October 1914, in AVPRI, fond 151, opis' 482, del' 4068, list' 222–223.

2. The original *bon mot* was uttered before the Reichstag on 5 December 1876. It has been misquoted ever since. For a discussion, see Margaret Lavinia Anderson, "'Down in Turkey, Far Away,'" p. 111.

3. Fromkin, *Peace to End All Peace,* p. 25.

4. Girs to Sazonov, 14/27 July 1914, reproduced in *Tsarskaia Rossiia v mirovoi voine,* v. 1, pp. 4–5; and as document 154 in IBZI, v. 5, pp. 125–126.

5. Sazonov to Benckendorff, 17/30 July 1914, document 281 in IBZI, v. 5, p. 195.

6. Initially widely praised by the British press for proactively detaining the Turkish warships ("Bravo Winston!" a headline in the *Tatler* proclaimed on 12 August 1914), Churchill was later widely blamed for provoking Turkey's entry into the war. See Fromkin, *Peace to End All Peace,* p. 54 and *passim.*

7. Aksakal, *Ottoman Road to War in 1914,* p. 107.

8. Girs to Sazonov, 22 July/4 August 1914, document 557 in IBZI, v. 5, p. 322.

9. Aksakal, *Ottoman Road to War in 1914,* pp. 108–109.

10. These terms were first published in Ulrich Trumpener, *Germany and the Ottoman Empire 1914–1918,* p. 28. For further discussion, see also Aksakal, *Ottoman Road to War in 1914,* p. 115 and *passim;* and McMeekin, *Berlin-Baghdad Express,* chapter 5.

11. Asquith recalled this conversation (which he had recorded in his diary) in his memoirs; it has firmly entered the historical literature, in popular accounts such as Barbara Tuchman's *Guns of August* (p. 185) and David Fromkin's *Peace to End All Peace,* p. 66. For a better-informed scholarly analysis of the context of Churchill's threat, see Miller, *Straits,* p. 282.

12. Sazonov to Girs, 27 July/9 August 1914, document 38 in IBZI, v. 6, p. 35. Emphasis added.

13. The story about the German crews teasing the Russian Embassy staff appears in *Ambassador Morgenthau's Story,* p. 79. For a more detailed discussion of the whole episode, see McMeekin, *Berlin-Baghdad Express,* chapter 5.

14. Airapetov, "Sud'ba Bosforskoi ekspeditsii," p. 182.

15. Cited in Aksakal, *Ottoman Road to War in 1914,* p. 103.

16. Girs to Sazonov, 19 August 1914, reproduced in TRMV, v. 1, p. 28.

17. Girs to Sazonov, 20 July/2 August 1914, in AVPRI, fond 151, opis' 482, del' 4068, list' 8.

18. Girs to Sazonov, 23 July/5 August 1914 (no. 628), original in AVPRI, fond 151, opis' 482, del' 4068, list' 10; also reproduced as document 8 in IBZI, v. 6:1, p. 5.

19. Girs to Sazonov, 23 July/5 August 1914, follow-up to no. 628, in AVPRI, fond 151, opis' 482, del' 4068, list' 13.

20. Yanushkevitch (from Stavka) to Sazonov, 27 July/9 August 1914, in AVPRI, fond 151, opis' 482, del' 4068, list' 29 (and back).

21. Girs to Sazonov, 30 July/12 August 1914, document 84 in IBZI, v. 6:1, p. 59.

22. Benckendorff to Sazonov, reporting on his conversation with Grey, 2/15 August 1914, in AVPRI, fond 151, opis' 482, del' 4068, list' 55 (and back).

23. Sazonov to Stavka, 9/22 August 1914, forwarding Erzurum consul's report, in AVPRI, fond 151, opis' 482, del' 4068, list' 88.

24. Girs to Sazonov, 10/23 August 1914, in AVPRI, fond 151, opis' 482, del' 4068, list' 95.

25. For examples of an intercepted Austrian message, see, for example, Girs to Sazonov, 15/28 September 1914. For Romanian intelligence passed on from the Germans, see Girs to Sazonov, 17/30 September 1914. Both documents in AVPRI, fond 151, opis' 482, del' 4068, list' 174, 180.

26. Girs to Sazonov, 19 September/2 October 1914, in AVPRI, fond 151, opis' 482, del' 4068, list' 183. He claims that he got this information "from the German Ambassador" (i.e., Wangenheim), but presumably this means indirectly, by way of either the Romanian ambassador or Pallavicini.

Other Girs reports to Sazonov list his source as "Otsiuda," a not terribly creative code which literally means "from here." On most, but not all, occasions, the source was Pallavicini's intercepted telegrams. But in some cases, the only possible source is someone deep inside the Ottoman government.

27. Girs to Sazonov, 19 September/2 October 1914 (no. 1291), in AVPRI, fond 151, opis' 482, del' 4068, list' 184.

28. Girs to Sazonov, no. 1314, 20 September/3 October 1914, in AVPRI, fond 151, opis' 482, del' 4068, list' 186.

29. Girs to Sazonov, 21 September/4 October 1914, in AVPRI, fond 151, opis' 482, del' 4068, list' 187. On the 11 October 1914 war council, see also Trumpener, *Germany and the Ottoman Empire,* p. 49; and McMeekin, *Berlin-Baghdad Express,* chapter 5.

30. As Girs reported to Sazonov the previous day, 27 September/10 October 1914, in AVPRI, fond 151, opis' 482, del' 4068, list' 215.

31. Girs to G. N. Trubetskoi, 28 September/11 October 1914, in AVPRI, fond 151, opis' 482, del' 4068, list' 222–225.

32. Girs to Sazonov, 17 and 19 October 1914, in AVPRI, fond 151, opis' 482, del' 4068, list' 230 and 233.

33. Girs to Sazonov 7/20 October 1914, in AVPRI, fond 151, opis' 482, del' 4068, list' 234.

34. Ketlinskii to Sazonov, 8/21 October 1914, in AVPRI, fond 151, opis' 482, del' 4068, list' 235.

35. Airapetov, "Sud'ba Bosforskoi ekspeditsii," p. 191.

36. Girs to Sazonov, no. 1570, 12/25 October 1914, in AVPRI, fond 151, opis' 482, del' 4068, list' 244.

37. As reported by Ambassador Pallavicini from Pera, 30 and 31 October 1914, in HHSA, Liasse Krieg 21a Türkei, box 942. The detail about the *Goeben* firing 308 shells is in Airapetov, "Sud'ba Bosforskoi ekspeditsii," p. 191.

38. I have mostly followed my own account, from *Berlin-Baghdad Express,* chapter 5. See also Aksakal, *Ottoman Road to War in 1914,* pp. 178–183; and Trumpener, *Germany and the Ottoman Empire,* pp. 55–61.

39. As they did in winter 1916–1917, when the *Goeben* went down for long-term repairs. See chapter 9 below.

40. Turkish authors who lament the collapse of the Ottoman Empire, such as Yusuf Hikmet Bayur, sometimes blame Enver for thrusting his countrymen unnecessarily into a European conflict in which they had no real stake. See especially, in this vein, Bayur, *Türk İnkılabı Tarihi.*

41. The legal correspondence between the Russian Embassy and the Sublime Porte was replete with these sorts of onerous protests, which had only accelerated in the months prior to the First World War. See, for example, the cases of Chamuel Ostachinsky and Benjamin Aténélachvili, over which Russia exerted terrible pressure over the winter of 1913–14. Correspondence in BOA, HR-H, Dosya 579.

42. Yasamee, "Ottoman Empire," pp. 257–258.

43. Ibid. Said Halim Pasha seems to have indicated that both he and Djavid would resign together at the 1 November 1914 meeting; but neither did. And when Djavid did resign on 5 November, the grand vizier did not follow suit.

44. Conversation cited in Aksakal, *Ottoman Road to War in 1914,* p. 172.

45. Signed proclamation of war against Turkey by Tsar Nicholas II, 20 October/2 November 1914, in leaflet form, in RGVIA, fond 2000, opis' 1, del' 3796, list' 192.

5. THE RUSSIANS AND GALLIPOLI

1. Paléologue to Delcassé, 4 March 1915, in the Nicholas de Basily collection, box 9, folder marked "Paléologue, Maurice—1915. Documents," Hoover Institution Archives.

2. On the Germans' promotion of jihad against the Entente powers, see McMeekin, *Berlin-Baghdad Express,* especially chapter 6.

3. From the biographical notes in box 3 of the Nicholas de Basily collection, Hoover Institution Archives. See also Basily's memoirs, *Diplomat of Imperial Russia 1903–1917,* pp. 3–4.

4. Bazili, "O tselyakh' nashikh' v Prolivakh," circa November 1914, in *Konstantinopol i Prolivyi,* p. 158 and pp. 161–162 (and note 1). A reliable English translation of this document, labeled "Our Goals in Regard to the Straits," is available in Basily's memoirs, *Diplomat of Imperial Russia 1903–1917,* pp. 153–183. Because the phrasing is significant, I have performed my own translations of most of the following passages, highlighting the Russian original in parenthesis where it seems appropriate.

5. Basily, *Diplomat of Imperial Russia 1903–1917,* pp. 158–159, and, for the bits about the Trojan peninsula, Gallipoli, and Adrianople, pp. 178–180.

6. Ibid., pp. 165–166.

7. Airapetov, "Sud'ba Bosforskoi ekspeditsii," p. 182. Technically, the *Goeben* had by now been renamed the *Yavuz Sultan Selim.* But in most inter-Allied correspondence, Souchon's dreadnought continued to be referred to by its original, German name. For simplicity's sake, I have followed the same practice.

8. Bazili, "O tselyakh' nashikh' v Prolivakh," pp. 169–170.

9. Airapetov, "Sud'ba Bosforskoi ekspeditsii," p. 204; Bobroff, *Roads to Glory,* pp. 120–121, 123–124.

10. As reported by Lord Salisbury to Mr. Cross, 15 June 1878, reproduced in Lady Gwendolen Cecil (his daughter), *Life of Robert Marquis of Salisbury,* v. 2, p. 282.

11. Paléologue "diary entry" for 21 November 1914, in *La Russie des Tsars,* v. 1, pp. 198–200. See also chapter 3 above.

12. Benckendorff to Sazonov, 27 October/9 November 1914, in KP, v. 1, pp. 227–228. The gist of this document is also summarized (although not reproduced in anywhere near the original length) as document 484 in IBZI, v. 6:2, p. 422.

13. Citations in Fromkin, *Peace to End All Peace,* p. 75.

14. Benckendorff to Sazonov, 31 October/13 November 1914, in KP, v. 1, pp. 231–232.

15. Grey aide-mémoire, sent by Benckendorff to Sazonov, 1/14 November 1914, in AVPRI, fond 151, opis' 482, del' 4116, list' 3.

16. Sazonov to Benckendorff, 5/18 November 1914, in KP, v. 1, pp. 234–235.

17. Cited in Bobroff, *Roads to Glory,* p. 121.

18. Citations in Miller, *Straits,* pp. 347–348, 359–361. See also Fromkin, *Peace to End All Peace,* pp. 125–131; and Churchill to Stavka, by way of Buchanan/Sazonov, 7/20 January 1915, in KP, v. 2, pp. 129–130; also document 43 in IBZI, v. 7:1, pp. 42–43.

19. Kudashev aide-mémoire, transcribed from the remarks of Grand Duke Nicholas to General Williams and transmitted to Sazonov, 18/31 December 1914, in KP, v. 2, no. 11, pp. 128–129.

20. Stolitsa to Stavka, 16/29 December 1914, 17/30 December 1914 (twice), and 19 December 1914/1 January 1915, all in AVPRI, fond 151, opis' 482, del' 4113, list' 10, 12–14.

21. Stolitsa to Stavka, 21 December 1914/3 January 1915, and follow-up on 6 January confirming the rescinding of the evacuation orders, in AVPRI, fond 151, opis' 482, del' 4113, list' 16–17. Turkish casualties at Sarıkamış have often been exaggerated. For example Fromkin, in *Peace to End All Peace* (p. 121), says that "Of the perhaps 100,000 men who took part in the

attack, 86 percent were lost." The original source for most exaggerations of the Ottoman casualty count at Sarıkamış seems to be Maurice Larcher's *La Guerre turque dans la guerre mondiale*. The most accurate estimates from Ottoman sources come to 23,000 battlefield deaths, another 10,000 who died from wounds, 7,000 taken prisoner, and 10,000 other casualties, leaving 42,000 "effectives" by 14 February 1915 out of a prebattle force a bit more than twice that size. See Erickson, *Ordered to Die*, pp. 59–60; and also Erickson, "The Armenians and Ottoman Military Policy, 1915," 148.

22. Sazonov to Izvolsky, 21 October/3 November 1914, in AVPRI, fond 187, opis' 524, del' 3175, list' 52.

23. See McMeekin, *Berlin-Baghdad Express*, chapter 13.

24. Sazonov to Izvolsky, 3 November 1914, in AVPRI, fond 187, opis' 524, del' 3175, list' 54 and 55.

25. Kudashev aide-mémoire, transcribed from the remarks of Grand Duke Nicholas to General Williams and transmitted to Sazonov, 18/31 December 1914, in KP, v. 2, no. 11, pp. 128–129.

26. Erickson, *Ordered to Die*, pp. 59–60.

27. Kudashev aide-mémoire, in KP, v. 2, no. 11, 128–129. *Nichego*—a Russian phrase meaning literally "nothing," but which can also convey something like "no big deal" in contemporary American English—was the phrase the grand duke used here, and with roughly that colloquial meaning *(. . . to pust' ne predprinimayut nichego)*.

28. Cited in Miller, *Straits*, p. 352.

29. The Witte quote footnoted here is cited in Mankoff, "Russia and the Polish Question," p. 198. Mankoff's translation.

30. Paléologue to Delcassé, 4, 5, and 6 March 1915, telegrams all copied in the original ms handwriting, in the Nicholas de Basily collection, Hoover Institution Archives, folder marked "Paléologue, Maurice—Documents," box 9.

31. Poincaré to Paléologue, 9 March 1915, no. 320, in *Documents diplomatiques français* tome 1 (1915), p. 419.

32. Churchill to Stavka, by way of Buchanan/Sazonov, 7/20 January 1915, in KP, v. 2, pp. 129–130; also document 43 in IBZI, v. 7:1, pp. 42–43. Miller, in *Straits* (pp. 396–398) does take note of Churchill's directive to Stavka, claiming (without giving a source for this assertion) that "the Russians were shocked to find that they were to be required at all." Miller further notes that Churchill knew by 27 January 1915 that "the Russians would take no active part" in the Dardanelles campaign. But he does not mention the subsequent communications between Stavka and the British Admiralty relating to Eberhart, the chain of command, and so on. While his study is by far the most exhaustive to date of the British side of the Straits/Dardanelles question, Miller does not use Russian sources (nor French ones, for that matter).

33. Izvolsky to Sazonov, 10/23 February 1915; Benckendorff to Sazonov, 12/25 February 1915, and Sazonov passing on the previous to Kudashev at Stavka, 15/28 February and 16 February/1 March 1915, in AVPRI, fond 138, opis' 467, del' 472/492, list' 2, 5, 7, 10–11.

34. Sazonov to Stavka, 16 February/1 March 1915, in AVPRI, fond 138, opis' 467, del' 467/486, list' 4–5.

35. Sazonov to Benckendorff (for Kitchener), passing on Stavka, 18/31 March 1915, in AVPRI, fond 138, opis' 467, del' 472/492, list' 49.

36. Churchill reproduced his own 24 March 1915 directive to de Robeck, cited here, in *World Crisis,* v. 2, pp. 239–241.

37. Ibid., p. 539.

38. As Fromkin points out, in *Peace to End All Peace,* p. 132.

39. For analysis, see McMeekin, *Berlin-Baghdad Express,* chapter 10.

40. Airapetov, "Sud'ba Bosforskoi ekspeditsii," pp. 207, 210.

41. Sazonov to Stavka, 15/28 February and 16 February/1 March 1915, and Stavka response to same (passing on Russian Admiralty), in AVPRI, fond 138, opis' 467, del' 472/492, list' 10–12.

42. Eberhart-Kudashev-Sazonov-Churchill-Carden, 26 February/11 March 1915, in AV-PRI, fond 138, opis' 467, del' 472/492, list' 28.

43. Sazonov to Benckendorff, 16/29 March 1915, in AVPRI, fond 138, opis' 467, del' 472/492, list' 46. Subsequent communications between Eberhart and Carden continued on in the old, clunky, and indirect vein all through April and May; it seems clear that no reliable direct wireless link was ever established. On the *Goeben*'s location in early April, see Airapetov, "Sud'ba Bosforskoi ekspeditsii," p. 218.

44. Sazonov passing on de Robeck to Eberhart, 5/18 and 7/20 April 1915, in AVPRI, fond 138, opis' 467, del' 472, list' 57, 59.

45. Serafimov, passing on Eberhart from Dedeagatch, 12/25 April 1915, in AVPRI, fond 138, opis' 467, del' 472, list' 60. In a sign of the priority the Russians attached to this message, it was sent not via Petrograd and London, but directly to Dedeagatch, the Bulgarian border town which served as a hub for Allied spies gathering intelligence on Turkey.

46. Sariyer today is the northernmost district of Istanbul on the European shoreline of the Bosphorus. But the term also refers to the whole area where the Bosphorus meets the Black Sea, stretching fifteen or twenty miles around the northeastern corner of Thrace. Beykos, likewise, can refer to the entire northwestern corner of Asiatic Turkey where it meets the Bosphorus and Black Sea. The Russian shells could therefore have been launched at almost any point along either coastline. Considering that no serious damage was registered by either the Russians or Turks, it is likely Eberhart's half-hearted 25 April 1915 attack was not directed at any major forts or shore batteries.

47. Citations from Moorehead, *Gallipoli,* pp. 141–142.

48. Man'kovskii, passing on Eberhart, 20 April/3 May 1915 (at 12:50 pm), in AVPRI, fond 138, opis' 467, del' 472, list' 61. For the number of shells fired, see Airapetov, "Sud'ba Bosforskoi ekspeditsii," p. 218.

49. Sazonov to Stavka, 30 April/13 May 1915, in AVPRI, fond 138, opis' 467, del' 472, list' 63.

50. In his otherwise sensible analysis of Russian Straits policy, Bobroff, citing Sazonov's memoirs, claims the news about Britain's plans for a Dardanelles campaign affected him "painfully." This is a curious remark. Shame at allowing one's ally to do all the heavy lifting there might have been; but not enough shame for Sazonov to renounce Russia's claims on the Straits. Bobroff, *Roads to Glory,* p. 125. In a similar vein, Horst Linke emphasizes Sazonov's desire that "the Straits and Constantinople not be taken without meaningful Russian participation" in operations, while neglecting to note how many golden opportunities the Russians had to participate, and yet did not. Linke, *Zaristische Russland und der erste Weltkrieg,* p. 195.

51. Airapetov, "Sud'ba Bosforskoi ekspeditsii," pp. 211–212.

52. Kudashev to Sazonov (for the Allies), passing on Eberhart, 2/15 May 1915, in AVPRI, fond 138, opis' 467, del' 472, list' 67. For the Greek offer of troops discussed in the footnote, see Fromkin, *Peace to End All Peace*, p. 135; and Ambassador Buchanan aide-mémoire, 6 March 1915, in KP, v. 2, pp. 259–261.

53. Turkish casualty figures were exaggerated for many years in British and Australian accounts of the campaign because they did not trust official Ottoman estimates and so doubled or tripled them. Even official estimates, however, come out higher than those for the Allies (at least those for soldiers killed; in terms of wounded, the figures were very close on both sides).

6. RUSSIA AND THE ARMENIANS

1. Sazonov to Tiflis command (with a copy to War Minister Sukhomlinov), 13/26 August 1914, in RGVIA, fond 2000, opis' 1, del' 3851, list' 24.

2. Curiously, as the Dardanelles operation was being planned in January 1915, Churchill wrote a letter to Grey complaining that overindulgence of the Russians—particularly their implied veto over any Greek participation in any future Gallipoli campaign—would mean that "a million men will die through the prolongation of the war," forcing Britain into "paying all the future into Russian hands." The letter, alas, was never sent—and its contents evidently later forgotten by Churchill, who could summon up little but gallantry towards the pitiable Russians after 1917. Cited in Fromkin, *Peace to End All Peace*, p. 128.

3. Donald Bloxham, in his acclaimed recent study *The Great Game of Genocide*, does take careful note (pp. 71–91) of Russian designs on eastern Turkey, including the formation of partisan bands of Armenians in the Caucasus border areas. He also notes the request of Armenian revolutionaries from Zeytun for arms, lodged with the Russian military command in Tiflis. Bloxham remarks, apropos all this, that "the Russian role in fostering an explosive situation does need to be highlighted." Still, Russia plays at most a secondary role in Bloxham's narrative, which turns almost entirely on the "genocide" question of Ottoman premeditation and/ or guilt for the Armenian massacres of 1915. Likewise, Taner Akçam's *A Shameful Act* (2006) concedes that "the issue of Armenian volunteers serving with the Russians is very important," but adds that this importance lies only in "its impact on the Unionist leaders"—that is, on Ottoman policy. For both Bloxham and Akçam, Russian foreign policy, as such, is an afterthought.

Many Soviet Armenian scholars, such as S. M. Akopian, in *Zapadnaia Armeniia v planakh imperialisticheskikh derzhav* (1969) and A. O. Arutiunian in *Kavkazskii front 1914–1917 gg.* (1971), have thoroughly explored the Russian imperial context of the wartime Armenian deportations, but this is not generally true of Russian-Armenians writing on the "genocide" in western languages, who tend to downplay the Russian role in the story. A notable exception to this rule is Ronald Suny, in *Armenia in the Twentieth Century* (1983).

More representative of the general Armenian line today are the books of Vahakn Dadrian and (with some exceptions) Richard Hovannisian. In *The History of the Armenian Genocide* (orig. 1995; six editions so far, and counting) Dadrian devotes all of six pages to Russia's role in "the Armenian disaster"—and these cover the pre–World War I period exclusively. Hovannisian, in "The Armenian Question in the Ottoman Empire," his principal article in the volume he edited recently on *The Armenian People from Ancient to Modern Times* (2004), does provide a fairly extensive discussion of Russia's Armenian policy—but again, only in the period *preceding* the First World War. It is not that Hovannisian does not know about the Russian angle in World War I—in fact he covered this subject rather extensively forty years ago in "The Allies and Armenia, 1915–18" (1968). Rather, he seems to have let it all slip down the memory hole in his later works, after becoming something like an official spokesman for the Armenian cause in American academe.

For example, in *The Armenian Genocide. History, Politics, Ethics* (1992), edited by Hovannisian—a kind of compilation of state-of-the-art research on the subject at a time when a great deal of it was being produced—there are separate articles by fourteen different scholars, not a single one of which examines Russian policy towards the Armenians, as will at least one article (by Peter Holquist) in a forthcoming volume edited by Ronald Suny, Fatma Müge Göçek, and Norman Naimark, entitled *A Question of Genocide: Armenians and Turks at the End of the Ottoman Empire* (2011). From zero to one: a significant improvement.

Of course, Turkish authors (and generally pro-Turkish western authors, like Justin McCarthy and more recently Guenter Lewy) have long taken note of the Russian side of the story, which is essential to any argument which challenges the "genocide" narrative. This is true even of Turkish scholars, like Akçam and Fuat Dündar, who hew more closely to the Armenian genocide narrative. Dündar's recent book, *Crime by Numbers: The Role of Statistics in the Armenian Question,* often mentions the Russian-Armenian threat to provide necessary context, even if generally dismissing its importance.

4. Cited in Lewy, *Armenian Massacres in Ottoman Turkey,* p. 20.

5. Cited in Nalbandian, *The Armenian Revolutionary Movement,* p. 83.

6. Lewy, *Armenian Massacres in Ottoman Turkey,* pp. 20–26. Bloxham, in *Great Game of Genocide,* gives a figure of "80,000 to 100,000 Armenians [killed] directly" and "tens of thousands indirectly in 1894–96," but gives no direct source for these figures, which seem extraordinarily high—higher even than the wildest contemporary estimates.

7. In this vein, see (for a recent version of the theme) Henry Kissinger, *Diplomacy,* pp. 161–164 (in which he sets up Gladstone's Midlothian campaign as the precursor for twentieth-century "Wilsonianism"); or for more classic statements of the story, Shannon, *Gladstone and the Bulgarian Agitation 1876;* and Matthew, *Gladstone: 1809–1898,* esp. vol. 2.

8. Gladstone was somewhat coy about the Russian invasion. He did not endorse it so much as seek to embarrass Disraeli, by way of introducing various resolutions denouncing Ottoman brutality in Bulgaria into the House of Commons, into not doing anything much to oppose it. It is an interesting question whether Gladstone would have supported or opposed a British declaration of war if the Russians had actually occupied Constantinople in 1878. By issuing a threat to prevent this from happening, Disraeli thus saved Gladstone from the horns of his own dilemma—in this way making possible Gladstone's return to power in 1880.

9. Ottoman demography is, of course, a highly contested and politically explosive subject. But there are certain undisputed facts worth mentioning. Contrary to common belief, in the early twentieth century the Armenians nowhere constituted a clear majority in eastern Turkey, the Transcaucasus, or northwestern Persia, although there were areas of very heavy concentration (like the Van-Bitlis area and Ottoman Cilicia). One could certainly make the case that the Armenians were the most important group in the area culturally, owing to their long and well-

chronicled history and to their much higher levels of literacy and education than local Muslims; or also economically, as a kind of widely resented "market-dominant minority." But these are subjective, not objective, arguments about the true ethnic "composition" of the region. For the politics surrounding various population estimates, see Fuat Dündar's excellent new study, *Crime by Numbers.*

10. Reynolds, "The Ottoman-Russian Struggle for Eastern Anatolia and the Caucasus, 1908–1918," pp. 169–174.

11. Chirkov to Girs from Van, 30/31 May 1913 (reporting on the events of 20 May), in AVPRI, fond 180, opis' 517/2, del' 3573, list' 191.

12. On Russia and the Kurds, for the best analysis in English, see especially Reynolds, "The Ottoman-Russian Struggle for Eastern Anatolia and the Caucasus, 1908–1918," p. 116 and *passim.* Reynolds, in turn, has drawn heavily on the magisterial study by M. S. Lazarev of the *Kurdskii Vopros (1891–1917).*

13. Cited in Reynolds, "The Ottoman-Russian Struggle for Eastern Anatolia and the Caucasus, 1908–1918," p. 111.

14. Ibid., p. 116.

15. Muraviev? to Tiflis command, from Urmia, 7/20 January 1913, report on activities of 15 to 31 December 1912, in AVPRI, fond 180, opis' 517/2, del' 3573, list' 1.

16. Orlov to Girs, 14/27 February 1913, in AVPRI, fond 180, opis' 517/2, del' 3573, list' 17.

17. Chirkov to Girs, 7 March 1913 (twice), in AVPRI, fond 180, opis' 517/2, del' 3573, list' 22, 24–27. On Abdurrezak, see also Reynolds, "The Ottoman-Russian Struggle for Eastern Anatolia and the Caucasus, 1908–1918," p. 106.

18. Kirsanov to Girs (from Mosul), 7 March 1913, in AVPRI, fond 180, opis' 517/2, del' 3573, list' 38–39 (and backs).

19. "Otchet o zasedaniyakh soveta armyanskoi revolutsionnoi partii 'Dashnaktsyun', proiskhodivshikh' v' Berline, v' kontse Marta mesyatsa tekushchago goda," sent in by Okhrana agent to St. Petersburg, 27 April 1914, in GARF, fond 529, opis' 1, del' 7, list' 22.

20. Olferiev to Girs, 18/31 March 1913, in AVPRI, fond 180, opis' 517-2, del' 3573, list' 53–55.

21. Olferiev to Girs from Van, 25 March/7 April 1913, in AVPRI, fond 180, opis' 517-2, del' 3573, list' 85. For analysis, see also Reynolds, "The Ottoman-Russian Struggle for Eastern Anatolia and the Caucasus, 1908–1918," pp. 175–176.

22. Olferiev to Girs, 18/31 March 1913, in AVPRI, fond 180, opis' 517-2, del' 3573, list' 53–55.

23. Olferiev to Girs from Van, 25 March/7 April 1913, in AVPRI, fond 180, opis' 517-2, del' 3573, list' 85.

24. Chirkov to Girs, from Van vilayet, 30 May/12 June 1913, in AVPRI, fond 180, opis' 517-2, del' 3573, list' 191.

25. Neratov to Girs, copies to Paris and London, 21 May/2 June 1913, in AVPRI, fond 172, opis' 514/2, del' 633, list' 2.

26. Sazonov to ambassadors in London, Paris, Berlin, Vienna, Rome, Constantinople, 30 May/12 June 1913, in AVPRI, fond 172, opis' 514/2, del' 633, list' 11.

27. "Secret telegram" from Ambassador Girs to Alexander Izvolsky, Imperial Russian Ambassador to Paris, copied to S. D. Sazonov, 4/17 October 1913, in AVPRI, fond 172, opis' 514-2, del' 633, list' 19.

28. As Richard Hovannisian notes in "The Armenian Question in the Ottoman Empire," in *The Armenian People from Ancient to Modern Times,* v. 2, p. 237.

29. This warning was made "more than once." See multiple citations in Reynolds, "The Ottoman-Russian Struggle for Eastern Anatolia and the Caucasus, 1908–1918," p. 125, fn. 114.

30. Chirkov to Girs from Bitlis, 14/27 May 1913, in AVPRI, fond 180, opis' 517/2, del' 3573, list' 59.

31. Chirkov to Girs from Bitlis, 6/19 October 1913, in AVPRI, fond 180, opis' 517/2, del' 3573, list' 269.

32. Letter of Zavène Der-Yéghiayan, the Armenian Metropolitan of Bitlis, to Russian Consul Shirkov, 3/17 March 1914, in AVPRI, fond 180, opis' 517/2, del' 3573, list' 326–327 (and backs). See also McMeekin, *Berlin-Baghdad Express,* chapter 14; and Reynolds, "The Ottoman-Russian Struggle for Eastern Anatolia and the Caucasus, 1908–1918," p. 125 and *passim.*

33. Shirkov to Girs from Bitlis, 23 March/5 April 1914, in AVPRI, fond 180, opis' 517/2, del' 3573, list' 369. See also McMeekin, *Berlin-Baghdad Express,* chapter 14; and Reynolds, "The Ottoman-Russian Struggle for Eastern Anatolia and the Caucasus, 1908–1918," pp. 127–130.

34. Letter from Dr. G. C. Reynolds, Secretary of the American Mission Board, to S. Olferieff (Olferiev), 25 March 1913, in AVPRI, fond 180, opis' 517–2, del' 3573, list' 72.

35. Chalabian, *General Andranik and the Armenian Revolutionary Movement,* pp. 215–217.

36. Shaw, *Ottoman Empire in World War I,* p. 93.

37. Prêtre, K. Elisée, S. Seradjian, L. Pachalian, and A. Tschobaniany?, on behalf of the Église Arménienne of Paris, 29 August 1914, in AVPRI, fond 187, opis' 524, del' 3176, list' 43. This folder alone contains dozens of similar letters.

38. Shaw, *Ottoman Empire in World War I,* pp. 93–95. For the detail about the Erzurum desertions, see the last report of the (departing) Russian consul Adamov before he left Turkey, 19 October/1 November 1914, in RGVIA, fond 2000, opis' 1, del' 3860, list' 608–609.

39. Sazonov memorandum on the Armenian question to Grand Duke Nicholas, circa mid-October 1915, in ΛVPRI, fond 151, opis' 482, del' 3480, list' 28 (and back), 29.

40. Chalabian, *General Andranik,* p. 217.

41. Yudenich to Yanushkevitch at Stavka, 18/31 August 1914, in RGVIA, fond 2000, opis' 1, del' 3851, list' 12 (and back), 13. On the recruitment of Armenian volunteers (including tsarist subjects) into the Russian army, see also Linke, *Zaristische Russland und der erste Weltkrieg,* pp. 208–209.

42. Sazonov to Sukhomlinov, 23 July/5 August 1914, in RGVIA, fond 2000, opis' 1, del' 3851, list' 17 (and back).

43. Sazonov to Tiflis command (copy to Sukhomlinov), 13/26 August 1914, in RGVIA, fond 2000, opis' 1, del' 3851, list' 24.

44. Yudenich ms signed report "O snabzhenii oruzhiem" turetskikh' armyan'," dated 16/29 August 1914, in RGVIA, fond 2000, opis' 1, del' 3851, 10 (and back), 11.

45. Demirel, *Birinci dünya harbinde Erzurum ve çevresinde Ermeni hareketleri (1914–1918),* p. 17.

46. The most thorough examination of these activities is that of Stanford Shaw, in *Ottoman Empire in World War I,* p. 430 and *passim.*

47. See Reynolds, "The Ottoman-Russian Struggle for Eastern Anatolia and the Caucasus, 1908–1918," p. 270.

48. Ibid., pp. 273–274; and Mahmed Yusuf Dzhafarov to Grand Duke Nicholas, received 23 February 1915, forwarded to Sazonov, in AVPRI, fond 151, opis' 482, del' 4113, list' 42–47.

49. Vorontsov-Dashkov to the War Ministry in St. Petersburg, 7/20 September 1914, in RGVIA, fond 2000, opis' 1, del' 3851, list' 68 (back).

50. Adamov report upon leaving Erzurum, 19 October/1 November 1914, in RGVIA, fond 2000, opis' 1, del' 3860, list' 613–614.

51. Vvedenskii to Tiflis command from Urmia, 1/14 December 1914, in RGVIA, fond 2000, opis' 1, del' 3851, list' 71.

52. Savinskii from Sofia, 8/21 December 1914, Savinskii passing on Varna consul, 5/18 December 1914, Poklevskii from Bucharest, 25 December 1914/7 January 1915, all in RGVIA, fond 2000, opis' 1, del' 3851, list' 3, 72, 77; and Bakhmetev from Washington D.C., 30 October/12 November 1914, in RGVIA, fond 2000, opis' 1, del' 3860, list' 164, all sent to Tiflis command by way of Sazonov.

53. Sazonov circular to Sofia and Washington (later copied), 8/21 November 1914, in RGVIA, fond 2000, opis' 1, del' 3851, list' 79.

54. Yudenich (and his staff officers) to Stavka, 22 August/4 September 1914 and undated (though presumably the same date), in RGVIA, fond 2000, opis' 1, del' 3851, list' 35, 36 (and backs). The main weapon on offer was the American-designed and originally British-built Berdan rifle. Somewhat shorter than the standard Russian infantry rifle, it was used primarily by mounted Cossacks (or Kurds), although it was not intended to be fired on horseback.

55. In this vein, see Sazonov to Tiflis command (copy to Sukhomlinov), 13/26 August 1914, in RGVIA, fond 2000, opis' 1, del' 3851, list' 24; Sazonov to Tiflis command, 5/18 September and 12/25 September 1914, in RGVIA, fond 2000, opis' 1, del' 3851, list' 45, 46.

56. Gul'kevich to Tiflis command by way of Vorontsov-Dashkov, 4/17 December 1914, in RGVIA, fond 2000, opis' 1, del' 3851, list' 65.

57. Vorontsov-Dashkov to Stavka from Tiflis, 7/20 February 1915, in RGVIA, fond 2000, opis' 1, del' 3851, list' 82.

58. See Bloxham, *Great Game of Genocide,* p. 81; Lewy, *Armenian Massacres in Ottoman Turkey,* pp. 103–104.

59. Neratov to Benckendorff, 28 March/10 April 1915, passing on Tiflis command/Stavka, in RGVIA, fond 2000, opis' 1, del' 3851, list' 93. On the Dörtyol landings, see Erickson, "The Armenians and Ottoman Military Policy," p. 156.

60. Stolitsa to Sazonov from Tiflis command, 3/16 April 1915, in RGVIA, fond 2000, opis' 1, del' 3851, list' 94.

61. Erickson, "The Armenians and Ottoman Military Policy," p. 156.

62. This document is cited by Akçam in *A Shameful Act,* pp. 141–142. Here as elsewhere in his narrative, Akçam takes note of evidence of collaboration between the Russian army and Ottoman Armenians, but only insofar as this evidence was used by the Turks to justify deportations. Whether or not the evidence was *true* does not seem to concern him.

63. Summary of rebel activity by Şükrü, in Van, for the Ottoman Third Army, circa April 1915, in ATASE, 528–2061, 21 (1–18). Also reproduced in TCGB, *Arşiv Belgeleriyle Ermeni Faaliyetleri 1914–1918,* v. 1 (cited passages on p. 114). As we saw above, the main border towns

where the Russians were assembling their Armenian guerrilla bands were indeed Oltu, Sarıkamış, and Gizman (Kâğızman); the Ottomans missed only Igdyr. The Turkish estimate of the striking power of these bands ("machine guns and artillery") was certainly exaggerated, but this is not exactly surprising in a wartime situation when the instinct of most commanders is to prepare for the worst.

64. Ibid. See also Erickson, "The Armenians and Ottoman Military Policy," pp. 156, 150–152; and Reynolds, "The Ottoman-Russian Struggle for Eastern Anatolia and the Caucasus, 1908–1918," pp. 263–264.

65. I have basically followed my own account here from *Berlin-Baghdad Express,* chapter 14, which draws on Erickson, "The Armenians and Ottoman Military Policy," and Reynolds, "The Ottoman-Russian Struggle for Eastern Anatolia and the Caucasus, 1908–1918," along with the "eyewitness" articles, cited below, in *Mshak* (note 67) and *Russkoe Slovo* (note 69).

66. Passed on by Stolitsa to Stavka from Tiflis, 29 April/12 May 1915, in AVPRI, fond 151, opis' 482, del' 3505, 4. With characteristic deceit, Sazonov forwarded this message on to his ambassadors in Paris and London, but only after deleting the word "Russian," so that it appeared more an innocent appeal for humanitarian sympathy than evidence of treasonous contact with Turkey's enemy in arms—which of course it was. That this method of communication was typical is confirmed in Ottoman army files, which mention at least one secret letter from an Armenian guerrilla commander intercepted by the Ottomans, "found sewn into the jacket" of a messenger named Fika. See ATASE April 1915 intelligence summary, ATASE, 528-2061, 21 (1–18), pp. 114–115.

67. *Mshak* cover story, 30 September 1915, as translated (into Russian) and clipped by Tiflis command and forwarded to Sazonov and Grand Duke Nicholas, in AVPRI, fond 151, opis' 482, del' 3480, 20.

68. Telegram from "the Armenians of Van" to Vorontsov-Dashkov, sent via Begri-Kala, 7/20 May 1915, in AVPRI, fond 151, opis' 482, del' 3505, list' 6. On the role of Armenian deserters in the taking of Van, see also the report by the Austrian ski instructor sent to train the Ottoman Third Army in mountain warfare, in packet labeled "Copia pro actis zu Einsichtstück der k.u.k. Marine-Sektion vom 2. VIII. 1915," passed on from the Pera Embassy, 16 July 1915, in HHSA, Liasse Krieg 21a. Türkei, box 944.

69. "Vozstanie v' Vane," in *Russkoe Slovo* no. 141 (20 June/3 July 1915), clipped in AVPRI, fond 151, opis' 482, del' 3505, list' 7–8.

70. Akçam, *A Shameful Act,* p. 140.

71. Dündar, *Crime by Numbers,* pp. 72–73.

72. Akçam, *A Shameful Act,* p. 159.

73. Talaat's instructions to Enver spoke only of the need to close down Hunchak and Dashnak committees known to have participated in revolutionary or partisan activity, and to search for weapons caches. Armenians suspected of treasonous activity, though, Talaat told Enver, "shall be sent to the military courts immediately." In light of previous discussions between Enver, Djemal, and Talaat about targeted relocations, however, Enver may well have thought that deportation was what Talaat was really getting at. Legally speaking, the Armenians in question were "relocated" elsewhere inside the Ottoman Empire (mostly to Syria), not "deported" beyond its borders. Because "relocation" has the sound of a euphemism, I use these terms interchangeably here.

74. The original text of Talaat's 24 April 1915 instructions to Enver is in ATASE, BDH

401–1580, 1–3, also reproduced in TCGB, *Arşiv Belgeleriyle Ermeni Faaliyetleri 1914–1918*, v. 1, pp. 127–129. For further details, see also Erickson, "The Armenians and Ottoman Military Policy," p. 164, and footnotes 114–116, same page.

75. Decree by "Minister of Internal Affairs" Talaat Pasha, on the "Coercive political circumstances necessitating the relocation and transfer of the Armenians," 31 May 1915, ATASE, BDH 361-1445, 1–4; also reproduced in TCGB, *Arşiv Belgeleriyle Ermeni Faaliyetleri 1914–1918*, v. 1, pp. 131–137. Akçam, in *A Shameful Act* (pp. 197–199) is dismissive of the "so-called 'Armenian uprisings' in eastern Anatolia," as of the claims that Armenian rebels had cached significant quantities of weapons. While he is surely right that the Ottoman military and government exaggerated the scale of the uprisings to justify the terrible atrocities of the Armenian deportation campaign, the Adamov report cited above suggests that there were significant weapons caches throughout eastern Turkey, just as Ottoman military files claim. It is interesting that, to refute Turkish claims of a substantial Armenian threat in Erzurum—where Ottoman Third Army headquarters was located—Akçam cites a report by the German consul there, Scheubner-Richter (the same who would later be felled by Hitler's side marching through Munich after the Beer Hall Putsch). The *Russian* consul at Erzurum, Adamov—who would have been far better informed about Armenian activities—reported otherwise.

76. On the exemptions, and how often they were disregarded, see Bloxham, *Great Game of Genocide*, pp. 89, 124–125; and Lewy, *Armenian Massacres in Ottoman Turkey*, pp. 180, 184, 205–206. On the controversies surrounding Armenian artisans working on the Baghdad Railway, see McMeekin, *Berlin-Baghdad Express*, pp. 254–258.

77. McMeekin, *Berlin-Baghdad Express*, p. 253.

78. Dündar, *Crime by Numbers*, p. 151. Interestingly, Guenter Lewy, in *Armenian Massacres in Ottoman Turkey* (pp. 240–241), came out with a very similar number, of 642,000, although he had not seen original Ottoman sources as has Dündar. The small discrepancy between these figures suggests that we may not be that far away from a rough consensus estimate. (Although neither is Armenian, Dündar is regarded as being closer to the Armenian "side," much as Lewy is seen as closer to the Turkish one.)

Official Turkish government estimates of Armenian casualty rates are much lower than these, of course, but they are not quite as exculpatory as one might expect. An "Armenian deportation registry" published by the Turkish General Staff several years ago, based on internal sources, lists 987,569 Armenians "recorded in registries" in the cities subject to the deportation campaign of 1915, of which 413,067 were "subject to relocation." The registry further notes the numbers of Armenians killed in clashes with government forces in certain areas (6,500 in Trabzon province, nearly 9,000 in Erzurum). In the case of Bitlis province, scene of some of the worst violence of 1915, the military estimated that as many as 89,500 of 109,521 Armenians, or nearly 80 percent, "either died in the clashes, or ran away." Even the Turkish General Staff will thus admit that more than 100,000 Armenians died or disappeared during the deportation battles of 1915, over and above the 413,067 officially deported (of whom we know a large percentage perished en route, something the Turkish General Staff publication makes no effort to deny). The Ottoman army registry of the deportations was published in TCGB, *Arşiv Belgeleriyle Ermeni Faaliyetleri 1914–1918*, v. 1, pp. 147–170, figures on pp. 147, 159. The key page is also reproduced as appendix 12 in Dündar, *Crime by Numbers*, p. 197.

79. Mankoff, "Russia and the Polish Question," pp. 239–240.

80. Fuller, *The Foe Within,* p. 3.

81. See Stone, *Eastern Front,* pp. 182–185.

7. THE RUSSIANS IN PERSIA

1. A. A. Baratov, "Bor'ba v' Persii vo vremeni revoliutsii v' Rossii," circa spring 1917, in the Baratov collection, Hoover Institution Archives, box 3.

2. See Quai d'Orsay memorandum labeled "Russie-Angleterre. Juillet 1914," in QO Russie Politique Etrangère, vol. 50; and Siegel, *Endgame,* esp. chapter 8 on the "Death of the Anglo-Russian Agreement: 1914."

3. Reade to Grey, 17 December 1914, in PRO, FO 371/2094.

4. On all this, see Fromkin, *A Peace to End All Peace,* esp. Part II ("Kitchener of Khartoum Looks Ahead").

5. Siegel, *Endgame,* p. 187 (for the Grey citation) and p. 189 (for the troop figure).

6. Buchanan aide-mémoire to Sazonov, 20 October/2 November 1914, document 449 in IBZI, v. 6:2, p. 1.

7. Benckendorff to Sazonov, 27 October/9 November 1914, in KP, v. 1, 227–228.

8. Benckendorff to Sazonov, 31 October/13 November and 1/14 November 1914, both in KP, v. 1, pp. 232–234.

9. See Benckendorff to Sazonov, passing on Grey, 9/22 December 1914, document 678 in IBZI, v. 6:2, pp. 575–576.

10. See chapter 5 above.

11. Benckendorff to Sazonov, passing on Grey, 9/22 December 1914, document 678 in IBZI, v. 6:2, p. 575.

12. Townley to Grey, 8 October 1914, telegram no. 469, in PRO, FO 438/3.

13. Korostovets to Sazonov, 26 November/9 December 1914, document 630 in IBZI, v. 6:2, pp. 537–538.

14. Benckendorff to Sazonov (twice), 10/23 December 1914, documents 684 and 685, in IBZI, v. 6:2, pp. 580–581.

15. Sazonov to Benckendorff, 27 December 1914/9 January 1915, document 739 in IBZI, v. 6:2, pp. 633–634.

16. Stolitsa from Tiflis, 17/30 December 1914 (twice), and 19 December 1914/1 January 1915, in AVPRI, fond 151, opis' 482, del' 4113, list' 12–16 and following.

17. Townley to Grey, 1 January 1915, in PRO, FO 438/6.

18. Townley to Grey, 3 January 1915, in PRO, FO 438/6.

19. Stolitsa to Stavka, 24 December 1914/6 January 1915, in AVPRI, fond 151, opis' 482, del' 4113, list' 18.

20. Vorontsov-Dashkov to Stavka from Tiflis, 7/20 September 1914; and Vvedenskii to Tiflis command from Urmia, 1/14 December 1914, both in RGVIA, fond 2000, opis' 1, del' 3851, list' 68 (and back), 71.

21. See McMeekin, *Berlin-Baghdad Express,* chapters 13 and 16.

22. Townley to Grey, 28 January 1915, no. 166, in PRO, FO 438/6.

23. Buchanan to Grey, 5 January 1915, no. 24, in PRO, FO 438/6.

24. Siegel, *Endgame,* pp. 187–188.

25. Smith, *Russian Struggle for Power,* pp. 229–232.

26. Townley to Grey, 23 March 1915, in PRO, FO 438/6.

27. Sazonov to Benckendorff, 27 December 1914/9 January 1915, document 739 in IBZI, v. 6:2, 633–634.

28. Marling to Grey, 12 and 20 May 1915, in PRO, FO 438/6.

29. Von der Goltz to Zimmermann from Constantinople, 30 January 1915, and Wangenheim from Pera, 1 and 6 February 1915, in PAAA, R 21035.

30. Sarre to Nadolny, 20 April 1915, in PAAA, R 21042.

31. Marling to Grey, 20 May 1915, in PRO, FO 438/6.

32. Hohenlohe from Constantinople, 23 September 1915, in PAAA, R 21049; and Lossow/ Wangenheim to Nadolny, 21 October 1915, in PAAA, R 21051.

33. Buchan, *Greenmantle,* p. 32.

34. See, for example, Grey/Buchanan aide-mémoire, 7/20 January 1915, document 42 in IBZI, v. 6:2, p. 42.

35. Sazonov to Benckendorff, 27 December 1914/9 January 1915, document 739 in IBZI, v. 6:2, 633–634.

36. Korostovets to Sazonov, 29 January/11 February 1915, document 181 in IBZI, pp. 166–167.

37. Sazonov to Etter, in Teheran, 9/22 May 1915, document 811 in IBZI, v. 7:2, p. 783; and (for the Stavka bit) Sazonov to Etter in Teheran, 29 April/12 May 1915, twice, documents 737 and 738 in IBZI, v. 7:2, p. 719. For the request for 10,000 troops, see Yanushkevitch to Sazonov, 26 July/8 August 1915, and Sazonov passing on to Etter in Teheran, documents 465 and 467 in IBZI, v. 8:2, pp. 448–449, 451. See also Klemm, for the Political Department of the Foreign Ministry, to Gov-General Baranovskii in Turkestan, 26 April 1915/9 May 1915, document 716 in IBZI, v. 7:2, p. 703.

38. See Sazonov to Vorontsov-Dashkov, 26 July/8 August 1915, document 457 in IBZI, v. 8:2, pp. 442–443 (and notes 1–2 on p. 443). See also Gehrke, *Persien in der deutschen Orientpolitik,* vol. 1, pp. 140–141.

39. Sazonov to Vorontsov-Dashkov, 3/16 September 1915, document 715; and also Sazonov aide-mémoire for Buchanan and Paléologue, 11 September 1915, document 688, both in IBZI, v. 8:2, pp. 638, 663.

40. For the September estimate of Russian forces at Kazvin, see the Memorandum of Yevreinov, the Russian Consulate Dragoman in Teheran, 27 August/9 September 1915, document 679 in IBZI, v. 8:2, p. 632. For estimates of the (official) Russian deployment numbers, see Strelianov, *Korpus Generala Baratova 1915–1918 gg.,* pp. 13, 22 (the first page gives a figure of 13,000 for the expeditionary force as of Nov.-Dec. 1915, the second as of April 1916—about 25,000). Allen and Muratoff, *Caucasian Battlefields,* pp. 321–324, gives a rough estimate of the initial deployment at around 14,000 including cavalry, along with the figures on troops already deployed on the Van front and in Urmia province (about 5,000 each). For a reckoning of Russian troop numbers by the main German guerrilla commander in Luristan (about 25,000), see Lührs, *Gegenspieler des Obersten Lawrence,* pp. 166, 191–192.

41. Strelianov, *Korpus Generala Baratova,* pp. 10–11.

42. Cited by Hopkirk, *On Secret Service East of Constantinople,* p. 175.

43. Strelianov, *Korpus Generala Baratova,* pp. 10–11. According to Strelianov's estimates

from Russian sources, before evacuating the city the Germans had 7,000 rifles, 30,000 bombs, "an unknown quantity of machine-guns," and about 2 million rounds in Teheran. From what I have seen in the German sources, these numbers sound suspiciously high. Still, it does seem plausible that the nervous young shah surrendered as much to Russian bluff as to a realistic assessment of the balance of forces arrayed against him. And of course, Baratov had more troops on the way, however small and unimposing the "advance guard" marching on Teheran actually was.

44. N. N. Baratov, "Extract from the Order to Russian Expeditionary Corps in Persia," 10 June 1918, in Hoover Institution Archives, Baratov collection, box 3; and Strelianov, *Korpus Generala Baratov,* pp. 13–20.

45. N. N. Baratov, "Bor'ba v' Persii vo vremeni revoliutsii v' Rossii," circa spring 1917, in the Baratov collection, Hoover Institution Archives, box 3.

46. Strelianov, *Korpus Generala Baratova.*

47. See especially, in this vein, Hopkirk, *On Secret Service East of Constantinople* (1994), which devotes several detailed chapters to Persian developments in the world war without once mentioning Baratov; and Antony Wynn's more recent *Persia in the Great Game* (2004), an entire *book* about Persia which devotes much of its second half to the intrigues of Sir Percy Sykes and his overrated South Persia Rifles, which likewise does not mention Baratov once. Wynn does treat Sykes's claim to have "won the war in Persia single-handed" with the skepticism it deserves—but he does not seem to realize that the Russians, under Baratov, wielded a force in the country ten times larger than the South Persia Rifles at the height of its negligible strength. There are few better examples of the western amnesia attending nearly everything Russia did in the First World War.

48. Strelianov, in *Korpus Generala Baratova,* includes some fairly imposing estimates of the Turco-Germano-Swedish-Persian forces opposing Baratov's expeditionary force in northern Persia—which he estimates (p. 17) at "25,000 in all." Curiously, this is the exact same number of *Russian troops* the German guerrilla commander Hans Lührs claims to have been arrayed against him in the theater. The difference between the two estimates is this: Lührs's guess was actually right on the money; Strelianov himself (p. 22) gives a figure of 566 Russian officers and 24,270 troops under Baratov as of 1 April 1916. By contrast, 25,000 is a wild exaggeration of the number of armed men the "Germans" were able to deploy against Baratov. The only significant armed force in Persia, the Swedish-officered Gendarmes, numbered at most 12,000; and of these very few ever engaged in combat against the Russians. Lührs himself helped command irregular bands in Luristan, but these never numbered more than a few thousand at a time. The Turks did deploy troops at times near the border towns of Hanekin and Kasri-Shirin, but again, never more than several thousand at most. For a discussion of the German "footprint" in wartime Persia, see McMeekin, *Berlin-Baghdad Express,* chapter 16.

49. Allen and Muratoff, *Caucasian Battlefields,* pp. 386–387.

50. Baratov, "Extract from the Order to Russian Expeditionary Corps in Persia," 10 June 1918, in Hoover Institution Archives, Baratov collection, box 3, pp. 4–6.

51. Strelianov, *Korpus Generala Baratova,* pp. 24 (for the Yudenich message to Baratov footnoted) and 41–46; and Baratov, "Extract from the Order to Russian Expeditionary Corps in Persia," 10 June 1918, in Hoover Institution Archives, Baratov collection, box 3, p. 10.

52. Erickson, *Ordered to Die,* pp. 120–137. On the Caucasian front generally, see also Reynolds, *Shattering Empires.*

53. This according to Baratov's own recollections, in his "Extract from the Order to Russian Expeditionary Corps in Persia," 10 June 1918, in Hoover Institution Archives, Baratov collection, box 3, pp. 11–12. On the British requests for Baratov's cooperation during the Mesopotamian offensive of winter 1917, see Allen and Muratoff, *Caucasian Battlefields,* pp. 443–444. As they remark sardonically, "General Maude judged the advance of his Russian allies as rather slow." Strelianov, in *Korpus Generala Baratova* (p. 60) claims that Russian action near Kermanshah had some diversionary impact on the Ottoman withdrawal from Baghdad, but he cites no evidence for this assertion.

54. See McMeekin, *Berlin-Baghdad Express,* chapters 16 and 18.

8. PARTITIONING THE OTTOMAN EMPIRE

1. Sazonov aide-mémoire, 29 February/13 March 1916, signed by Tsar Nicholas II, 1/14 March 1916, no. LXXVII in RAT, pp. 160–161.

2. The original Russian-language version of the Sazonov aide-mémoire is reproduced as no. XVI in RAT, pp. 118–119.

3. Paléologue to Delcassé, 10AM on 6 March 1915 (reporting on the previous day's conversation), original ms version reproduced in photocopied form, Hoover Institution Archives, Nicolas de Basily collection, box 9.

4. Citation in Fromkin, *Peace to End All Peace,* p. 138.

5. Paléologue aide-mémoire, 8 March 1915, no. XX in RAT, pp. 122–123.

6. Sazonov to Stavka, 22 February/7 March 1915; Paléologue aide-mémoire, 27 February/12 March 1915, and follow-up Sazonov aide-mémoire responding to Paléologue, 28 February/13 March 1915, all in AVPRI, fond 138, opis' 467, del' 477, list' 6, 7, 8.

7. Paléologue "verbal note" to Sazonov, 10 April 1915, no. XXXVII in RAT, p. 134.

8. To his considerable credit, David Fromkin, in *Peace to End All Peace,* calls it the "Sykes-Picot-Sazonov Agreement." And yet Fromkin, for all his appreciation of Russia's contributory role in the proceedings, uses no Russian sources, print or archival.

9. Erickson, *Ordered to Die,* p. 151.

10. Fromkin, *Peace to End All Peace,* pp. 189–199. For further details see also Hovannisian, "The Allies and Armenia, 1915–1918," pp. 159–160.

11. A thorough summary of inter-allied correspondence surrounding Djemal's (mythical) peace offer, in a file dated 29 and 30 December 1915, can be found in PRO, FO 371/2492; the basic gist is also reproduced (in French translation) in a French Foreign Ministry aide-mémoire dated 26 December 1915, in *Documents diplomatiques français,* Tome III (1915), no. 692, pp. 829–830 (see also the long explanatory footnote on pp. 849–850). Zavriev's original come-on was delivered to Sazonov via S. A. Poklevskii, the Russian minister in Bucharest, 28 November/11 December 1915, reproduced as no. L in RAT, pp. 141–142. For plausible (but ultimately unconvincing) popular renderings of the story which credits Djemal's "offer" as genuine, see Hopkirk, *On Secret Service East of Constantinople,* pp. 129–130; and Fromkin, *Peace to End All Peace,* pp. 214–215. Horst Linke, in *Zaristische Russland und der erste Weltkrieg,* treats the offers as genuine, as does Ronald Bobroff, although the latter does note that it was abnormally favorable to the Russians. Bobroff, *Roads to Glory,* p. 143.

12. Kress, *Mit den Türken zum Suezkanal,* p. 73. On the French connection to the Arab

conspiracy, see Djemal, *Memoirs of a Turkish Statesman,* p. 197; and on the business about Talaat, Djemal, and the British hostages, see U.S. Ambassador Morgenthau to the Secretary of State in Washington, 12 December 1914, in NA, M 353, roll 6; and McMeekin, *Berlin-Baghdad Express,* chapter 6.

13. Zavriev letter to the Russian Foreign Ministry, 7/20 March 1915, from Petrograd (Moika 30), in AVPRI, fond 151, opis' 482, del' 3480, list' 4 (back), 5.

14. A. A. Neratov to Izvolsky and Benckendorff, 4/17 April 1915, reproduced as no. XXXIX in RAT, p. 135.

15. Izvolsky to Sazonov, 1/14 June 1915, and Benckendorff to Sazonov, 2/15 June 1916, nos. XLIII and XLV in RAT, pp. 137–138.

16. Poklevskii to K. N. Gul'kevich, 12/25 December 1915, no. LIII in RAT, pp. 143–144. Only much later did Sazonov, after Buchanan and Paléologue asked for his source for the "Djemal" offer, name Zavriev as his supposed intermediary. See Paléologue to Briand, 31 December 1915, reproduced in *Documents diplomatiques français* Tome III (1915), in fn to no. 706, on p. 849.

17. See Fromkin, *Peace to End All Peace,* p. 189.

18. See Benckendorff to Sazonov, passing on Nicolson's objections to a Djemal deal, 10/23 January 1916, no. LXVII, in RAT, p. 151.

19. Briand to French Ambassadors in London, Rome, and Petrograd, 29 December 1915, no. 706 in DDF 1915, Tome III, p. 847–848, and fn. (pp. 848–849); and, for the French dismissal of the whole idea (but willingness to at least entertain the possibility of talking to Djemal), see Izvolsky to Sazonov, passing on Briand, 19 December 1914/1 January 1915, no. LXI in RAT, pp. 148–149.

20. "Foreign Ministry Diary entries" *(Dnevnik Ministerstva Inostrannyikh Del')* for 25 February/9 March 1916, in KA, v. 32 (part of Tome encompassing volumes 31–33, published 1928–1929), p. 19.

21. Diary entry for 26 February/10 March 1916, in ibid., pp. 20–21.

22. Buchanan aide-mémoire, reporting on Sir Mark Sykes's presentation of the modified map prepared according to Sazonov's instructions, 11 March 1916, no. LXXV in RAT, p. 157.

23. "Diary entry" for 27 February/11 March 1916, in KA, v. 32, p. 21.

24. See Sykes' clarification on the Armenian question to the original Sykes-Picot draft, submitted to Sazonov via Buchanan, 12 March 1916, no. LXXVI in RAT, pp. 158–159.

25. Buchanan aide-mémoire, 13 March 1916, no. LXXVIII in RAT, pp. 161–162. The remark about Wolf as "public enemy number one of Tsarist Russia" is usually attributed to Chimen Abramsky.

26. Sazonov aide-mémoire, 4/17 March 1916, no. LXXX in RAT, pp. 163–164.

27. "Diary entry" for 4/17 March 1916, second meeting (Sykes and Sazonov only), in KA, v. 32, p. 23.

28. Minutes of the 17/30 March 1916 meeting at the Foreign Ministry, reproduced in both KA, v. 32, pp. 26–27, and, in a slightly more detailed version, as no. XCVII in RAT, pp. 174–175; for the Sinop business see also Grigorevich explanatory memorandum, 20 March/2 April 1916, no. XCVIII in RAT, pp. 175–177 (the passages cited in the text on p. 177).

29. Minutes of the 17/30 March 1916 meeting at the Foreign Ministry, in RAT, p. 175.

30. Ibid.

31. Sazonov aide-mémoire drafted for Paléologue, 13/26 April 1916, no. CLLL in RAT, pp. 185–186.

32. Sazonov aide-mémoire, 29 February/13 March 1916, signed by Tsar Nicholas II, 1/14 March 1916, no. LXXVII in RAT, pp. 160–161.

33. See Paléologue to Briand, 1 April 1916 (4:30 pm), copy of ms original, in the Hoover Institution Archives, Nicholas de Basily collection, box 9.

34. Briand to Paléologue on the Polish question, 15 April 1916, and Paléologue reply to Briand, reporting on his conversations with Sazonov, 18 April 1916, both copies of ms originals, in the Hoover Institution Archives, Nicholas de Basily collection, box 9.

This time Sazonov's threat was less explicit—Witte himself had died on 13 March 1915, literally a week after serving Sazonov as a perfect foil to get his way over Constantinople and the Straits. Still, the French were no less worried a year later that Sazonov would be forced out of office by Stürmer, who not only had a Germanic name but was part of Witte's circle—as in fact transpired in July 1916, when Stürmer replaced Sazonov as foreign minister.

35. Paléologue "Note" to Sazonov, 26 April 1916, no. CIV in RAT, pp. 187–188; Cambon to Grey, 15 May 1916 (received 16 May), and Grey to Cambon, 16 May 1916, in Butler and Woodward, eds., *Documents on British Foreign Policy 1919–39*, 1st series, v. 4, pp. 244–247. On Sazonov's conditions attached to Russia's acceptance of France's existing railway concessions, see Smith, *Russian Struggle for Power 1914–1917*, pp. 378–379.

36. On all this, see Fromkin, *Peace to End All Peace*, pp. 190–191.

37. Izvolsky to Sazonov, 18 April/1 May 1916, no. CV in RAT, p. 188.

38. Hovannisian, "The Allies and Armenia, 1915–18," p. 163.

39. Pechkov report, 29 June 1916, forwarded from the field by Tiflis command to Sazonov, in AVPRI, fond 151, opis' 482, del' 3481, list' 33.

40. Hovannisian, "The Allies and Armenia, 1915–18," p. 163.

41. "Russia's Conquests in Armenia," in the *Manchester Guardian,* 18 September 1916, clipped in AVPRI, fond 151, opis' 482, del' 3481, list' 39.

42. Cited in Hovannisian, "The Allies and Armenia, 1915–18," p. 164.

43. Sazonov to Grand Duke Nicholas, 14/27 June 1916, no. CXL in RAT, pp. 207–209.

44. Grand Duke Nicholas to Sazonov from Tiflis, 3/16 July 1916, in AVPRI, fond 151, opis' 482, del' 3481, list' 15–16 (and backs). Emphasis added. Also reproduced as no. CXLIV in RAT, pp. 211–212. For the long quotation here I have largely followed the able translation of Richard Hovannisian, in "The Allies and Armenia, 1915–18," with slightly different emphases.

45. Sazonov letter to Grand Duke Nicholas, circa mid-October 1916, in AVPRI, fond 151, opis' 482, del' 3480, list' 26 (back).

46. And even, improbably, by an Ottoman corps comprising nearly seven whole army divisions, which had been transferred by Enver to the Galician front as a way of showing the Central powers that Turkey was fully their co-belligerent.

9 · 1917

1. Cited by Richard Stites in "Miliukov and the Russian Revolution," foreword to Miliukov, *The Russian Revolution,* p. xii.

2. "Prikaz' zaklyuchitel'nii voiskam' Otdelnago Kavkazkago Kavaleriiskago Korpusa . . .

Generala ot' Kavalerii Baratova," 10 June 1918, in the Hoover Institution Archives, Baratov collection, box 3, folder 3–5 ("Russian Expeditionary Force. Farewell to Troops"), p. 15.

3. The Russians' Lake Narotch offensive was a terrible failure and cost the army some 100,000 casualties. Terrible as these losses were, however, they did not compare to those at Verdun and the Somme. And in a way, Lake Narotch was salutary, in that it inspired Brusilov's reorganization of army doctrine and tactics, which would emerge with considerable success that summer. See Stone, *Eastern Front,* pp. 227–231.

4. See Komarnicki, *Rebirth of the Polish Republic,* p. 82 and *passim.*

5. Mankoff, "Russia and the Polish Question, 1907–1917," pp. 199–200.

6. Paléologue to Briand, 18 April 1916, Hoover Institution Archives, Nicholas de Basily collection, box 9.

7. This episode is brilliantly recounted in Smith, *Russian Struggle for Power, 1914–1917,* pp. 392–393, 400–404.

8. Mankoff, "Russia and the Polish Question, 1907–1917," p. 298.

9. On Stürmer's "loss of nerve," see Smith, *Russian Struggle for Power 1914–1917,* pp. 440–441. On the Miliukov speech and its political implications, see Pipes, *The Russian Revolution,* pp. 254–255. For a thorough debunking of Stürmer's supposed Germanophile sympathies—especially the idea that he was appointed in order to work out a separate peace with Germany—see Kulikov, *Biurokraticheskaia elita Rossiiskoi Imperii nakanune padeniya starogo poryadka (1914–1917),* p. 246 and *passim.*

10. Stone, *Eastern Front 1914–1917,* p. 282.

11. Pipes, *Russian Revolution,* pp. 257–258.

12. Paléologue to Briand, 31 October 1916, in the Bazili collection, Hoover Institution Archives, box 9.

13. Airapetov, "Sud'ba Bosforskoi ekspeditsii," pp. 241–243.

14. Ibid., pp. 243–245.

15. Erickson, *Ordered to Die,* pp. 165–166.

16. Baratov, "Extract from the Order to Russian Expeditionary Corps in Persia," p. 12; and "Prikaz' zaklyuchitel'nyi voiskam' Otdelnago Kavkazkago Kavaleriiskago Korpusa . . . Generala ot' Kavalerii Baratova," p. 15, both dated 10 June 1918, both in the Hoover Institution Archives, box 3, folder 3–5 ("Russian Expeditionary Force. Farewell to Troops").

17. Erickson, *Ordered to Die,* p. 166.

18. As noted in ibid., p. 160. See also Reynolds, "The Ottoman-Russian Struggle," pp. 250–251. A. O. Aratiunian, in *Kavkazskii front 1914–1917,* does devote a long chapter to 1917 (pp. 250–290), but it deals mostly with politics.

19. For the Alekseev proposal footnoted, see Kudashev to Sazonov, 5/18 February 1916, in KA, v. 28, p. 29 and *passim.*

20. Bazili to Pavel Nikolaevich Miliukov, "top secret," 23 March/ 6 April 1917, in AVPRI, fond 138, opis' 467, del' 493/515, list' 4–6 (and backs), and attached report by Captain A. D. Bubnov (same date), the latter (along with a copy of the former) available in the Nicolas de Basily collection, Hoover Institution Archives, box 11. For further details on the status of the *Goeben* and *Breslau,* and more on both Alekseev and Bubnov, especially, see Airapetov, "Sud'ba Bosforskoi ekspeditsii," pp. 236–245.

21. Bazili to N. N. Pokrovskii, from Stavka, 26 February/11 March 1917, in AVPRI, fond 138, opis' 467, del' 493/515, list' 1 (and back).

22. Bazili to Miliukov, 23 March/6 April 1917, in AVPRI, fond 138, opis' 467, del' 493/515, list' 4–6 (and backs).

23. Guchkov telegram to Stavka, 19 March/1 April 1917, in the Bazili collection, Hoover Institution Archives, box 11.

24. Alekseev to Sevastopol, 21 March/3 April 1917, in the Bazili collection, Hoover Institution Archives, box 11. On Denikin's involvement, see Denikin/Bazili report to Miliukov from Stavka, 8/21 April 1917, in AVPRI, fond 138, opis' 467, del' 493, list' 12–16.

25. On all this, and for the detail about Nicholas II addressing his abdication to Alekseev, see Pipes, *Russian Revolution,* pp. 316–317.

26. The tsar's abdication letter was addressed not to the Duma, or the provisional government, but to General Alekseev. Because Alekseev had read and approved Bazili's text before Nicholas II saw it, one might almost say that Alekseev wrote it to himself. See Bazili, *Diplomat of Imperial Russia 1903–1917,* chapter 5 ("The Abdication of Nicholas II"), pp. 121–125. Bazili also reproduces the original Russian-language draft.

27. Klembovskii to Black Sea fleet command, 20 March/2 April 1917, in the Bazili collection, Hoover Institution Archives, box 11. Klembovskii was later chosen by Kerensky to replace General Kornilov, following the notorious "Kornilov affair" of August 1917. He turned down the offer.

28. Pipes, *Russian Revolution,* p. 402.

29. On anti-German paranoia and "spy mania" in Petrograd, which seems to have first taken off in the wake of Russia's Great Retreat of 1915, see especially Fuller, *The Foe Within* (2006).

30. Cited in Pipes, *Russian Revolution,* p. 253.

31. Bazili to N. N. Pokrovskii, from Stavka, 26 February/11 March 1917, in AVPRI, fond 138, opis' 467, del' 493/515, list' 1 (back). For Sazonov to the service chiefs in November 1912, see chapter 1 above.

32. Cited by Richard Stites in "Miliukov and the Russian Revolution," foreword to Miliukov, *The Russian Revolution,* p. xii.

33. Baratov, "Bor'ba v' Persii vo vremeni Revoliutsii," in the Baratov collection, Hoover Institution Archives, box 3, pp. 2–3, 9; and Strelianov, *Korpus Generala Baratova,* pp. 81–83. Curiously, Strelianov does not mention the Kara-Tepe operation Baratov discusses (vaguely—without even mentioning specific dates) in his memoir account, but Strelianov does cite General Maude's requests for a diversionary strike on Mosul, passed on by Stavka—along with Baratov's refusal, on two occasions, to comply. It seems unlikely that the Kara-Tepe offensive amounted to much.

34. Baratov, "Bor'ba v' Persii vo vremeni Revoliutsii," in the Baratov collection, Hoover Institution Archives, box 3, pp. 2–3, 9; and, for the elegiac paeans to his Cossacks, Baratov collection, box 3, folder 3–5 ("Russian Expeditionary Force. Farewell to Troops"), p. 15.

35. Cited in Kazemzadeh, *Struggle for Transcaucasia,* p. 61.

36. Wildman, *The End of the Russian Imperial Army,* vol. 2, p. 141.

37. Airapetov, "Sud'ba Bosforskoi ekspeditsii," pp. 248–252.

38. Cited in Pipes, *Russian Revolution,* p. 413.

39. "Rukovodiashchiia ukazaniia General'-Komissaru oblastei Turtsii, zanyatyikh' po pravu voinyi," adjusted by the provisional government in light of the "peace without annexa-

tions" declaration by Ispolkom, dated 15/28 May 1917, in AVPRI, fond 151, opis' 482, del' 3481, list' 81–82.

40. Baratov, heartbroken by the October Revolution and fearful for his life after disobeying countless Bolshevik decrees in the months that followed it, took up a British offer of protection in June 1918, making his way to London by way of India. Lieutenant-General L. F. Bicherakhov, who commanded what was left of the expeditionary force in Persia after Baratov departed, was so bitterly anti-Bolshevik that he would later join Andrey Vlasov's notorious Russian Liberation Army which collaborated with the Nazis in the Second World War.

General Yudenich joined the Whites with relish after the Bolshevik seizure of power. He would later spearhead the White offensive from Estonia against Petrograd in fall 1919, famously repulsed by Trotsky's Reds near Tsarskoe Selo. Denikin and Kolchak would command, respectively, the Volunteer Army in south Russia, and the Siberian People's Army, in the Russian Civil War.

CONCLUSION

1. Sazonov to Tsar Nicholas II, 23 November/6 December 1913, in AVPRI, fond 138, opis' 467, del' 461, list' 27–28 (and backs).

2. PBM, box 1, chapter 7, pp. 9–10.

3. Sazonov, *Fateful Years,* pp. 204–205.

4. See McMeekin, *History's Greatest Heist.*

5. Ibid., esp. chapter 5. A number of the most important documents have been published in English, in Zeman et al., *Germany and the Revolution in Russia, 1915–1918.*

6. As in the studies by Strelianov, of *Korpus Generala Baratov,* and Airapetov, "Sud'ba Bosforskoi ekspeditsii," of Russian Straits policy.

7. Churchill, *World Crisis,* vol. 2, pp. 539–540.

8. In this light, see the collected works of E. H. Carr—as channeled, perhaps somewhat unfairly, in Norman Stone's notorious obituary for the same, in the *London Review of Books* 5 (1) (10 January 1983): 3–8.

9. For this sort of pseudo-Marxist reasoning, see Geyer, *Russian Imperialism.*

10. Fromkin, *Europe's Last Summer,* p. 305.

11. And as Stalin nearly did in 1946–47, when his demands for privileged Russian access to the Straits, and the Turkish provinces of Ardahan and Batum, helped push Turkey into the western alliance. In yet another nod to the unshakeable hold of traditional Russian foreign policy prerogatives, Stalin also, famously, refused to withdraw Soviet troops from "Persian Azerbaijan." Truman in 1946–47, unlike Asquith and Grey in 1914–15, refused to indulge Russian pretensions in Turkey and Persia, which refusal may accurately be said to have inaugurated the Cold War.

12. Friedman, *Germany, Turkey, and Zionism,* pp. 253 and 239, n. 33.

13. Ferguson, *Pity of War* (1997); Charmley, *Splendid Isolation?* (1999).

Bibliography

ARCHIVES AND PRINCIPAL COLLECTIONS

Arkhiv Vneshnei Politiki Rossiiskoi Imperii (AVPRI). Moscow, Russia.
Fond 135. Osobyi politicheskii otdel. Miscellaneous.
Fond 138, opis' 467. Sekretnyi arkhiv ministra.
    Del' 461/480. Correspondence with the Black Sea fleet, pertaining to amphibious operations against Constantinople. February 1912 to December 1913.
    Del' 462/481. "Zhurnal osobogo soveshchaniya 8 February 1914. Turetskii flot." And correspondence relating to plans for amphibious operations against Constantinople, 8/21 February 1914–13/26 June 1914.
    Del' 467/486. Correspondence on the Straits and Gallipoli, 13/26 February to 4 September 1915.
    Del' 472/492. More correspondence on the Straits and Gallipoli, 10/23 February to 12/25 August 1915.
    Del' 476/496. Correspondence with Paris and London on Constantinople and the Straits.
    Del' 493/515. Bazili. Dokladnyie zapiski.
Fond 151, opis' 482. Politicheskii arkhiv.
    Del' 3505. "Vozstanie armyan' v Vane, vyizvannyim turetskimi zhestokami." 1915.
    Del' 3480–3481. "Armyane. Budushchee ustroistvo Armyanii." 1915–.
    Del' 4068. "Politicheskie i vnutrenyie polozhenie Turtsii do razryiva. Peregovoryi s Turtsiei."
    Del' 4073. "Polozhenie vnutri Turtsii vo vremya voinyi s neyu." 1914–1917.
    Del' 4113. "Turtsiya." 1914–1916.
    Del' 4116. "Russko-turetskie voennyie deistvie." 1914.
Fond 172, opis' 514/2. Posol'stvo v Vene.
    Del' 633. "Turtsiya. Armeniya." 1913–1914.
    Del' 636. "Sekretnyie telegrammyi." 1914.
    Del' 636a. "Posol'stvo v Saraevo." 1914–1916.
Fond 180. Posol'stvo v Konstantinopole.
    Del' 3573. General correspondence for 1912–1914.

Fond 187, opis' 524. Posol'stvo v Parizhe.
  Del' 3135. "Guerre I. Action diplomatique. Origines de la guerre. Correspondence
    guerrière. Italie. Roumanie." 1914.
  Del' 3176. "Varia (1908–1914)."
Fond 149, Opis' 502b. Turetskii stol. Opis' 502b. Miscellaneous.

Askeri Tarih ve Stratejik Etüt Başkanlığı Arşivi (ATASE). Ankara, Turkey.
BDH (First World War Collection).

Başbakanlık Osmanlı Arşivleri (BOA). Istanbul, Turkey.
Hariciye Nezareti Hukuk Kismi (HR-H). Sublime Porte Correspondence.
  Box 329. "Almanya. Muhtelif Yazişmalar." 1914–1918.
  Box 425. "Fransa. Muhtelif Yazişmalar." March–October 1914.
  Box 579. "Rusya. Muhtelif Yazişmalar." 13 April 1912–28 October 1914.
Dahiliye Nezareti. Şifre Kalemi (DH-ŞFR). Ottoman government telegrams.
  Boxes 47–48. Wartime communiqués. 1914–1916.

Deutsches Bundesarchiv Berlin (DBB), Lichterfelde, Berlin, Germany.
R 901. Auswärtiges Amt.

Gosudarstvennyi Arkhiv Rossiiskoi Federatsii (GARF). Moscow, Russia.
Fond 529, opis' 1. "Byuro zaveduyushchego zagranichnoi agenturoi departmenta politsii
v Konstantinopole." (Okhrana files). 1911–1914.

Haus-, Hof- und Staatsarchiv (HHSA), Vienna, Austria.
Politisches Archiv I. Liasse Krieg (früh. Interna IXXX). 1 Teil.
  Kartons 810–812. Correspondence related to the Sarajevo incident and the July
    crisis. June–July 1914.
Politisches Archiv III. Preußen.
  Karton 171. Berichte, Weisungen, Varia 1914. Berichte 1915.
Politisches Archiv X. Russland.
  Karton 133. Berichte 1908 IX–XII. Weisungen, Varia 1908–1909.
  Karton 134. Berichte 1909 I–IX.
  Karton 138. Berichte, Weisungen, Varia 1912.
  Karton 139. Berichte, Weisungen, Varia 1913.
  Karton 149. Russland Liasse VIIIb, IX, X.

Kriegsarchiv Wien (KW). Vienna, Austria.
Generalstab. Militärattachees Konstantinopel.
Evidenzbüro. Türkei.
  Karton 3502. 1914. Telegramme, Berichte v. Jänner-August
  Karton 3506. 1914. Resumes d. Vertraulichen Nachrichten-Italien, Russland, Balkan.

National Archives of the United Kingdom (PRO). Kew Gardens, London, UK.
FO 371. Foreign Office Correspondence.
  Boxes 2093–96. Russia correspondence, 1914.
  Boxes 2135–41. Turkey Files, 1914 (up to Turkey's entry into war).
  Boxes 2445–50. Russia (War) correspondence, 1914–

Box 2481. Turkey (War) correspondence, 1914–

Boxes 2147, 2482–2492, 2769–2772, 2781, 3046–3060, 3391–3399. Turkey (War) Files, 1914–1918.

FO 438

Boxes 5–8. Further Correspondence Relating to the War. 1915.

WO 33

Box 712. "Report on Certain Aspects of the Military Situation in Russia. During February–March 1915."

Box 714. European War. Secret Telegrams, Series B (1914–15).

Box 731. War Office Correspondence, esp. 1914–1918.

Politisches Archiv des Auswärtigen Amtes (PAAA), Berlin, Germany.

Akten betreffend: Allgemeine Angelegenheiten Oesterreich. (secr).

R 8545–8552. Secret corr. with Austria. 1 January 1913–February 1920.

Acten betreffend. Allg. Angelegenheiten Russlands. (Russland 61.)

R 10066–74. 1 January 1908–31 March 1917.

Acten betreffend. Allg. Angelegenheiten Russlands. Russland 61 secr.

R 10136–38. 1 January 1888–January 1920.

Akten betreffend: Eisenbahnen in Rußland.

R 11010–11. 1 July 1908–31 December 1914.

Akten betreffend: Die Jüden in Russland.

R 10503–4. 1 January 1912–August 1919.

Akten betreffend den Krieg 1914 (allgemeine).

R 19865–74. 28 June 1914–31 July 1914.

Akten betreffend: das Verhältnis Rußlands zu Oesterreich.

R 10894–98. 1 April 1904–January 1920.

Geheime Acten betreffend: die russische Presse.

R 10544. 1 October 1909–February 1920.

Innere Zustände Polen.

R 10834. 1 July 1914–31 December 1914.

Krieg 1914. Unternehmungen und Aufwiegelungen gegen unserer Feinde.

R 20942. ("Durch die Juden").

R 29050. (Ukraine).

R 20974. (Polen).

R 21008–21025. (Kaukasus).

R 21028–21062. (Afghanistan und Persien).

Das Verhaeltnis der Tuerkei zu Deutschland. (Tuerkei 152).

R 13742–13760. 1898–1918.

Quai d'Orsay Archives (QO), Paris, France.

Correspondence politique et commerciale dite "nouvelle série," 1896–1918.

Allemagne.

Files 51–52. Dossier General. 1913–1914.

File 62. Politique étrangère. Relations avec la Russie. 1905–1914.

Autriche-Hongrie.

Files 29–30. 29 October 1908–1914.

Files 31–33. Conflit austro-serbe (correspondence relating to the Sarajevo incident and the July crisis).

Guerre 1914–1918. Russie.

File 1. Dossier General. I. 28 Juillet 1914–31 Decembre 1915.

Russie.

File 4. Politique Intérieure. Dossier général. 1906–1914.

Files 8–11. Politique Intérieure. Pologne. 1896–1914.

Files 32–42. Politique Etrangère. Alliance franco-russe. 1896–1918.

File 50. Politique Etrangère. Relations avec Angleterre 1906–1914.

Rossiiskii Gosudarstvennyi Voenno-Istoricheskii Arkhiv (RGVIA). Moscow, Russia.

Fond 428. Opis' 1. Avstro-vengriya.

Del' 162. Svedeniya o sostoyanii, chislennosti i dislokatsii avstro-vengerskoi armii. 9 November 1909–20 February 1914.

Del' 187. Spiski sluzhashchikh' v politicheskikh i politseiskikh uchrezhdeniyakh Galitsii. 1 January 1914.

Del' 188. Materialyi gazetyi "Nemetsko-vengerskaya korrespondentsiya" o vnutrennem polozhenii v Vengrii, o sobyityakh v Konstantinopole, i polozhenii v Serbii i Bolgarii. 14 March 1913–20 February 1914.

Del' 190. Spisok na poluchenie dovol'stviya voenno-sluzhashchikh 18-go pekhotnogo polka avstro-vengerskoi armii. July 1914.

Fond 432. Opis' 1. Germaniya.

Del' 607. Mobilizatsionnaya instruktsiya dlya Vestgotskogo polka polkovoi ekspeditsii germanskoi armii. 1912.

Del' 608. Materialyi o meropriyatiyakh 6 germanskogo korpusa po okhrane granits na 1913 i mobilizatsionnyi god. 9 January 1913.

Fond 165. Opis' 1. Kuropatkin.

Del' 1394. Perepiska 30 June 1908–24 February 1921.

Del' 5255. Dnevniki Kuropatkina A. K. za 1906–1915 gg.

Del' 5256. Dnevniki Kuropatkina A. K. za 1915–1917 gg.

Fond 450. Opis' 1. Turtsiia.

Del' 118–131. Correspondence with "voennyi agent" in Constantinople, 1897–1906.

Fond 2000. Opis' 1. Glavnoe upravlenie General'nago Shtaba. (Stavka).

Del' 2219. Materialyi o podgotovke i provedenii desantnyikh operatsii na Chernom more v sluchae voinyi s Turtsiei. 6 July 1909–12 November 1911.

Del' 2220. Desantnaya Ekspeditsia. 18 April 1912–15 November 1912.

Del' 2221. To zhe. Dessantnaya ekspedits. Podgotovka ekspeditsii snabzheniya i drug. 25 September 1912–15 September 1913.

Del' 2222. To zhe. Dessantnaya ekspeditsiya. O dessantnyikh operatsiyakh v Chernom more na 1914 g. 31 January 1914–31 May 1914.

Del' 2247. Zapiska N. A. Bazili: 'O tselyakh Rossii na prolivakh.'

Del' 3796. Dokladyi po GUGSh, perepiska so shtabom Kavkazskogo voennago okruga i spravochnyie materialyi o voennyikh' prigotovleniyakh i sostave voiskovyikh chastei okruga; mobilizatsii turetskoi armii, ee sostave, sosredotochenii i boevyikh deistviyakh' na Kavkazskom fronte; opisanie ukreplenii Bosfora i Dardanell.

Del' 3810. Otcheta i zaklyucheniya o polevoi ofitzerov gen. Schtaba Kavkazskago okruga. Spisok. Turtsii i Persii. 22 May 1909–16 August 1914.

Del' 3844. Doklad po GUGSH, doneseniya nachal'nika Konsul'skogo konvoya v Azerbaidzhane, perepiska s Ministerstvom inostrannyikh del. i shtabom Kavkazskago voennogo okruga o turetsko-persidskom pogranichnom konflikte i rabote Razgranichitel'noi Komissii po provedeniyu turetsko-persidskoi granitse. 25 July 1912–29 November 1914.

Del' 3845. Doklad I soobrazheniya GUGSh I Ministerstva inostrannyikh del' ob osnovnyikh usloviyakh mira mezhdu Turtsiei i Balkanskimi gosudarstvami s tochki zreniya voennyikh interesov Rossii. 22 November 1912–15 March 1914.

Del' 3846. Svodki svedenii shtaba Kavkazskogo voennogo okruga a vnutripoliticheskom polozhenii Turtsii; kompletovanii i boevoi gotovnosti ee armii i stroitel'stve Bagdadskoi xh.d. 23 September 1913–21 September 1914.

Del' 3848. Perepiska so shtabom Kavkazskom voennogo okruga i russkim voennyim agentom v Turtsii o planakh razpolozheniya turetskoi armii v 1914 g., izdanii i rassyilke voenno-statisticheskikh materialov o Turtsii. . . . Vooruzhennyiya silyi Turtsii. 1 November 1913–8 September 1914.

Del' 3851. Perepiska s Mob. Otdelom, shtabom Kavkazskogo voennogo okruga i russkim diplomaticheskimi predstavitelyami v Turtsii i Persii o podgotovke k vooruzhennomu vosstaniyu turetskikh armyan, aiserov i kurdov protiv turok. 31 July 1914–9 April 1915.

Del' 3852. Doneseniya shtabov Verkhovnogo glavnokomanduyushchego, 7 i Kavkazskoi armii, russkikh diplomaticheskikh predstavitelei v Egipte i Frantsii i voennyikh agentov v Bolgarii, Gretsii, Rumyinii, o vnutripolitcheskom polozhenii Turtsii, Gretsii i Egipta i dislokatsii turetskoi armii. 6 February–25 April, 1915.

Del' 3860. Doneseniya shtaba Kavkazskoi armii, russkikh diplomaticheskikh predstavitelei i voennyikh agentov v Turtsii, Persii, Balkanskikh gosudarstvakh i Frantsii o vnutripoliticheskom polozhenii v Turtsii i Persii, vstuplenii Turtsii v mirovuyu voinu, mobilizatsii armii i khode boevyikh deistvii. 15 October 1914–17 January 1915.

Del' 3861. Svodki svedenii shtabov Kavkazskoi I 7 armii o sostave i gruppirovke turetskoi armii. 5 November 1914–8 June 1915.

Del' 3888. Razvedyivatel'nyie materialyi o sostoyanii turetskoi armii, voennom politicheskom i ekonomicheskom polozhenii Turtsii, Germanii, Bolgarii i Palestinyi. 1915–1916.

Del' 3890. Perepiska so shtabom Kavkazskoi armii i doneseniya shtaba Turkestanskogo voennogo okruga i russkogo voennogo agenta v Gretsii o formirovanii i dislokatsii turetskoi armii, voennom polozhenii na persidskom fronte i deistviyakh germanskikh otryadov v Afganistane. 9 January 1916–9 July 1917.

Vincennes. Service Historique de la Défense (VSHD). Vincennes, Paris, France.
7 N 1478. Attachés militaires. Russie. 1910–1914.
7 N 1487. Attachés militaires. Russie. 1912–1914.
7 N 1538. Attachés militaires. Russie. 1902–1914.
7 N 1559. Attachés militaires. Russie 1917–1919. Mission au Caucase. Corr. Arménie.

7 N 1649. Attaché militaires. Turquie. 1917–1919. Caucase et Arménie.

7 N 2150. Section d'Afrique. 1915–1918. Subventions aux corps de partisans d'Orient . . . Irréguliers, Arméniens, etc.

PRINTED AND ONLINE WORKS, INCLUDING MEMOIRS

Adamov, E. A., ed. *Konstantinopol' i prolivyi.* 2 vols. Moscow: Izdanie Litizdata NKID, 1925–1926.

———. *Razdel aziatskoi Turtsii. Po sekretnyim dokumentam b. Ministerstva inostrannyikh del.* Moscow: Izdanie Litizdata NKID, 1924.

Airapetov, O. R., ed. "Na Vostochnom napravlenii. Sud'ba Bosforskoi ekspeditsii v pravlenie imperatora Nikolaia II." In *Poslednaia voina imperatorskoi Rossii: sbornik statei,* ed. Airapetov, 158–252. Moscow: Tri kvadrata, 2002.

———. *Vneshnaia politik Rossisskoi imperii, 1801–1914.* Moscow: Iz-vdo "Europa," 2006.

Akopian, S. M. *Zapadnaia Armeniia v planakh imperialisticheskikh derzhav v period pervoi mirovoi voinyi.* Yerevan: Izdatel'stvo akademii nauk armyanskoi SSR, 1967.

Aksakal, Mustafa. *The Ottoman Road to War in 1914: The Ottoman Empire and the First World War.* Cambridge: Cambridge University Press, 2008.

Akçam, Taner. *A Shameful Act: The Armenian Genocide and the Question of Turkish Responsibility,* trans. Paul Bessemer. New York: Metropolitan Books, 2006.

Albertini, Luigi. *The Origins of the War of 1914.* 3 vols. New York: Oxford University Press, 1952–1957.

Allen, W. E. D., and Paul Muratoff. *Caucasian Battlefields: A History of the Wars on the Turco-Caucasian Border, 1828–1921.* Cambridge: Cambridge University Press, 1953.

Anderson, Margaret Lavinia. "'Down in Turkey, Far Away': Human Rights, the Armenian Massacres, and Orientalism in Wilhelmine Germany." *Journal of Modern History* 79 (March 2007): 80–111.

Aratiunian, A. O. *Kavkazskii front 1914–1917.* Yerevan: Izdatelstvo "Aiastan," 1971.

Bachmann, Klaus. *Ein Herd der Feindschaft gegen Rußland. Galizien als Krisenherd in Den Beziehungen der Donaumonarchie mit Rußland (1907–1914).* Vienna: Verlag für Geschichte und Politik Wien, 2001.

Bakhturina, A. Iu. *Okrainyi rossiiskoi imperii: gosudarstvennoe upravlenie i natsional'naia politika v godyi pervoi mirovoi voinyi (1914–1917 gg).* Moscow: Rosspen, 2004.

———. *Politika Rossiiskoi Imperii v vostochnoi Galitsii v godyi pervoi mirovoi voiny.* Moscow: Airo-XX, 2000.

Basily, Nicolas de (N. A. Bazili). *Nicolas de Basily, Diplomat of Imperial Russia.* Stanford, California: Hoover Institution Press, 1973.

Bayur, Yusuf Hikmet. *Türk İnkılabı Tarihi.* 3 vols. Ankara: Türk Tarih Kurumu Basimevi, 1940–1967.

Berghahn, V. R., ed. *Germany and the Approach of War in 1914.* London: Macmillan, 1973.

Bitter, Ludwig, et al., eds. *Österreich-Ungarns Aussenpolitik von der bosnischen Krise 1908 bis zum Kriegsausbruch 1914.* 9 vols. Vienna: Österreichischer Bundesverlag für Unterricht, Wissenschaft und Kunst, 1930.

Bloxham, Donald. *The Great Game of Genocide: Imperialism, Nationalism, and the Destruction of the Ottoman Armenians.* Oxford: Oxford University Press, 2005.

Bobroff, Ronald Park. *Roads to Glory: Late Imperial Russia and the Turkish Straits.* London: I. B. Tauris, 2006.

Bodger, Alan. "Russia and the End of the Ottoman Empire." In *The Great Powers and the End of the Ottoman Empire,* ed. Marian Kent. London: Frank Cass, 1984.

Buchan, John. *Greenmantle.* London: Penguin, 2001.

Buchanan, Sir George. *My Mission to Russia, and Other Diplomatic Memories.* London: Cassell, 1923.

Butler, Rohan, and E. L. Woodward, eds. *Documents on British Foreign Policy 1919–1939.* 65 vols. London: H. M. S. O., 1946–1989.

Cecil, Lady Gwendolen. *Life of Robert Marquis of Salisbury.* 4 vols. London: Hodder and Stoughton, 1921–.

Chalabian, Antranig. *General Andranik and the Armenian Revolutionary Movement.* Southfield, Mich.: Antranig Chalabian, 1988.

Charmley, John. *Splendid Isolation? Britain, the Balance of Power and the Origins of the First World War.* London: Hodder and Stoughton, 1999.

Churchill, Winston. *The World Crisis.* 4 vols. New York: Scribner, 1923–1929.

———. *The Unknown War: The Eastern Front.* New York: C. Scribner's Sons, 1931.

Dadrian, Vahakn N. *The History of the Armenian Genocide: Ethnic Conflict from the Balkans to Anatolia to the Caucasus.* New York: Berghahn Books, 1995.

Danilov, I. N. (Jurij Daniloff). *Russland im Weltkriege,* trans. Rudolf Freiherrn von Campenhausen. Jena: Frommannsche Buchhandlung (Walter Biedermann), 1925.

"Démembrement de l'Autriche." In *Kurjer Warszawski,* 17 April 1914.

Demirel, Muammer. *Birinci dünya harbinde Erzurum ve çevresinde Ermeni hareketleri (1914–1918).* Ankara: 1996.

Djemal, Ahmad, Pasha. *Memoirs of a Turkish Statesman, 1913–1919.* New York: George H. Doran, 1922.

Dobrorolski, Sergei. *Die Mobilmachung der russischen Armee 1914.* Berlin: Deutsche Verlagsgesellschaft für Politik und Geschichte, 1922.

Documents diplomatiques français (1871–1914). 41 vols. Paris: Imprimerie Nationale, 1929–1959.

Documents diplomatiques français. 1915. 3 vols. Brussels: Peter Lang, 2004.

Documents on Ottoman Armenians. 2 vols. Ankara: Turkish Directorate General of Press and Information, 1982–1983.

Dündar, Fuat. *Crime by Numbers: The Role of Statistics in the Armenian Question (1878–1918).* New Brunswick, N.J.: Transaction, 2010.

Erdmann, Karl Dietrich, ed. *Kurt Riezler: Tagebücher, Aufsätze, Dokumente.* Göttingen: Vandenhoeck und Ruprecht, 1972.

Erickson, Edward. "The Armenians and Ottoman Military Policy, 1915." *War in History* 15, no. 2 (2008): 141–167.

———. "Armenian Massacres: New Records Undercut Old Blame." *Middle East Quarterly* 11, no. 3 (Summer 2006): 67–75.

———. *Ordered to Die: A History of the Ottoman Army in the First World War.* Westport, Connecticut: Greenwood Press, 2001.

Fay, Sidney. *The Origins of the First World War.* 2 vols., 2nd edition. New York: Macmillan, 1935.

Ferguson, Niall. *The Pity of War.* New York: Basic Books, 1999.

Fischer, Fritz. *Germany's Aims in the First World War.* New York: Norton, 1967.

——. *Griff nach der Weltmacht. Die Kriegszielpolitik des Kaiserlichen Deutschland, 1914–1918.* Düsseldorf: Droste Verlag, 1961.

——. *Krieg der Illusionen. Die deutsche Politik von 1911 bis 1914.* Düsseldorf: Droste Verlag, 1969.

——. "Twenty-Five Years Later: Looking Back at the 'Fischer Controversy' and Its Consequences." *Central European History* 21, no. 3 (September 1988): 207–223.

——. *World Power or Decline: The Controversy over Germany's Aims in the First World War.* New York: Norton, 1974.

Friedman, Isaiah. *Germany, Turkey, and Zionism, 1897–1918.* New Brunswick, N.J.: Transaction, 1998.

Fromkin, David. *A Peace to End All Peace: Creating the Modern Middle East, 1914–1922.* New York: H. Holt, 1989.

——. *Europe's Last Summer: Who Started the Great War in 1914?* New York: Alfred A. Knopf, 2004.

Fuller, William C., Jr. *Civil-Military Conflict in Imperial Russia 1880–1914.* Princeton: Princeton University Press, 1985.

——. *The Foe Within: Fantasies of Treason and the End of Imperial Russia.* Cornell: Cornell University Press, 2006.

——. *Strategy and Power in Russia, 1600–1914.* New York: Free Press, 1992.

Gatrell, Peter. *Government, Industry, and Rearmament in Russia, 1900–1914: The Last Argument of Tsarism.* Cambridge: Cambridge University Press, 1994.

Gehrke, Ulrich. *Persien in der Deutschen Orientpolitik während des ersten Weltkrieges.* 2 vols. Stuttgart: W. Kohlhammer, 1960.

Geiss, Imanuel. *Der lange Weg in die Katastrophe: die Vorgeschichte des Ersten Weltkrieges, 1815–1914.* Munich: Piper, 1990.

——. *July 1914: The Outbreak of the First World War: Selected Documents.* New York: Scribner, 1967.

Geyer, Dietrich. *Russian Imperialism: The Interaction of Domestic and Foreign Policy 1860–1914.* New Haven: Yale University Press, 1987.

Gooch, G. P., and Harold Temperley, eds. *British Documents on the Origins of the War of 1914.* 13 vols. London: H. M. S. O., 1926–1938.

Die Grosse Politik der Europäischen Kabinette 1871–1914. Sammlung der Diplomatischen Akten des Auswärtigen Amtes. Berlin: Deutsche Verlagsgesellschaft für Politik und Geschichte, 1927.

Hamilton, Richard, and Holger Herwig, eds. *Decisions for War, 1914–1917.* New York: Cambridge University Press, 2004.

——. *The Origins of World War I.* New York: Cambridge University Press, 2003.

Hoeniger, Robert. *Russlands Vorbereitung zum Weltkrieg auf Grund unveröffentlicher Russischer Urkunden.* Berlin: E. S. Mittler, 1919.

Holquist, Peter. *Making War, Forging Revolution: Russia's Continuum of Crisis, 1914–1921.* Cambridge, Mass.: Harvard University Press, 2002.

Hopkirk, Peter. *The Great Game: On Secret Service in High Asia.* London: Murray, 1990.

——. *On Secret Service East of Constantinople: The Plot to Bring Down the British Empire.* London: John Murray, 1994.

Hovannisian, Richard. "The Allies and Armenia, 1915–18." *Journal of Contemporary History* 3, no. 1 (January 1968): 145–168.

———, ed. *The Armenian Genocide: History, Politics, Ethics*. New York: Macmillan, 1992.

———, ed. *The Armenian Genocide in Perspective*. New Brunswick, N.J.: Transaction, 1986.

———. "The Armenian Question in the Ottoman Empire." In *The Armenian People from Ancient to Modern Times,* ed. Hovannisian. 2 vols. New York: MacMillan, 1997–.

Jarausch, Konrad. "The Illusion of Limited War: Chancellor Bethmann Hollweg's Calculated Risk, July 1914." *Central European History* 2, no. 1 (March 1969): 48–76.

Karpat, Kemal. *Ottoman Population 1830–1914: Demographic and Social Characteristics.* Madison: University of Wisconsin Press, 1985.

Karsh, Efraim, and Inari Karsh. *Empires of the Sand: The Struggle for Mastery in the Middle East, 1789–1923.* Cambridge, Mass.: Harvard University Press, 1999.

Kazemzadeh, Firuz. *The Struggle for Transcaucasia, 1917–1921.* New York: Philosophical Library, 1951.

Keiger, John F. V. *France and the Origins of the First World War.* New York: St. Martin's Press, 1983.

———. "France." In *Decisions for War, 1914,* ed. Keith Wilson, 121–150. New York: St. Martin's Press, 1995.

———. *Raymond Poincaré.* Cambridge: Cambridge University Press, 1997.

Kennan, George. *Fateful Alliance: France, Russia, and the Coming of the First World War.* New York: Pantheon Books, 1984.

Kennedy, Paul. *The Rise and Fall of the Great Powers: Economic Change and Military Conflict from 1500 to 2000.* New York: Vintage, 1987.

Khalidi, Rashid. *Resurrecting Empire: Western Footprints and America's Perilous Path in the Middle East.* Boston: Beacon Press, 2004.

Kissinger, Henry. *Diplomacy.* New York: Simon and Schuster, 1994.

Kokovtsev, V. N. *Out of My Past: The Memoirs of Count Kokovtsov, Russian Minister of Finance, 1904–1914. Chairman of the Council of Ministers, 1911–1914.* Ed. H. H. Fisher. Trans. Laura Matveev. Stanford: Stanford University Press, 1935.

Komarnicki, Titus. *Rebirth of the Polish Republic: A Study in the Diplomatic History of Europe, 1914–1920.* London: W. Heinemann, 1957.

Korsun, N. G. *Alashkertskaia i Khamadanskaia operatsii na Kavkazskom fronte mirovoi voiny v 1915 godu.* Moscow: Gos. voen. izd-vo Narkomata oborony Soiuza SSR, 1940.

Krasnyi Arkhiv. Istoricheskii zhurnal. 106 vols. Moscow: Gospolitizdat, 1922–1941.

Kress von Kressenstein, Friedrich. *Mit den Türken zum Suezkanal.* Berlin: Vorhut-Verlag, 1938.

Krivoshein, K. A. *A. V. Krivoshein (1857–1921 g.) Ego znachenie v istorii Rossii nachala XX veka.* Paris: s.n., 1973.

Kulikov, S. V. *Biurokraticheskaia elita Rossiiskoi Imperii nakanune padeniya starogo poryadka (1914–1917).* Ryazan: 2004.

Kurat, Akdes Nimet. *Türkiye ve Rusya.* Ankara: Kültür Bakanlığı, 1990.

Laqueur, Walter. *A History of Zionism.* New York: Schocken Books, 1972.

Larcher, Maurice. *La Guerre turque dans la guerre mondiale.* Paris: E. Chiron, 1926.

Lazarev, M. S. *Kurdskii vopros (1891–1917).* Moscow: Izdatel'stvo "Nauka," 1972.

Lewy, Guenter. *The Armenian Massacres in Ottoman Turkey: A Disputed Genocide.* Salt Lake City: University of Utah Press, 2005.

Lieven, D. C. B. *Empire: The Russian Empire and Its Rivals.* New Haven: Yale University Press, 2002.

———. *Nicholas II: Emperor of All the Russias.* London: J. Murray, 1993.

———. *Russia and the Origins of the First World War.* New York: St. Martin's Press, 1983.

Linke, Horst Günther. *Das Zaristische Russland und der erste Weltkrieg. Diplomatie und Kriegsziele 1914–1917.* Munich: Wilhelm Fink Verlag, 1982.

Lohr, Eric. *Nationalizing the Russian Empire: The Campaign against Enemy Aliens during World War I.* Cambridge, Mass.: Harvard University Press, 2003.

———. "The Russian Army and the Jews: Mass Deportation, Hostages, and Violence during World War I." *Russian Review* 60 (July 2001): 404–419.

Lührs, Hans. *Gegenspieler des Obersten Lawrence.* Berlin: Otto Schlegel, 1936.

Mango, Andrew. *Atatürk.* London: John Murray, 1999.

Mankoff, Jeffrey. "Russia and the Polish Question, 1907–1917: Nationality and Diplomacy." Ph.D. diss., Yale University, 2006.

Massie, Robert K. *Nicholas and Alexandra.* New York: Atheneum, 1967.

Matthew, H. C. G. *Gladstone: 1809–1898.* 2 vols. Oxford: Clarendon Press, 1986.

McCarthy, Justin, et al. *The Armenian Rebellion at Van.* Salt Lake City: University of Utah Press, 2006.

McDonald, David MacLaren. *United Government and Foreign Policy in Russia 1900–1914.* Cambridge, Mass.: Harvard University Press, 1992.

McMeekin, Sean. *The Berlin-Baghdad Express: The Ottoman Empire and Germany's Bid for World Power, 1898–1918.* London: Penguin/Allen Lane, 2010.

———. *History's Greatest Heist: The Bolshevik Looting of Russia.* New Haven: Yale University Press, 2008.

Menning, Bruce. *Bayonets before Bullets: The Imperial Russian Army, 1861–1914.* Bloomington: Indiana University Press, 1992.

———. "The Offensive Revisited: Russian Preparation for Future War, 1906–1914." In *Reforming the Tsar's Army: Military Innovation in Imperial Russia from Peter the Great to the Revolution,* ed. Menning and David Schimmelpeninck van der Oye. New York: Cambridge University Press, 2004.

Miliukov, Paul N. *The Russian Revolution.* 3 vols. Gulf Breeze, Fl.: Academic International Press, 1978–.

Miller, Geoffrey. *Straits: British Policy towards the Ottoman Empire and the Origins of the Dardanelles Campaign.* Hull: University of Hull Press, 1997.

Miller, Margaret. *The Economic Development of Russia 1905–1914, with Special Reference to Trade, Industry, and Finance.* New York: A. M. Kelly, 1967.

Moltke, Helmuth Johann Ludwig von. *Erinnerungen, Briefe, Dokumente 1877–1916. Ein Bild vom Kriegsausbruch, erster Kriegsführung und Persönlichkeit des ersten militärischen Führern des Krieges.* Stuttgart: Der kommende Tag, 1922.

Mombauer, Annika. *The Origins of the First World War: Controversies and Consensus.* New York: Longman, 2002.

Moorehead, Alan. *Gallipoli.* London: H. Hamilton, 1956.

Moranian, Suzanne Elizabeth. "Bearing Witness: The Missionary Archives as Evidence of the Armenian Genocide." In *The Armenian Genocide,* ed. Richard Hovannisian, 103–128.

Morgenthau, Henry. *Ambassador Morgenthau's Story.* New York: Doubleday, 1918.

———. *Secrets of the Bosphorus.* London: Hutchinson, 1918.

Nalbandian, Louise. *The Armenian Revolutionary Movement: The Development of Armenian Political Parties through the Nineteenth Century.* Berkeley: University of California Press, 1963.

Neilson, Keith, with Roy Arnold Prete. *Coalition Warfare: An Uneasy Accord.* Ontario: Wilfred Laurier University Press, 1984.

———. "Russia." In *Decisions for War, 1914,* ed. Keith Wilson, 97–120. New York: St. Martin's Press, 1995.

"Un nouveau Dreadnought pour la navire turque." *Le Matin,* 29 April 1914.

Orel, Sinasi, and Süreyya Yuca. *The Talât Pasha "Telegrams": Historical Fact or Armenian Fiction?* Nicosia: K. Rustem and Brother, 1986.

Paléologue, Maurice. *An Ambassador's Memoirs.* Trans. F. A. Holt. 3 vols. London: Hutchinson, 1923–1925.

———. *La Russie des Tsars pendant la Grande Guerre.* 3 vols. Paris: Plon-Nourrit, 1921.

Pares, Bernard. *The Fall of the Russian Monarchy: A Study of the Evidence.* New York: Knopf, 1939.

Pipes, Richard. *The Russian Revolution.* New York: Alfred Knopf, 1990.

Pokrovskii, M. N., ed. *Drei Konferenzen (zur Vorgeschichte des Krieges).* Berlin: Arbeiterbuchhandlung, 1920.

———. *Internationale Beziehungen im Zeitalter des Imperialismus.* 8+ vols. Berlin: R. Hobbing, 1931–.

———. *Tsarskaia Rossiia v mirovoi voine.* Vol. 1. Leningrad: 1926.

Poincaré, Raymond. *The Memoirs of Raymond Poincaré.* Trans. Sir George Arthur. 4 vols. London: W. Heinemann, 1926–.

Pomiankowski, Joseph. *Der Zusammenbruch des Ottomanischen Reiches. Erinnerungen an die Türkei aus der Zeit des Weltkrieges.* Zurich: Amalthea, 1928.

Rauchensteiner, Manfried. *Der Tod des Doppeladlers. Österreich-Ungarn und der Erste Weltkrieg.* Vienna: Verlag Styria, 1993.

Reynolds, Michael A. "The Ottoman-Russian Struggle for Eastern Anatolia and the Caucasus, 1908–1918." Ph.D. diss., Princeton University, 2003.

———. *Shattering Empires: The Clash and Collapse of the Ottoman and Russian Empires.* New York: Cambridge University Press, 2011.

"Russia's Conquests in Armenia." *Manchester Guardian,* 18 September 1916.

Sazonov, S. D. *Fateful Years, 1909–1916: The Reminiscences of Serge Sazonov, Russia's Minister for Foreign Affairs: 1914.* London: J. Cape, 1928.

Schilling, Baron M. F., ed. *How the War Began: Being the Diary of the Russian Foreign Office from the 3rd to the 20th (Old Style) of July, 1914.* Trans. Major W. Cyprian Bridge. London: G. Allen and Unwyn, 1925.

Schmidt, Stefan. *Frankreichs Aussenpolitik in der Julikrise 1914: Ein Beitrag zur Geschichte des Ausbruchs des Ersten Weltkrieges.* Munich: Oldenbourg, 2009.

Shannon, Richard. *Gladstone and the Bulgarian Agitation 1876.* London: Nelson, 1963.

Shaw, Stanford. *The Ottoman Empire in World War I*. Ankara: Turkish Historical Society, 2006.

Siegel, Jennifer. *Endgame: Britain, Russia, and the Final Struggle for Central Asia*. London: I. B. Tauris, 2002.

Smith, C. Jay, Jr. *The Russian Struggle for Power, 1914–1917: A Study of Russian Foreign Policy during the First World War*. New York: Philosophical Library, 1956.

Sondhaus, Lawrence. *Naval Warfare, 1815–1914*. New York: Routledge, 2001.

Spring, Derek. "Russia and the Coming of War." In *The Coming of the First World War*, ed. R. J. W. Evans and Hartmut Pogge von Strandmann. Oxford: Clarendon Press/Oxford University Press, 1983.

———. "Russian Imperialism in Asia in 1914." *Cahiers du monde russe et soviétique* 20, no. 3/4 (July–December 1979): 305–322.

Steinberg, John W. *All the Tsar's Men: Russia's General Staff and the Fate of Empire, 1898–1914*. Baltimore, Md.: Johns Hopkins University Press, 2010.

Stevenson, David. *Cataclysm: The First World War as Political Tragedy*. New York: Basic Books, 2004.

———. *The First World War and International Politics*. New York: Oxford University Press, 1988.

Stites, Richard. "Miliukov and the Russian Revolution." In Paul N. Miliukov, *The Russian Revolution*. Ed. Richard Stites. Trans. Tatyana Stites and Richard Stites.

Stone, Norman. *The Eastern Front 1914–1917*. New York: Charles Scribner's Sons, 1975.

———. "Moltke-Conrad: Relations between the Austro-Hungarian and German General Staffs, 1909–1914." *Historical Journal* 9, no. 2 (1966): 201–228.

———. *World War One: A Short History*. London: Allan Lane, 2007.

Strelianov, Pavel Nikolaevich. *Korpus Generala Baratova 1915–1918 gg*. Moscow, 2002.

Strachan, Hew. *The First World War*. New York: Viking, 2004.

Suny, Ronald. *Armenia in the Twentieth Century*. Chico, Calif.: Scholars Press, 1983.

———. "Empire and Nation: Armenians, Turks and the End of the Ottoman Empire." *Armenian Forum* 1, no. 2 (1998): 17–51.

TCGB (T. C. GenelKurmay Başkanlığı). *Arşiv Belgeleriyle Ermeni Faaliyetleri 1914–1918*. 4 vols. Ankara: Genelkurmay Basim Evi, 2005.

Trumpener, Ulrich. *Germany and the Ottoman Empire, 1914–1918*. Princeton: Princeton University Press, 1968.

Tuchman, Barbara. *The Guns of August*. New York: Macmillan, 1962.

Turner, L. C. F. *Origins of the First World War*. London: Edward Arnold, 1970.

———. "The Russian Mobilization in 1914." *Journal of Contemporary History* 3, no. 1 (January 1968): 65–88.

Von Hagen, Mark. "The Great War and the Mobilization of Ethnicity in the Russian Empire." In *Post-Soviet Political Order: Conflict and State Building*, ed. Barnett R. Rubin and Jack Snyder. London: Routledge, 1998.

"Vozstanie v' Vane." In *Russkoe Slovo* 141 (20 June/3 July 1915).

Weber, Frank G. *Eagles on the Crescent: Germany, Austria, and the Diplomacy of the Turkish Alliance, 1914–1918*. Ithaca: Cornell University Press, 1970.

Wendland, Anna Veronika. *Die Russophilen in Galizien. Ukrainische Konservative zwischen Österreich und Rußland 1848–1915*. Vienna: Verlag der Österreichischen Akademie der Wissenschaften, 2001.

Wildman, Allan K. *The End of the Russian Imperial Army.* 2 vols. Princeton: Princeton University Press, 1980/1987.

Würthle, Friedrich. *Die Spur führt nach Belgrad. Die Hintergründe des Dramas von Sarajevo 1914.* Vienna: Fritz Molden, 1975.

Wynn, Antony. *Persia in the Great Game.* London: John Murray, 2004.

Yasamee, F. A. K. "Ottoman Empire." In *Decisions for War, 1914,* ed. Keith Wilson, 229–268. New York: St. Martin's Press, 1995.

Zechlin, Egmont. *Die deutsche Politik und die Juden im Ersten Weltkrieg.* Göttingen: Vandenhoeck und Ruprecht, 1969.

Zeman, Z. A. B., ed. *Germany and the Revolution in Russia, 1915–1918: Documents from the Archives of the German Foreign Ministry.* London: Oxford University Press, 1958.

Acknowledgments

This book could not have been written without generous financial support from the Brady-Johnson Program in Grand Strategy at Yale University. I extend gratitude to Professors Paul Kennedy, John Gaddis, and Charlie Hill for offering me the Henry Chauncey '57 Fellowship which enabled me to spend such a pleasant—and productive—time at Yale. Although he is no longer with the program, Ted Bromund was instrumental in facilitating a smooth transition as I moved to the States. At International Security Studies, Ann Carter-Drier, Susan Hennigan, and Kathleen Murphy made me feel right at home, while clearing away administrative hurdles with panache.

At Bilkent, I must thank my department chair, Professor Ersel Aydınlı, along with Professors Nedim Karakayalı and Emre Özgen, and the Social Sciences Dean (now Provost), Professor Metin Heper, for generously granting me two whole years of leave. The Rector (now Chairman), Ali Doğramacı, has supported me for many years, and he graciously offered Bilkent's support for the book, even though I was primarily in residence at Yale while writing it. Norman Stone provided the inspiration for this project with his pathbreaking study of the *Eastern Front 1914–1917*. Nur Bilge Criss, Ali Tekin, Paul Williams, and Hasan Ali Karasar have kindly stayed in touch during my leave time from Bilkent, keeping me abreast of what is going on. Likewise Sandy Berkovski and James Alexander, whose amusing reports of Ankara life have kept me in good cheer as my wife and I prepared to return. Our department secretary, Pınar Şener, has been tireless in forwarding my mail and otherwise keeping the Bilkent fires burning. And our new chair, Pınar Bilgin, has offered me all possible support.

Among scholars whose own research I have drawn on, I must single out Mike Reynolds, on whose Princeton dissertation, "Russo-Ottoman Struggle for Eastern Anatolia and the Caucasus" (now published by Cambridge University Press as *Shattering Empires*) I have relied in both of my last two books. Mike also generously forwarded some important material from Princeton. Ronald Bobroff's recent study *Roads to Glory: Late Imperial Russia and the Turkish Straits* in some ways prefigures my principal theme, although Bobroff shied away from my bolder conclusions about Russia's war aims and their relation to the outbreak of war in 1914. Likewise Oleg Airapetov's "Sud'ba Bosforskoi ekspeditsii," which is the only work I have seen which extends its analysis of tsarist Russian Straits policy into 1917 (Bobroff's does not). I have also drawn heavily on Mustafa Aksakal's groundbreaking research on the Ottoman entry into World War I, as I did in my last book. Jesse Kaufmann generously excerpted his Stanford dissertation on "Sovereignty and the Search for Order in German-Occupied Poland." Jeff Mankoff's unpublished Yale dissertation on "Russia and the Polish Question, 1907–1917" was an invaluable resource. I was also fortunate enough to be able to discuss Russo-Polish affairs with Jeff on many occasions in the ISS offices. Andrey Ivanov was a great sounding board for my ideas and excellent company during my time in New Haven; he also scanned several long articles for me, unavailable in Turkey, after I returned to Bilkent. Professor Paul Bushkovitch also shared his encyclopedic knowledge of tsarist Russian history. Ethan Rundell was an entertaining host in Paris, as always. Ethan also heroically saved my attaché bag, with research materials and laptop, from the clutches of an amazingly brazen café thief in the Marais. Bravo, Ethan!

I am grateful to Joyce Seltzer of Harvard University Press for believing in this book and bringing it home. Thanks also to Kate Brick for cleaning up my prose and to Philip Schwartzberg, Meridian Mapping, for drawing the maps.

As always, my wife Nesrin deserves her own paragraph. She has read the manuscript from start to finish, saving me from numerous errors. As she is my target reader, I do hope that her good opinion of the book heralds well for it; but of course she bears no responsibility for anything in it. I would not be able to write at all without Nesrin's unflagging support and generosity of spirit.

Index

Abdul Hamid II, 17, 24, 143, 149; and coun-
terrevolution, 145; fall of, 17, 24
Abrurrezak Bey, 148–149
Adamov, A. A., 162, 164
Adamov report, 162, 164, 276n50, 278n75
Adana, 146, 166, 171; and Armenian deporta-
tions, 171
Adrianople (Edirne), 26, 118, 136; in First
Balkan War, 26; and Russian territorial
claims, 118
Aegean Sea and Aegean Islands, 3, 104, 107,
118, 160; Russian claims to, 118
Aehrenthal, Baron Alois Lexa von, 16, 28,
36, 117, 146, 250n21, 258n43; and first
Bosnian crisis, 16, 28, 36
Afghanistan, 7, 14, 176, 184, 186, 193, 250n14;
and Anglo-Russian Accord of 1907, 14,
250n14; and German "holy war" plans,
184, 186, 193; and Great Game intrigue, 176
Ahmad Shah, 186, 188
Airapetov, Oleg, 247n4, 254n73
Akçam, Taner, 170–171, 272n3, 276n62,
278n75
Albania, 27, 88, 90, 96
Albertini, Luigi, 47, 55–56, 246n1, 256n4;
questions foreknowledge of Sarajevo plot,
47, 256n4, 257n17

Alekseev, General M. V., 93, 217–218, 223–
225, 227, 232, 285n20; and abdication of
tsar, 224, 286n26; advocates separate
peace, 223n
Aleppo, 144, 165–166, 168
Alexander III, 79
Alexandra Feodorovna (Alix of Hesse), 217,
236, 259n49
Alsace-Lorraine, 54, 77; and French revanchist territorial ambition, 54, 90, 232
Amanus Mountains, 15, 172
Anatolia, 7, 12, 14, 17, 19, 25, 95, 121, 147, 150–
153, 156, 161, 168, 171–172, 194, 202–203,
205, 212, 218, 220, 224, 227; occupied by
Russian troops, 202–203, 205, 212, 227;
and Russian imperial ambition, 7, 12, 19,
95, 156, 161; as WWI conflict zone, 168,
171–172, 218, 220, 224, 278n75
Anglo-Russian Accord of 1907, 14, 99, 175,
185, 250n14
Ankara, 15, 17, 97, 121, 161, 172, 192, 204–205,
208–209, 213, 220, 222; deportations of
Armenians from, 172
Anzac troops, 137–139, 168
Apis. *See* Dimitrijević, Colonel Dragutin
Arabia, 11–12, 197, 200, 210, 227; in British
thinking, 11–12, 197